The Arts in Mind

The Arts in Mind

Pioneering Texts of a Coterie of British Men of Letters

Ruth Katz and Ruth HaCohen, editors

Transaction Publishers
New Brunswick (U.S.A.) and London (U.K.)

Library of Congress Catalog Number: 2001048083
ISBN: 0-7658-0106-X
Printed in the United States of America

Library of Congress Cataloging-in-Publication Data

The arts in mind : pioneering texts of a coterie of British men of letters / Ruth Katz and Ruth HaCohen, editors.
     p. cm.
     Companion v. to: Tuning the mind.
     Includes bibliographical references and index.
     ISBN 0-7658-0106-X (alk. paper)
     1. Aesthetics, British—18th century. I. Katz, Ruth, 1927- II. HaCohen, Ruth. III. Tuning the mind.

BH221.G7 A78 2001
701'.1—dc21   2001048083

Contents

The Arts in Mind
Pioneering Texts of a Coterie of British Men of Letters

Introduction

A major shift in deliberations concerning the arts took place in the eighteenth century. Once the fine arts were grouped together , in a realm seemingly governed by rules different from those governing science, the need to spell out these rules was keenly felt. Thus the century abounds with treatises that sought to extract from comparisons and correspondences among the arts the overriding principles, which differentiates Art from other walks of life. This burst of scholarly activity resulted in the incorporation of aesthetics among the classic branches of philosophy, heralding, moreover, the cognitive turn in epistemology.

Deliberations on the arts, all along, entertained conjectures concerning the working of the mind. Perception, for one, was an integral part of the artistic endeavor, taken into consideration by artists, in one from or another, even while they believed that they were imitating nature. However, with the rise of the systematic study of perception in the eighteenth century, the mimetic tradition was forced to give way to concerns with the ways in which art constructs that which it aims to achieve. The Aristotelian notion that art is a kind of making gradually occupied center stage.

If art resides in the making, how is it that the mind can comprehend such constructions, and even, where necessary, infer what it is that they refer to? It was questions of this kind that were opened for re-examination in the eighteenth century. Among the many treatises dealing with these subjects, it its primarily the British texts that led in the direction of modern cognitive concerns. It is only now, however, in the floodlights of the study of mental processes that the British contributions may be fully assessed, rectifying an oversight in the historical accounts of seminal contributions to the understanding of art.

All of this, and more, was discussed in our own book, *Tuning the Mind: The Prefiguration of the Cognitive Turn by the Arts..* In the book we discussed the deliberations over art in the context of wider cultural and philosophical issues which, in turn, stem from major shift of worldview and ideals at the time. In our examination of the large treasury of historical sources, the texts assembled in the present volume loomed large and seemed unfairly neglected. The writers of these texts functioned as an "invisible college," constituting an important British "school" that contributed significantly, and unusually, to the prefiguration of the cognitive turn by the arts. This is why we decided to resurrect the writings of this group of men of letters, and to make them available to readers, who are better equipped that their eighteenth -century predecessors, to assess their significance. Yet, it should also be noted that the educated reader of these times possessed the skills necessary for delving deep into such writings, even though they were incapable, by definition, of fully understanding their historical significance. This volume, therefore, is annotated so as to facilitate the present-day reading of these texts. We believe that today's reader will gain fresh insights into contemporary questions in addition, of course, to a new look at the past.

Readers of our *Tuning of the Mind* especially welcome. they are here. invited to become better acquainted with the kinds of texts which guided our thinking. The elaborate annotations are meant to serve a double function: they are expected to elucidate ambiguities and hidden assumptions in the texts, as well as to reveal the processes of thought which led to our major claims. Such objectives are best served, we believe, by allowing those whom one wishes to convince, to follow closely the problems raised by the various details, even if the task of delineating a comprehensive picture composed of scattered details is thereby made more difficult. Nevertheless, like the treatises themselves, we too, mutatis mutandis, place value on the kinds of arguments enlisted, the data which constrain them, and the rigor required to highlight the texture of the fabric one weaves.

The texts we deal with are neither obscure nor forgotten; in fact, some of them, have already been discussed before. However, most of the histories which deal with eighteenth-century thought avail themselves only of a selection of the ideas expressed in these writings, based on various assortments that seemed of special interest to them. We know of no study, other than this one, that deals with most of these texts in their entirety, treating them as a unique corpus highly relevant to the development of aesthetic theory, particularly as far as perceptual and cognitive aspects are concerned. Moreover, as explicated in *Tuning the Mind*, we believe that the writers of these treatises, as a group, have initiated some major breakthroughs that underlie the systematic study of the mind.

It is not for want of serious scholarship that the major contributions of the group were overlooked. If Draper and Rogerson failed to recognize them, this is largely due to the fact that both were literary people and neither was sufficiently versed in musical matters and in aesthetic theory. Schueller, who was concerned with the history of ideas, approached these treatises in an attempt to unveil inherited assumptions in order to safeguard the continuity of the "great chain of being." Even Kristeller, who was fully aware of the issues which these treatises raised, overlooked the new type of argumentation involved. Cassirer, on the other hand, more than anybody else, was aware of the paradigmatic change in epistemology and aesthetic theory to which our writers contributed, but his analysis fails to define them as a group per se. In his comprehensive synthesis of eighteenth century thought, Cassirer does not make room for a detailed investigation of treatises whose outward appearance conceals their philosophical interest.

To be sure, changing perspectives is a consequence of changing times; it is anachronistic and unfair to demand of studies published half a century ago or earlier, to show awareness of that which seems central nowadays. The hindsight of the "mind's new science" and crucial developments in aesthetic theory, enable us not only to detect the modernity of the kind of argumentation which characterize these texts, but to unveil, as well, the shared solutions which follow from the very formulation of their problems. There is no doubt in our minds that these writings, as a whole, successfully connect incommensurable subjects by means of the new conceptual framework which they have created. Our annotations, therefore, focus on the argumentation, trying to elucidate the inner logic of each treatise as well as its relatedness to the other treatises. Through the "conversation" which we have constructed among these writers, we hope to indicate some of the roads we have ourselves traversed.

The reader will notice that our annotations do not dwell on esoteric titles, authors or mythological figures that do not directly contribute to the clarification of the argument. At the same time, we do elucidate certain assumptions which were implicit in the texts and attempt to show how they evolved. Thus, our construction includes conceptualizations unknown to those who participated in bringing about the major turn. This is in the nature of historical writing, of course, but deserves special awareness in order to avoid anachronisms, or worse, the coercion of the data.

Whereas the discussion concerning the arts was widespread and included reputable figures in both Germany and France we decided to limit ourselves to members of the English group, and among them we chose only those who directly contributed to the arguments which constitute part of the new "paradigm". "Estimate" John Brown's Dissertation, for example, is not included because its main arguments are foreign to the general spirit of the other treatises; moreover, it lacks the readiness to view old problems in fresh ways. The same holds true for some of the other treatises which were not included, such as Sir William Jones' and Anselm Bayly's. The treatises included are representative of the changed climate of opinion which entailed new issues such as those of perception, symbolic function, the role of history in worldmaking etc. Our selection from each treatise is guided by our desire to preserve the major claims and their attendant argumentation in their entirety. For example, all of Webb is included, since each and every part of his essay relates to his attempt to bridge music and passion via movement. Beattie, on the other hand, whose eclectic method led to unnecessary deviations and extensions is not presented in toto; instead, the central issues that concern us are so presented. The sections deleted from the various treatises do not contradict our focal points, they are simply less relevant to our discussion.

A word must be said about placing Shaftesbury and Hutcheson at the head of our list. Neither was directly a member of the group, yet their writings had an enormous influence on the group, and set in broad terms the agenda for the investigations of its members, providing them with a major frame of reference. Above all, as already discussed, Shaftesbury and Hutcheson set into motion the kind of questions which attempt to relate aesthetic norms to artistic constraints as revealed by the various media and by the nature of their perception. Employing 'beauty' as a major concept for the explication of central issues in moral philosophy accorded the arts centrality within culture. The fact that the deliberations concerning art not only continued but actually flourished is due in large measure to the legitimation which these thinkers bestowed upon it.

Since our group constitutes an "invisible college," representative of an important trend of thought in the second half of the eighteenth century, we wished also to convey the Spirit of the visual aspects of the treatises. Even with the advanced technology nowadays, it proved difficult to scan the treatises and still allow for the complicated editing which seemed necessary. Indeed, the editing required a number of interpolations: 1) the interpolation of translations of texts which appear in the treatises in Greek, Latin and other languages, 2) the interpolation of our own annotations, and 3) the differentiation between our annotations and the author's own footnotes. In order to compensate the reader for the too modern appearance, we tried to add some "visual substance" which does not appear in the original treatises, though it is alluded to and sometimes discussed at length. Our writers obviously did not feel the need to supply the reader with pictorial and musical examples since they assumed that those who have taken the trouble to read them were familiar with the examples which they saw fit to mention. Without offending our readers, the vast expansion of the world of knowledge no longer allows us to take such things for granted. Thus we added some musical and visual illustrations of works which were suggested by the texts. We also allowed ourselves to correct obvious typographical errors in the originals, since we saw no advantage in preserving them intact. For the reader's convenience, we differentiate between our annotations and the authors' footnotes through arabic numbers and alphabetical signs respectively, and by typographical differences between the original and the interpolated texts. Since the present volume maybe viewed as a companion to *Tuning the Mind* we refer to the latter in our annotations as Vol. I.

This brings us to the pleasant task of thanking Mrs. Jane Singer for her expert help in the production of the manuscript; Mr. Eitan Kornik for locating the passages that required translation in authorized translations, our friend Professor Raanana Meridor, who examined some of Mr. Kornik's original translations and made valuable suggestions, Ms. Andrea Rothstein for modernizing the Greek typography and Ms. Yellena Ginzburg for locating the visual examples which we saw fit to include. Finally, we are grateful to the grants we have received from the Hebrew University, one from the Robert H. and Clarice Smith Center of Art History and the other from the Authority of Research and Development — which made all of this possible.

Anthony Ashely Cooper

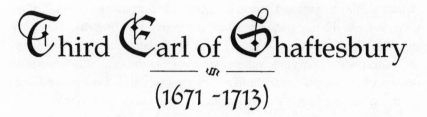

Third Earl of Shaftesbury

(1671 -1713)

As an earnest student and ardent lover of liberty, the 3rd Earl of Shaftesbury
was an enthusiast in the cause of virtue. The topics which most interested him
in his unfortunately brief life were philosophy, politics, morals and religion. In
spite of ill health, he held various political offices and was even offered the
secretaryship of state by William III, an offer he was compelled to decline.
During several extended sojourns in Holland and Italy, he came into close con-
tact with artistic and philosophical associations which exercised a marked influence on his thought, to which he brought a profound classical education. The
latter he owed, in no small measure, to Locke, who was entrusted with over-
seeing his early education.

Shaftesbury's major contribution lies in the field of ethics. In his various
attacks on the principle of egoism, central to Hobbes' social theory, he tried to
assail the irreconcilable antagonism between social duty and self-love. Instead
of presenting the principle of social duty as abstract reason, liable to conflict
with natural self-love (as explicated by some of his contemporaries), he tried
to exhibit the naturalness of man's social affections, and to demonstrate the
normal harmony between these and his self-regarding impulses. Shaftesbury
was perhaps the first to transfer the center of ethical interest from the rational
apprehension of either abstract moral distinctions or laws of divine legislation
to emotional impulses that prompt us to perform our social duties. Hobbes
might have been right, argued Shaftesbury, were it possible to consider man as
a wholly self-sufficient individual. However, since man, by definition, must be
considered as part of a larger system, we call him good only "when his impulses and dispositions are so balanced as to tend towards the good of the whole."
Goodness is not attributed to man because his acts have beneficial results, but
because his dispositions or affections "tend of themselves to promote the good

or happiness of human society." Moral goodness in "sensible creatures" implies disinterested affections whose direct object is the good of others. Goodness of character, thus, consists in a certain harmony of self-regarding and social affections. Virtue is the recognition of moral goodness for its own sake. The pleasure one takes in goodness is due to what Shaftesbury calls the Moral Sense. This susceptibility compares with our susceptibility to Beauty (as opposed to deformity) in external things. In like manner, it furnishes a direct impulse to good conduct and proves the coincidence between virtue and happiness.

Shaftesbury's theories contributed to a major turning point in ethical thought whereby the introspective study of the human mind — observations of the actual ways of its impulses and sentiments — replaced the considerations of abstract rational principles. Psychological experiences became, thereby, the basis of ethics. Many of Shaftesbury's suggestions influenced Hutcheson and were further developed by him, and in their turn, they influenced Hume's speculations concerning utilitarianism.

Though avidly engaged in both writing and re-writing of some of his essays, Shaftesbury appears to have published very few of them before his untimely death. His *Characteristics of Man, Manners, Opinions and Times* appeared for the first time in 1711 and contained his major treatises. Shortly before his death he also formed an outline for a discourse on the art of painting, sculpture, etching etc., but did not live to accomplish it.

Shaftesbury preferred to pose as a gentleman rather than as a pedant of the scholastic kind. His style and manner were guided by the same criterion of harmony with which he tried to refute Hobbes and from which he attempted to deduce that the virtue of benevolence is indispensable to morality. It is, in fact, the close parallel which he drew between the moral and the aesthetic which concerns us most. While Shaftesbury enlisted the faculty which apprehends beauty in the sphere of art in order to exemplify the workings of the faculty that determines the value of human actions, it is through his explication of the moral sense that we gain insight into his aesthetic theory. Both faculties, in essence, are primarily emotional and non-reflective, though in the process of development they become rationalized by education and use. The distinction between beauty and deformity, like that between right and wrong, is part of the constitution of human nature. The harmonious in art stands apart from external dictates as does morality from theology. Mental dictates are the incentive of beauty just as the voice of conscience is the incentive of morality; both reside in the mind which aims at perfect harmony for its own sake. Guided by internal notions of harmony, the artist may be viewed as a "maker" of coherent wholes, in which the constituent parts are subjugated to that which is "proportioned in itself" — the work of art. The unique nature of Shaftesbury's thought did not elude his contemporaries, as exemplified in the following lines from Thomson's "Seasons":

> The generous Ashley thine, the friend of man;
> Who scann'd his nature with a brother's eye,
> His weakness prompt to shade, to raise his aim,
> To touch the finer movements of the mind,
> And with the moral beauty charm the heart.

Indeed, the influence of Shaftesbury's theories in the fields of ethics and aesthetics was considerable, both at home and abroad. The list of important thinkers who were inspired by Shaftesbury is impressive indeed. In England it comprised people like Hutcheson, Hume and Butler, in France — Voltaire, Diderot and Montesquieu, and in Germany — Lessing, Mendelssohn and Herder. His special relationship with Leibniz will come to the fore in our annotations of the excerpts from Shaftesbury's writings.

The British group which we chose to present here, though less known both collectively and individually, is heavily indebted to Shaftesbury in its aesthetic outlook and public concerns. While almost none of them separately had the standing of some of the philosophers we mentioned, their impact as a group was considerable. Shaftesburian "resonances" reverberate in many of their arguments, especially in those which were central to the cognitive shift in the theory of art which they helped to effect. Relegating aesthetic criteria to the mind while maintaining their psychological substratum is an elaboration of the Shaftesburian conception of Sense; it bridges the sensual, on the one hand, with the "making of sense" on the other.

SOLILOQUY

OR

ADVICE TO AN AUTHOR

PART I, SECTION 3 [1]

I MUST confess there is hardly any where to be found a more insipid Race of Mortals, than those whom we Moderns are contented to call Poets, for having attain'd the chiming Faculty of a Language, with an injudicious random use of Wit and Fancy. But for the Man, who truly and in a just sense deserves the Name of *Poet*, and who as a real Master, or Architect in the kind, can describe both Men and Manners, and give to an *Action* its just Body and Proportions; he will be found, if I mistake not, a very different Creature. Such a *Poet* is indeed a second *Maker;* a just PROMETHEUS, under JOVE. Like that Sovereign Artist or universal Plastick Nature, he forms *a Whole*, coherent and proportion'd in it-self, with due Subjection and Subordinacy of constituent Parts. He notes the Boundarys of the Passions, and knows their exact *Tones* and *Measures;* by which he justly represents them, marks *the Sublime* of Sentiments and Action, and distinguishes *the Beautiful* from *the Deform'd*, *the Amiable* from *the Odious*. The moral Artist, who can thus imitate the Creator, and is thus knowing in the inward Form and Structure of his Fellow-Creature, will hardly, I presume, be found unknow-

---------- ⟟ ----------

1. The text is taken from *Characteristics of Man, Manners, Opinions and Times*, vol. I, 1732: 207-8. We did not include Shaftsbury's footnotes in our selection.

ing in *Himself*, or at a loss in those Numbers which make the
Harmony of a Mind. For *Knavery* is mere *Dissonance* and
Disproportion. And tho Villains may have strong *Tones* and nat-
ural Capacitys of Action; 'tis impossible that * true *Judgment* and
Ingenuity shou'd reside, where *Harmony* and *Honesty* have no
being.[2]

PART II, SECTION 2[3]

In the days of ATTICK *Elegance*, as Works were then truly of
another Form and Turn, so Workmen were of another Humour,
and had their Vanity of a quite contrary kind. They became
rather affected in endeavouring to discover the pains they had

——————— ◊ ———————

2. Shaftesbury here makes some of his major statements concerning art and the artist.
Like Baumgarten (Vol. I: 182ff.), he prefers to focus on the poet, whom he sees as representing all those who are equally engaged in "bringing about" works of art.
However, unlike Baumgarten, who does not differentiate between poets and painters,
Shaftesbury considers the poet closer to the "study of the graces and perfection of the
mind," because he copies "life" (notions of) and not "bodies" (objects; cf. same section p. 206.)

The idea that the artist is a "maker" guided by internal notions of "harmony" which
form coherent wholes, is no doubt Shaftesbury's main contribution to modern aesthetics. It integrates Aristotelian conceptions regarding art as a "coming into being"
(whose origin is in the "maker" and not in the "thing made"; see *Nichomacian Ethics*,
book vii, sec. 4) with Neoplatonic speculations concerning Beauty, transferring both
the metaphysical (the harmonious relations) as well as the physical (the imitated reality) into the creative mind. This transference will guide all of the subsequent writers to
whom we attribute a growing awareness of the "operations of the mind" and its role
in the arts.

The idea of the Whole, which Shaftesbury refers to, harbors the idea of organicity the
"subjection and subordinacy of constituent parts" to that which is "proportion'd in itself," i.e. the work of art. Proportion, in turn, is guided by a "sense" of harmony the
"inward form and structure" of human-creatures. These ideas reveal Shaftesbury's kinship with Leibniz, whose "pre-established harmony" connected the ontological with
the epistemological through intuition (see Vol. I: 170 and the following fn. 10).

Interestingly, Baumgarten's aesthetic theory, which was, by his own admission, largely inspired by Leibniz, transferred that level of perfection which transcends mere perceptions — the well proportioned — into artistic products. Indeed, Baumgarten and
Shaftesbury share the attempt to grant empirical anchorage to the normative, thus differentiating between the nature of perception in general and the nature of aesthetic
perception in particular.

3. *Characteristics* Vol. I pp. 233–240.

taken to be correct. They were glad to insinuate how laboriously, and with what expence of Time, they had brought the smallest Work of theirs (as perhaps a single *Ode* or *Satire*, an *Oration* or *Panegyrick*) to its perfection. When they had so *polish'd* their Piece, and render'd it so natural and easy, that it *seem'd* only a lucky Flight, a Hit of Thought, or flowing Vein of Humour; they were then chiefly concern'd lest it shou'd *in reality* pass for such, and their Artifice remain undiscover'd. They were willing it shou'd be known how serious their Play was; and how elaborate their Freedom and Facility: that they might say as the agreeable and polite Poet, glancing on himself,

> *Ludentis speciem dabit & torquebitur——*
>
> > Hor. Epist. 2. lib. 2.
>
> *And*
> ——————————— *Ut fibi quivis*
> *Speret idem, sudet multum, frustraque laboret*
> *Ausus idem, tantum series juncturaque pollet.*
>
> > Id. de Arte Poet.

[one that any writer might hope to achieve, but would sweat tears of blood in his efforts and still not manage it — such is the power of words that are used in the right places and in the right relationships]

SUCH Accuracy of Workmanship requires a CRITICK'S *Eye*. 'Tis lost upon a vulgar Judgment. Nothing grieves *a real Artist* more than that indifference of the Publick, which suffers *Work* to pass *uncriticiz'd*. Nothing, on the other side, rejoices him more than the nice View and Inspection of the accurate *Examiner* and *Judg of Work*. 'Tis the mean *Genius*, the slovenly Performer, who knowing nothing of *true Workmanship*, endeavours by the best outward Gloss and dazling Shew, to turn the Eye from a direct and steddy Survey of his Piece.

WHAT is there which an expert *Musician* more earnestly desires, than to perform his part in the presence of those who are knowing in his Art? 'Tis to *the Ear* alone he applies himself;

the critical, the nice Ear. Let his Hearers be of what *Character* they please: Be they naturally austere, morose, or rigid; no matter, so they are *Criticks*, able to censure, remark, and sound every Accord and Symphony. What is there mortifies the good *Painter* more, that when amidst his admiring Spectators there is not one present, who has been us'd to compare the Hands of different Masters, or has *an Eye* to distinguish the Advantages or Defects of every Style? Thro' all the inferior orders of *Mechanicks*, the Rule is found to hold the same. In every Science, every Art, the real *Masters*, or *Proficients*, rejoice in nothing more, than in the thorow Search and Examination of their Performances, by all the Rules of Art and nicest *Criticism*. Why therefore (in the MUSES name!) is it not the same with our Pretenders to the Writing Art, our *Poets*, and *Prose-Authors* in every kind? Why in this Profession are we found such *Critick-Haters*, and indulg'd in this unlearned Aversion; unless it be taken for granted, that as Wit and Learning stand at present in our Nation, we are still upon the foot of *Empiricks* and *Mountebanks?*

FROM these Considerations, I take upon me absolutely to condemn the fashionable and prevailing Custom of inveighing against CRITICKS, as the common Enemys, the Pests, and Incendiarys of the Commonwealth of Wit and Letters. I assert, on the contrary, that they are the *Props* and *Pillars* of the Building; and that without the Encouragement and Propagation of such a Race, we shou'd remain as GOTHICK *Architects* as ever.

IN THE weaker and more imperfect Societys of Mankind, such as those compos'd of federate *Tribes*, or mix'd *Colonys*, scarce settled in their new Seats, it might pass for sufficient Good-fortune, if the People prov'd only so far Masters of Language, as to be able to understand one another, in order to confer about their Wants, and provide for their common Necessitys. Their expos'd and indigent State cou'd not be prefum'd to afford 'em either that full Leisure, or easy Disposition which was requisite to raise 'em to any Curiosity of Speculation. They who were neither safe from Violence, nor secure of Plenty, were unlikely to engage in unnecessary Arts. Nor cou'd it be expected they shou'd turn their Attention towards the Numbers of their Language, and the harmonious Sounds which they accidentally emitted. But when, in process of time, the Affairs of the Society were settled on an easy and secure Foundation; when *Debates* and *Discourses* on these Subjects of common Interest, and publick Good, were grown familiar; and the *Speeches* of prime Men, and Leaders, were consider'd, and compar'd together: there wou'd naturally be observ'd not only a more agreeable Measure of sound, but a happier and more easy Rangement of Thoughts, in one Speaker, than in another.

IT may be easily perceiv'd from hence, that *the Goddess* PERSUASION must have been in a manner the Mother of *Poetry*, *Rhetorick*, *Musick*, and the other kindred Arts. For 'tis apparent, that where chief Men, and Leaders had the strongest Interest *to persuade;* they us'd the highest endeavours *to please.* So that in such *a State* or *Polity* as has been describ'd, not only the best Order of Thought, and Turn of Fancy, by the most soft an inviting Numbers must have been employ'd, to charm *the Publick Ear*, and to incline *the Heart,* by the Agreeableness of Expression.

ALMOST all the antient *Masters* of this sort were said to have been MUSICIANS. And *Tradition*, which soon grew fabulous, cou'd not better represent the first *Founders* or *Establishers* of these larger Societys, than as real *Songsters*, who by the power of their Voice and Lyre, cou'd charm the wildest Beasts, and draw the rude Forests and Rocks into the Form of fairest Citys. Nor can it be doubted that the same *Artists*, who so industriously apply'd themselves to study the Numbers of *Speech*, must have made proportionable Improvements in the Study of mere sounds and *natural Harmony;* which, of it-self, must have considerably contributed towards the softning the rude Manners and harsh Temper of their new People.

IF therefore it so happen'd in these *free* Communitys, made by Consent and voluntary Association, that after a-while, the Power of *One*, or of *a Few*, grew prevalent over the rest; if FORCE took

place, and the Affairs of the Society were administer'd without
their Concurrence, by the influence of *Awe* and *Terror:* it follow'd, that these pathetick Sciences and Arts of Speech were little cultivated, since they were of little use. But where PERSUA-
SION was the chief means of guiding the Society; where the
People were to be convinc'd before they acted; there *Elocution*
became considerable; there *Orators* and *Bards* were heard; and
the chief Genius's and *Sages* of the Nation betook themselves to
the Study of those Arts, by which the People were render'd more
treatable in a way of Reason and Understanding, and more subject to be led by Men of Science and Erudition. The more these
Artists courted the Publick, the more they instructed it. In such
Constitutions as these, 'twas the interest of the Wise and Able,
that the Community shou'd be Judges of Ability and Wisdom.
The high Esteem of Ingenuity was what advanc'd the Ingenious
to the greatest Honours. And they who rose by Science, and
Politeness in the higher Arts, cou'd not fail to promote that *Taste*
and *Relish* to which they ow'd their personal Disctinction and
Pre-eminence.

HENCE it is that those *Arts* have been deliver'd to us in such
perfection, by *free Nations;* who from the Nature of their
Government, as from a proper Soil, produc'd the generous
Plants: whilst the mightiest Bodys and vastest Empires, govern'd
by *Force*, and *a despotick Power*, cou'd, after Ages of Peace and
Leisure, produce no other than what was deform'd and barbarous of the kind.

WHEN the *persuasive* Arts were grown thus into repute, and
the Power of moving the Affections become the Study and
Emulation of the forward *Wits* and aspiring *Genius's* of the
Times; it wou'd necessarily happen that many Genius's of equal
size and strength, tho less covetous of publick Applause, of
Power, or of Influence over Mankind, wou'd content themselves
with the *Contemplation* merely of these enchanting Arts. These
they wou'd the better enjoy, the more they refin'd their *Taste*,
and cultivated their *Ear.* For to all Musick there must be an Ear
proportionable. There must be an Art of *Hearing* found, ere the

performing Arts can have their due effect, or any thing exquisite in the kind be felt or comprehended. The just Performers therefore in each Art wou'd naturally be the most desirous of improving and refining the publick Ear; which they cou'd no way so well effect as by the help of those latter *Genius's*, who were in a manner their *Interpreters* to the People; and who by their Example taught the Publick to discover what was just and excellent in each Performance.[4]

4. Shaftesbury's advice to authors — "makers" in the field of literature — includes the topic of criticism and its importance for the creative act. In the opening paragraphs of section II (not included here), Shaftesbury discloses the state of criticism in England at the time. From his somewhat sociological discussion it appears 1) that literary criticism, evidently, was an upcoming field of endeavor, 2) that writers seem to have enjoyed freedom of expression and 3) that a strained atmosphere apparently characterized the relationship between critics and writers.

In the following sections, Shaftesbury dismisses the vulnerability of writers as misplaced, calling for indulgence and a better understanding of the role of criticism. 'Perfection,' he tells us, is achieved through workmanship, endeavor and, not least, through judgment which rests on knowledge. It is the latter which creative writing has in common with constructive criticism. But since writers focus primarily on the act of creation, they stand to benefit from those who preoccupy themselves with the act of reflection. Shaftesbury tells us that critics constitute an ideal audience; they are, in fact, the true addressees of genuine and thoughtful writers. On the whole, a community of discourse develops between creators and their connoisseurs, guaranteeing the artistic quality that serves the "public good." The presence of critics, moreover, is the sign of a society that has already developed beyond basic necessities and is able to afford the "unnecessary arts." The latter, Shaftesbury tells us, require "leisure," i.e. conditions conducive to "curiosity and speculation." The idea that culture, and especially the arts, thrives better under conditions of "plenty" will be picked up by Shaftesbury's followers, especially Harris.

Whether tacit or explicit, such ideas invariably imply policy suggestions of sorts, aiming to insure social melioration. The refinement of culture, however, is not achieved through coercion but rather through "persuasion," says Shaftesbury. Where persuasion is the "chief means of guiding the society," the arts prosper because of their own "persuasive powers." The arts, in other words, both benefit from and contribute to the public good. The critic, in Shaftesbury's brief socio-cultural account, thus plays a double role as guardian and mediator. While protecting the public and the arts from "mere pretenders," the critic also promotes and interprets the "just performers."

AN INQUIRY CONCERNING VIRTUE OR MERIT

BOOK I, SECTION 3 [5]

*B*UT to proceed from what is *Goodness*, and lies within the reach and capacity of all *sensible Creatures*, to that which is call'd VIRTUE or MERIT, and is allow'd to *Man* only.

Reflex Affection.

In a Creature capable of forming general Notions of Things, not only the outward Beings which offer themselves to the Sense, are the Objects of the Affection; but the very *Actions* themselves, and the *Affections* of Pity, Kindness, Gratitude, and their Contrarys, being brought into the Mind by Reflection, become Objects. So that, by means of this reflected Sense, there arises another kind of Affection towards those very Affections themselves, which have been already felt, and are now become the Subject of a new Liking or Dislike.

THE Case is the same in *mental* or *moral* Subjects, as in ordinary *Bodys*, or the common Subjects of *Sense*. The Shapes, Motions, Colours, and Proportions of these latter being presented to our Eye; there necessarily results a *Beauty or Deformity, according to the different Measure, Arrangement and Disposition of their several Parts. So in *Behaviour* and *Actions*, when presented to our Understanding, there must be found, of necessity, an apparent Difference, according to the Regularity or Irregularity of the Subjects.

Moral Beauty and Deformity.

THE MIND, which is Spectator or Auditor of *other Minds*, cannot be without its *Eye* and *Ear;* so as to discern Proportion, distinguish Sound, and scan each Sentiment or Thought which comes before it. It can let nothing escape its Censure. It feels the Soft and Harsh, the Agreeable and Disagreeable, in the Affections; and finds a *Foul* and *Fair,* a *Harmonious* and a *Dissonant,* as really and truly here, as in any musical Numbers, or in the outward Forms or Representations of sensible Things. Nor can it * with-hold its *Admiration* and *Extasy,* its *Aversion* and

———— ఴ ————

5. *Characteristics* Vol II. pp. 28–30; pp. 42–45.

Scorn, any more in what relates to one than to the other of these Subjects. So that to deny the common and natural Sense of a SUBLIME and BEAUTIFUL in Things, will appear an Affectation merely, to any-one who considers duly of this Affair.

Now as in the *sensible* kind of Objects, the Species or Images of Bodys, Colours, and Sounds, are perpetually moving before our Eyes, and acting on our Senses, even when we sleep; so in the *moral* and *intellectual* kind, the Forms and Images of Things are no less active and incumbent on the Mind, at all Seasons, and even when the real Objects themselves are absent.

IN these vagrant Characters or Pictures of *Manners*, which the Mind of necessity figures to it-self, and carrys still about with it, the Heart cannot possibly remain neutral; but constantly takes part one way or other. However false or corrupt it be within it-self, it finds the difference, as to Beauty and Comeliness, between one *Heart* and another, one *Turn of Affection*, one *Behaviour*, one *Sentiment* and another; and accordingly, in all disinterested Cases, must approve in some measure of what is natural and honest, and disapprove what is dishonest and corrupt.[6]

———— ⚘ ————

6. The first part of Shaftesbury's *Inquiry* deals with the question of virtue and its relation to religion.

Distinguishing between virtue and goodness, he argues that immediate inclination towards the good "lies within the reach and capacity of all sensible creatures," since it is in the interest of the species. 'Virtue' or 'merit,' on the other hand, is allowed only to man. Virtue, claims Shaftesbury, is part of the faculty of reflection which forms the general notion of things, especially that of actions and affections. Once introduced into the mind, actions and affections become objects of moral evaluation. Shaftesbury attributes the act of approval or disapproval to a moral sense a "sense of right and wrong." What is of special interest in the preceding pages (included here) is the connection which Shaftesbury establishes between the ethical and the beautiful, between moral judgment and aesthetic judgment. The "harmonious" sense, manifested in "forms or representations of sensible things" is, accordingly, the very sense, or a sense similar to it, on which moral evaluations are based. Thus "right vs. wrong," not unlike "beauty vs. deformity," is assessed by the mind's disposition to kinds of "proportions" "regularity" of sorts.

In the second part of the treatise, Shaftesbury grounds man's obligation to virtue in his conduciveness to happiness. He likewise resorts to aesthetic notions with regard to natural vs. unnatural affections.

. . .

Moral
Sense.

THERE is in reality no rational Creature whatsoever, who knows not that when he voluntarily offends or does harm to anyone, he cannot fail to create an Apprehension and Fear of like harm, and consequently a Resentment and Animosity in every Creature who observes him. So that the Offender must needs be conscious of being liable to such Treatment, from every-one, as if he had in some degree offended All.

THUS Offence and Injury are always known as punishable by every-one; and equal Behaviour, which is therefore call'd MERIT, as rewardable and well-deserving from every-one. Of this even the wickedest Creature living must have a *Sense*. So that if there be any further meaning in this *Sense* of Right and Wrong; if in reality there be any *Sense* of this kind which an absolute wicked Creature has not; it must consist in a real Antipathy or Aversion to *Injustice* or *Wrong*, and in a real Affection or Love towards *Equity* and *Right*, for its own sake, and on the account of its own natural Beauty and Worth.

'TIS impossible to suppose a mere sensible Creature originally so ill-constituted, and unnatural, as that from the moment he comes to be try'd by sensible Objects, he shou'd have no one good Passion towards his Kind, no foundation either of Pity, Love, Kindness, or social Affection. 'Tis full as impossible to conceive, that a rational Creature coming first to be try'd by rational Objects, and receiving into his Mind the Images or Representations of Justice, Generosity, Gratitude, or other Virtue, shou'd have no *Liking* of these, or *Dislike* of their contrarys; but be found absolutely indifferent towards whatsoever is presented to him of this sort. A Soul, indeed, may as well be without *Sense*, as without Admiration in the Things of which it has any knowlededg. Coming therefore to a Capacity of seeing and admiring in this new way, it must needs find a Beauty and a Deformity as well in Actions, Minds, and Tempers, as in Figures, Sounds or Colours. If there be no *real* Amiableness or Deformity in moral Acts, there is at least *an imaginary one* of full force. Tho perhaps the Thing itself shou'd not be allow'd in Nature, the

Imagination or Fancy of it must be allow'd to be from Nature alone. Nor can any thing besides Art and strong Endeavour, with long Practice and Meditation, overcome such a *natural Prevention,* or *Prepossession* of the Mind, in favour of this moral Distinction.

Moral Sense.

SENSE of Right and Wrong therefore being as natural to us as *natural Affection* itself, and being a first Principle in our Constitution and Make; there is no speculative Opinion, Persuasion or Belief, which is capable *immediately* or *directly* to exclude or destroy it. That which is of original and pure Nature, nothing beside contrary Habit and Custom (a second Nature) is able to displace. And this Affection being *an original one* of earliest rise in the Soul or affectionate Part; nothing beside contrary Affection, by frequent check and controul, can operate upon it, so as either to diminish it in part, or destroy it in the whole.

How impari'd:

By opposite Affection, or Antipathy;

'TIS evident in what relates to the Frame and Order of our *Bodys;* that no particular odd Mein or Gesture, which is either natural to us, and consequent to our Make, or accidental and by Habit acquir'd, can possibly be overcome by our immediate Disapprobation, or the contrary Bent of our Will, ever so strongly set against it. Such a Change cannot be effected without extraordinary Means, and the intervention of Art and Method, a strict Attention, and repeated Check. And even thus, Nature, we find, is hardly master'd; but lies sullen, and ready to revolt, on the first occasion. Much more is this *the Mind's* Case in respect of that natural Affection and anticipating Fancy, which makes the sense of Right and Wrong. 'Tis impossible that this can instantly, or without much Force and Violence, be effac'd, or struck out of the natural Temper, even by means of the most extravagant Belief or Opinion in the World.[7]

Not by Opinion merely.

———— ᵴ ————

7. Elsewhere, Shaftesbury explicates the relationship between the virtuous, the beautiful and happiness. In the present section, he deals with "beauty itself." His treatment concerns form and the power to form, a capacity which is innate to man. These are hierarchically ordered inasmuch as the latter has power to potentiate the potential, i.e. the power of activation. Thus, in the absence of a forming power, Shaftesbury considered mere forms to be "dead forms." Those forms which reveal intelligence i.e. actions and operations, are "forms which form," for they contain the "effects of the
(CONT.)

THE MORALIST

PART III, SECTION 2 [8]

. . .

O THEOCLES! said I, well do I remember now the Terms in which you engag'd me, that Morning when you bespoke my *Love* of this *mysterious Beauty.* You have indeed made good your part of the Condition, and may now claim me for *a Proselyte.* If there be any seeming Extravagance in the case, I must comfort myself the best I can, and consider that all sound *Love* and *Admiration* is * ENTHUSIASM: "The Transports of *Poets,* the Sublime of *Orators,* the Rapture of *Musicians,* the high Strains of the *Virtuosi;* all mere ENTHUSIASM! Even *Learning* it-self, the Love of *Arts* and *Curiositys,* the Spirit of *Travellers* and *Adventurers; Gallantry, War, Heroism;* All, all ENTHUSIASM!" ———— 'Tis enough: I am content to be this *new Enthusiast,* in a way unknown to me before.

And I, reply'd THEOCLES, am content you shou'd call this *Love*

———   ———

(CONT.)   mind and Mind itself." The power to form, Shaftesbury argues, stems from "mere nature," and is innate to man as such. Innateness, however, does not imply ready-made designs, only the power to judge them. The kind of judgment employed rests on cultivation and knowledge. For Shaftesbury, the mind is neither a tabula rasa nor an aggregate of given forms; mental processes, rather, rest on some basic propensities with which the mind is endowed and which enable such operations. Thus, beauty does not reside in matter, but in that which beautifies it, which in turn, resides in the design or form bestowed upon it. This forming power, Shaftesbury insists, resides in the mind, and represents in a nutshell the core of his aesthetic theory. It frees art from "pre-established" configurations, replacing imitation by original creation, and thereby granting art an honorable place in man's rational existence.

Characteristics was sent to Leibniz (among others) for criticism upon its appearance in 1711. Despite some criticism, Leibniz states approvingly that he was surprised to find "a number of thoughts" which agree with his own "principles." About the *Philosophical Rhapsody* in particular, which he called "the sanctuary of the most sublime philosophy," he wrote: "I had expected merely to find a philosophy like Mr. Locke's but was led beyond Plato and Descartes. If I had seen this work before my *Theodicy* was published I should have profited as I ought and should have borrowed its great passages." (See his remarks on the *Characteristics* in Leibniz 1969: 633.)

8. *Characteristics,* vol. II, pp. 400–428.

of ours ENTHUSIASM: allowing it the Privilege of its Fellow-Passions. For is there a fair and plausible *Enthusiasm,* a reasonable *Extasy* and *Transport* allow'd to other Subjects, such as Architecture, Painting, Musick; and shall it be exploded *here?* Are there Senses by which all those other Graces and Perfections are perceiv'd? and none by which this higher Perfection and Grace is comprehended? Is it so preposterous to bring that *Enthusiasm* hither, and transfer it from those *secondary* and *scanty* Objects, to this *original* and *comprehensive* One? Observe how the Case stands in all those other Subjects of Art or Science. What difficulty to be in any degree knowing! How long ere a true *Taste* is gain'd! How many things shocking, how many offensive at first, which afterwards are known and acknowledg'd the highest *Beautys!* For 'tis not instantly we acquire the *Sense* by which these Beautys are discoverable. *Labour* and *Pains* are requir'd, and *Time* to cultivate a natural Genius, ever so apt or forward. But Who is there once thinks of cultivating *this* Soil, or of improving any Sense or Faculty which Nature may have given of *this* kind? And is it a wonder we shou'd be dull then, as we are, confounded, and at a loss in *these* Affairs, blind as to *this* higher Scene, *these* nobler Representations? Which way shou'd we come to understand better? which way be knowing in *these* Beautys? Is Study, Science, or Learning necessary to understand all Beautys else? And for *the Sovereign* BEAUTY is there no Skill or Science requir'd? In Painting there are *Shades* and *masterly Strokes,* which the Vulgar understand not, but find fault with: in Architecture there is *the Rustic;* in Musick *the Chromatick* kind, and skilful Mixture of *Dissonancys.* And is there nothing which answers to this, in *The* WHOLE?

Arts.

A Judgment, Taste.

Improvement.

Chief Science.

I MUST confess, said I, I have hitherto been one of those Vulgar, who cou'd never relish *the Shades, the Rustick,* or *the Dissonancys* you talk of. I have never dreamt of such *Masterpieces* in NATURE. 'Twas my way to censure freely on the first view. But I perceive I am now oblig'd to go far in the pursuit of *Beauty;* which lies very absconded and deep: and if so, I am well assur'd that my *Enjoyments* hitherto have been very shallow. I have dwelt, it seems, all this while upon the Surface, and enjoy'd

Beauty

only a kind of slight superficial Beautys; having never gone in
search of *Beauty it-self,* but of what I *fansy'd* such. Like the rest
of the unthinking World, I took for granted that what I liked was
beautiful; and what I rejoic'd in, was my *Good.* I never scrupled
loving what I fansy'd; and aiming only at the Enjoyment of what
I lov'd, I never troubled my-self with examining what *the Subjects*
were, nor ever hesitated about their *Choice.*

BEGIN then, said he, and *chuse.* See what the *Subjects* are; and
which you wou'd prefer; which honour with your Admiration,
Love and Esteem. For by these again you will be honour'd in
your turn. Such, PHILOCLES, as is the Worth of these Companions,
such will your Worth be found. As there is Emptiness or Fulness
here, so will there be in your Enjoyment. See therefore where
Fulness is, and where *Emptiness.* See in what Subject resides *the
chief Excellence:* where BEAUTY reigns: where 'tis *intire, perfect,
absolute;* where *broken, imperfect, short.* View these terrestrial
Beautys, and whatever has the appearance of Excellence, and is
able to attract. See that which either really is, or stands as in the
room of *Fair, Beautiful,* and *Good:* "A Mass of Metal; a Tract of
Land; a Number of Slaves; a Pile of Stones; a human Body of certain Lineaments and Proportions." Is this the highest of the kind?
Is BEAUTY founded then in *Body* only; and not in *Action, Life,* or
Operation?

. . .

THUS THEN, said he, (smiling) Whatever Passion you may have
for *other Beautys;* I know, good PHILOCLES, you are no such
Admirer of *Wealth* in any kind, as to allow much Beauty to it;
especially in a rude Heap or Mass. But in Medals, Coins, Imbost-
work, Statues, and well-fabricated Pieces, of whatever sort, you
can discover *Beauty,* and admire the kind. True, said I; but not
for the *Metal's* sake. 'Tis not then *the Metal* or *Matter* which is
beautiful with you.   No.   But *the Art.*   Certainly.
The Art then is the *Beauty.*   Right.   And *the Art* is
that which beautifies.   The same.   So that the
Beautifying, not the Beautify'd, is the really *Beautiful.*   It
seems so.   For that which is beautify'd, is beautiful only by

the accession of something beautifying: and by the recess or withdrawing of the same, it ceases to be beautiful. Be it. In respect of Bodys therefore, *Beauty* comes and goes. So we see. Nor is the Body it-self any Cause either of its coming or staying. None. So that there is no principle of Beauty in *Body.* None at all. For Body can no-way be the Cause of Beauty to it-self. No-way. Nor govern nor regulate it-self. Nor yet this. Nor mean nor intend it-self. Nor this neither. Must not *that* therefore, which means and intends for it, regulates and orders it, be the Principle of Beauty to it? Of necessity. And what must that be? MIND, I suppose; for what can it be else?

HERE then, said he, is all I wou'd have explain'd to you before: "that *the Beautiful, the Fair, the Comely*, were never in the *Matter*, but in the *Art* and *Design;* never in *Body* it-self, but in the *Form* or *forming Power.*" Does not the beautiful *Form* confess this, and speak the Beauty of *the Design*, whene'er it strikes you? What is it but *the Design* which strikes? What is it you admire but MIND, or the Effect of *Mind?* 'Tis *Mind* alone which forms. All which is void of *Mind* is horrid: and Matter formless is *Deformity it-self.*

OF all *Forms* then, said I, Those (according to your Scheme) are the most amiable, and in the first Order of Beauty, which have a power of making other Forms themselves: From whence methinks they may be styl'd *the forming Forms.* So far I can easily concur with you, and gladly give the advantage to *the human Form*, above those other Beautys of Man's Formation. The Palaces, Equipages and Estates shall never in my account be brought in competition with the original *living Forms* of Flesh and Blood. And for the other, the *dead* Forms of Nature, the Metals and Stones, however precious and dazling; I am resolved to resist their Splendour, and make abject Things of 'em, even in their highest Pride, when they pretend to set off human Beauty, and are officiously brought in aid of *the Fair.*

DO you not see then, reply'd THEOCLES, that you have establish'd *three* Degrees or Orders of Beauty? As how?

Orders of Beauty

First Or-der.

Why first, *the dead Forms*, as you properly have call'd 'em, which bear a Fashion, and are form'd, whether by Man, or Nature; but have no forming Power, no Action, or Intelligence.   Right.   Next, and as the *second* kind, *the*

Second Or-der.

forms which form; that is which have Intelligence, Action, and Operation.   Right still.

Here therefore is double Beauty. For here is both the Form (the *Effect* of Mind) and *Mind* it-self: The first kind low and despicable in respect of this other; from whence the dead Form receives its Lustre and force of Beauty. For what is a mere *Body*, tho a human one, and ever so exactly fashion'd, if *inward* Form be wanting, and the Mind be monstrous or imperfect, as in an *Idiot*, or *Savage?* This too I can apprehend, said I; but where is the *third* Order?

HAVE patience, reply'd he, and see first whether you have dis-cover'd the whole Force of this *second* Beauty. How else shou'd you understand the Force of Love, or have the Power of Enjoyment? Tell me, I beseech you, when first you nam'd these *the forming Forms*, did you think of no other Productions of theirs besides the *dead Kinds*, such as the Palaces, the Coins, the Brazen or the Marble Figures of Men? Or did you think of some-thing nearer *Life?*

I COU'D easily, said I, have added, that these *Forms* of ours had a Virtue of producing *other living Forms*, like themselves. But this Virtue of theirs, I thought was from *another Form* above them, and cou'd not properly be call'd *their* Virtue or Art; if in reality there was a *superior Art*, or something *Artist-like*, which guided their Hand, and made Tools of them in this specious Work.

HAPPILY thought, said he! You have prevented a Censure which I hardly imagin'd you cou'd escape. And here you have unawares discover'd that *third* Order of Beauty, which forms not

Third Or-der.

only such as we call mere Forms, but even *the Forms which form*. For we our-selves are notable Architects in Matter, and can shew lifeless Bodys brought into Form, and fashion'd by our own Hands: but that which fashions even Minds themselves, contains in it-self all the Beautys fashion'd by those Minds; and is consequently the Principle, Source, and Fountain of all *Beauty*.

It seems so.

THEREFORE whatever Beauty appears in our *second* Order of Forms, or whatever is deriv'd or produc'd from thence, all this is eminently, principally and originally in this *last* Order of *Supreme* and *Sovereign Beauty.*

True.

THUS Architecture, Musick, and all which is of human Invention, resolves itself into this *last* Order.

Right, said I: and thus all the *Enthusiasms* of other kinds resolve themselves into ours. The fashionable Kinds borrow from us, and are nothing without us: We have undoubtedly the Honour of being *Originals.*

NOW therefore say again, reply'd THEOCLES; Whether are those Fabricks of *Architecture, Sculpture,* and the rest of that sort, the greatest Beautys which Man forms; or are there greater and better? None which I know, reply'd I. Think, think again, said he: and setting aside those Productions which just now you excepted against, as Master-pieces *of another Hand;* think What there are which more immediately proceed from us, and may more truly be term'd *our Issue.* I am barren, said I, for this time: you must be plainer yet, in helping me to conceive. How can I help you, reply'd he? Wou'd you have me be conscious for you, of that which is immediately *your own,* and is solely in, and from *your-self?* You mean my *Sentiments,* said I. Certainly, reply'd he: and together with *Beauty moral.* your *Sentiments,* your *Resolutions, Principles, Determinations, Actions;* whatsoever is handsom and noble in the kind; whatever flows from your good *Understanding, Sense, Knowledg* and *Will;* whatever is ingender'd in your *Heart,* (good PHILOCLES!) or *Offsrping. Genera- tion.* derives it-self from your *Parent-*MIND, which unlike to other *Parents,* is never spent or exhausted, but gains Strength and Vigor by producing. So *You,* my Friend! have prov'd it, by many a Work: not suffering that fertile Part to remain idle and unactive. Hence those good Parts, which from a natural Genius you have rais'd by due Improvement. And here, as I cannot but admire the pregnant Genius, and *Parent-*Beauty; so am I satisfy'd of the *Offspring,* that it is and will be ever beautiful.

I Took the Compliment, and wish'd (I told him) the Case were really as he imagin'd, that I might justly merit his Esteem and Love. My Study therefore shou'd be to grow *beautiful*, in his way of *beauty;* and from this time forward I wou'd do all I cou'd

Source

to propagate that lovely Race of mental Children, happily sprung from such a high Enjoyment, and from a Union with what was *Fairest* and *Best.* But 'tis you, Theocles, continu'd I, must help my labouring Mind, and be as it were the Midwife to those Conceptions; which else, I fear, will prove abortive.

You do well, reply'd he, to give me the Midwife's part only: For the Mind conceiving *of it-self,* can only be, as you say, *assist-*

Pregnan-cy

ed in the Birth. Its *Pregnancy* is from its *Nature.* Nor cou'd it ever have been thus *impregnated* by any other *Mind,* than that which form'd it at the beginning; and which, as we have already prov'd, is Original to all *mental,* as well as *other Beauty.*

Do you maintain then , said I, that these *mental* Children, the

Innate Ideas.

Notions and Principles, of *Fair, Just,* and *Honest,* with the rest of these *Ideas,* are *innate?*

Anatomists, said he, tell us that the Eggs, which are Principles in Body, are *innate;* being form'd already in the *Fœtus* before the Birth. But *When* it is, whether *before,* or *at,* or *after* the Birth, or at *What* time after, that either these, or other Principles, Organs of Sensation, or Sensations themselves, are *first* form'd in us, is a matter, doubtless, of curious Speculation, but of no great Importance. The Question is, whether the Principles spoken of are *from Art,* or *Nature?* If from *Nature* purely; 'tis no matter for the Time: nor would I contend with you, tho you shou'd deny *Life* it-self to be *innate,* as imagining it follow'd rather than pre-ceded the moment of Birth. But this I am certain of; that *Life,* and the *Sensations* which accompany Life, come when they will, are form *mere Nature,* and nothing else. Therefore if you dislike

Instinct

the word *Innate,* let us change it, if you will, for Instinct; and call *Instinct,* that which *Nature* teaches, exclusive of *Art, Culture,* or *Discipline.*

Content, said I.

Leaving then, reply'd he, those admirable speculations to the *Virtuosi,* the *Anatomists,* and *School-Divines;* we may safely aver, with all their Consents, that the several Organs, particularly those of Generation, are form'd by *Nature*. Whether is there also from Nature, think you, any *Instinct* for the after-Use of them? Or whether must *Learning* and *Experience* imprint this use? 'Tis imprinted, said I, enough in Conscience. The Impression, or *Instinct*, is so strong in the Case, that 'twou'd be absurdity not to think it *natural*, as well in our own Species, as in other Creatures; amongst whom (as you have already taught me) not only the mere engendring of the Young, but the various and almost infinite Means and Methods of providing for them, are all foreknown. For thus much we may indeed discern in the preparatory Labours and Arts of these wild Creatures; which demonstrate their anticipating *Fancys*, *Pre-conceptions*, or *Pre-sensations;* if I may use a word you taught me yesterday. *Genera-tion.* *Pre-con-ceptions.*

I ALLOW your Expression, said THEOCLES, and will endeavour to show you that the same *Pre-conceptions*, of a higher degree, have place in human Kind. Do so, said I, I intreat you: For so far am I from finding in my-self these Pre-conceptions of *Fair* and *Beautiful*, in your sense, that methinks, till now of late, I have hardly known of any thing like them in Nature. How then, said he, wou'd you have known that *outward Fair* and *Beautiful* of human Kind; if such an Object (a fair fleshly one) in all its Beauty, had *for the first time* appear'd to you, by your-self, this morning, in these Groves? Or do you think perhaps you shou'd have been unmov'd, and have found no difference between *this Form* and *any other;* if first you had not been *instructed?*

I HAVE hardly any Right, reply'd I, to plead this last Opinion, after what I have own'd just before.

WELL then, said he, that I may appear to take no advantage against you; I quit the dazling *Form*, which carrys such a Force of *complicated Beautys;* and am contented to consider separately each of those *simple* Beautys, which taken all together, create this wonderful effect. For you will allow, without doubt, that in respect of *Bodys*, whatever is commonly said of the unexpress-ible, the unintelligible, the *I-know-not-what* of Beauty; there can lie no Mystery here, but what plainly belongs either to *Figure*, *Colour*, *Motion* or *Sound*. Omitting therefore the *three* latter, and their dependent Charms; let us view the Charm in what is sim- *Beauty of Body*

plest of all, *mere Figure.* Nor need we go so high as Sculpture,
Architecture, or the Designs of those who from this Study of
Beauty have rais'd such delightful Arts. 'Tis enough if we con-
sider the simplest of Figures; as either a round *Ball,* a *Cube,* or
Dye. Why is even an Infant pleas'd with the first View of these
Proportions? Why is the *Sphere* or *Globe,* the *Cylinder* and
Obelisk prefer'd; and the irregular Figures, in respect of these,
rejected and despis'd?

I AM ready, reply'd I, to own there is in certain *Figures* a natural Beauty, which the Eye finds as soon as the Object is presented to it.

Beauty of   Is there then, said he, a natural Beauty of *Figures?* and is there
Soul,   not as natural a one of ACTIONS? No sooner the Eye opens upon
As real,   *Figures,* the Ear to *Sounds,* than straight *the Beautiful* results, and
And neces-   *Grace* and *Harmony* are known and acknowledg'd. No sooner
sarily mov-   are ACTIONS view'd, no sooner the *human Affections* and
ing.   *Passions* discern'd (and they are most of 'em as soon discern'd
                 as felt) than straight *an inward* EYE distinguishes, and sees *the*
Idea Na-   *Fair* and *Shapely,* the *Amiable* and *Admirable,* apart from *the*
tural   *Deform'd, the Foul, the Odious,* or the *Despicable.* How is it pos-
                 sible therefore not to own, "That as these *Distinctions* have their
                 Foundation *in Nature,* the Discernment it-self is *natural,* and
                 from NATURE *alone?"*

If this, I told him, were as he represented it; there cou'd never,
I thought, be any Disagreement among Men concerning Actions
and Behaviour: as which was *Base,* which *Worthy;* which
Handsom, and which *Deform'd.* But now we found perpetual
Variance among Mankind; whose Differences were chiefly
founded on this Disagreement in Opinion; "The one *affirming,*
the other *denying,* that this, or that, was *fit* or *decent."*

The Fit,   EVEN by this then, reply'd he, it appears there is Fitness and
and De-   Decency in actions; since *the Fit* and *Decent* is in this
cent.   Controversy ever pre-suppos'd: And whilst Men are at odds
                 about the Subjects, the Thing it-self is universally agreed. For
                 neither is there Agreement in Judgments about other *Beautys.*
                 'Tis controverted "Which is the finest *Pile,* the loveliest *Shape,* or
                 Face:" But without controversy, 'tis allow'd "There is a BEAUTY of

each kind." This no-one goes about to *teach*: nor is it *learnt* by *Standard* any; but *confess'd* by All. *All* own the *Standard, Rule,* and *own'd.* *Measure:* But in applying it to Things, Disorder arises, Ignorance prevails, Interest and Passion breed Disturbance. Nor can it otherwise happen in the Affairs of Life, whilst that which interests and engages Men as *Good,* is thought different from that which they admire and praise as *Honest.* ――― But with us, PHILOCLES! 'tis better settled; since for our parts, we have already decreed, "That *Beauty* and *Good* are still the same. *Good.*

. . .

AND NOW, what say you, PHILOCLES, continu'd he, to this Defense I have been making for you? 'Tis grounded, as you see, on the Supposition of your being deeply ingag'd in this philosophical Cause. But perhaps you have yet many Difficultys to get over, ere you can so far take part with *Beauty,* as to make this to be your *Good.*

I HAVE no difficulty so great, said I, as not to be easily remov'd. My Inclinations lead me strongly this way: for I am ready enough to yield there is no real *Good* beside *the Enjoyment of Beauty.* And I am as ready, reply'd THEOCLES, to yield There is no real Enjoyment of Beauty beside what is *Good.* Excellent! But upon reflection, I fear I am little beholden to you for your Concession. As how? Because shou'd I offer to contend for any Enjoyment of Beauty out of your mental Way, you wou'd, I doubt, call such Enjoyment of mine *absurd;* as you did once before. Undoubtedly, I shou'd. For what is it shou'd *Mental* enjoy, or be capable of Enjoyment, except MIND? Or shall we say, *Body Enjoy-* *enjoys?* By the help of *Sense,* perhaps; not otherwise. Is BEAU- *ment.* TY, then, *the Object of Sense?* Say how? Which way? For otherwise the help of *Sense* is nothing in the Case: And if *Body* be of *Body.* it-self incapable, and *Sense* no help to it, to apprehend or enjoy Beauty, there remains only the MIND which is capable either to apprehend or to *enjoy.*

TRUE, said I; but show me, then, "Why BEAUTY may not be *the Sense.* Object of the Sense?"* Shew me first, I intreat you, "*Why, Where,* or in *What* you fansy it may be so?" Is it not *Beauty* which first excites the Sense, and feeds it afterwards in

the Passion we call *Love?*   Say in the same manner,
"That it is *Beauty* first excites the Sense, and feeds it afterwards
in the Passion we call *Hunger.*" —— You will not say it. The
Thought, I perceive, displeases you. As great as the Pleasure is
of good Eating, you disdain to apply the Notion of *Beauty* to the
good Dishes which create it. You wou'd hardly have applauded the preposterous Fancy of some luxurious ROMANS of old,
who cou'd relish a Fricassee the better for hearing it was compos'd of Birds which wore a beautiful Feather, or had sung deli-
ciously. Instead of being incited by such a historical Account of
Meats, you wou'd be apt, I believe, to have less Appetite, the
more you search'd their Origin, and descended into the *Kitchin*-
Science, to learn the several Forms and Changes they had under-
gone, ere they were serv'd at this elegant voluptuous Table. But
tho the *Kitchin*-Forms be ever so disgraceful, you will allow that
the *Materials* of the Kitchin, such, for instance, as the *Garden*
furnishes, are really fair and beautiful in their kind. Nor will you
deny beauty to the wild *Field,* or to these *Flowers* which grow
around us, on this verdant Couch. And yet, as lovely as are these
Forms of Nature, the shining *Grass,* or silver'd *Moss,* the flowry
Thyme, wild *Rose,* or *Honey-suckle:* 'tis not their BEAUTY allures
the neighbouring Herds, delights the brouzing Fawn, or Kid, and
spreads the Joy we see amidst the feeding Flocks: 'Tis not the
Form rejoices; but that which is beneath the Form: 'tis
Savouriness attracts, *Hunger* impels; and *Thirst,* better allay'd by
the clear Brook than the thick Puddle, makes the *fair* NYMPH to
be prefer'd, whose form is otherwise flighted. For never can the
Form be of real force where it is uncontemplated, unjudg'd of,
unexamin'd, and stands only as the accidental Note or Token of
what appeases provok'd Sense, and satisfies the brutish Part. Are
you persuaded of this, good PHILOCLES? or rather than not give
Brutes the advantage of *Enjoyment,* will you allow them also a
Mind and rational Part?

Not so, I told him.

IF BRUTES therefore, said he, be incapable of knowing and
enjoying Beauty, as being *Brutes,* and having SENSE only (the
brutish part) for their own share; it follows, "That neither can
MAN by the same *Sense* or brutish Part, conceive or enjoy *Beauty;*

But all the *Beauty* and *Good* he enjoys, is in a nobler way, and by the help of what is noblest, his MIND and REASON." Here lies *Reason.* his *Dignity* and highest *Interest*: Here his *Capacity* toward Good and Happiness. His *Ability* or *Incompetency*, his *Power* of Enjoyment, or his *Impotence*, is founded in this alone. As this is *sound, fair, noble, worthy;* so are its Subjects, Acts and Employments. For as the *riotous* MIND, captive to *Sense*, can never enter in competition, or contend for Beauty with the *virtouos* MIND of Reason's Culture; so neither can the *Objects* which allure the former, compare with those which attract and charm the latter. An when *each* gratifies it-self in the Enjoyment and Possession of its Object; how evidently fairer are the Acts which join the *latter Pair*, and give a *Soul* the Enjoyment of what is *generous* and *good?* This at least, PHILOCLES, you will surely allow, that when you place a Joy elsewhere than in the Mind; *the Enjoyment* it-self will be no beautiful Subject, nor of any graceful or agreeable Appearance. But when you think how *Friendship* is enjoy'd, how *Honour, Gratitude, Candour, Benignity*, and all internal Beauty; how all the *social* Pleasures, *Society* it-self, and all which constitutes the Worth and Happiness of Mankind; you will here surely allow Beauty in the *Act*, and think it worthy to be view'd, and pass'd in review often by the glad Mind, happily conscious of the generous Part, and of its own Advancement and Growth in Beauty.

Comparison of Objects, and Enjoyments.

THUS, PHILOCLES, (continu'd he, after a short Pause) thus have I presum'd to treat of *Beauty* before so great a Judg, and such a skilful Admirer as your-self. For taking rise from Nature's Beauty, which transported me, I gladly ventur'd further in the Chase; and have accompany'd you in search of Beauty, as it relates to us, and makes our highest *Good*, in its sincere and natural Enjoyment. And if we have not idly spent our hours, nor rang'd in vain thro' these deserted Regions; it shou'd appear from our strict Search, that there is nothing so divine as BEAUTY: which belonging not to *Body*, nor having any Principle or Existence except in MIND and REASON, is alone discover'd and acquir'd by this diviner Part, when it inspects *it-self*, the only Object worthy of it-self. For whate'er is void of Mind, is *Void* and *Darkness* to the *Mind's* EYE. This languishes and grows dim, whene'er

Recapitulation.

detain'd on foreign Subjects; but thrives and attains its natural
Vigour, when employ'd in Contemplation of what is like it-self.
'Tis thus the *improving* MIND, slightly surveying other Objects,
and passing over Bodys, and the common Forms, (where only a
Shadow of Beauty rests) ambitiously presses onward to its
Source, and views *the Original* of Form and Order in that which

Knowledg
of our-
selves.
Interest.

is intelligent.   And thus, O PHILOCLES! may we improve and
become Artists in the kind; learning "To know *Our-selves*, and
what *That* is, which by improving, we may be sure to advance
our Worth, and real Self-Interest."   For neither is this *Knowledg*
acquir'd by Contemplation of Bodys, or the outward Forms, the
View of Pageantrys, the Study of Estates and Honours: nor is He

Ability.

to be esteem'd that self-improving Artist, who makes a Fortune
out of these; but he, *He* only, is the *wise* and *able* Man, who with
a slight regard to these Things, applies himself to cultivate another Soil, builds in a different Matter from that of Stone or Marble;
and having righter Models in his Eye, becomes in truth the
Architect of *his own Life* and *Fortune;* by laying within himself
the lasting and sure Foundations of *Order, Peace,* and *Concord.*
—— But now 'tis time to think of returning home. The Morning
is far spent.   Come! Let us away, and leave these uncommon
Subjects; till we retire again to these remote and unfrequented
Places.

MISCELLANEOUS REFLECTIONS

ON THE PRECEEDING TREATISES, AND OTHER CRITICAL SUBJECTS

SECTION III, CHAPTER 2 [9]

S OMETHING therefore shou'd, methinks, be further
thought of, in behalf of our generous Youths, towards the
correcting of their TASTE, or *Relish* in the Concerns of *Life*.
For this at last is what will influence. And in this respect *the
Youth* alone are to be regarded. Some hopes there may be still

———— ✍ ————

9. *Characteristics*, vol. III, pp. 178–187.

conceiv'd of *These*. The rest are confirm'd and harden'd in their way. A middle-ag'd Knave (however devout or orthodox) is but a common Wonder: an old-one is no Wonder at all: but a young-one is still (thank Heaven!) somewhat extraordinary. And I can never enough admire what was said once by a worthy Man at the first appearance of one of these young able Prostitutes, "That he even trembled at the sight, to find Nature capable of being turn'd so soon: and That he boded greater Calamity to his Country from this single Example of *young* Villany, than from the Practices and Arts of all the *old* Knaves in being."

LET us therefore proceed in this view, addressing our-selves to the grown *Youth* of our polite World. Let the Appeal be to these, whose *Relish* is retrievable, and whose *Taste* may yet be form'd in *Morals;* as it seems to be, already, in *exterior Manners* and *Behaviour.*

THAT there is really A STANDARD of this latter kind, will imme-diately, and on the first view, be acknowledg'd. The Contest is only, "Which is *right:* — which the *un-affected* Carriage, and *just* Demeanour: and Which the *affected* and *false*." Scarce is there any-one, who pretends not to know and to decide What is *well-bred* and *handsom*. There are few so affectedly clownish, as absolutely to disown *Good-breeding*, and renounce the Notion of a BEAUTY in *outward Manners* and *Deportment*. With such as these, wherever they shou'd be found, I must confess, I cou'd scarce be tempted to bestow the least Pains or Labour, towards convincing 'em of a *Beauty* in *inward Sentiments* and *Principles.*

WHOEVER has any Impression of what we call *Gentility* or *Politeness*, is already so acquainted with the DECORUM and GRACE of things, that he will readily confess a Pleasure and Enjoyment in the very *Survey* and *Contemplation* of this kind. Now if in the way of polite Pleasure, *the Study* and *Love* of BEAUTY be essen-tial; *the Study* and *Love* of SYMMETRY and ORDER, on which *Beauty* depends, must also be essential, in the same respect.

'TIS impossible we can advance the least in any *Relish* or *Taste* of outward Symmetry and Order; without acknowledging that the proportionate and regular State is the truly *prosperous* and natural in every Subject. The same Features which make

Deformity, create Incommodiousness and Disease. And the same Shapes and Proportions which make Beauty, afford Advantage, by adapting to Activity and Use. Even in the imitative or *designing* Arts, (to which our author so often refers) the *Truth* or *Beauty* of every Figure or Statue is measur'd from the Perfection of Nature, in her just adapting of every Limb and Proportion to the Activity, Strength , Dexterity, Life and Vigor of the particular Species or Animal *design'd*.

THUS *Beauty* and *Truth* are plainly join'd with the Notion of *Utility* and *Convenience*, even in the Apprehension of every ingenious Artist, the *Architect*, the *Statuary*, or the *Painter*. 'Tis the same in the *Physician's* way. Natural *Health* is the just Proportion, *Truth*, and regular Course of things, in a Constitution. 'Tis *the inward Beauty of the* BODY. And when the Harmony and just Measures of the rising Pulses, the circulating Humours, and the moving Airs or Spirits are disturb'd or lost, *Deformity* enters, and with it, *Calamity* and *Ruin*.

SHOU'D not this, one wou'd imagine, be still the same Case, and hold equally as to *the* MIND? Is there nothing *there* which tends to Disturbance and Dissolution? Is there no natural Tenour, Tone, or Order of the Passions or Affections? No *Beauty,* or *Deformity* in this *moral* kind? Or allowing that there really is; must it not, of consequence, in the same manner imply *Health* or *Sickliness, Prosperity* or *Disaster?* Will it not be found in this respect, above all, "That what is BEAUTIFUL is *harmonious* and *proportionable;* what is harmonious and proportionable, is TRUE; and what is at one both *beautiful* and *true,* is, of consequence, *agreeable* and GOOD?"

WHERE then is this BEAUTY or *Harmony* to be found? How is this SYMMETRY to be discover'd and apply'd? Is it any other *Art* than that of PHILOSOPHY, or *the Study of inward Numbers and Proportions,* which can exhibit this in Life? If no other; Who, then, can possibly have a TASTE of this kind, without being beholden to PHILOSOPHY? Who can admire the *outward* Beautys, and not recur instantly to the *inward,* which are the most real and essential, the most naturally affecting, and of the highest Pleasure, as well as Profit and Advantage?

IN so short a compass does that Learning and Knowledge lie, on which *Manners* and *Life* depend. 'Tis *We our-selves* create and form our TASTE. If we resolve to have it *just;* 'tis in our power. We may esteem and value, approve and disapprove, as we wou'd wish. For who wou'd not rejoice to be always equal and consonant to himself, and have constantly that Opinion of things which is natural and proportionable? But who dares search OPIN-ION to the bottom, or call in question his *early* and *prepossessing* TASTE? Who is so just to himself, as to recal his FANCY from the power of *Fashion* and *Education,* to that of REASON? Cou'd we, however, be thus courageous; we shou'd soon settle in our-selves such an *Opinion* of GOOD as wou'd secure to us an *invari-able, agreeable,* and *just* TASTE in Life and Manners.[10]

10. These selected paragraphs from *Miscellaneous* (one of the last treatises, which first appeared in the complete edition of *Characteristics* in 1711), represents Shaftesbury's overall philosophical view, bridging between man as a natural creature and man as a cultural agent. It brings together some of the major issues that occupied him in his earlier work. By nature, as we have seen, man's mind is endowed with the ability to make distinctions, guided by a predilection towards the harmonious — the ordered -which is necessary for apprehension. But whereas few are those who do not readily recognize outward deformities, there are many who overlook the inward proportionate beauties. This gap can be overcome by those who are not yet so "confirmed and hardened" by habituation, as to be unable to accept change.

But if man is endowed by nature with a harmonious sense, as Shaftesbury believed, what gives rise to those deformations of judgment that call for correction? Shaftesbury does not fully explicate this point.

His analogy between the beautiful and the ethical, noted in previous sections, now seems somewhat problematic, if the beautiful serves as a sole criteria for moral judgments and the establishment of truth.

As influential as Shaftesbury was in providing a counter-theory to Hobbes and in opening new vistas for aesthetic and moral deliberations, he was also trapped in a kind of circular explication which both Hume and Kant later tried to resolve. Nonetheless, the centrality that he accorded the reflective powers of the mind, and to the immediate inclination of sensible creatures towards "goodness" constitute an optimistic view, according to which man is capable, through his own endeavors, to bring about that which he is by nature empowered to accomplish. This is what civilization is all about.

Interestingly, Leibniz attributed great importance to Shaftesbury's discourse on taste, precisely because "taste as distinguished from understanding," says Leibniz, "consists

(CONT.)

A LETTER CONCERNING DESIGN[11]

J CAN my-self remember the Time, when, in respect of MUSICK, our reigning Taste was in many degrees inferior to the *French*. The long Reign of Luxury and Pleasure under King CHARLES the Second, and the foreign Helps and study'd Advantages given to *Musick* in a following Reign, cou'd not raise our Genius the least in this respect. But when the Spirit of the Nation was grown more *free*, tho engag'd at that time in the fiercest War, and with the most doubtful Success, we no sooner began to turn our-selves towards *Musick*, and enquire what ITALY in particular produc'd, than in an instant we outstrip'd our Neighbours the FRENCH, enter'd into a Genius far beyond theirs, and rais'd our-selves an *Ear*, and *Judgment*, not inferior to the best now in the World.

IN the same manner, as to PAINTING. Tho we have as yet nothing of our own native Growth in this kind worthy of being mention'd; yet since the Publick has of late begun to express a Relish for Ingravings, Drawings, Copyings, and for the original Paintings of the chief *Italian* Schools, (so contrary to the modern *French*) I doubt not that, in very few years, we shall make an equal progress in this other Science. And when our Humour turns us to cultivate these designing Arts, our Genius, I am persuaded, will naturally carry us over the slighter Amusements, and lead us to that higher, more serious, and noble Part of *Imitation*, which relates to *History, Human Nature*, and *the chief Degree or Order of* BEAUTY; I mean that of the *Rational* life, distinct from the merely *vegetable* and *sensible*, as in Animals, or Plants; according to those several Degrees or Orders of Painting, which your Lordship will find suggested in this extemporary *Notion* I have sent you.

(CONT.) ——— ᚾ ———

of confused perceptions for which one cannot give an adequate reason.... Tastes are formed by nature and by habits. To have good taste, one must practice enjoying the good things which reason and experience have already authorized. Young people need guidance in this." (Leibniz 1969: 634).

11. *Characteristics* Vol III, pp. 398-405.

As for ARCHITECTURE, 'tis no wonder if so many noble Designs of this kind have miscarry'd amongst us; since the Genius of our Nation has hitherto been so little turn'd this way, that thro' several Reigns we have patiently seen the noblest publick Buildings perish (if I may say so) under the Hand of one single Court-Architect; who, if he had been able to profit by Experience, wou'd long since, at our expence, have prov'd the greatest Master in the World. But I question whether our Patience is like to hold much longer. The Devastation so long committed in this kind, has made us begin to grow rude and clamorous at the hearing of a new Palace spoilt, or a new Design committed to some rash or impotent Pretender.

'TIS the good Fate of our Nation in this particular, that there remain yet two of the noblest Subjects for Architecture; our Prince's *Palace*, and our *House of Parliament*. For I can't but fansy that when *Whitehall* is thought of, the neighbouring *Lords* and *Commons* will at the same time be plac'd in better Chambers and Apartments, than at present; were it only for Majesty's sake, and as a Magnificence becoming the Person of the Prince, who here appears in full Solemnity. Nor do I fear that when these new Subjects are attempted, we shou'd miscarry as grosly as we have done in others before. Our *State*, in this respect, may prove perhaps more fortunate than our *Church*, in having waited till a national Taste was form'd, before these Edifices were undertaken. But the Zeal of the Nation cou'd not, it seems, admit so long a Delay in their Ecclesiastical Structures, particularly their *Metropolitan*. And since a Zeal of this sort has been newly kindled amongst us, 'tis like we shall see from afar the many Spires arising in our great City, with such hasty and sudden growth, as may be the occasion perhaps that our immediate Relish shall be hereafter censur'd, as retaining much of what Artists call the *Gothick* Kind.

HARDLY, indeed, as the Publick now stands, shou'd we bear to see a *Whitehall* treated like a *Hampton-Court* , or even a new Cathedral like St. PAUL'S. Almost every-one now becomes concern'd, and interests himself in such publick Structures. Even those Pieces too are brought under the common Censure, which, tho rais'd by private Men, are of such a Grandure and Magnificence, as to become National Ornaments. The ordinary Man may build his Cottage, or the plain Gentleman his Country-house according as he fansys: but when a great Man builds, he will find little Quarter from the Publick, if instead of a beautiful Pile, he raises, at a vast expence, such a false and counterfeit Piece of Magnificence, as can be justly arraign'd for its Deformity by so many knowing Men in Art, and by the whole *People*, who, in such a Conjuncture, readily follow their Opinion.

IN reality *the People* are no small Partys in this *Cause.* Nothing moves successfully without 'em. There can be no PUBLICK, but where they are included. And without *a Publick Voice,* knowingly guided and directed, there is nothing which can raise a true Ambition in the Artist; nothing which can exalt the Genius of the Workman, or make him emulous of after-Fame, and of the approbation of his *Country,* and of *Posterity.* For with *these* he naturally, as a *Freeman,* must take part: in *these* he has a passionate Concern, and Interest, rais'd in him by the same Genius of *Liberty,* the same *Laws* and *Government,* by which his Property, and the Rewards of his Pains and Industry are secur'd to him, and to his Generation after him.

EVERY thing co-operates, in such a *State,* towards the Improvement of *Art* and *Science.* And for the *designing Arts* in particular, such as *Architecture, Painting,* and *Statuary,* they are in a manner link'd together. The Taste of one kind brings necessarily that of the others along with it. When the *free* Spirit of a Nation turns it-self this way, Judgments are form'd; Criticks arise; the publick Eye and Ear improve; a right Taste prevails, and in a manner forces its way. Nothing is so improving, nothing so natural, so *con-genial* to the liberal Arts, as that reigning Liberty and high Spirit of a People, which from the Habit of judging in the highest Matters for themselves, makes 'em freely judg of other Subjects, and enter thorowly into the Characters as well of *Men* and *Manners,* as of the *Products* or *Works* of Men, in Art and Science. So much, my Lord, do we owe to the Excellence of our National Constitution, and Legal Monarchy; happily fitted for Us, and which alone cou'd hold together so mighty a People; all sharers (tho at so far a distance from each other) in the Government of *themselves;* and meeting under *one* Head in *one* vast *Metropolis;* whose enormous Growth, however censurable in other respects, is actually a Cause that Workmanship and Arts of so many kinds arise to such perfection.

WHAT Encouragement our higher Powers may think fit to give these growing Arts, I will not pretend to guess. This I know, that 'tis so much for their advantage and Interest to make themselves the chief Partys in the Cause, that I wish no Court or Ministry, besides a truly virtuous and wise one, may ever concern themselves in the Affair. For shou'd they do so, they wou'd in reality do more harm than good; since 'tis not the Nature of a Court (such as Courts generally are) to improve, but rather corrupt *a Taste.* And what is in the beginning set wrong by their Example, is hardly ever afterwards recoverable in the Genius of a Nation.

CONTENT therefore I am, my Lord, that BRITAIN stands in this respect as she now does. Nor can one, methinks, with just reason regret her having hitherto made no greater advancement in these affairs of art. As her *Constitution* has grown, and been establish'd, she has in proportion fitted her-self for other Improvements. There has been no Anticipation in the Case. And in this surely she must be esteem'd wise, as well as happy; that ere she attempted to raise her-self any other Taste or Relish, she secur'd her-self a right one in *Government.* She has now the advantage of beginning in other Matters, on a new foot. She has her *Models* yet to seek, her *Scale* and *Standard* to form, with deliberation and good choice. Able enough she is at present to shift for her-self; however abandon'd or helpless she has been left by those whom it became to assist her. Hardly, indeed, cou'd she procure a single *Academy* for the training of her Youth in Exercises. As good Soldiers as we are, and as good Horses as our Climate affords, our Princes, rather than expend their Treasure this way, have suffer'd our Youth to pass into a foreign Nation, to learn to ride. As for other *Academys,* such as those for Painting, Sculpture, or Architecture, we have not so much as heard of the Proposal; whilst the Prince of our rival Nation raises Academys, breeds Youth, and sends Rewards and Pensions into foreign Countrys, to advance the Interest and Credit of his own. Now if, notwithstanding the Industry and Pains of this foreign Court, and the supine Un-concernedness of our own, the National Taste however rises, and already shews it-self in many respects beyond that of our so highly assisted Neighbours; what greater Proof can there be of the Superiority of Genius in one of these Nations above the other?[12]

---

12. Very optimistic, this last section has the air of a quasi manifesto. Shaftesbury is both encouraged and encouraging; he is pleased with Britain's progress in matters of culture and civic life, and also reassuring as far as her future development is concerned. The public good, as we have noticed, was neither overlooked nor ignored in our earlier sections, but in this section the public receives attention of a different sort: here Shaftesbury tries to enlist its 'voice.' This shift of emphasis seems to place responsibility also upon those who stood mainly to benefit from cultural growth and refinement, as we were told earlier. Indeed, what turns Shaftesbury into such an optimistic philosopher is his benevolent belief in man's ability to help himself help others to help him to help them... Does this interdependent activity represent the essential dynamics of cultural growth?

Francis Hutcheson*
(1694 – 1747)

Hutcheson, like Shaftesbury, may be regarded as one of the earliest modern writers on aesthetics. Of Scottish descent, his father and grandfather were ministers of congregations in Northern Ireland. Hutcheson attended various academic institutions, and, like Shaftesbury, opted for a broad education which included philosophy, classics, literature and theology. After six years at the University of Glasgow (1710–1716), he returned to Ireland and opened a private academy at Dublin.

While at Dublin (1716–1729), Hutcheson published the four essays by which he is best known, including *An Inquiry Concerning Beauty, Harmony and Design.* He enjoyed great popularity among his pupils and colleagues as teacher as well as scholar. In 1729 Hutcheson was appointed to the Chair of Moral Philosophy at the University of Glasgow where he spent the remainder of his life.

In his writings Hutcheson dealt with metaphysics, logic and ethics. His importance, however, like that of Shaftesbury, is due almost entirely to his contribution to the field of ethics, though his philosophy of mind constituted a major link between Locke and the Scottish School. Like Shaftesbury, he strongly opposed Hobbes' social theory and its underlying premise concerning man's self-love, favoring the position according to which benevolent feelings form an irreducible, original part of man's nature. For Hutcheson as for Shaftesbury, the test of virtuous action is in its tendency to promote the general welfare of society.

---

*The text presented here is based on Peter Kivy's scholarly edition of Hutcheson's text (Martinus Nijhoff, the Hague 1973). We omitted his critical footnotes and the brackets he used to call the reader's attention to the comparisons he made of different versions of the original text.

The basic agreement between Hutcheson and Shaftesbury applies not only to the functions assigned to the moral sense, but also to the analogy between beauty and virtue, which implies that man is endowed with a special sense by which he perceives beauty. This reflexive, internal sense presupposes the action of the external senses. Yet beauty, with its attendant pleasure, may also be discerned, for example, in matters such as universal truth or moral principles and actions, which do not involve the external senses, as do sensible objects. While insisting on the naturalness of the sense of beauty and its antecedent standing, Hutcheson, like Shaftesbury, leaves ample room for education, convention, individual tastes and the like.

While falling short of Shaftesbury's aristocratic style, Hutcheson contributes to the broadening and tightening of Shaftesbury's ideas, although he, too, leaves certain internal inconsistencies unresolved (see annotations). Thus, the real nature of the process which leads to judgment and subsequent action is not sufficiently clarified, nor is the distinction between perception and sensations. Taken together, however, Shaftesbury and Hutcheson contributed not only to the development of some of the most important modern schools of ethics, but of aesthetics as well.

To reiterate, Hutcheson believed that man is possessed of a variety of senses, internal as well as external. Repudiating the doctrine of innate ideas, Hutcheson, like Shaftesbury, refers all of our ideas to these senses. "Any determination of our minds to receive ideas independent of our will, and to have perception of pleasure and pain" is Hutcheson's definition of a sense. Given this definition, Hutcheson must assume the existence of a number of senses, beyond the five external ones that are commonly recognized.

While the moral sense and the sense of beauty have received the greater part of scholarly attention, there seems to be no limit to the number of internal senses of this kind. Hutcheson himself assumed the existence of a goodly number of them. What is interesting about these additional senses is that they are, at one and the same time, designative and immediate, direct and nonreflective, i.e. monolithic in character. Were we to subordinate the internal senses to the external ones, it would necessarily imply the augmentation of the latter by cognitive operations which will enable them to accomplish the functions of the former. Moreover, the transformation of material in thought, necessitated by designative targets, might threaten to divest sensations of cognitive content. Sensations, however, may be "possessed" by affective qualities — experienced and learned — which may assist or guide newly-imagined targets, in terms of affective "fitness."

Indeed, among modern attempts to study the workings of the mind, the "intelligence" of perception and the "transformations" of thought materials loom large. Thus, it is becoming increasingly clear that the cognitive operations of thinking do not commence after perception has taken place but are essential ingredients of perception itself. Moreover, there is an increasing evidence for the productive role of the anticipatory properties of affect in thought.

We maintain (see Part I) that the arts, in theory and practice, grappled with these issues long before they gained saliency elsewhere. If contemporary research on vision increasingly makes room for the Mind as part of the eye, it is within the precinct of art that awareness of the Eye as part of the mind grew, essentially dealing with the same problem. Similarly, if understanding of creativity involves an examination of the Anticipatory Properties of affect, it is within art that Affective Qualities to "move the minds" of its addressees were created and debated.

Indeed, the attempt to illuminate the nature of Human Nature and its power as an agent of investigation and understanding is what concerns us most in Shaftesbury's and Hutcheson's writings. Their writings constitute inquiries into a remodeled theory of knowledge. Though epistemological questions invariably imply a reasoning mind, they focused on the thing explained and not on the explainer. The interest in Human Nature yielded new insights into the workings of the mind which does the explaining.

Shaftesbury and Hutcheson were keen observers of art. They brought a profound understanding to its properties and domain. Enlisting art as they did not only further the understanding of art but also contributed to those important attempts which eventually led to today's concerted effort to study the working of the mind.

AN

INQUIRY

INTO THE
ORIGINAL of our IDEAS
OF
BEAUTY and *VIRTUE*;
In Two TREATISES.

IN WHICH
The Principles of the late Earl of SHAFTSBURY are explain'd and defended, against the Author of the *Fable of the Bees*:

AND THE
Ideas of *Moral Good* and *Evil* are establish'd, according to the Sentiments of the antient *Moralists*.

With and Attempt to introduce a *Mathematical Calculation* in Subjects of *Morality*.

Itaque eorum ipsorum quæ aspectu sentiuntur, nullum aliud animal pulchritudinem, venustatem, convenientiam partium sentit: Quam similitudinem natura ratioque ab oculis ad animum transferens, multo etiam magis pulchritudinem, constantiam, ordinem in consiliis, factisque conservandum putat: Quibus ex rebus conflatur & efficitur id quod quærimus honestum: Quod etiamsi nobilitatum non sit, tamen honestum sit: quodque etiamsi a nullo laudetur, natura est laudabile. Formam quidem ipsam & faciem honesti vides, quæ si oculis cerneretur, mirabiles amores excitaret sapientiæ.

Cie. de Off. .ib. 1. *e.* 4

[And so no other animal has a sense of beauty, loveliness, harmony in the visible world; and Nature and Reason, extending the analogy of this from the world of sense to the world of spirit, find that beauty, consistency, order are far more to be maintained in thought and deed....It is from these elements that is forged and fashioned that moral goodness which is the subject of this inquiry — something by its own nature, we correctly maintain, it merits praise, even though it be praised by non...You see here...the very form and as it were the face of Moral Goodness; "and if," as Plato says, "it could be seen with the physical eye, it would awaken a marvelous love of wisdom."

(Translation by Walter Miller as appearing in Kivy's edition)]

PREFACE TO THE TWO INQUIRIES

There is no part of philosophy of more importance than a just knowledge of human nature and its various powers and dispositions. Our late inquiries have been very much employed about our understanding, and the several methods of obtaining truth. We generally acknowledge that the importance of any truth is nothing else than its moment, or efficacy to make men happy, or to give them the greatest and most lasting pleasure; and wisdom denotes only a capacity of pursuing this end by the best means. It must surely then be of the greatest importance to have distinct conceptions of this end itself, as well as of the means necessary to obtain it, that we may find out which are the greatest and most lasting pleasures, and not employ our reason, after all our laborious improvements of it, in trifling pursuits. It is to be feared, indeed, that most of our studies, without this inquiry, will be of very little use to us; for they seem to have scarce any other tendency than to lead us into speculative knowledge itself. Nor are we distinctly told how it is that knowledge, or truth, is pleasant to us.

This consideration put the author of the following papers upon inquiring into the various pleasures which human nature is capable of receiving. We shall generally find in our modern philosophic writings nothing farther on this head than some bare division of them into *Sensible*, and *Rational*, and some trite commonplace arguments to prove the latter more valuable than the former. Our sensible pleasures are slightly passed over and explained only by some instances of tastes, smells, sounds, or such like, which men of any tolerable reflection generally look upon as very trifling satisfactions. Our rational pleasures have had much the same kind of treatment. We are seldom taught any other notion of rational pleasure than that which we have upon reflecting on our possession, or claim to those objects which may be occasions of pleasure. Such objects we call advantageous; but advantage, or interest, cannot be distinctly conceived till we know what those pleasures are which advantageous objects are apt to excite, and what senses or powers of perception we have with respect to such objects. We may perhaps find such an inquiry of more importance in *morals*, to prove what we call the reality of virtue, or that it is the surest happiness of the agent, than one would first imagine.

In reflecting upon our *external senses*, we plainly see that our perceptions of pleasure or pain do not depend directly upon our will. Objects do not please us according as we incline they should. The presence of some objects necessarily pleases us, and the presence of others as necessarily displeases us. Nor can we by our will any otherwise procure pleasure or avoid pain than by procuring the former kind of objects and avoiding the latter. By the very frame of our nature the one is made the occasion of delight and the other of dissatisfaction.

The same observation will hold in all our other pleasures and pains. For there are many other sorts of objects which please or displease us as necessarily, as material objects do when they operate on our organs of sense. There are few objects which are not thus constituted the necessary occasion of some pleasure or pain. Thus we find ourselves pleased with a regular form, a piece of architecture or painting, a composition of notes, a theorem, an action, an affection, a character. And we are conscious that this pleasure necessarily arises from the contemplation of the idea which is then present to our minds, with all its circumstances, although some of these ideas have nothing of what we commonly call sensible perception in them; and in those which have, the pleasure arises from some *uniformity, order, arrangement, imitation,* and not from the simple ideas of *colour* or *sound* or *mode of extension* separately considered.

These determinations to be pleased with certain complex forms the author chooses to call *senses,* distinguishing them from the powers which commonly go by that name by calling our power of perceiving the *beauty* of regularity, order, harmony, an *internal sense,* and that determination to approve affections, actions, or characters of rational agents, which we call *virtuous,* he marks by the name of a *moral sense.*

His principal design is to show that human nature was not left quite indifferent in the affair of virtue, to form to itself observations concerning the advantage or disadvantage of actions, and accordingly to regulate its conduct. The weakness of our reason, and the avocations arising from the infirmities and necessities of our nature, are so great that very few men could ever have formed those long deductions of reason which show some actions to be in the whole advantageous to the agent, and their contraries pernicious. The Author of nature has much better furnished us for a virtuous conduct than some moralists seem to imagine, by almost as quick and powerful instructions as we have for the preservation of our bodies. He has given us strong affections to be the springs of each virtuous action, and made virtue a lovely form, that we might easily distinguish it from its contrary, and be made happy by the pursuit of it.

This moral sense of beauty in actions and affections may appear strange at first view. Some of our moralists themselves are offended at it in my Lord Shaftesbury, so much are they accustomed to deduce every approbation or aversion from rational views of private interest (except it be merely in the simple ideas of the external senses) and have such a horror at *innate ideas*, which they imagine this borders upon. But this moral sense has no relation to innate ideas, as will appear in the second Treatise. Our gentlemen of good taste can tell us of a great many senses, tastes, and relishes for beauty, harmony, imitation in painting and poetry; and may not we find too in mankind a relish for a beauty in characters, in manners? It will perhaps be found that the greater part of the ingenious arts are calculated to please some natural powers pretty different either from what we commonly call *reason*, or the external senses.

In the first Treatise the author perhaps in some instances has gone too far in supposing a greater agreement of mankind in their sense of beauty than experience will confirm; but all he is sollicitous about is to show that there is some sense of beauty natural to men; that we find as great an agreement of men in their relishes of forms as in their external senses, which all agree to be natural; and that pleasure or pain, delight or aversion, are naturally joined to their perceptions. If the reader be convinced of this, it will be no difficult matter to apprehend another superior sense, natural also to men, determining them to be pleased with actions, characters, affections. This is the moral sense which makes the subject of the second Treatise.

The proper occasions of perception by the external senses occur to us as soon as we come into the world, whence perhaps we easily look upon these senses to be natural; but the objects of the superior senses of beauty and virtue generally do not. It is probably some little time before children reflect or at least let us know that they reflect upon proportion and similitude, upon affections, characters, tempers, or come to know the external actions which are evidence of them. Hence we imagine that their sense of beauty, and their moral sentiments of actions must be entirely owing to instruction and education; whereas it is as easy to conceive how a character, a temper, as soon as they are observed, may be constituted by nature the necessary occasion of pleasure, or an object of approbation, as a taste or a sound, though these objects present themselves to our observation sooner than the other.[1]

. . .

——————— ⟡ ———————

1. In his preface, Hutcheson presents the major argument of his treatise, in broad terms. Inquiries into "human nature and its various powers and dispositions," are important for the understanding of Understanding, including the comprehension of the methods man employs for obtaining truth. In other words, it is important for a sound theory of knowledge.

Since the importance of truth resides in its ability to make man happy, Hutcheson undertook the study of pleasure, i.e., the study of what pleases and how. The underlying hypothesis guiding this study concerns uniformity, order, arrangement and the like, which presumably give rise to pleasure. His inquiry, he tells us, rests on the conviction that the Author of nature gave virtue a "lovely form" to make man happy. Human nature, he postulates, must have been likewise furnished with regulative propensities, whereby "strong affection" (the determination to be pleased) leads to virtuous action. Man, concludes Hutcheson, like Shaftesbury whom he acknowledges, is endowed by nature with the will to pursue virtue; order, harmony and design are instrumental in this pursuit.

Beauty and virtue, for Hutcheson, are thus inseparably related to each other by Nature's design; God, it seems, must have chosen to be guided by the very "senses" with which he saw fit to endow man. Indeed, the universe, for Hutcheson, is as we shall see, a macro creation of "uniformity amidst variety."

Based on an a priori belief in an ordered world, Hutcheson's deductive method is no longer viable, even without entertaining the new theories concerning Chaos. However, the search for coherence and that which coheres in mental processes may still benefit from some of Hutcheson's propositions, whether in the field of aesthetics or cognitive psychology.

TREATISE I
AN INQUIRY CONCERNING BEAUTY, ORDER, HARMONY, DESIGN

Section I:

CONCERNING SOME POWERS OF PERCEPTION, DISTINCT FROM WHAT IS GENERALLY UNDERSTOOD BY SENSATION.

To make the following observations understood, it may be necessary to premise some definitions, and observations, either universally acknowledged, or sufficiently proved by many writers both ancient and modern, concerning our perceptions called *sensations*, and the actions of the mind consequent upon them.

Sensation

I. Those ideas which are raised in the mind upon the presence of external objects, and their acting upon our bodies, are called *sensations*. We find that the mind in such cases is passive, and has not power directly to prevent the perception or idea, or to vary it at its reception, as long as we continue our bodies in a state fit to be acted upon by the external object.

Different senses

II. When two perceptions are entirely different from each other, or agree in nothing but the general idea of sensation, we call the powers of receiving those different perceptions different *senses*. Thus seeing and hearing denote the different powers of receiving the ideas of colours and sounds. And although colours have great differences among themselves, as also have sounds, yet there is a greater agreement among the most opposite colours, than between any colour and a sound. Hence we call all colours perceptions of the same sense. All the several senses seem to have their distinct organs, except *feeling*, which is in some degree diffused over the whole body.

Mind, how active

III. The mind has a power of *compounding* ideas which were received separately; of *comparing* objects by means of the ideas, and of observing their *relations* and *proportions*; of *enlarging* and *diminishing*

its ideas at pleasure, or in any certain *ratio* or degree; and of considering *separately* each of the simple ideas, which might perhaps have been
impressed jointly in the sensation. This last operation we commonly call
abstraction.

Substances

IV. The ideas of corporeal substances are compounded of the various
simple ideas jointly impressed when they presented themselves to our
senses. We define substances only by enumerating these sensible ideas;
and such definitions may raise a clear enough idea of the substance in
the mind of one who never immediately perceived the substance, provided he has separately received by his senses all the simple ideas
which are in the composition of the complex one of the substance
defined. But if there be any simple ideas which he has not received, or
if he wants any of the senses necessary for the perception of them, no
definition can raise any simple idea which has not been before perceived by the senses.

Education. Instruction

V. Hence it follows that when instruction, education, or prejudice of
any kind raise any desire or aversion toward an object, this desire or
aversion must be founded upon an opinion of some perfection, or some
deficiency in those qualities for perception of which we have the proper senses. Thus if beauty be desired by one who has not the sense of
sight, the desire must be raised by some apprehended regularity of figure, sweetness of voice, smoothness, or softness, or some other quality
perceivable by the other senses, without relation to the ideas of colour.

Pleasure, Pain

VI. Many of our sensitive perceptions are pleasant, and many painful,
immediately, and that without any knowledge of the cause of this pleasure or pain, or how the objects excite it, or are the occasions of it, or
without seeing to what farther advantage or detriment the use of such
objects might tend. Nor would the most accurate knowledge of these
things vary either the pleasure or pain of the perception, however it
might give a rational pleasure distinct from the sensible; or might raise
a distinct joy from a prospect of farther advantage in the object, or aversion from an apprehension of evil.

Different ideas

VII. The simple ideas raised in different persons by the same object are probably some way different when they disagree in their approbation or dislike, and in the same person when his fancy at one time differs from what it was at another. This will appear from reflecting on those objects to which we have now an aversion, though they were formerly agreeable. And we shall generally find that there is some accidental conjunction of a disagreeable idea which always recurs with the object, as in those wines to which men acquire an aversion after they have taken them in an emetic preparation, we are conscious that the ideas is altered from what it was when that wine was agreeable, by the conjunction of the ideas of loathing and sickness of the stomach. The like change of idea may be insensibly made by the change of our bodies as we advance in years, or when we are accustomed to any object, which may occasion an indifference toward meats we were fond of in our childhood, and may make some objects cease to raise the disagreeable ideas which they excited upon our first use of them. Many of our simple perceptions are disagreeable only through the too great intenseness of the quality: thus moderate light is agreeable, very strong light may be painful; moderate bitter may be pleasant, a higher degree may be offensive. A change in our organs will necessarily occasion a change in the intenseness of the perception at least, nay sometimes will occasion a quite contrary perception: thus a warm hand shall feel that water cold which a cold hand shall feel warm.

We shall not find it perhaps so easy to account for the diversity of fancy about more complex ideas of objects, (including many) in which we regard many ideas of different senses at once, as (some) perceptions of those called *primary qualities*, and some *secondary*, as explained by Mr. Locke: for instance, in the different fancies about architecture, gardening, dress. Of the two former, we shall offer something in Section VI. As to dress, we may generally account for the diversity of fancies from a like conjunction of ideas. Thus if either from anything in nature, or from the opinion of our country or acquaintance, the fancying of glaring colours be looked upon as an evidence of levity, or of any other evil quality of mind, or if any colour or fashion be commonly used by rustics, or by men of any disagreeable profession, employment, or temper, these additional ideas may recur constantly with that of the colour or fashion, and cause a constant dislike to them in those who join the additional ideas, although the colour or form be no way disagreeable of themselves, and actually do please others who join no such ideas to them. But there appears no ground to believe such a diversity in human minds, as that the same simple idea or perception should give pleasure to one and pain to another, or to the same person at different times, not to say that it seems a contradiction that the same simple idea should do so.

Complex ideas

VIII. The only pleasure of sense which many philosophers seem to consider is that which accompanies the simple ideas of sensation. But there are far greater pleasures in those complex ideas of objects, which obtain the names of *beautiful, regular, harmonious*. Thus every one acknowledges he is more delighted with a fine face, a just picture, than with the view of any one colour, were it as strong and lively as possible; and more pleased with a prospect of the sun arising among settled clouds, and colouring their edges with a starry hemisphere, a fine landscape, a regular building, than with a clear blue sky, a smooth sea, or a large open plain, not diversified by woods, hills, waters, buildings. And yet even these latter appearances are not quite simple. So in music, the pleasure of fine composition is incomparably greater than that of any one note, how sweet, full, or swelling soever.

Beauty, Harmony

IX. Let it be observed that in the following papers the word *beauty* is taken for *the idea raised in us*, and a *sense* of beauty for *our power of receiving this idea. Harmony* also denotes *our pleasant ideas arising from composition of sounds*, and a *good ear* (as it is generally taken) a *power of perceiving this pleasure*. In the following sections, an attempt is made to discover what is the immediate occasion of these pleasant ideas, or what real quality in the objects ordinarily excites them.

Internal sense

X. It is of no consequence whether we call these ideas of beauty and harmony perceptions of the external senses of seeing and hearing, or not. I should rather choose to call our power of perceiving these ideas an *internal sense*, were it only for the convenience of distinguishing them from other sensations of seeing and hearing which men may have without perception of beauty and harmony. It is plain from experience that many men have in the common meaning the senses of seeing and hearing perfect enough. They perceive all the *simple ideas* separately, and have their pleasures; they distinguish them from each other, such as one colour from another, either quite different, or the stronger or fainter of the same colour, when they are placed beside each other, although they may often confound their names when they occur apart form each other, as some do the names of green and blue. They can tell in separate notes, the higher, lower, sharper or flatter, when separately sounded; in figures they discern the length, breadth, wideness of each line, surface, angle; and may be as capable of hearing and seeing at great distances as any men whatsoever. And yet perhaps they shall find no pleasure in musical compositions, in painting, architecture, natural landscape, or but a very weak one in comparison of what others enjoy from the same objects. This greater capacity of receiving such pleasant ideas we commonly call a *fine genius* or *taste*. In music we seem universally to acknowledge something like a distinct sense from the external one of hearing, and call it a *good ear;* and the like distinction we should probably acknowledge in other objects, had we also got distinct names to denote these *powers* of perception by.

Different from external

XI. We generally imagine the brute animals endowed with the same sort of powers of perception as our external senses, and having sometimes greater acuteness in them; but we conceive few or none of them with any of these sublimer powers of perception here called *internal senses*, or at least if some of them have them, it is in a degree much inferior to ours.

There will appear another reason perhaps hereafter for calling this power of perceiving the ideas of beauty an *internal sense*, from this, that in some other affairs where our external senses are not much concerned, we discern a sort of beauty, very like, in many respects, to that observed in sensible objects, and accompanied with like pleasure. Such is that beauty perceived in theorems, or universal truths, in general causes, and in some extensive principles of action.

XII. Let one consider, first, that "tis probable a being may have the full power of external sensation, which we enjoy, so as to perceive each colour, line, surface, as we do; yet, without the power of *comparing*, or of discerning the similitudes of proportions. Again, it might discern these also, and yet have no pleasure or delight accompanying these perceptions. The bare idea of the form is something separable from pleasure, as may appear from the different *tastes* of men about the beauty of forms, where we don't imagine that they differ in any ideas, either of the primary or secondary qualities. *Similitude, proportion, analogy* or *equality* of proportion are objects of the understanding, and must be actually known before we know the natural causes of our pleasure. But pleasure perhaps is not necessarily connected with perception of them, and may be felt where the proportion is not known or attended to, and may not be felt where the proportion is observed. Since then there are such different powers of perception, where what are commonly called *external* senses are the same, since the most accurate knowledge of what the external senses discover may often not give the pleasure of beauty or harmony which yet one of a good taste will enjoy at once without much knowledge, we may justly use another name for these higher and more delightful perceptions of beauty and harmony, and call the *power* of receiving such impressions an *internal sense*. The difference of the perceptions seems sufficient to vindicate the use of a different name, especially when we are told in what meaning the word is applied.

Its pleasures necessary and immediate

This superior power of perception is justly called a *sense* because of its affinity to the other senses in this, that the pleasure does not arise from any *knowledge* of principles, proportions, causes, or of the usefulness of the object, but strikes us at first with the idea of beauty. Nor does the most accurate knowledge increase this pleasure of beauty, however it may superadd a distinct rational pleasure from prospects of advantage, or from the increase of knowledge.

XIII. And farther, the ideas of beauty and harmony, like other sensible ideas, are *necessarily* pleasant to us, as well as immediately so.

Neither can any resolution of our own, nor any prospect of advantage or disadvantage, vary the beauty or deformity of an object. For as in the external sensations, no view of interest will make an object grateful, nor view of detriment distinct from immediate pain in the perception, make it disagreeable to the sense. So propose the whole world as a reward, or threaten the greatest evil, to make us approve a deformed object, or disapprove a beautiful one: dissimulation may be procured by rewards or threatenings, or we may in external conduct abstain from any pursuit of the beautiful, and pursue the deformed, but our *sentiments* of the forms, and our *perceptions*, would continue invariably the same.

This sense antecedent to, and distinct from prospects of interest

XIV. Hence it plainly appears that some objects are *immediately* the occasions of this pleasure of beauty, and that we have senses fitted for perceiving it, and that it is distinct from that *joy* which arises upon prospect of advantage. Nay, do not we often see convenience and use neglected to obtain beauty, without any other prospect of advantage in the beautiful form than the suggesting the pleasant ideas of beauty? Now this shows us that however we may pursue beautiful objects from self-love, with a view to obtain the pleasures of beauty, as in architecture, gardening, and many other affairs, yet there must be a *sense* of beauty, antecedent to prospects even of this advantage, without which sense these objects would not be thus advantageous, nor excite in us this pleasure which constitutes them advantageous. Our sense of beauty from objects, by which they are constituted good to us, is very distinct from our desire of them when they are thus constituted. Our desire of beauty may be counter-balanced by rewards of threatenings, but never our *sense* of it, even as fear of death may make us desire a bitter potion, or neglect those meats which the sense of taste would recommend as pleasant, but cannot make that potion agreeable to the *sense*, or meat disagreeable to it, which was not so antecedently to this prospect. The same holds true of the sense of beauty and harmony; that the pursuit of such objects is frequently neglected, from prospects of advantage, aversion to labour, or any other motive of interest does not prove that we have no *sense* of beauty, but only that our desire of it may be counter-balanced by a stronger desire. So gold outweighing silver is never adduced as proof that the latter is void of gravity.

XV. Had we no such sense of beauty and harmony, houses, gardens, dress, equipage might have been recommended to us as convenient, fruitful, warm, easy, but never as *beautiful*. And in faces I see nothing which could please us but liveliness of colour and smoothness of surface. And yet nothing is more certain than that all these objects are recommended under quite different views on many occasions. "tis true, what chiefly pleases in the countenance are the indications of moral dispositions; and yet, were we by the longest acquaintance fully convinced of the best moral dispositions in any person, with that countenance we now think deformed, this would never hinder our immediate dislike of the form, or our liking other forms more. And custom, education, or example could never give us perceptions distinct from those of the senses which we had the use of before, or recommend objects under another conception than grateful to them. But of the influence of custom, education, example, upon the sense of beauty, we shall treat below.

Beauty original or comparative

XVI. Beauty in corporeal forms is either *original* or *comparative;* or, if any like the terms better, *absolute* or *relative*. Only let it be observed that by absolute or original beauty is not understood any quality supposed to be in the object which should of itself be beautiful, without relation to any mind which perceives it. For beauty, like other names of sensible ideas, properly denotes the *perception* of some mind; so *cold, hot, sweet, bitter*, denote the sensations in our minds, to which perhaps there is no resemblance in the objects which excite these ideas in us, however we generally imagine otherwise. The ideas of beauty and harmony, being excited upon our perception of some primary quality, and having relation to figure and time, may indeed have a nearer resemblance to objects than these sensations, which seem not so much any pictures of objects as modifications of the perceiving mind; and yet, were there no mind with a sense of beauty to contemplate objects, I see not how they could be called beautiful. We therefore by absolute beauty understand only that beauty which we perceive in objects without comparison to anything external, of which the object is supposed an imitation or picture, such as that beauty perceived from the works of nature, artificial forms, figures. Comparative or relative beauty is that which we perceive in objects commonly considered as *imitations* or *resemblances* of something else. These two kinds of beauty employ the three following sections.

Section II:
OF ORIGINAL OR ABSOLUTE BEAUTY

Sense of men

I. Since it is certain that we have *ideas* of beauty and harmony, let us examine what *quality* in objects excites these ideas, or is the occasion of them. And let it be here observed that our inquiry is only about the qualities which are beautiful to *men*, or about the foundation of their sense of beauty. For as was above hinted, beauty has always relation to the sense of some mind; and when we afterwards show how generally the objects which occur to us are beautiful, we mean that such objects are agreeable to the sense of men, for there are many objects which seem no way beautiful to men, and yet other animals seem delighted with them: they may have senses otherwise constituted than those of men, and may have the ideas of beauty excited by objects of a quite different form. We see animals fitted for every place, and what to men appears rude and shapeless, or loathsome, may be to them a paradise.

II. That we may more distinctly discover the general foundation or occasion of the ideas of beauty among men, it will be necessary to consider it first in its simpler kinds, such as occurs to us in regular figures; and we may perhaps find that the same foundation extends to all the more complex species of it.

Uniformity with variety

III. The figures which excite in us the ideas of beauty seem to be those in which there is *uniformity amidst variety*. There are many conceptions of objects which are agreeable upon other accounts, such as *grandeur, novelty, sanctity,* and some others, which shall be mentioned hereafter. But what we call beautiful in objects, to speak in the mathematical style, seems to be in compound ratio of uniformity and variety: so that where the uniformity of bodies is equal, the beauty is as the variety; and where the variety is equal, the beauty is as the uniformity. This may seem probable, and hold pretty generally.

Variety

First, the variety increases the beauty in equal uniformity. The beauty of an equilateral triangle is less than that of the square, which is less than that of a pentagon, and this again is surpassed by the hexagon. When indeed the number of sides is much increased, the proportion of them to the radius, or diameter of the figure, or of the circle to which regular polygons have an obvious relation, is so much lost to our observation, that the beauty does not always increase with the number of sides, and the want of parallelism in the sides of heptagons, and other figures of odd numbers, may also diminish their beauty. So in solids, the eicosiedron surpasses the dodecaedron, and this the octaedron, which is still more beautiful than the cube, and this again surpasses the regular pyramid. The obvious ground of this is greater variety with equal uniformity.

Uniformity

The greater uniformity increases the beauty amidst equal variety in these instances: an equilateral triangle, or even an isosceles, surpasses the scalenum; a square surpasses the rhombus or lozenge, and this again the rhomboides, which is still more beautiful than the trapezium, or any figure with irregular curve sides. So the regular solids surpass all other solids of equal number of plane surfaces. And the same is observable not only in the five perfectly regular solids, but in all those which have any considerable uniformity, as cylinders, prisms, pyramids, obelisks, which please every eye more than any rude figures, where there is no unity or resemblance among the parts.

Compound ratio

Instances of the compound ratio we have in comparing circles or spheres with ellipses or spheroids not very eccentric, and in comparing the compound solids, the exotaedron, and eicosidodecaedron, with the perfectly regular ones of which they are compounded; and we shall find that the want of that most perfect uniformity observable in the latter is compensated by the greater variety in the former, so that the beauty is nearly equal.

IV. These observations would probably hold true for the most part, and might be confirmed by the judgment of children in the simpler figures, where the variety is not too great for their comprehension. And however uncertain some of the particular aforesaid instances may seem, yet this is perpetually to be observed, that children are fond of all regular figures in their little diversions, although they be no more convenient or useful for them than the figures of our common pebbles. We see how early they discover a taste or sense of beauty in desiring to see buildings, regular gardens, or even representations of them in pictures of any kind.

Beauty of nature

V. The same foundation we have for our sense of beauty in the works of nature. In every part of the world which we call beautiful there is a surprising uniformity amidst an almost infinite variety. Many parts of the universe seem not at all designed for the use of man; nay, it is but a very small spot with which we have any acquaintance. The figures and motions of the great bodies are not obvious to our senses, but found out by reasoning and reflection, upon many long observations; and yet as far as we can by sense discover, or by reasoning enlarge our knowledge and extend our imagination, we generally find their structure, order, and motion agreeable to our sense of beauty. Every particular object in nature does not indeed appear beautiful to us; but there is a great profusion of beauty over most of the objects which occur either to our senses, or reasonings upon observation. For not to mention the apparent situation of the heavenly bodies in the circumference of a great sphere, which is wholly occasioned by the imperfection of our sight in discerning distances, the forms of all the great bodies in the universe are nearly spherical, the orbits of their revolutions generally elliptic, and without great eccentricity, in those which continually occur to our observation. Now these are figures of great uniformity, and therefore pleasing to us.

Further, to pass by the less obvious uniformity in the proportion of their quantities of matter, distances, times of revolving, to each other, what can exhibit a greater instance of uniformity amidst variety than the constant tenour of revolutions in nearly equal times, in each planet around its axis, and the central fire, or sun, through all the ages of which we have any records, and in nearly the same orbit? Thus after certain periods all the same appearances are again renewed. The alternate successions of light and shade, or day and night, constantly pursuing each other around each planet, with an agreeable and regular diversity in the times they possess the several hemispheres, in the summer, harvest, winter, and spring, and the various phases, aspects, and situations of the planets to each other, their conjunctions and oppositions, in which they suddenly darken each other with their conic shades in eclipses, are repeated to us at their fixed periods with invariable constancy. These are the beauties which charm the astronomer, and make his tedious calculations pleasant.

> *Molliter austerum studio fallente laborem.*
> [Horace, *Satires,* Book II, Satire ii, verse 12: "Where the excitement pleasantly beguiles the hard toil" (trans. H.R. Fairclough, as appearing in Kivy's edition)]

. . .

Proportion

X. There is a farther beauty in animals, arising from a certain proportion of the various parts to each other, which still pleases the sense of spectators, though they cannot calculate it with the accuracy of a statuary. The statuary knows what proportion of each part of the face to the whole face is most agreeable, and can tell us the same of the proportion of the face to the body, or any parts of it, and between the diameters and lengths of each limb. When this proportion of the head to the body is remarkably altered, we shall have a giant or a dwarf; and hence it is that either the one or the other may be represented to us even in miniature, without relation to any external object, by observing how the body surpasses the proportion it should have to the head in giants, and falls below it in dwarfs. There is a farther beauty arising from that figure which is a natural indication of strength; but this may be passed over, because our approbation of this shape flows from an opinion of advantage, and not from the form itself.

The beauty arising from mechanism apparently adapted to the necessities and advantages of any animal, which pleases us even though there be no advantage to ourselves ensuing from it, will be considered under the head of *Relative Beauty*, or *Design*.[2]

...

Harmony

XIII. Under *original beauty* we may include *harmony*, or *beauty* of *sound*, if that expression can be allowed, because harmony is not usually conceived as an imitation of anything else. Harmony often raises pleasure in those who know not what is the occasion of it; and yet the foundation of this pleasure is known to be a sort of uniformity. When the several vibrations of one note regularly coincide with the vibrations of another they make an agreeable composition; and such notes are called *concords*. Thus the vibrations of any one note coincide in time

———— ⚘ ————

2. In an attempt to give more substance to Shaftesbury's conception of the sense of beauty as both immediate and rational, Hutcheson enlists notions derived from a number of venerable philosophical traditions. Thus he links (via a sort of Leibnizian conception of the mind as "calculator") Locke's theory of ideas and their association with the scholastic notion of 'uniformity amidst variety' and Aristotle's understanding of 'mimesis.' Rationality is granted to 'beauty' by relating it to complex ideas (Locke) which integrate numerous basic sensations ('variety'). This integration is immediate, resting, as it does, on the unconscious, computative powers of the mind (Leibniz). Beauty, conceived as unity, is thus a quality effected by a sort of algorithm. The more sensations it connects, the greater the unity it achieves. The unity, however, may vary in kind and degree of perfection (given the "algorithm" applied), determining the character of each of the units which constitute the variety. (We shall overlook for the moment the challenge that such a conclusion raises with regard to the notion of immediacy.) At any rate, relating affect, as an intervening variable, to the pleasure that beauty entails, enables Hutcheson to entertain the possibility that contextual influences — habits, conventions and education — are participatory factors in the overall artistic experience. The subjective standard of taste is thus distinct from the sense of beauty, which functions as the objective criterion of aesthetic judgment, though the two may be made compatible by cultural norms. The "harmonious proportions," consequently, are not a direct cause of pleasure, but constitute a point of reference for affective response. Moreover, the divergence of tastes remains consistent with the universality of the aesthetic sense.

This gives rise to "reflexive" processes as well as to reflective ones, related to direct

(CONT.)

with two vibrations of its octave; and two vibrations of any note coincide with three of its fifth, and so on in the rest of the concords. Now no composition can be harmonious in which the notes are not, for the most part, disposed according to these natural proportions. Besides which, a due regard must be had to the *key*, which governs the whole, and to the *time* and *humour* in which the composition is begun, a frequent and inartificial change of any of which will produce the greatest and most unnatural discord. This will appear by observing the dissonance which would arise from tacking parts of different tunes together as one, although both were separately agreeable. A like uniformity is also observable among the *basses, tenors, trebles* of the same tune.

There is indeed observable, in the best compositions, a mysterious

———— ♫ ————

(CONT.)

and indirect mechanisms, respectively. Contemplating the cause of artistic pleasure might itself give pleasure, not unlike the pleasure which Descartes attributed to "intellectual emotions." Adam Smith, as we shall see, will elaborate this idea, arguing that in art, "the pleasing wonder of ignorance is accompanied with the still more pleasing satisfaction of science. We wonder and are amazed by the effect; and we are pleased ourselves, and happy to find that we can comprehend, in some measure, how that wonderful effect is produced" (see this part p. 389). The contemplation of artistic objects, however, takes a secondary place in Hutcheson, who does not grant reflection the ability to change immediate aesthetic judgments. This unwillingness to entertain the idea that reflection is part of the judgment of beauty is puzzling, in as much as Hutcheson extends the applicability of the latter to non-sensible ideas as well, e.g. scientific theorems. His attempt to include mimesis within the sphere of immediate aesthetic pleasure lands him in the same pitfall, since the comparison implied by mimesis postulates an understanding of abstract concepts and their application (see also section IV and fn. 4 below).

Despite the novelties he introduces, Hutcheson appears as a man of the seventeenth century by virtue of his inclusion, à la Kepler, of the *un*perceived harmony of the spheres among his examples of Nature's beauties (Shaftesbury, too, conceived the universe in such terms; see *Characteristics* ii: 372). It becomes clear that, by enlisting the regularity of recurring patterns, he still, like Rameau, views artistic objects as natural phenomena, given to our perception through "pre-established mechanisms." Hence the centrality of "original beauty" (Kant's eventual "independent beauty") receives in his theoretical framework, compared to the subsidiary position allotted to "relative beauty". Yet, like other thinkers influenced by the "new science," Hutcheson puts art on a par with scientific method, equating artistic cohesion with scientific cohesion. In this connection, however, Hutcheson provides a new insight, namely, that scientific theories ought to be judged not only by rational criteria but by aesthetic criteria as well. At any rate, the questions regarding the difference between conception and perception, the "made" and the "given," still calls for further investigation and analysis.

effect of discords: They often give as great a pleasure as continued harmony, whether by refreshing the ear with variety, or by awakening the attention, and enlivening the relish for the succeeding harmony of concords, as shades enliven and beautify pictures, or by some other means not yet known. Certain it is, however, that they have their place, and some good effect in our best compositions. Some other powers of music may be considered hereafter.

XIV. But in all these instances of beauty let it be observed that the pleasure is communicated to those who never reflected on this general foundation, and that all here alleged is this, that the pleasant sensation arises only from objects in which there is *uniformity amidst variety*. We may have the sensation without knowing what is the occasion of it, as a man's taste may suggest ideas of sweets, acids, bitters, though he be ignorant of the forms of the small bodies, or their motions, which excite these perceptions in him.[3]

. . .

Works of art

VII. As to the works of art, were we to run through the various artificial contrivances or structures, we should constantly find the foundation of the beauty which appears in them to be some kind of uniformity or unity of proportion among the parts, and of each part to the whole. As there is a great diversity of proportions possible, and different kinds of uniformity, so there is room enough for that diversity of fancies observable in architecture, gardening, and such like arts in different nations: they all have uniformity, though the parts in one may differ from those in another. The Chinese or Persian buildings are not like the

———————— *ℳ* ————————

3. Given Hutcheson's theoretical premises, it is hardly surprising to find that his first artistic example of 'original beauty' comes from music. Seventeenth-century acoustical findings reverberate in his argument. As far as aesthetics is concerned, however, Hutcheson does not go much beyond Zarlino, who also adhered to the principle of 'uniformity amidst variety', utilizing variety for his own theoretical needs. "Harmony," thus, "can arise only from things that are among themselves diverse" (Strunk, II, p. 43). Zarlino was also the first to emphasize the role of the dissonance in the aesthetic "uniformity" of the musical experience, an argument which served Kepler in his astronomical investigations and led to his conception of "recurring patterns."

Grecian and Roman, and yet the former has its uniformity of the various parts to each other, and to the whole, as well as the latter. In that kind of architecture which the Europeans call regular, the uniformity of parts is very obvious, the several parts are regular figures, and either equal or similar at least in the same range: the pedestals are parallelopipedons or square prisms; the pillars, cylinders nearly; the arches circular, and all those in the same row equal; there is the same proportion everywhere observed in the same range between the diameters of pillars and their heights, their capitals, the diameters of arches, the heights of the pedestals, the projections of the cornice, and all the ornaments in each of our five orders. And though other countries do not follow the Grecian or Roman proportions, yet there is even among them a proportion retained, a uniformity and resemblance of corresponding figures; and every deviation in one part from that proportion which is observed in the rest of the building is displeasing to every eye, and destroys or diminishes at least the beauty of the whole.

VII. The same might be observed through all other works of art, even to the meanest utensil, the beauty of every one of which we shall always find to have the same foundation of *uniformity amidst variety*, without which they appear mean, irregular, and deformed.[4]

Section IV:
OF RELATIVE OR COMPARATIVE BEAUTY

Comparative beauty

I. If the preceeding thoughts concerning the foundation of *absolute beauty* be just, we may easily understand wherein *relative beauty* con-

───────── ∽ ─────────

4. The "mathematical" foundation of proportions, the constancy of diverse comparative relations (ratios), so basic in Hutcheson's aesthetic theory, enables him to cope with a "diversity of fancies," including cultural differences, without forgoing the universality manifested in each. The "uniformity amidst variety" principle, however, neither explains the *causes* of diverse cultural choices, nor the stylistic changes within them. Whereas architecture's "harmonious proportions" may be obvious, the "delight" which accompanies the understanding of universal theorems should not be confused with the unveiling of the non-obvious "uniformities" in both science and the arts. Sensations no more provide "sufficient reasons" for the explanation of uniformities than do uniformities ("sufficient reasons") for the explanation of sensations (see section III, articles V & VI which were not included in our selection).

sists. All beauty is relative to the sense of some mind perceiving it; but what we call *relative* is that which is apprehended in any object commonly considered as an *imitation* of some original. And this beauty is founded on a conformity, or a kind of unity between the original and the copy. The original may be either some object in nature, or some established idea; for if there be any known idea as a standard, and rules to fix this image or idea by, we may make a beautiful imitation. Thus a statuary, painter, or poet may please with an Hercules, if his piece retains that grandeur, and those marks of strength and courage which we imagine in that hero.

And farther, to obtain comparative beauty alone, it is not necessary that there be any beauty in the original. The imitation of absolute beauty may indeed in the whole make a more lovely piece, and yet an exact imitation shall still be beautiful, though the original were entirely void of it. Thus the deformities of old age in a picture, the rudest rocks or mountains in a landscape, if well represented, shall have abundant beauty, though perhaps not so great as if the original were absolutely beautiful, and as well represented. Nay, perhaps the novelty may make us prefer the representation of irregularity.

Description in poetry

II. The same observation holds true in the descriptions of the poets either of natural objects or persons; and this relative beauty is what they should principally endeavour to obtain, as the peculiar beauty of their works. By the *Moratae Fabulae*, or the greek [ἤθη] of Aristotle, we are not to understand virtuous manners, but a just representation of manners or characters as they are in nature, and that the actions and sentiments be suited to the characters of the persons to whom they are ascribed in epic and dramatic poetry. Perhaps very good reasons may be suggested from the nature of our passions to prove that a poet should not draw his characters perfectly virtuous. These characters indeed abstractly considered might give more pleasure, and have more beauty than the imperfect ones which occur in life with a mixture of good and evil; but it may suffice at present to suggest against this choice that we have more lively ideas of imperfect men with all their passions, than of morally perfect heroes such as really never occur to our observation, and of which consequently we cannot judge exactly as to their agreement with the copy. And farther, through consciousness of our own state we are more nearly touched and affected by the imperfect characters, since in them we see represented, in the persons of others, the contrasts of inclinations, and the struggles between the passions of self-love and those of honour and virtue which we often feel in our own breasts. This is the perfection of beauty for which Homer is justly admired, as well as for the variety of his characters.

Probability, Simile, Metaphor

III. Many other beauties of poetry may be reduced under this class of *relative beauty*. The *probability* is absolutely necessary to make us imagine *resemblance*. It is by resemblance that *similitudes, metaphors*, and *allegories* are made beautiful, whether either the subject of the thing compared to it have beauty or not; the beauty indeed is greater when both have some original beauty or dignity as well as resemblance, and this is the foundation of the rule of studying *decency* in metaphors and similes as well as likeness. The *measures* and *cadence* are instances of harmony, and come under the head of absolute beauty.

Proneness to compare

IV. We may here observe a strange proneness in our minds to make perpetual comparisons of all things which occur to our observation, even of those which are very different from each other. There are certain resemblances in the motions of all animals upon like passions, which easily found a comparison; but this does not serve to entertain our fancy. Inanimate objects have often such positions as resemble those of the human body in various circumstances. These airs or gestures of the body are indications of certain dispositions in the mind, so that our very passions and affections, as well as other circumstances, obtain a resemblance to natural inanimate objects. Thus a tempest at sea is often an emblem of wrath; a plant or tree drooping under the rain of a person in sorrow; a poppy bending its stalk, or a flower withering when cut by the plow resembles the death of a blooming hero; an aged oak in the mountains shall represent an old empire; a flame seizing a wood shall represent a war. In short, everything in nature, by our strange inclination to resemblance, shall be brought to represent other things, even the most remote, especially the passions and circumstances of human nature in which we are more nearly concerned; and to confirm this and furnish instances of it one need only look into Homer or Virgil. A fruitful fancy would find in a grove, or a wood an emblem for every character in a commonwealth, and every turn of temper or station in life.

Intention

V. Concerning that kind of comparative beauty which has a necessary relation to some established idea, we may observe that some works of art acquire a distinct beauty by their correspondence to some universally supposed intention in the artificers, or the persons who employed him. And to obtain this beauty sometimes they do not form their works so as to attain the highest perfection of original beauty separately considered, because a composition of this relative beauty, along with some degree of the original kind, may give more pleasure than a more perfect original beauty separately. Thus we see that strict regularity in laying out of gardens in parterres, vistas, parallel walks, is often neglected to obtain an imitation of nature even in some of its wildness. And we are more pleased with this imitation, especially when the scene is large and spacious, than with the more confined exactness of regular works. So likewise in the monuments erected in honour of deceased heroes, although a cylinder, or prism, or regular solid may have more original beauty than a very acute pyramid or obelisk, yet the latter pleases more by answering better to supposed intentions of stability and being conspicuous. For the same reason, cubes or square prisms are generally chosen for the pedestals of statues, and not any of the more beautiful solids, which do not seem so secure from rolling. This may be the reason too why columns or pillars look best when made a little taper from the middle, or a third from the bottom, that they may not seem top-heavy and in danger of falling.

VI. The like reason may influence artists in many other instances to depart from the rules of original beauty as above laid down. And yet this is no argument against our sense of beauty being founded, as was above explained, on uniformity amidst variety, but only an evidence that our sense of beauty of the original kind may be varied and overbalanced by another kind of beauty.

VII. This beauty arising from correspondence to intention would open to curious observers a new scene of beauty in the works of nature, by considering how the mechanism of the various parts known to us seems adapted to the perfection of that part, and yet in subordination to the good of some system or whole. We generally suppose the good of the greatest whole, or of all beings, to have been the intention of the Author of nature, and cannot avoid being pleased when we see any part of this design executed in the systems we are acquainted with. The observations already made on this subject are in everyone's hand, in the treatise of our late improvers of *mechanical philosophy*. We shall only observe here that everyone has a certain pleasure in seeing any design well executed by curious mechanism, even when his own advantage is no way concerned, and also in discovering the design to which any complex machine is adapted, when he has perhaps had a general knowledge of the machine before, without seeing its correspondence or aptness to execute any design.[5]

The arguments by which we prove reason and design in any cause from the beauty of the effects are so frequently used in some of the highest subjects that it may be necessary to inquire a little more particularly into them, to see how far they will hold, and with what degree of evidence.

5. As we have noted above (fn. 1), Hutcheson's view of relative beauty necessarily postulates previous knowledge, thus including intervening conceptual variables into the aesthetic experience. His account of beauty in descriptive poetry, for example, includes affects, which were formerly only related to pleasure. Hutcheson is able to justify variety in the imitated model without having to enlarge his theoretical base by introducing the notion of the "well represented," for it likewise relates coherence to ordered relations of sorts. Resemblance, therefore, the core of imitation in art, turns into a basic principle that may include, among other things, rhetorical figures — allegories, anthropomorphisms, etc. — and the manifestation of all kinds of intentional designs. Among the latter Hutcheson includes English Gardens, which, though artificial, are conceived as "wild" nature, and Nature, however untouched, is conceived as an artificial machine. Both, he says, reveal their author's manipulation, which plays a central part in the inner relations exemplified by each object. Beyond these typical eighteenth-century examples, Hutcheson's argument is of importance for subsequent discussions concerning the role of intention in art, its formation as well as the assessment of its signification.

...

Section VI:

OF THE UNIVERSALITY OF THE SENSE OF BEAUTY AMONG MEN

Internal sense not an immediate source of pain

I. We before insinuated that all beauty has a relation to some perceiving power. And, consequently, since we know not how great a variety of senses there may be among animals, there is no form in nature concerning which we can pronounce that it has no beauty; for it may still please some perceiving power. But our *Inquiry* is confined to men; and before we examine the *universality* of this sense of beauty, or their agreement in approving uniformity, it may be proper to consider whether, as the other senses which give us pleasure do also give us pain, so this sense of beauty does make some objects disagreeable to us, and the occasion of pain.

That many objects give no pleasure to our sense is obvious: many are certainly void of beauty. But then there is no form which seems necessarily disagreeable of itself, when we dread no other evil from it, and compare it with nothing better of the kind. Many objects are naturally displeasing, and distasteful to our external senses, as well as others pleasing and agreeable, as smells, tastes, and some separate sounds; but as to our sense of beauty, no composition of objects which give not unpleasant simple ideas, seems positively unpleasant or painful of itself, had we never observed anything better of the kind. Deformity is only the absence of beauty, or deficiency in the beauty expected in any species. Thus bad music pleases rustics who never heard any better, and the finest ear is not offended with tuning of instruments, if it be not too tedious, where no harmony is expected; and yet much smaller dissonancy shall offend amidst the performance, where harmony is expected. A rude heap of stones is no way offensive to one who shall be displeased with irregularity in architecture, where beauty was expected. And had there been a species of that form which we now call ugly or deformed, and had we never seen or expected greater beauty, we should have received no disgust from it, although the pleasure would not have been so great in this form as in those we now admire. Our sense of beauty seems designed to give us positive pleasure, but not positive pain or disgust, any farther than what arises from disappointment.

Approbation and dislike from associations of ideas

II. There are indeed many faces which at first view are apt to raise dislike; but this is generally not from any deformity which of itself is positively displeasing, but either from want of expected beauty, or much more from their carrying some natural indications of morally bad dispositions, which we all acquire a faculty of discerning in countenances, airs, and gestures. That this is not occasioned by any form positively disgusting will appear from this, that if upon long acquaintance we are sure of finding sweetness of temper, humanity, and cheerfulness, although the bodily form continues, it shall give us no disgust or displeasure; whereas if anything were naturally disagreeable, or the occasion of pain, or positive distaste, it would always continue so, even although the aversion we might have toward it were counterbalanced by other considerations. There are horrors raised by some objects, which are only the effect of fear of ourselves, or compassion towards others, when either reason, or some foolish association of ideas, makes us apprehend danger, and not the effect of anything in the form itself; for we find that most of those objects which excite horror at first, when experience or reason has removed the fear, may become the occasions of pleasure, as ravenous beasts, a tempestuous sea, a craggy precipice, a dark shady valley.

Associations

III. We shall see hereafter that associations of ideas make objects pleasant and delightful which are not naturally apt to give any such pleasures; and the same way, the casual conjunctions of ideas may give a disgust where there is nothing disagreeable in the form itself. And this is the occasion of many fantastic aversions to figures of some animals, and to some other forms. Thus swine, serpents of all kinds, and some insects really beautiful enough, are beheld with aversion by many people who have got some accidental ideas associated to them. And for distastes of this kind no other account can be given.

Universality of this sense

IV. But as to the universal agreement of mankind in their sense of beauty from uniformity amidst variety, we must consult experience. And as we allow all men reason, since all men are capable of understanding simple arguments, though few are capable of complex demonstrations, so in this case it must be sufficient to prove this sense of beauty universal if all men are better pleased with uniformity in the simpler instances than the contrary, even when there is no advantage observed attending it; and likewise if all men, according as their capacity enlarges, so as to receive and compare more complex ideas, have a greater delight in uniformity, and are pleased with its more complex kinds, both original and relative.

Now let us consider if ever any person was void of this sense in the simpler instances. Few trials have been made in the simplest instances of harmony, because as soon as we find an ear incapable of relishing complex compositions, such as our tunes are, no farther pains are employed about such. But in figures, did ever any man make choice of a trapezium, or any irregular curve, for the ichnography or plan of his house, without necessity, or some great motive of convenience? Or to make the opposite walls not parallel, or unequal in height? Were ever trapeziums, irregular polygons or curves, chosen for the forms of doors or windows, though these figures might have answered the uses as well, and would have often saved a great part of the time, labour, and expense to workmen which is now employed in suiting the stones and timber to the regular forms? Among all the fantastic modes of dress, none was ever quite void of uniformity, if it were only in the resemblance of the two sides of the same robe, and in some general aptitude to the human form. The pictish painting had always relative beauty, by resemblance to other objects, and often those objects were originally beautiful. However justly we might here apply Horace's censure of impertinent descriptions in poetry:

> Sed non erat his locus.
> ["For such things there is a place, but not just now" (Horace, De Arte Poetica, line 19, translated by H.R. Fairclough, as appearing in Kivi's edition)]

But never were any so extravagant as to affect such figures as are made by the casual spilling of liquid colours. Who was ever pleased with an inequality of heights in windows of the same range, or dissimilar shapes of them? With unequal legs or arms, eyes or cheeks in a mistress? It must however be acknowledged that interest may often counterbalance our sense of beauty in this affair as well as in others, and superior good qualities may make us overlook such imperfections.

Real beauty alone pleases

V. Nay farther, it may perhaps appear that regularity and uniformity are so copiously diffused through the universe, and we are so readily determined to pursue this as the foundation of beauty in works of art, that there is scarcely anything ever fancied as beautiful where there is not really something of this uniformity and regularity. We are indeed often mistaken in imagining that there is the greatest possible beauty, where it is but very imperfect; but still it is some degree of beauty which pleases, although there may be higher degrees which we do not observe; and our sense acts with full regularity when we are pleased, although we are kept by a false prejudice from pursuing objects which would please us more.

A Goth, for instance, is mistaken when from education he imagines the architecture of his country to be the most perfect; and a conjunction of some hostile ideas may make him have an aversion to Roman buildings, and study to demolish them, as some of our reformers did the popish buildings, not being able to separate the ideas of the superstitious worship from the forms of the buildings where it was practised. And yet it is still real beauty which pleases the Goth, founded upon uniformity amidst variety. For the Gothic pillars are uniform to each other, not only in their sections, which are lozenge-formed, but also in their heights and ornaments. Their arches are not one uniform curve, but yet they are segments of similar curves, and generally equal in the same ranges. The very Indian buildings have some kind of uniformity, and many of the Eastern nations, though they differ much from us, yet have great regularity in their manner, as well as the Romans in theirs. Our Indian screens, which wonderfully supply our imaginations with ideas of deformity, in which nature is very churlish and sparing, do want indeed all the beauty arising from proportion of parts and conformity to nature; and yet they cannot divest themselves of all beauty and uniformity in the separate parts. And this diversifying the human body into various contortions may give some wild pleasure from variety, since some uniformity to the human shape is still retained.[6]

...

An internal sense does not presuppose innate ideas

X. But let it be observed here once for all that an *internal sense* no more presupposes an *innate idea,* or principle of knowledge, than the *external.* Both are *natural* powers of *perception,* or determinations of the mind to receive necessarily certain ideas from the presence of objects. The *internal sense is a passive power of receiving ideas of beauty from all objects in which there is uniformity amidst variety.* Nor does there seem anything more difficult in this matter than that the mind should be always determined to receive the idea of *sweet* when particles of such a form enter the pores of the tongue, or to have the idea of *sound* upon any quick undulation of the air. The one seems to have as little connection with its idea as the other; and the same power could with equal ease constitute the former the occasion of ideas as the latter.

Associations cause of disagreements

XI. The *association of ideas* above hinted at is one great cause of the apparent diversity of fancies in the sense of beauty, as well as in the external senses, and often makes men have an aversion to objects of beauty, and a liking to others void of it, but under different conceptions than those of beauty or deformity. And here it may not be improper to

6. Hutcheson further qualifies what he means by universality and by the immediacy of the internal sense. The mind, as it turns out, must be tuned to harmony in order to sense not only the "harmonious" but the disharmonious as well. Pain is immediate only as far as simple ideas are concerned; sensing deformity, on the other hand, needs a certain frame of reference, an acquaintance with a better possible formation. Again, Hutcheson is unable to escape the conceptual in his consideration of the perceptual: His attempts to demonstrate the constancy of his principles in their diverse realizations seem, despite his intent, to grant specific cultural and psychological factors an importance equal to that of the sense natural to man in general.

give some instances of some of these associations. The beauty of trees, their cool shades, and their aptness to conceal from observation have made groves and woods the usual retreat to those who love solitude, especially to the religious, the pensive, the melancholy, and the amorous. And do not we find that we have so joined the ideas of these dispositions of mind with those external objects that they always recur to us along with them? The cunning of the heathen priests might make such obscure places the scene of the fictitious appearances of their deities; and hence we join ideas of something divine to them. We know the like effect in the ideas of our churches, from the perpetual use of them only in religious exercises. The faint light in Gothic buildings has had the same association of a very foreign idea which our poet shows in his epithet,

> A dim religious light.
> (Milton, *Il Penseroso*)

In like manner it is known that often all the circumstances of actions, or places, or dresses of persons, or voice, or song, which have occurred at any time together, when we were strongly affected by any passion, will be so connected that any one of these will make all the rest recur. And this is often the occasion both of great pleasure and pain, delight and aversion to many objects which of themselves might have been perfectly indifferent to us; but these approbations, or distastes, are remote from the ideas of beauty, being plainly different ideas.

Music, how it pleases differently

XII. There is also another charm in music to various persons, which is distinct from harmony and is occasioned by its raising agreeable passions. The human voice is obviously varied by all the stronger passions: now when our ear discerns any resemblance between the air of a tune, whether sung or played upon an instrument, either in its time, or modulation, or any other circumstance, to the sound of the human voice in any passion, we shall be touched by it in a very sensible manner, and have melancholy, joy, gravity, thoughtfulness excited in us by a sort of *sympathy* or *contagion*. The same connection is observable between the very air of a tune and the words expressing any passion which we have heard it fitted to, so that they shall both recur to us together, though but one of them affects our senses.

Now in such a diversity of pleasing or displeasing ideas which may be joined with forms of bodies, or tunes, when men are of such different dispositions, and prone to such a variety of passions, it is no wonder that they should often disagree in their fancies of objects, even although their sense of beauty and harmony were perfectly uniform; because many other ideas may either please or displease, according to persons' tempers and past circumstances. We know how agreeable a very wild country may be to any person who has spent the cheerful days of his youth in it, and how disagreeable very beautiful places may be if they were the scenes of his misery. And this may help us in many cases to account for the diversities of fancy, without denying the uniformity of our internal sense of beauty.[7]

...

Final causes of the internal senses

II. As to the *final causes* of this internal sense, we need not inquire whether, to an almighty and all-knowing Being, there be any real excellence in regular forms, in acting by general laws, in knowing by general theorems. We seem scarce capable of answering such questions anyway; nor need we inquire whether other animals may not discern uni-

———— ✍ ————

7. In these three sections Hutcheson indirectly addresses the question of artistic meaning. As his argument proceeds, it becomes increasingly clear that the internal sense he posits is hardly able to deal with the symbolic or even with the suggestive in art. In line with the British empiricists, he maintains that an internal sense is a "passive power," a content-free propensity. Contents are attached to works of art via the shared associations of collective symbols and via private, personal tastes. Interestingly, Hutcheson turns to music for illustration, renouncing the conception of music's expressive contents as innate ideas, a theory adhered to by the contemporary "Affektenlehre" group (see Vol. I: 131-2). Introducing his concept of "resemblance" into the theory which views the expressivity of music in relation to the inflections of the voice, he demystifies the "echo" metaphor, which has governed this theory since Galilei, subjecting it to specific cognitive investigation. He thus enlists an additional "sense," that of sympathy, a concept which likewise underwent psychological demystification at the time. Thus, music, which served Hutcheson as a prime example of the harmonious, is also chosen for the delineation of the limits of the latter. Reverberating the famous Zarlino–Galilei debate, Hutcheson thus unwittingly transcends the conception of art as the embodiment of the beautiful and shows a recognition of the cognitive complexity of the artistic domain.

formity and regularity in objects which escape our observation, and may not perhaps have their senses constituted so as to perceive beauty from the same foundation which we do, in objects which our senses are not fit to examine or compare. We shall confine ourselves to a subject where we have some certain foundation to go upon and only inquire if we can find any reasons worthy of the great Author of nature for making such a connection between regular objects and the pleasure which accompanies our perceptions of them; or, what reasons might possibly influence him to create the world as it at present is as far as we can observe, everywhere full of regularity and uniformity.

Let it be here observed that as far as we know concerning any of the great bodies of the universe, we see forms and motions really beautiful to our senses; and if we were placed in any planet, the apparent courses would still be regular and uniform, and consequently beautiful to us. Now this gives us no small ground to imagine that if the senses of their inhabitants are in the same manner adapted to their habitations and the objects occurring to their view as ours are here, their senses must be upon the same general foundation with ours.

But to return to the questions, what occurs to resolve them may be contained in the following propositions.

1. The manner of knowledge by universal theorems, and of operation by universal causes, as far as we can attain it, must be most convenient for beings of limited understanding and power, since this prevents distraction in their understandings through the multiplicity of propositions, and toil and weariness to their powers of action; and consequently their reason, without any sense of beauty, must approve of such methods when they reflect upon their apparent advantage.

2. Those objects of contemplation in which there is uniformity amidst variety are more distinctly and easily comprehended and retained than irregular objects because the accurate observation of one or two parts often leads to knowledge of the whole. Thus we can from a pillar or two, with an intermediate arch and cornice, form a distinct idea of a whole regular building, if we know of what species it is and have its length and breadth. From a side and solid angle we have the whole regular solid. The measuring one side gives the whole square, one radius the whole circle, two diameters an oval, one ordinate and abscis-

sa the parabola. Thus also other figures, if they have any regularity, are in every point determined from a few data, whereas it must be a long attention to a vast multiplicity of parts which can ascertain or fix the idea of any irregular form, or give any distinct idea of it, or make us capable of retaining it, as appears in the forms of rude rocks, and pebbles, and confused heaps, even when the multitude of sensible parts is not so great as in the regular forms; for such irregular objects distract the mind with variety, since for every sensible part we must have a quite different idea.

3. From these two propositions it follows that beings of limited understanding and power, if they act rationally for their own interest, must choose to operate by the simplest means, to invent general theorems, and to study regular objects, if they be as useful as irregular ones, that they may avoid the endless toil of producing each effect by a separate operation, of searching out each different truth by a different inquiry, and of imprinting the endless variety of dissimilar ideas in irregular objects.

4. But then beside this consideration of interest there does not appear to be any necessary connection, antecedent to the constitution of the Author of nature, between regular forms, actions, theorems, and that sudden sensible pleasure excited in us upon observation of them, even when we do not reflect upon the advantage mentioned in the former proposition. And so possibly the Deity could have formed us so as to have no immediate pleasure from such objects, or connected pleasure form those of a quite contrary nature. We have a tolerable presumption of this in the beauties of various animals; they give some small pleasure indeed to everyone who views them, but then everyone seems far more delighted with the peculiar beauties of its own species than with those of a different one, which seldom raise any desire. This makes it probable that the pleasure is not the necessary result of the form itself, otherwise it would equally affect all apprehensions in what species soever, but depends upon a voluntary constitution adapted to preserve the regularity of the universe, and is probably not the effect of necessity but choice in the Supreme Agent who constituted our senses.

From the divine goodness

5. Now from the whole we may conclude that supposing the Deity so kind as to connect sensible pleasure with certain actions or contemplations beside the rational advantage perceivable in them, there is a great moral necessity from his goodness that the internal sense of men should be constituted as it is at present so as to make uniformity amidst variety the occasion of pleasure. For were it not so, but on the contrary, if irregular objects, particular truths and operations pleased us, beside the endless toil this would involve us in, there must arise a perpetual dissatisfaction in all rational agents with themselves, since reason and interest would lead us to simple general causes while a contrary sense of beauty would make us disapprove them. Universal theorems would appear to our understanding the best means of increasing our knowledge of what might be useful, while a contrary sense would set us on the search after particular truths. Thought and reflection would recommend objects with uniformity amidst variety, and yet this perverse instinct would involve us in labyrinths of confusion and dissimilitude. And hence we see how suitable it is to the sagacious bounty which we suppose in the Deity to constitute our internal senses in the manner in which they are, by which pleasure is joined to the contemplation of those objects which a finite mind can best imprint and retain the ideas of with the least distraction; to those actions which are most efficacious and fruitful in useful effect; and to those theorems which most enlarge our minds.

Reason of general laws

III. As to the other question, What reason might influence the Deity, whom no diversity of operation could distract or weary, to choose to operate by simplest means and general laws, and to diffuse uniformity, proportion, and similitude through all the parts of nature which we can observe?, perhaps there may be some real excellence in this manner of operation, and in these forms, which we know not. But this we may probably say, that since the divine goodness, for the reasons above mentioned, has constituted our sense of beauty as it is at present, the same goodness might have determined the Great Architect to adorn this stupendous theatre in a manner agreeable to the spectators, and that part which is exposed to the observation of men so as to be pleasant to them, especially if we suppose that he designed to discover himself to them as wise and good, as well as powerful; for thus he has given them greater evidences through the whole earth of his art, wisdom, design, and bounty, than they can possibly have for the reason, counsel, and good-will of their fellow creatures, with whom they converse, with full persuasion of these qualities in them, about their common affairs.

As to the operations of the Deity by general laws, there is still a farther reason from a sense superior to these already considered, even that of virtue, or the beauty of action, which is the foundation of our greatest happiness. For were there no general laws fixed to the course of nature, there could be no prudence or design in men, no rational expectation of effects from causes, no schemes of action projected, or any regular execution. If, then, according to the frame of our nature, our greatest happiness must depend upon our actions, as it may perhaps be made appear it does, the universe must be governed not by particular wills but by general laws upon which we can found our expectations and project our schemes of action. Nay farther, though general laws did ordinarily obtain, yet if the Deity usually stopped their effects whenever it was necessary to prevent any particular evils, this would effectually and justly supersede all human prudence and care about actions, since a superior mind did thus relieve men from their charge.[8]

———— ⁄♫ ————

8. In these last paragraphs, Hutcheson highlights and summarizes three major points which he repeatedly enlists in the course of the treatise. These comprise: (1) the relationship between pleasure and aesthetic order, (2) the applicability of this order to a wide range of phenomena, from the sensual to the scientific and (3) the recognition that order, as an aesthetic principle, is unique to man's mental constitution. The first guarantees a compatibility between the affective and the rational, avoiding, as it were, a "cognitive dissonance." The second is tantamount to a unified system of knowledge and action. The third relates the first and the second to a theological stand. Though the aesthetic principle, recognized as unique to man, appears to circumscribe Hutcheson's epistemological scope, he leaves room in the essay for other kinds of mental constructions. Instead of a Kantian conclusion, Hutcheson, in his last observations, exhibits a typical seventeenth-century anthropocentric view. The Creator, accordingly, revealed himself to man by enabling him to grasp Creation through its comprehensible manifestations. Though the sky was long believed to be "untuned," by that time, the harmony of the spheres, nonetheless, is still "heard" in Hutcheson's writings. It seems that for Hutcheson, as for several others, the a priori abstract structure, implied by world harmony, still constituted a viable base for investigation of the physical as well as the spiritual and of the links between them.

$\mathcal{H}$ildebrand $\mathcal{J}$acob

(1693-1739)

Hildebrand Jacob was the only son of Sir John Jacob and Lady Catherine Barry. As a gentleman of leisure, he devoted much time to all kinds of literary activities, including writing. Of his several poems, the "Curious Maid" (1720) was frequently imitated and parodied; his tragedy "The Fatal Constancy" was performed five times at the Drury Lane Theatre. He also translated from and into French several literary works of which Abbé Prèvost's *Manon Lescaut* is best known. His broad literary interests and knowledge led him into the aesthetic realm as well; his *Of the Sister Arts: an Essay* and *How the mind is raised to the Sublime* was published in 1734 and 1735 respectively. Subsequently, he gathered his scattered writings in one volume, wishing to convince his friends that he was more than just the author of "some perhaps less pardonable Productions." Jacob's tour to Paris, Vienna and the chief towns of Italy, between 1728 and 1729, was typical of a man of his standing; one cannot fail to notice the penetrating and lasting impressions of this tour in the present *Essay* which is fully presented in this volume.

Undoubtedly, Jacob's main achievement resides in this essay, which constituted one of the first attempts in modern times to subject poetry, painting and music to a correspondence theory. Arguing for basic aesthetic principles shared by the three arts, he also insisted on distinctions, due to their different media. Departing from the Neoplatonic dogma, still held by contemporary French writers, he ushered the "Lessing conception" about the "limits" of artistic media, which all of the later writers in our group implicitly shared. This, and more, is aptly expressed in the seemingly innocent title of his essay: *Of the Sister Arts*. The "sisterhood" of the *three* arts, which was later taken for granted, was, in fact, Jacob's single-handed success to unify music and painting — unrelated arts — through a common "sibling." Only a man acquainted with both the French and English legacies, could coordinate the former two pairs within one family. The sisterhood of music and poetry was most explicitly expressed by Milton, whom Jacob admired; that of painting and poetry (related to the *ut pictura poesis* paradigm), by Du Fresnoy's Latin poem *De arte graphica* which Jacob probably knew well. What is most significant about Jacob's integration, is his attempt to render the poetic imagery into theoretical concepts of philosophical standing. Such attempts, as we observed in the first part of this book, were typical of our British writers.

Milton's image of the relationship between poetry and music is expressed in his poem *At A Solemn Music*: "Blest pair of Sirens, pledges of Heav'n's joy/ Sphere-born harmonious Sisters, Voice and Verse,/ Wed your divine sounds, and mixt power employ...." Themselves already a metamorphosis of the celestial sirens (related to the unheard music of heaven) and the earthly sirens (the Homerian tempters of voyagers on earth), Milton's sphere-born harmonious sisters, are an "ultimate image of Heaven's music, capable of reconciling men through their imagination with the divine." (Hutton 1951). While Voice and Verse, music and poetry, were not distinguished by earlier writers as two different "personae," in Milton they acquire full autonomy. Considered autonomous, Milton's wish for their union becomes meaningful. For Jacob, their autonomy turned into a basic premise, enabling him to view the perfection of music in its own terms. Harmoniousness, for Jacob, is thus related to autonomy, itself related to the imagery generated by each of the arts. In the final analysis, it is the unique imagery which determines the nature of each of the arts. Developing this argument in a consistent way, Jacob could not help but refute the basic premises of *ut pictura poesis*.

The idea of the sisterhood of Poetry and Painting was supplied by Du Fresnoy — the oracle of painters for at least one hundred and twenty years — in the following lines (with the attached translation of Dryden):

> Ut Pictura Poesis erit; siilisque Poesi
> Sit pictura; refert par aemula quaeque sororem
>
> Alternantque vices et nomina; muta poesis
> Dicitur haec, Pictura loquens solet illa vocari.
>
> Painting and Poesy are two Sisters, which are so
> like in all things, that they mutually lend to each
> other both their name and Office. One is call'd a
> dumb Poesy, and the other a speaking Picture.

While Jacob was probably acquainted with Dryden's as well as De Piles' translations of the poem, he felt free to interpret the idea of resemblances among the arts in his own way, emphasizing the *theoretical* implications of comparisons among the arts, rather than the actual similarity. Critical thought, Jacob tells us, is itself a creative act, as such it may function as a guiding force in bringing about successful artistic works and convincing styles. New works of art, however, may suggest new premises, calling for the broadening of old theories, or, at times, for their total replacement by others.

Jacob tried to get the most out of the different sources that were at his disposal, surveying the arts from as many points of view as he could possibly find. He discusses epistemological aspects while cognizant of ontological ones; he deals with perceptual questions while accepting cultural constraints; he assessed historical processes within anthropological frames of reference. Though he never mentions Shaftesbury, his cultural interests are akin to the latter's, although his own account of the arts is more specific. The variety of subjects Jacob touches upon in a relatively short text is typical of preliminary treatises of this kind. Still, the insights he provided set an entire agenda for later thinkers, though they were inclined to concentrate on fewer subjects, even a single one, with greater rigor.

Part of Jacob's essay appeared in French; what influence it exerted across the Channel is difficult to assess. He is never mentioned by name even by our group, though it is quite improbable that his *Essay* was not read by most of its members.

OF THE

SISTER ARTS, &C.

ℐf it be allow'd with *Cicero* that all *Arts* are *related*, we may safely conclude that *Poetry, Painting,* and *Music* are closely ally'd.[1] From this near Resemblance to each other they have been commonly call'd the *Sister Arts*, which is so great, that it is difficult to discourse upon either of them, particularly on the two First, without a mutual borrowing of *Images*, and *Terms*, insomuch that one of these *Arts* cannot well be explain'd, without giving some Insight into the other at the same Time.[2]

———— ☾ ————

1. Jacob, it seems, uses Cicero as an authority in the sense of "everybody knows that...." Cicero is enlisted to provide a *proper* stepping stone for the presentation of his own arguments concerning the nature of the relationships among the arts. As elaborated in Vol. I, what the ancients understood by art differs considerably from what subsequent generations understood by the term. Moreover, the standing of each of the arts and the relations among them underwent many changes. The leap, therefore, from Cicero's general statement concerning human activities (like carpentry and medicine) to Jacob's "closely ally'd" arts (poetry, painting, music) is surprising, even though Jacob is not perturbed by it. It is precisely this leap, which instigated the sort of clarifications and deliberations, which eventually led to the turn from *ut pictura poesis* to *ut musica poesis*.

2. The claim that Du Fresnoy's poem constituted a base for Jacob's argument, is lent additional reinforcement in these lines. Yet Du Fresnoy's postulate concerning referentiality in the arts ("each to her sister doth refer"; Will's translation, 1754, as quoted in Lipking 1970) is viewed by Jacob as a result of the theoretical difficulties peculiar to the phenomena under discussion. Indeed, one may argue, in retrospect, that the need for "the mutual borrowing of images and terms" derives from the absence, at the time, of a conceptual language suited to deal with artistic phenomena from a higher theoretical level.

Almost all the *Parts* of *Poetry* are found in *Painting*. *Harmony*, which is the *Essence* of *Music*, is, as it were, the *Dress* or *Cloath*ing of *Poetry*, and *Painting* is a kind of *dumb Harmony*,[3] which charms and sooths us thro' our *Eyes*, as *Music* does thro' our *Ears*. *Poetry* is much nearer ally'd to *Painting* than to *Music*. *Lyric Poetry* approaches more to *Music*, than any other *Species* of it, as *Dramatic* and *Pastoral* Poetry do to *Painting*.[4] *Harmony* does the Office of a *Lucina* to the *Poet* and *Painter*, helping the Production of their Labours; and scarce any of those who have succeeded in these *Arts*, have been insensible of the *Power* of *Sounds*. [5]

The nearer the *Poet* approaches to the *Painter*, the more perfect he is; and the more perfect the *Painter*, the more he imitates the *Poet*, in drawing the *Manners* and *Passions* with *Life* and *Spirit*. The *Painter* is to *animate* a *Form*, and the *Poet* to lend a *Form* to *Sentiment* and *Diction:* One is to give *Life* to beautiful *Proportion*, and the other *Strength* and *Figure* to sublime *Thought:* The *Painter, like Prometheus*, lights up a *Spirit* in the *Body*, while the *Poet* seeks a *Body*, to *maintain* and *support* that

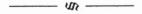

3. Jacob accepts the above-mentioned rules of the aesthetic discourse for the sake of further elaboration. "Painting is *dumb harmony*," is, of course, a paraphrase of Simonides' comment: "painting is mute poetry, and poetry is speaking pictures." What Jacob adds by this insight to the ongoing discussion will be elucidated in fn. 5.

4. Accepting the premises of *ut pictura poesis*, Jacob is willing, nonetheless, to tamper with the different alliances among the arts. Though he views parts of poetry as a kind of eloquent painting, he considers lyric poetry more akin to music. This readiness to differentiate between poetic "species," in connection with correspondences, is one of the cornerstones for the eventual paradigmatic shift to *ut musica poesis*.

5. This last paragraph partly clarifies what the various arts have in common according to Jacob. All the arts require a sort of internal "congeniality" which presides over their constructedness. This congeniality plays the role of the Goddess of Birth (Lucina), as it were; it emerges from within as part and parcel of the creative act, as Shaftesbury believed. That music should serve Jacob as a prime model in this connection, is hardly surprising. While still in line with the tradition of the harmony of the spheres, Jacob gives it an interesting twist. Harmony, accordingly, does not transcend the arts but emanates from them, as a force which guides their very construction.

Spirit, which is one of *Homer's* greatest Praises; for, by the *Fire* of his great *Genius*, he has given *Form* to almost all *Things*, and made them appear, as it were, *alive*.[6]

As these *Arts* proceed chiefly from the same Principles, *Imitation* and *Harmony*, so they are mutually assistant to each other, and ought to dwell much together; yet however they may be reciprocally oblig'd to each other, and agree so well in the main, they have their *separate* Beauties too.

Poetry not only can express the external Signs of the Operation of the Mind, which are so livelily represented by *Painting*; but also its finest *abstracted* Thoughts, and most *pathetic* Reflections. *Painting* cannot convey its *Images* in such *great Numbers*, and with so *quick* and *unwearied* a *Succession* as *Poetry* does; and there are almost innumerable *Images* in *Poetry*, which *Painting* is not capable of forming, and which are often the greatest Ornaments in *Poetry*. What *Painter* can give us the *Image*, for example, which *Horace* has done in these Words,[7]

> *Et nova Febrium*
> *Terris incubuit Cohors.*
>
> Ode 3. Lib. 1.

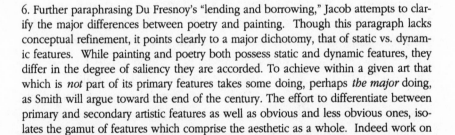

6. Further paraphrasing Du Fresnoy's "lending and borrowing," Jacob attempts to clarify the major differences between poetry and painting. Though this paragraph lacks conceptual refinement, it points clearly to a major dichotomy, that of static vs. dynamic features. While painting and poetry both possess static and dynamic features, they differ in the degree of saliency they are accorded. To achieve within a given art that which is *not* part of its primary features takes some doing, perhaps *the major* doing, as Smith will argue toward the end of the century. The effort to differentiate between primary and secondary artistic features as well as obvious and less obvious ones, isolates the gamut of features which comprise the aesthetic as a whole. Indeed work on the correspondences and differences among the arts contributed in no small way to the establishment of aesthetics as a separate branch within philosophy.

7. To the principle of harmony, discussed in these two paragraphs, Jacob adds the principle of imitation, which belongs to another venerable tradition. Here, again, he is willing to address anew an old subject, in order to arrive at helpful distinctions. Not unlike Baumgarten, he shifts from the imitated object to its artistic representations—to the images thus created. Hence it becomes clear that poetry deals with *numerous* images, while painting creates a *single* image, thus explicating the basis of the dynamic-static dichotomy which he alluded to earlier.

[and an army of feverish diseases hitherto unbeknown
weighed heavily upon the lands]

This represents a *dreadful, active Image* to the Imagination, and
is one of those *many*, which are absolutely out of the Province
of the *Pencil.* A great *Painter* might, perhaps, form a very beautiful *Design* from the Description which *Virgil* gives of *Venus*,
when she discovers herself to *Æneas* in the first book of the
Æneid.

> *Dixit, & avertens rosea cervice refulsit,*
> *Ambrosiæque comæ divinum vertice odorem*
> *Spiravere: pedes vestis defluxit ad imos,*
> *Et vera incessu patuit Dea——*

[She spoke. She turned away; and as she turned, her neck
Glowed to a rose-flush, here crown of ambrosial hair breathed out
A heavenly fragrance, her robe flowed down, down to her feet,
An in gait she was all a goddess. (l. 402–405)]

But to reduce the *intire Image*, which these three or four Verses
convey to the Mind, to *Light* and *Shadow*, is impossible. What a
Complexity of beautiful *Images* are here charm'd up into the
Mind, as it were, by the *Magic* of a few Words? It is in the *brightest Ideas* that *Virgil* thus represents the *Transfiguration*, if one
may so say, of this *Goddess*, while she breaks forth from her
Disguise, into that Blaze and Refulgency of Heavenly *Beauty*,
with all the *Ensigns* of her *Divinity.* What a happy *Attitude* has
the *Poet* chose for this Purpose? With what *Grace* and *Majesty* do
we behold her turning from *Æneas*, and brightning by Degrees
into that glorious *Form* which confess'd her no less than the
Queen of *Love* herself? [8]

---------- ᕫ ----------

8. Explaining the multiplicity of images in poetry vs. the single image of painting, Jacob
reveals an additional insight: The many images may amount to a kind of "transfiguration"; the dynamics of the change it involves is an indivisible aesthetic quality.

It may, perhaps, be said in Favour of *Painting* and *Music*, that they may be look'd upon as *universal Languages*, being to be understood and comprehended every where; and that *Poetry* and *Music* have this Advantage over *Painting*, that as many *Copies* may be taken of them as the *Printer* or *Transcriber* pleases, and that all of them shall be equally perfect with the *Original*; but there are much fewer good Judges of *Poetry* than of *Painting* or *Music*. *Music* is a great and very sudden *Mover* and *Refiner* of the *Passions*; its *Operations* are *intense*; but as it consists only of *Sounds*, to which no other *Ideas* are annexed, its *Impressions* are soon and easily *defac'd*. [9]

It is certain, that, by universal Consent, *Poetry* is the most *elegant* Pleasure, and the most *pleasing* Instruction; a more elevated and harmonious *Philosophy*, inviting more sweetly, and, consequently, more powerfully to that true Wisdom which makes our Happiness. It is the Child of *Nature* and of *Science*, dress'd up in all the choicest of their Beauties; in all Ages it has liv'd, and has had its Nourishment with *Learning*, and with *Learning* too it has constantly decay'd and dwindled into *Barbarism*. We are oblig'd to the *Poets* for the most *lively Pictures* of human Dispositions and Affections. *Horace* declares *Poetry more instructive* than *Philosophy* itself; for it is not only design'd to divert and move. *Poets* were originally those *Divines* and *Philosophers* who *tam'd* Mankind, taught them *Arts* and *Sciences*, gave them *Laws* and fitted them for *Society*; and it is for this Reason chiefly, that *Poetry* has been always so much esteem'd by the greatest Men and wisest *Philosophers*. There is no Doubt, but that *poisonous Morals* may more easily be insinuated and recommended by the *Charms* of *Poetry* as well as *sound*

---

9. Note again the flexibility with which Jacob addresses the issue of the relationships among the arts: Whereas painting and music are epistemologically allied, he relates poetry and music ontologically. Distinctions of this kind help locate the work of art in the symbolic system to which it belongs. Such issues have been elaborated by Goodman, Wolterstorff and other eminent philosophers in our own time.

Instruction, which made a certain *Philosopher* compare *Poetry* to the land of *Ægypt*, equally abounding with *wholsome* and *unwholesome* Herbs; but no body will impute this to *Poetry* itself; but to those who make a wrong Use of it. [10]

Tho' *Music* may give the Mind no *Instruction* immediately from itself; yet it helps greatly to *mend* the *Heart* in general, and elevate it to the doing of great and generous Actions: It disposes the Soul for the Reception of such Precepts as tend to *Humanity* and *Benevolence;* it charms and softens us, like *Beauty*, which, tho' generally incapable of giving Instruction, serves to *refine* our *Passions*, and excite and raise us to the Performance of *brave* and *noble* Exploits. The *Grecians* in the Education of their *Children* took great Care that they should be instructed in *Music*; they were of Opinion, that it contributed much to the framing of them to *Virtue;* and we find, that for a long Time, they had no *Music* but what was proper for forming of Youth to *Morality*, and for *singing* the *Praises* of *Heroes* and great Men. *Hercules, Achilles, &c.* were all taught *Music*; it employ'd their leisure Hours, when the Toils of War were ended; they sung the *Gods* and Deeds of valiant Men. *Poets* and *Musicians* were of old the same Persons. *Socrates* apply'd himself to the *Lyre* towards the End of his Life; and his Disciple *Plato* says, that *Music* has as much Influence on the *Mind* as *Air* has over the *Body. Aristotle* thought it not below him to treat of that *Art*, and *Pythagoras* imagin'd it so useful, that he enjoin'd it as a Duty to his Scholars, to *compose* their Minds

10. As though taken out of Hume's contemporary sensational *Treatise of Human Nature*, Jacob adds an additional distinction in relation to music. This distinction involves *unnamed*, though fully recognized, perceptions ('impressions'), alongside *named* perceptions, codified in appropriate signs ('ideas'). Viewing music as consisting of impressions rather than ideas, enabled Jacob to explain music's immediacy as well as its fugacity. The implications of this distinction will be elaborated by Harris and Webb, and their repercussions will be felt in the works of Kant and his followers.

with it the first Thing they did in a Morning, and the last Thing when they went to sleep at Night.[11]

A *Painter* was of old look'd on as a *common Good*. These *Artists* thought their *Works* too much conceal'd, if they were not exhibited in *public Places*. Some of them chose rather to give their *Labours gratis* to their Country, than to set any Value upon them. *Zeuxis* is said by *Pliny* to have done so, esteeming his Productions invaluable, and the vast Prices we find the *Ancients* gave for *Pictures* and *Statues* are evident Arguments of the Veneration they held them in. The Art of *Painting* is not so easy, or so mechanical a Thing as some seem to imagine. To become a good *Painter*, a great *Genius* is requisite, sound *Judgment* and a fine *Imagination*, joyn'd with long Practice, Patience and Industry. The *Painter*, as well as the *Poet* must be an *Enthusiast* in his *Art*, to succeed in it as he ought; his Mind must be turn'd for a true Relish of what is *great, beautiful*, and *surprizing*; he ought to have a *quick* and *lively* Discernment, and must be easily struck with the *Beauty* and *Proportion* of all the Objects he meets with. A *Painter* must sacrifice almost all his time to his *Art*, and scarce let a Day pass without *doing something*; he ought to *love* his *Profession*, and prefer the *Truth* and *Perfection* of it to any *Interest* besides. He must have an *Idea* of *perfect Nature*, and his Business sometimes may lay out of *Nature* itself, tho' not so often as the *Poet's*. The *Disposition* of the *whole* requires great *Judgment*, as well as it does, before that, to chuse a *proper*

———— ⟨π ————

11. Moving from the relations and differences among the arts to the discussion of value, Jacob engages in a new kind of comparison based on the refinements he introduced in the first part of his treatise. He ascribes to music the power to make man receptive to that which poetry is able to deliver—ideas. He acknowledges the legacies from which he borrows: The Pythagorean-Platonic tradition according to which music *tunes* the soul, and the Horatian legacy, according to which poetry *instructs* the soul. However, by reducing the metaphysical soul to the mind—Locke's and Hume's rather than Plato's—he grants music and poetry a venerable place among cognitive activities. His previous distinction between 'impressions' and 'ideas' provides the content for the mental activities specific to each of the arts.

Subject; nor is it the least Secret in his *Art*, to know when to *leave off*, for which *Apelles* was so much commended.[12]

Some of the Ancients deriv'd the original Ideas of these Arts immediately from Heaven itself, so high was the Opinion they had of them.

It is not very material to know, which of these *Arts* was first produced. *Hieroglyphicks* seem to have been the earliest *Painting* as well as the first, and most ancient Way found out to transmit the Knowledge of Things to Posterity, before the Invention of *Letters:* It is easy to conceive, that the *first Essays* of this *Art* were very rude and imperfect.

The first *Poetry* we hear of was at Feasts and Sacrifices in the earliest Ages after the Labour and Toils of the Harvest and Vintage was ended. In these ancient Assemblies were sung the Praises of the *Gods* and great *Men*; so that, 'tis probable, *Music* must have been born at the same Time with this rude Kind of *Lyric Poetry*, and proceeded at first from a certain Fulness of *Heart,* from a Kind of *Exultation*, and overflowing of *Joy*, and *Mirth* on these Occasions. *Music*, perhaps, afterwards when the *Passions* of Men grew more *refin'd*, was made use of upon Occasions of Sorrow, at the Funerals, or Death of Kings, great Captains, &c., and in Private, to sooth the Grief of particular Men for the Loss of their Friends, Country, or whatever was dear to them; Lovers, Captives, and such as were in Sorrow and Affliction found their Consolation in it: It at length became more familiar, and frequently us'd; but it is likely, it was a considerable Time before it was strong enough to go alone, if we may so say, and to be utter'd without Words. *Vocal Music* was certainly long used

———— ✻ ————

12. Painting, Jacob tells us, is not just a craft; in addition to experience and diligence, it requires imagination and judgement. Linking himself with contemporary discussions concerning genius, Jacob again provides his own insights. Discussing imagination and judgement, he points to their complex interrelationship from a cognitive point of view. Though the painter must have an idea of "Perfect Nature," his art may be "out of nature itself." Indeed, art requires antecedent judgement, and an imaginative envisaging.

before *Instrumental Music* of any Kind was found out; but it seems, that *string'd* Instruments were invented, at least perfected, before *Wind Music*. *Vocal Music* has always been the *most esteem'd* of any other Kind, and the most difficult to bring to Perfection; and, as it is the most *natural to* Mankind, so it is the most *pleasing* and *agreeable*. It is probable that *Martial Music* is almost as old as *War* itself.

The first *Painters* began only with one Colour, then another was added, a third, and so on; in like Manner, the *Dramatic Poets* introduced but *one* single Person, at the Beginning of *Tragedy*, upon the *Stage*, after that, they brought in a *second*, and, at last, they were increas'd to *three;* but this Addition to *Tragedy*, which was originally purely a *Chorus*, and *Hymn* to the *Divinity*, constituted its true *Form* and *Perfection*, whereas, the *Variety* of *Colours*, on the contrary, hasten'd the *Decay* of *Painting*. The *Painters* soon began to depart from the *Justness*, and *Severity* of their *Art*; they found they could please at a cheaper Rate with the *Pageantry* of *Colours:* The Merit of their *severer* Labours was known but to a few; but the *Splendour* of their *Colours* attracted the Eyes of the *Multitude*, and the *Painters* were themselves debauch'd by it by Degrees, and lost their former true *Tast*. [13]

All these *Arts* have travel'd to us from the *East*, as indeed all *Learning* has done. *Painting* in *Ægypt* was at first rude, nor did it attain its *Perfection* till it was brought into *Greece*. The Schools of *Athens, Sicyon, Rhodes,* and *Corinth* were reckon'd the principal *Academies* for *Painting* amongst the *Greeks*. According to *Pliny*, this *Art* was already brought to Perfection in *Greece*, about the Eighteenth *Olympiad;* it was in its highest Glory about the

---------- ☙ ----------

13. Discussing the rise of the arts, Jacob discerns three of their major functions: communicative, expressive and social. These functions are not mutually exclusive and may undergo changes. Given his commitment to what he calls "universal languages," he ascribes to painting ("hieroglyphics") immediate communicative ability. Poetry, interestingly, is coupled with music as the two arts which express the "fullness of heart"; poetry, not only music, gives expression to a state of mind, since it does not merely describe external situations. Altogether, through their ability to lend form to functions, the arts partake in *creating* culture rather than *reflecting* it.

Time of *Alexander* the Great; but degenerated, when the *Roman* Empire flourish'd under *Augustus*, at which Time, *Poetry* was in its Hight in *Italy;* for these *Arts* have not always flourish'd together. Some Time after that, *Painting* broke forth again in its former Splendour in the Reigns of some succeeding *Emperors*, till the *Hunns* overrunning *Italy*, entirely destroy'd it with all other *Arts*, and *Learning*. In the *Fourteenth, Fifteenth,* and *Sixteenth* Centuries it recover'd itself, and came to a great Hight of *Perfection*. *Titian*, famous for his *Colouring*, was the first of the *Venetian* School that began to *adorn* his Works. *Coreggio*, celebrated for his *Graces*, did the same in *Lombardy;* as likewise did *Raphael* in the *Roman* School, noted for his *Designing; Carracio*, esteem'd for his *Contours*, or *Out-Lines* at *Bologna*, and *Andrea del Sarto* at *Florence*. But the *Roman* School neglected *Colouring* thro' their eager Imitation of the *Proportion*, Justness of *Design*, and *beautiful Nature*, which they found in the *Remains* of the *Ancients*. The *Painters*, who saw not those *Remains* of *Antiquity*, had always still a good deal of the old, *Gothic*, barbarous Style in their Works. At the *Recovery* of these *Arts* in *Europe, Painting* was much beforehand with *Poetry;* for *Poetry* requires so much more *Learning*, and so many more *Arts* to bring it to *Perfection*, that it was obliged to wait for the *Revival* of all the *Parts* of *Learning* before it could make any Figure.[14]

———— ꝯ ————

14. Despite its brevity and inaccuracy, the history which Jacob sees fit to account for, succeeds, nonetheless, to convey certain basic conceptual premises. In line with the eighteenth-century view of the centrality of history, he clarifies the relevance of the history of art to the understanding of art. The English, as Lipking (1971) showed, were especially interested in the historical "*Ordering of the Arts.*" What is unique to Jacob is that he singles out four basic factors that affect the unfolding of the history of the arts. All arts have (1) "rude" beginnings; they strive, each in its own way and its own time, to attain "perfection" (technical proficiency in handling artistic components in relation to artistic objectives). (2) Perfections are not necessarily maintained, they depend on circumstances that allow the arts to flourish. Moreover, (3) in the history of art, one needs to be cognizant of cultural-aesthetic preferences and, finally, (4) the arts do not flourish simultaneously as a group. All of these are interrelated and thus defy a clear notion of progress. According to Kristeller (1980), the awareness, at the time, that the arts could not be described in terms of progress, was a prime factor in separating them from science.

The *Moderns* seem to have surpass'd the *Ancients* in *Music* to so great a Degree, that they may be said, in some Measure, to be the *Inventers* of it; so great appears the *Difference* to have been between the *old*, and *new Music:* For in the Beginning amongst the *Greeks* it was very low, nor does it appear, that the *Ancients* had in their *Concerts* any *Variety* of *Parts*, except the same *Parts* may be called various, when they are *play'd* or *sung* an *Octave* higher or lower. As for Example, when a *Man* and a *Woman*, or *Boy* sing the same Thing together; for there is *naturally* between the *Voice* of a *Man* and that of a *Woman* or *Boy*, the Difference of a *Diapason* or *Octave*. So far *Nature* directed them; afterwards they found out the *Consonances*, as the *Diatessaron*, the *Diapente* or *Diapedesis*; and all the *Greeks* and *Latins* who have writ of *Music* from the earliest Times have never treated of any Thing in their Books beyond the *Nature* of these *Consonances*, till *Boëthius*, an accurate Interpreter of the *Ancients*, collected, examin'd, explain'd, corrected, and reconcil'd their *Opinions*; but advanced nothing of himself, treading directly in their Footsteps: He gave us the *Characters* of *Sounds*, in the Place of which we have now our *Notes*. Two hundred Years after him *Beda* writ two *Treatises*, one of the *Theory* and another of the *Practice* of *Music*, nor did he, any more than *Boëthius*, exceed the Bounds of the *Ancients*. He has given us, however, the *Forms* of the *Notes*, and the *Keys*, as likewise the *Musical Scale*, consisting of *Lines* and *Spaces* as used in the *Church* after the *Gregorian* method. However, *Music*, as to itself, was much in the same imperfect State, and made no considerable Advances, 'till about the End of the *Tenth Century*, when *Guido Aretinus*, a *Benedictin* Monk, and an excellent Musician, having carefully examin'd the Books of the *Ancients* upon this Subject, added to what they had done, and instituted a *better* and *easier Method* of *Music:* To this Man *Posterity* owes the *Perfection* of *Music*; for tho' it was not he who altogether perfected it, he open'd the Way to others who have done it since. About the *Thirteenth Century* flourished *Franco*, another *Musician*; and after him in the *Fourteenth Century*, *Jo.*

Tinctoris, Franchinus Gaffurius, and others; by whose *Labour* and *Writings* both *Theorical* [sic!] and *Practical Music* was wonderfully improv'd. At length one *J. Zarlinus* publish'd a Book of *Music* in *Italian* at *Venice* in the Year 1580, in which he surpass'd all those who went before him, and brought *Music* to much greater *Perfection* than it had yet arrived at; but, however, not to that Hight in which we now have it. Thus we find how long Music remain'd in its ancient *Simplicity*. However perfect the Art of *Music* may be at this day, it is confin'd to the more *Western* Parts of *Europe:* In the Countries where it had its *Birth*, it is in a much worse State than it was amongst the *Ancients*, and by all the best Accounts we have of the more *civiliz'd* and *polite Nations* of the *East*, this *Art* is in a very low *Condition* in that Part of the World, and yet they ascribe to it as wonderful Effects as the *Ancients* did to theirs; and if we may believe the most celebrated *Authors*, who have written of the *Savages* of *America*, even their *Music*, however rude it may appear to us, is in so great *Credit* amongst themselves, that they rarely make use of any other *Medicine*, and think their *Labours* sufficiently *reliev'd* by it.[15]

The *Moderns* may glory to have improv'd upon the ancient *Painters* by their Invention of *Copper Plates*; in their Knowledge of *Colouring*, of the *Ciaro Oscuro*, and of *Perspective*. What the

———— ♫ ————

15. Jacob uses music to exemplify what he means by attaining perfection. As noted above, perfection is closely linked to technical proficiencies in handling artistic components in relation to artistic objectives. Since music, unlike the other arts, also partakes in the construction of its basic parameters, it best conveys the broad possibilities of artistic control. Jacob seems to recognize that the "making of" and the "theorizing about" are more markedly intertwined in the case of music. Recognizing that the music he discusses is not universally enjoyed, he hastens to state that the powers he previously attributed to music are not reserved to Western music alone. "Perfection," Jacob believes, is, thus, relative to culture, as is, for that matter, the assessment of the powers of music. These last realizations were no doubt influenced by the growing anthropological awareness of the time.

Ancients seem most to have excell'd us in, is *Purity, Easiness,* and a beautiful and natural *Simplicity,* both in *Poetry* and *Painting.* The farther we look into past *Ages,* the more *true, simple* and *natural* we find their *Productions* of all Kinds: Every *Age* has by Degrees degenerated from the ancient *Simplicity;* the *Romans* had less of it than the *Grecians,* and we have little, or none of it remaining with us.

Poetry and *Painting* propose the most *beautiful* Works of *Nature* for the *Objects* of their *Imitation: Art* alone conceals her *Beauties;* a *Genius uncultivated,* and without *Art,* shews her, as it were, thro' a *Veil,* but confusedly, and to Disadvantage, in such a Manner as we regret the imperfect View we have of her; but where *Art* and *Genius* are happily *united,* they send her forth beauteous, amiable, and attended with the real *Graces. Art,* however, is to be employ'd with Caution, and consider'd as the *Handmaid,* or *Servant* of *Nature,* whose Office it is to heighten, and improve the *Beauties* of her *Mistress,* and, not by dressing her up *fantastically,* to hide her *Charms* in such a *Complexity,* as the wrong Judgments of some have mistaken for *Ornament.* Better is *Nature, loose* and *unattir'd* in all her *Wildness,* and *Luxuriancy,* amidst a Croud of *Errors,* than *bury'd* in the most exact *Labours;* for if she *appears* at all, it is to *charm* us.

The Misfortune is, that *Fancy* and *Judgment* are very differently employ'd; while the *first* is busy'd in *throwing* Things *together,* the *other* is perpetually *dividing* them again. *Fancy* importunately *intrudes* upon you her *Ware* of all Sorts; *flatters,* and *sooths* you, and *sollicites* your Reception of them; *insinuates* her *self,* and *Goods* into your *Favour,* and enhances the Worth of whatever she exposes to your View; 'till *Judgment,* that stern and rigid *Umpire* between you, examines them against the Light of *Reason;* rejects those; reforms these; throws others away as false, and unsound; receiving what he *likes* best at the lowest *Price* he can; and yet notwithstanding his great *Caution,* is sometimes egregiously *mistaken,* and *refuses* the greatest *Beauties,* when he takes most Pains not to be *impos'd* upon. So hard a Thing it is, to make a wholsome *League* between these two *Opposites,* which, however, are so *necessary* to each other.[16]

Painters as well as *Poets* are not only to choose what is *most beautiful* in *Nature* to imitate; but they are likewise to choose out of those *Beauties,* such as are most proper for, and agree best with their respective *Arts;* for, there are some Subjects fitter for *Painting,* and Others for *Poetry,* which may admit of *Imitation* in either *Art. Aristotle,* and *Horace* after him, advise the *Poets* to choose their Subjects out of known *Fables:* 'Tis plain, the *Painters* have much more need of following that *Rule.* [17]

 The Choice of a Subject being thus happily made, the *Artist* must be equally careful to *range* all its *Parts* in their proper *Order,* disposing each where they will be most *surprizing* and contribute most to the *Beauty* of the *whole:* He should respect the future Perfection of his work in the very *Embryo* of his Design, that every *Part* may arise from the same Foundation, and in that *just Order,* which *Nature* herself observes in her *Productions;* thus we should conceive all at once, and have a *Satisfaction* like that which arises from the happy *Combination* of the several *Parts* of a *Consort* of *Music.*

16. In the last three paragraphs Jacob addresses the question of artistic quality. Novelty, innovation, complexity and ornateness he tells us, do not guarantee artistic quality. On the contrary, they may be counterproductive. Quality is not achieved through unharnessed *Fancy,* but through fancy curbed by *Judgement,* through genius checked by reason. This last phrase will be explicated by Kant later in the century. Jacob also makes an important distinction, between the beautiful and the condition of the beautiful, the latter depending on *cultivated* artistic sensitivity, i.e., on the artist who knows how to separate the essential from the non-essential.

17. Though Jacob still drags along prevalent legacies, he is not restricted by them. We have already witnessed (fn. 4) his readiness to create new alliances among the arts, which do not conform to the premises of *ut pictura poesis.* Here, he arrives at a more fundamental principle, based on the many insightful observations he made with regard to the ways in which artistic media — their possibilities and limitations—dictate the choice of subject matter. Though Lessing will elaborate and develop this idea more convincingly, it is worth noting that Jacob may have been the first to turn upside down the Neoplatonic dictum according to which all the arts are supposed to deal with the same subject matter albeit in their own ways.

Painters, as well as *Poets*, ought to choose *warm* and *affecting Subjects*. It is an Instant of Time only which an *historical Piece* represents, and that *Representation* must be *active*, and *passionate*, or it will appear but *dead* and *cold*; so likewise must the Subject of a *Tragedy* be full of *Spirit*, and move the *Affections* briskly, or else, as it proposes an *immediate Action*, it will be as *languid*, and *dull* as the other. Thus *dramatic Poetry* is that Part of *Poetry* which nearest resembles *Painting*, not only because it exhibits the very *Action* itself; but because it aims more at the *Passions* than *Epic*, or any other kind of *Poetry*; for *Epic Poetry* works slowly, and arrives at its *End* thro' a long *Series* of *Things* and *Examples*, and this is one of *Aristotle's* Reasons why he prefers *Tragedy* to *Epic Poetry*, as performing its Work in *less Time*, and consequently, *more intensely*.

In *great Works* we don't so much consider what is *accurately finish'd* in each single *Part*, regarding rather the *Beauty* of the *whole*; but *smaller Works* in *Poetry*, and *Pictures* ought to be exquisitely *finish'd*: They have not *Length*, or *copiousness* enough to hide their *Faults*, or excuse their *Imperfections* by the Number of *Beauties* which a *greater Work* might be capable of, where little *Omissions* are sometimes even of use to set off great *Beauties*: Besides, these little *Subjects* require all *foreign* Ornaments that may be *conveniently* introduced to support them.

The *Subject* ought to be *clear* and *unconfused*; neither too *big* nor too *little*, that the Mind may *comprehend* it all with Pleasure, and, at the same Time, not too *easily*, and all at once. A *Play*, or *Picture* may have *too many Persons* in it; and an *epic Poem* may be embarrassed with too great a *Variety* of *Incidents*.

The different *Figures* which compose a *Picture*, as well as the different *Parts* which compose each *Figure*, ought to conspire to form one, entire *whole*: the same Thing, in Effect, is to be observ'd in *Poetry*, where every Thing is vicious, that does not necessarily, or probably conspire to the *Unity* of the *Composition*.[18]

There are some *Incidents* which are not proper to be expos'd or introduced either on the *Stage* or in the *Tablet*. A *Picture* may be too *horrid*, as well as a *Tragedy*; and such *Incidents* as *offend* the Sense, or *Shock* in any Manner, should be perform'd behind the *Scene*, or cast at the Back of the *Picture*, where the *Subject* will admit of it: Where it will not, that *Subject* is better neglected, as improper for *Imitation*.

Our *Religion* affords *properer* Subjects for *Painting* than for *Poetry*; nor can any great *Success* be expected from the *Subject* of an *Epic Poem*, which admits not of the *Ornaments* of the *Machinery* drawn from the *Heathen Mythology*; but the Mingling of the *Profane*, and *Christian Systems* together, which some of our most famous modern *Poets*, and *Painters* have not scrupled to do, is both *monstrous*, and *indecent*; and notwithstanding some have stood up with *warmth*, (perhaps with more *Zeal* than *Reason*) for the Introduction of *Religious Subjects* into the *greater Poetry*, they will not be found either so fit for the *Drama*, or *Epic Poetry*, as for the *Lyric*. They who would join *Poetry* to their *Devotion*, can do it no way more sublimely, and properly than by falling into the ancient Way of *Hymns:* It is to this Kind of *Poetry* that we owe most Part of those *great* and *sublime* Passages with which the *Scripture* so abounds.

18. Early in the treatise, Jacob suggests that all works of art require a kind of internal congeniality, which he calls Harmony. Here he states more explicitly what he may have had in mind: the particles of a work of art should contribute to and be guided by the unified whole. It is the whole which carries the artistic import and not the parts. The specific treatments of the parts depend on medium, genre and size of the work of art, each constituting a different kind of whole. Although these ideas derive in part from traditional approaches to rhetoric, especially that of Horace's *lucido ordo*, they harbor an important kernel of an eventual full-fledged theory of artistic organicism, which was to flourish only towards the end of the century. Though lacking in tightness of argument, Jacob's ideas may be considered as a contribution to the attempts to deal with artistic 'coherence.'

The same Rules which *Aristotle* lays down as necessary for the *Poets* to observe in the Formation of the *Manners* or *Characters* are equally instructive to the *Painters*. 'Tis first requir'd that they be well *denoted*; that the *Character* intended, should stand manifestly *express'd* and *distinguish'd*; which is of the most Importance, and the Foundation on which the other *Rules* are grounded. The next *Quality* desir'd in the *Manners*, is, that they be *agreeable* to the Age, Sex, Country &c. of the *Person* represented. Another *Condition* mention'd, is that they may be like those of the *Person*, whom they are intended to represent, whether it be an *Ajax*, or an *Ulysses*, an *Alexander*, or a *Cæsar*, or any other famous Personage, eminent in Story. The last *Precept* which this *Philosopher* lays down for the *Manners*, is that they be *equally maintain'd*, thro' the whole *Subject*, whether taken from *History*, or purely *invented*. The *Poets* in the forming of their *Characters*, as well as the *Painters* are not to copy from Particulars; but from the *Idea* of *Nature* in general: They must *draw* from the *original*. Not what *Nature* does in her more *common* Production; but what she does *sometimes, may*, or *ought* to do, should be the *Example* of the *Artist*. *Leonardo da Vinci* in his Treatise of *Painting*, gives Rules altogether conformable to this, proposing in General the most remarkable *characteristicks* of Youth, Age, &c. to the Consideration of the *Painters:* He is so very exact in Relation to the *Manners*, as to require, that the *Attitude* of a *Figure* be so conducted in all its Parts, that the *Intention* of the *Mind* may be seen in *every Member*. The same judicious *Painter* observes, that the *Motions* of the *Figures* should always shew the Degree of Strength, which they may be reasonably suppos'd to employ in their respective *Actions*. Thus let the *Poet* proportion the *Emotion* and *Passion* of his *Person* to the *Subject*, and present *Circumstance*, which is too often neglected: *Similes* and *moral Reflections* are very common upon the *Stage* in the hurry of a *Surprize*, or *Fight*; while *Rage*, and *Fury* are acted in *Cabinets*, and solitary *Woods*. The *Poet* ought to consider in every *Sentence* whether his *Person* speaks from the Bottom of *Nature*, or not, and to study the various *Motions*, and *Alterations* of the *Mind* as attentively as the good *Painter* does those of the *Body*, for as the *Painter* characterizes his *Figures* by *Attitudes*, and *Features*; so does the *Poet* characterize his *Persons* by *Sentiments*, and *Actions*.[19]

As all Things in a *Tragedy*, or *Heroic Poem* should contribute to illustrate the *Hero*, so in a *Picture* nothing ought to be made so shining and conspicuous, as to divert the Eye from the *principal Person*, which, in either *Art* must be placed in the most *eminent* Light, and be the most *exactly* finish'd. *Aristotle* advises the *Poets* to imitate *Painters* who preserve the *Similitude* in *Adorning* it. *Homer* has drawn *Achilles*, inexorable, fierce and cruel; but he has mingled with that, such a Magnanimity, and generous Concern for his *Friend*, that we are forc'd to *admire* him.

'Tis by the *Sentiments* that the *Manners* or *Characters* are denoted. Let the *Artist* improve his *Mind* by studying what the best *Authors* both of the Ancients, and Moderns have written, and furnish his *Imagination* with the *Examples* of such famous *Men* as are recorded in *History*, and from thence draw forth the *Ideas* of his *Heroes*, and *Thoughts* proper for great *Personages:* Let him thus inrich himself with sublime *Sentiments*, and sublime *Words*, and *Expressions* will follow of Course.

The *Diction* in *Poetry* answers to the *Colouring* in *Painting*, and its great *Lights*, and *Shadows* are as the *Ornaments* of *Language*; and as it is observ'd, that such of the *Painters* as are particularly famous for their *Colouring*, are seldom good *Designers*, so it may be remark'd amongst the *Poets* and other *Writers*, that they, who

---

19. The last paragraphs suggest an interesting overlap between two issues— 'decorum' and the dictates of the medium— which share the notion of fitness. Decorum stood for both stylistic and social dictates and implied convention as a necessary ingredient of the communicative act. Indeed, works of art depend on the expectations of those to whom they are addressed. Though related to stylistic dictates, decorum, or, for that matter, propriety, should not be confused with the "Lessing-argument," concerning the *limits* of the arts. Jacob, thus, calls our attention to the difference between, as well as to the interdependence of, communicative and cognitive issues.

aim at being carefully *finish'd* in their *Style*, and are very *curious* and *exact* in their *Words*, have rarely any thing *Great*, and *solid* in their *Compositions*.

Poets, and *Painters* never gratify more the Observers of their *Works*, than when they express themselves not so fully, but that these may find matter enough to exercise their own *Imaginations* upon: We are agreeably flatter'd by such *Discoveries*; and it is for this Reason, that the *Sketches*, or unfinish'd *Designs* of some great *Masters*, which are but lightly *touch'd*, seem sometimes to have more *Spirit*, and often *please* more than such as are perfected.

A *Break*, or *Pause* in *Poetry* is sometimes more *significant* than any Thing, that might have been said; so in *Music* a *Rest* in its proper *Place* has often a wonderful *Effect*, and from the *Beauty* of its *Surprize*, makes the *Suspension* of *Harmony* itself agreeable. The silence of *Ajax's* Shade to *Ulysses* in *Homer*, and that of *Dido* to *Æneas*, which *Virgil* has copy'd from the Former, are esteem'd Master Strokes of this Nature in *Poetry*.

Ease and Freedom both in *Writing* and *Painting*, like *good Nature*, *excuse* a great many *Faults*, which in such Cases are rather imputed to *Neglect,* or to the *Impetuosity* of *Genius*, than to the *Insufficiency* of the *Artist*: this *Ease* in Execution, which some call *Happiness*, may proceed sometimes from a natural *Disposition*; but more commonly from *Art* well conceal'd, like our Happiness in Life, is oftner the *Effect* of *Management* and *Discretion*, than of *meer* good *Fortune*.

The same *Attitudes* are not to be repeated in a Piece of *Painting*, or the same *Expressions* made frequent Use of in *Poetry*. *Leon. da Vinci* says, that a *Painter* by disregarding the *Diversity* of Proportions, seems to cast all his *Figures* in the same *Mould*, which he will have to be a Fault of the first Magnitude: In either *Art* there must be *Variety* to please.

Whenever a *Picture* is very much *inrich'd*, we may reasonably suspect that the main *Design*, and *Execution* are *poor*, and that the *Painter* endeavors, by this Means, to hide his *Imperfections*. *Theatrical* Ornaments, and pompous *Diction* are often employ'd to do the same good Office to bad *Poets*.[20]

There are at this Day very few or scarce any remains of the *Paintings* of the *Ancients*; but many of their finest *Statues* as perfect, and beautiful, as when they came out of the *Artists* Hands; from whence we may observe, that *Sculpture* has the same Advantage over *Painting*, that the dead, learned *Languages* have over the fluctuating, unfixt *Tongues* now in use; for as the Traces of the *Pencil*, and *Colours* in *Painting* fade quite away by time, so do the *Words* of these *Languages* in a few Ages become so *obsolete*, that it is with the greatest difficulty that their Meaning is then to be traced, if at all discover'd. Perhaps there is no *European* language so exposed to *Changes*, and *Innovations* as our own: It is to be hop'd, that we only adopt the *Flowers*, and *Graces* of other *Languages*; and thus this Liberty of *borrowing* from every *Tongue* we *hear*, will become of the greatest *Advantage* to our own.

20. In these last paragraphs Jacob lists a number of basic principles that must be obeyed if art is to succeed in practice: (1) Works of art should have clear focal points, for it is the focus that determines the choice and organization of the rest. (2) Art should imitate art, for art itself often sets the best examples for actual practice. (3) Art works should leave something for the imagination to render them complete. (4) Things unstated may at times create the desired effect through their very omission. (5) Artistic problems, once overcome, should be concealed in the finished work. The complete work should create an appearance of ease (*facilità*) in execution. (6) Art must assure variety to avoid boredom.

As we see, Jacob's principles are closely related to each other. The unity and import of the work of art rest on the wedding of the two components he introduced early in his essay — imagination and judgement. As we have learned in the course of the essay, imagination must submit to judgement and judgement must submit to cultivation. To be sure, some of Jacob's principles had already been discussed, since the Renaissance. Their new standing derives from their being included in a general theory that differentiates between premises and arguments, on the one hand, and their implications, on the other. Implications, when tested, constitute that which brings about the actual works of art. The latter, in turn, lend support to the premises on which those implications rest. Let us suggest a partial explanation as to why this is not a vicious circle: While exemplifying old conceptions, works of art often suggest new premises, causing the broadening of old theories, or giving rise to new ones.

Besides the Observance, or Neglect of the foregoing *Rules*, there are several *Accidents* which conspire to support, or ruin these *Arts*, which, like *tender* Plants, are too delicate to flourish in all *Seasons*, and in every *Place:* They require *generous* Encouragers, and Protectors; uninterrupted Quiet, and Leisure; Retirement, and Solitude; they are the Daughters of *Peace*, and are soon alarm'd and frighten'd away by the rude Voice of *Discord*, and contending *Factions*; but however they may be *lull'd* to sleep by *Luxury*, or *Sloth*; or *starv'd* for Want of due *Warmth*, and *Encouragement*, they are always to be waken'd again, and recover'd by the *Encouragement* of the *Great*.

A Man that would *succeed* in any of these *Arts*, must have his Mind pretty much at ease, and be consequently in tolerable Circumstances, and Master of his own Time, that he may find Leisure to *finish* his Works as they ought to be. *Poetry*, especially, is not to be look'd on as a Trade, or Profession to get ones Bread by; but is to be follow'd only on favourable Occasions for Pleasure, and Entertainment. The *Poet* should have recourse to his *Muse*, as to a *Mistress*, when *Inclination* invites him; he may then hope for more *beautiful* Productions, than when he is inslav'd to his *Art* by a strict *Necessity*; but we find on the Contrary, that this, which should be but a generous *Amusement*, becomes too often the *Refuge* of any needy *Scribler*, who has the least pretence to dabble in *Poetry*, and will venture to hurry out his *unfinish'd* Labours upon the good natur'd *Town*, letting the World know, how *soon*, and *easily* they were perform'd, as if there was a *real* merit in *Precipitation*. We find, on the other Hand, some vaunts of the *contrary* Practice amongst the *Ancients*. *Catullus* tells us in Commendation of his friend *Hel. Cinna*, that a *Piece* of his was *nine* Years in finishing. *Horace* in his Art of *Poetry*, blames the *Writers* of his Time for their Want of *Patience* to finish their *Works*, and there can be no greater Proof of the Justness of his Reprehension, than that not any of their *labours* have *liv'd* long enough, for us to see their *errors*.

Thus *Poetry* has suffer'd in the Opinion of many People from the *unworthy* Professors of it; but to contemn *Poetry*, is to condemn, in effect, the *Tastes* of the most learned, polite, and greatest Men

in all Ages; for such, from all *Antiquity*, have lov'd and encourag'd this, and the other fine *Arts*, and have oftentimes themselves
profess'd it; nor was it out of a foolish admiration of jingling
Numbers, and little *Points*; but thro' a laudable Love, and Respect, for
Reason, Morality, great, and beautiful Sentiments that the *Ancients* so
much encourag'd *Poetry*, and its Professors, who were generally
Persons of merit, and learning, and liv'd up to the *Maxims*, they
taught. The *Poets* who have writ *judiciously*, have led their Lives
with *Judgment* too; it was as conspicuous in their Manners, and
way of living, as in their *Works*; and, if *Horace* may be rely'd on, it
is necessary that a good *Poet* be a *Philosopher*. *Poetry* then should
not be charged with the *Faults* of some, who have *disgraced* it:
Whoever will consider it in its proper *Light*, will not find it so contemptible a Thing, as they would have it pass for, who know nothing of its *Worth*, and *Beauties*, the Ignorance of which is very common, notwithstanding that almost every Body thinks he has a Right
to judge of, and meddle with *Poetry*; and it is remarkably surprizing, that some of the most *learned* Men and most *knowing* Men
and most *knowing* in other Parts of *Literature*, should have been
so *blind*, and *deceived* in the Judgments they have made of
Poetry. Considering these Things, it is not much to be wonder'd at,
that there should be so many *lame* Productions in this *Art*, in which it
is so difficult to succeed well with all the Advantages of *Nature*, and
Study, as the *few* excellent Performances in it may witness.[21]

——————— ↻ ———————

21. Early in the essay, Jacob mentions that art requires suitable conditions in order to
flourish, and that history has amply shown that not all times and places were equally conducive to art. Here, after having listed his artistic principles, he takes up that
theme again but from the point of view of the creative artist. Discussing artistic conditions from this point of view enables Jacob to explicate more closely the conception
of art itself. Art, he tells us, is not to be identified with a trade, and cannot therefore,
be judged by the same criteria; for example, art cannot guarantee the number of productions and their timely delivery. Nor can the criticism of art be left in the hands of
those who are guided by criteria of utility which are alien to art. In addition to certain
capacities, art requires a suitable state of mind, which only a free and supportive envi-
ronment can guarantee. Such conditions should be secured, though only few people
participate in the creation and understanding of art. Jacob allows himself to advocate
special conditions designed for a lucky few, because he believes that these few contribute significantly to the making of culture for the many; civilizations are gauged by
their culture!

If *Poets*, and *Painters* are to propose the *Idea* of *perfect* Nature for their *Imitation*, it is absolutely necessary that they attain to that *Idea*; and how is that *Idea* to be acquir'd, but by studying the *Perfections* both of the *Body*, and the *Mind?* And where are these *Perfections* found in such Excellence, and Abundance as in the Works of the *Ancients?* In the Statues, Bas-relieves, and precious *Relicts* of the great Masters of old, and in the *Writings* of those learned Philosophers, Poets, and Historians, who have drawn the *Manners* and *Sentiments* of Mankind with the same Majesty, and Justness, as these great *Painters* did their *exterior* Forms, and the *visible* Beauties of *Nature?* But why, say some People, must we have Recourse to *Antiquity?* Have we not our *Organs* as perfect as the *Ancients* had? And is it unreasonable to suppose, that we may have *Ideas* as great, as beautiful, as just, and surprizing as they had? It may be true, that we have the same *Faculties*, and *Power* inherent in our Natures; and that they have thought wrong, who have imagin'd, that *Nature* herself, thro' her long operations, is become *tir'd*, and *decay'd*, and that now, in her *Weakness*, she throws out *imperfect* Creatures, and *weak* Minds. This yet is certain, that Mankind has every age invented new things, lost some *Arts*, and found out others, and that there has been a constant *Revolution*, and *succession* of *Arts*, as of every thing else; but that the *Ancients* were more excellent than we in most parts of these *Arts* of *Ornament*, is as manifest, as that *latter* Ages have invented many *useful Things* entirely unknown to them. That Majesty, that Truth, or Justness, that beautiful Simplicity, and natural Grace, so peculiar to the *Ancients*, are rarely to be met with in any Degree amongst the *Moderns*, and never but amongst such of them, as have imitated *Antiquity*; for it has been the *Fate* of these *latter* Ages, to *refine* so much upon *Nature*, that they have quite *lost Sight* of her, and that not only in relation to these *Arts* in Question; but in almost *every* Thing else. The *Ancients* endeavored to *improve Nature*; we seem, on the Contrary, to strive to *hide her* as much as possible; they consulted *Nature* in her self, and considering, in general, what she *could*, and *ought* to do, they copy'd her *Perfections*; nor was this so beautiful *Simplicity* of the *Ancients* confin'd to these *Arts*; but diffus'd it self thro' their *Manners*; nor should we, perhaps, have had any *Idea* of it at all; but from what remains we have found of it in their Works. Where these *Arts* chiefly flourish'd, the *Genius* of the People, their Government, and, perhaps, their Climate, and Situation, together with the turn of their Pleasures, and taste of their great Men, all seem'd to favour the *Advancement* of these *Arts*, to which may be added, their Religion, Superstition, and natural Love of the *Marvelous*. The *Scene* which is now carrying on upon the *Theatre* of what we call the *Polite World*, is of quite a different Nature from what it was in those Days; and increase of *Luxury*, and new *Inventions* have made, at present, so many Things necessary, which then were either held superfluous, or quite unknown, that the Condition of our Affairs seem to put Men rather upon providing for the *Conveniencies* of Life, than to afford them *Leisure*, to *finish* any considerable Work in these *Arts*, as it ought to be; or opportunity of thinking *justly*, and *sublimely* of Things which are chiefly intended for *Ornament*; and in an *Age* where Men are more distinguish'd by their *Acquisitions*, than by any real *Merit* of their own, there is a certain Pride, and Ambition in *accumulating*, which knows no Bounds, and necessarily introduces *mercenary* Views, and such *narrow* Ways of thinking, as *stifle* in the Mind all *Greatness* of Thought, and *Love* of these *Studies*.

Indolence, and *Sloth*, the Effects of *Luxury*, and *Ease*, are equally prejudicial to these *Arts*, and have brought on a Neglect of *Study*, and all *Rules*, by which means so many *imperfect*, and *unfinish'd* Performances in every one of these *Arts* are Daily precipitated into the *World*; and, what is worse, they who send these *lame* Productions so untimely abroad, not content to have transgress'd against all Sorts of *Rules* themselves, endeavour, as much as they can, to hinder others from following them, by descrying them as vain, and useless, in order to *support* their own *Errors:* They have endeavour'd to laugh away all *Rules*, and banish the *Truth* of *Arts* from amongst us; and Men are easily drawn from the *Practice* of what gives them any Prospect of *Trouble* in the *Pursuit:* We find it as difficult to submit our *Fancies*, as our

Passions to any *Regimen*; and the Misfortune is, that they, who have the *brightest* Imaginations, are generally the most *impatient* of *Rules*, and thus our greatest *Genius's* are, in a Manner, *overthrown* by their own *Strength*. There is a kind of native *Liberty* in *Fancy*, which abhors the Chain of *Rules*, and Management of *Art*; yet it is not in human Nature to *perfect* any Thing without some *Labour*, and *Patience*; but these *Precepts* they despise, are so founded upon *Nature*, that it is only by the Knowledge, and Observation of them, that they must at last, if ever, compass, what they are supposed, to intend, *viz.* to Work with *Ease*, and *Surety*. Many, who might be *excellent*, dare not, because they know not *precisely* what they ought to do; for a just *Confidence* is to be got only from a thorough *Knowledge* of the *Beauties* of the *Art*, and of the *Faults* that may be committed against it. This would, perhaps, be a Means, to cure that *Diffidence* which is most commonly found with those of the best *Parts*: This would hinder them, from *discreetly blotting* out sometimes the most *sublime* Thing they have writ, and the *boldest* Strokes of the *Pencil.* [22]

The Study of these *Arts* should be begun *early*, nor are the *Arts* themselves to be prosecuted in that Stage of Life in which the Mind may be reasonably suppos'd to have lost much of its

22. Deploring the state of the *"Moderns,"* compared to the *"Ancients,"* Jacob raises another set of variables which influence the both kind of art production and the artistic preference. The values and norms of a society, Jacob tells us, have a direct effect on artistic behavior. While Art has its own dictates, regardless of time, artistic production reflects particular moments in its history. Artists do not stand apart from society; rather, they are a part of society, affected by its values and norms. To put it somewhat differently, values and norms form the particular expectations a society might have of its artists. Thus, society may be judged by the art it has produced, as the art of the *Ancients* exemplifies.

What is interesting about this last deliberation is that Jacob clearly separates the aesthetic-philosophical from the historic-sociological. While maintaining the unity of culture, it is the separation of the aesthetic from the sociological which opens up possibilities for deliberate artistic change: Despite unfavorable societal attitudes, artistic behavior may improve through a "thorough knowledge of the beauty of art" and the study of models which exemplify "true art." This last statement justifies Jacob's entire endeavor, which amounts, after all, to an attempt to fathom the "Truth of Arts."

Strength and *Vigour.* That natural *Force* of *Imagination*, that *Fire*, or rather *Enthusiasm*, so necessary to the perfect *Execution* of these *Arts*, is not easily curb'd, and kept in Order by the Restraint of wholsome *Rules* in the Time of our *Youth*, or maintain'd to any Degree of Perfection, when old *Age* creeps upon us. *Longinus* discovers *Homer's* Decline in his *Odysses*, and we have more than one Example, amongst our *Poets*, of Authors, who have *surviv'd* their own *Genius.*

Temperance is as necessary as any thing else to him who would perform in either of these *Arts* to a Degree of Perfection. *Horace*, who introduces *Bacchus* teaching *Verse*, and favourable to *Poetry*, and the *Muses*, knew well, that cool *Reflection*, and *Patience* are requir'd, to *finish* any *considerable Design*; and however debauch'd *Petronius* may appear himself to have been, he is too good a *Critick*, not to have prescrib'd *Regularity* to the Person, who means to *write* any Thing to purpose; this *Virtue* was observed by the ancient *Sculptors*, and *Painters*, to mention only the famous *Protogenes*, who, when he sat about any *Work*, he was resolv'd to succeed in, lived, 'tis said, only upon *Lupines*, lest he should have *blunted* his *Faculties* by too high a *Diet.* *Wine*, indeed, may work upon the Mind, like a kind of *Enthusiastic* Rage, in *Starts*, and broken *Raptures*; but it must be by meer *Accident*, if it produces any Thing that way, that wants not a great deal of *Correction*. It is unsafe trusting to *Fancy* at any Time; but much more so, when *heighten'd* and *stretched* beyond its natural *Pitch* by the Fumes of intoxicating Liquor. [23]

These *Arts* anciently met with more *Encouragement* from *Great Men* than they do at present: They took a *Pride* in those Days in the *Knowledge* of them, and *respected*, and *honour'd* those who *profess'd* them; and formerly only such as were of *noble*

---

23. While repeating some of the ideas which he explicated earlier, Jacob concludes with a brief discussion of some aspects of socialization. No one is born a full-fledged artist, argues Jacob. The successful activation of one's natural artistic propensities depends on the right sort of cultivation at a proper time in his life.

Extraction, had Permission to exercise the *Art* of *Painting*. The *Professors* of these *Arts* should be *protected*, and *countenanced*, in order to inspire them with such *noble*, and *generous* Thoughts, as they ought to have. Men of *base*, and *servile* Sentiments can never produce any thing *Great*, and worthy of *Posterity* in any of these *Arts*; and the Company of People of *Low*, and *narrow* Minds ought to be avoided by them, as *contagious*: They should *imitate* Nothing but what is *Perfect*, and set the best *Patterns* before their Eyes. The *Ancients* seem'd in some Measure to prescribe this *Rule* to *Nature* her self, while they contrived to place the most *beautiful Statues*, and *Pictures* before their teeming *Matrons*, as tho' they intended thereby to *restore* those *Excellencies* to *Nature*, which they had originally *borrow'd* of her. This may serve to put *Artists* in mind, that they may receive no small Assistance from good *Examples*, and the assiduous *Contemplation* of the *Works* of the *Ancients*, while they would *form* their Minds to the *Production* of *great*, and *beautiful* Things. It should be their constant Care, to treasure up the *Perfections* of *Nature* in their *Memories*, that they may bring forth nothing themselves but what is truly *perfect*. But how few are capable of perceiving the Perfections of *Nature?* Such alone are qualified either for *judging* of, or *exercising* the *Sister Arts*; but this *Idea* of *perfect Nature* is to be *improv'd*, if not *entirely gain'd* by long *Study*, and *Familiarity* with the *fine* Works of the *Ancients*, and by *dwelling* on their several *Beauties*. [24]

Thus we have taken a *cursory* Survey of these *Arts*; said something, *in general*, of their *Relation*, and *Difference*; of their *Value, Rise,* and *Progress*; of the Necessity, Conformity, and Practice of the *principal Rules* by which they were brought to *Perfection*; whence it is they have *decay'd*; and how they may be *restor'd*.

F I N I S.

24. The last paragraph is, in fact, the "table of contents" of the entire essay. It has guided the division of its presentation.

James Harris
(1709 –1780)

Harris was educated at the grammar school of the precinct of the cathedral at Salisbury, where he was born. He later attended Wadham College at Oxford and on leaving the University he went on to study law. After the death of his father in 1733, he came into a fortune, including his father's house in Salisbury Close, and became a country magistrate. From 1761 until his death, he represented Christchurch in Parliament. From 1774 he was also Controller to the Queen.

Despite such official activities, and like so many of his fellow-countrymen, Harris was a man of letters with a decided bent towards the classics, especially Aristotle. He published a number of philosophical inquiries of which Hermes (1751) — a philosophical inquiry concerning universal grammar — is best known. In 1744 he published three treatises which attest to his combined love for philosophy and for the arts, especially music. *On Music, Painting and Poetry* is one of them.

In line with an established tradition, Harris' treatise tries to assess the relative merits of the arts by comparing them. Accepting the Aristotelian conception of art as imitation, he set out to gauge the success of the several arts in these terms. His methodology rests on the Lockian proposition according to which the senses are the source of all knowledge. At one and the same time, Harris is invariably concerned with that which supplies the *purpose* for change, i.e. with that which brings about the art product, the "final cause."

In a dialogue addressed to Shaftesbury, Harris examines some basic issues concerning art in general. His examination involves four questions — what is art, what is its subject, for the sake of what, and for what end — which he attempted to answer. However, prior to answering these questions, he justified the consideration of art in terms of the Aristotelian causes by showing that not every cause leads to art and that only intentional ones do. The requisite of intention, in turn, implies reason, volition and consciousness. He further qualifies intention in art by founding it in habit, in something learned and acquired, for "to every art there is a System of various approved Percepts." Thus, unlike Nature, Art is secondary and acquired, never "original," but a part of human nature, a part of "man becoming a cause intentional and habitual." Whereas facilities, powers, capacities, etc., are in themselves abstract — "obscure and hidden things" — action, energies and operations are open to the senses and can be observed.

As one examines Harris' treatise concerning the relative merits of the various arts, one should bear in mind the answers Harris gives to the four questions he posits in the dialogue. His answers can be summarized as follows: 1) Art is "a habitual power in Man, of becoming the cause of some effect according to a system of various and well-approved precepts." 2) The subject of art is contingent on that "which is within the reach of the human powers to influence." 3) Art operates for the sake of some absent good "relative to human life, and attainable by Man, but superior to his natural and uninstructed factulties." 4) The end of art is "either in some energy (a product the parts of which exist successively and "whose nature hath its being or essence in a transition") or in some work (a product whose parts exist all at once and "whose nature does not depend on a transition for its essence").

Through Shaftesbury is never mentioned in the *Dialogue Concerning Art*, Harris obviously takes issue with the former whose premises were decidely Platonic. This may well constitute the reason why Harris addressed his dialogue to Shaftesbury to begin with (see Vol. I). The dialogue at any rate, helps us understand why Harris was willing to suggest that the arts are bound to manipulate the elements perceived by sight and hearing, i.e., form and color, sound and movement respectively. By circumscribing the domain of the arts in this manner, Harris could also specify the subject matter which each of the arts is best qualified to handle. Thus Harris, like Jacob, contributes clarifications of the sort on which Lessing's thesis and other theories eventually rested.

Ironically, his systematic approach, which reflects his philosophical bent, reveals the shortcomings of his premises. Time and again, albeit unwittingly, Harris found himself breaking the frames he set for himself, challenging the very theories with which he began. It is not the degree of Harris' success, however, which concerns us here, nor does his centrality rest on his unchallenged acceptance by those who read him. The importance of his treatise lies rather in: 1) the kind of attempt it represents, 2) the systematic approach it employs, 3) some of its claims (which constitute starting points for subsequent discussions) and, not least, 4) the shortcomings it reveals. All these, separately and combined, contributed to that momentous discourse of the eighteenth century which tried to clarify aesthetic matters concerning the arts.

Contents

CHAPTER the FIRST.

INTRODUCTION——*Design and Distribution of the Whole Preparation for the following Chapters.*

CHAPTER the SECOND.

On *the Subjects which Painting imitates*——*On the Subjects which Music imitates*——*Comparison of Music with Painting.*

CHAPTER the THIRD

On *the Subjects which Poetry imitates, but imitates only thro'* natural *Media, or mere Sounds*——*Comparison of Poetry in this Capacity, first with Painting, then with Music.*

CHAPTER the FOURTH.

On *the Subjects which Poetry imitates, not by mere Sounds or natural Media, but by* Words significant; *the Subjects being such to which the Genius of each of the other two Arts is most* perfectly *adapted.*——*Its Comparison in these Subjects, first with Painting, then with Music.*

CHAPTER the FIFTH.

On *the Subjects which Poetry imitates by* Words *significant, being at the same time Subjects not adapter to the Genius of either of the other Arts*——*The Nature of these Subjects.*——*The* Abilities *of* Poetry *to imitate them.*——*Comparison of Poetry in respect of these Subjects, first with Painting, then with Music.*

CHAPTER the SIXTH.

On *Music considered not as an Imitation, but as deriving its Efficacy from* another *Source.*——*On its joint Operation by this means with Poetry.*——*An Objection to Music solved.*——*The Advantage arising to it, as well as to Poetry, from their being united.*——*Conclusion.*

A DISCOURSE**

On MUSIC, PAINTING, and POETRY.

CHAP. I.

*Introduction. —— Design and Distribution of the Whole. ——
Preparation for the following Chapters.*

ALL Arts have this in common, that *they respect Human
Life.* Some contribute to its *Necessities*, as Medicine and
Agriculture; others to its *Elegance*, as Music, Painting,
and Poetry.

Now, with respect to these two different *Species*, the *necessary*
Arts seem to have been *prior in time;* if it be probable, that Men
consulted how *to live* and *to support themselves*, before they
began to deliberate how *to render Life agreeable.* Nor is this
indeed unconfirmed by Fact, there being no Nation known so
barbarous and ignorant, as where the Rudiments of these *necessary* Arts are not in some degree cultivated. And hence possible
they may appear to be the *more excellent and worthy*, as having
claim to a *Preference*, derived from their *Seniority*.

THE Arts however of *Elegance* cannot be said to want
Pretensions, if it be true, that Nature framed us for *something*

——————— ∽ ———————

** Harris' own cross-references have been omitted here.

more than mere Existence. Nay, farther,* if *Well-being* be clearly preferable to *Mere-being,* and this without it be but a thing contemptible, they may have reason perhaps to aspire even to a *Superiority.* But enough of this, to come to our Purpose.[1]

§2. The Design of this Discourse is to treat of MUSIC, PAINTING, and POETRY; to consider in what they agree, and in what they *differ;* and WHICH UPON THE WHOLE, IS MORE EXCELLENT THAN THE OTHER TWO.

In entering upon this Inquiry, it is first to be observed, that the MIND is made conscious of the *natural World* and its Affections, and of other *Minds* and their Affections, by the several *Organs of the Senses.* [a][2] By the *same Organs,* these Arts exhibit to the

---

*   Ὁυ τὸ ζῆν περὶ πλείστου ποιητέον, Ἀλλὰ (sic) τὸ εὖ ζῆν. Plat. in Critone
[...that it is not living, but living well which we ought to consider most important.]
a. To explain some future Observations, it will be proper here to remark, that the MIND *from these Materials thus brought together, and from its own Operations on them, and in consequence of them, becomes fraught with* IDEAS —— and that MANY MINDS *so fraught, by a sort of* COMPACT *assigning to each* IDEA *some* SOUND *to be its* MARK *or* SYMBOL, *were the first* INVENTORS *and* FOUNDERS *of* LANGUAGE. See Vol. II, or *Hermes,* Lib. iii, cap. 3. 4.

 ∽

---

1. At the beginning of his treatise, Harris, like Jacob, turns to the Classical tradition for anchorage. He employs the word 'art' in its Greek sense, as a term covering all kinds of human activities. His distinctions within the latter, however, differ from those of the Greeks. Harris distinguishes between activities related to "mere-being" and those related to "well-being." By attaching the terms 'agreeable' and 'elegant' to the activities which concern well-being, Harris contributes to the growing awareness of the fine arts as a distinct group. Through this kind of rearrangement, Harris attributes to the arts a loftier level of existence, which is not only unique to mankind but embodies man's humanity. Hence his distinction between "seniority" and "superiority," related to "necessity" and "agreeableness" respectively. Thus, the place he allots to the arts lends justification to his query.

As Schueller pointed out, the eighteenth-century tendency to introduce hierarchies in man's activities was still part of the idea of the "great chain of being." This tendency is evident in Harris' treatment of the arts, particularly in his attempt to assess their relative superiority by comparing them. Like Jacob, Harris compares poetry, painting and music; and like him, Harris does not explain his choice, but takes it for granted. However, what had been still new with Jacob became almost an established fact with Harris, thus taking another step towards the transition from *ut pictura* poesis to *ut musica poesis.*

2. In his epistemological assumptions, Harris follows the Empiricists, especially Locke, viewing the senses as vehicles which transmit sense-data to the mind and which the

(CONT.)

Mind *Imitations*, and imitate either Parts or Affections of this *natural World*, or else the Passions, Energies, and other Affections of *Minds*. There is this Difference however between these *Arts* and *Nature*; that Nature passes to the Percipient thro' *all* the Senses; whereas these Arts use *only two* of them, that of Seeing and that of Hearing. And hence it is that the *sensible Objects* or *Media*, thro' which[b] they imitate, can be *such only*, as these two Senses are framed capable of perceiving; and these Media are *Motion, Sound, Colour,* and *Figure.* [3]

---

b. To prevent Confusion it must be observed, that in all these Arts there is a Difference between the *sensible Media, thro' which they imitate,* and the *Subjects imitated.* The sensible Media, thro' which they imitate, must be always *relative to that Sense, by which the particular Art applies to the Mind;* but the Subject imitated may be *foreign to that Sense, and beyond the Power of its Perception.* Painting, for instance, (as is shewn in this Chapter) has *no sensible Media,* thro' which it operates, except *Colour* and *Figure:* But as to *Subjects,* it may have Motions, Sounds, moral Affections and Actions; *none of which* are either *Colours* or *Figures,* but which however are *all capable of being imitated thro' them.*

(CONT.)   ———— ♍ ————

mind through its operations on them turns into ideas. Harris also adopts Locke's conception of language as a nominating agent of the ideas thus prepared by the mind. According to Harris, language also requires shared symbols — an agreement among many minds — in addition to the prerequisite of the operations of the mind. With regard to the epistemological standing of language, Harris is, no doubt, old-fashioned for his time. Vico, for example, at the same time, linked the development of ideas with that of symbol- making, as complementary parts of one and the same domain, i.e. culture. Condillac, for his part, tried to show that the very development of the powers of the mind is intertwined with that of language. The Lockian stand which artificially separated these two entities, may have prevented Harris from applying to the arts some of the more subtle aspects of the relationship between symbolic systems and ideas.

3. Harris claims, in no ambiguous terms, that the arts, like "natural" ideas, depend on the senses for the acquisition of knowledge. However, like Plato, he maintains that works of art do not constitute a first-order knowledge, for a work of art is related to another such object which, in its turn, depends on the very same senses. As is well known, though he spoke of art as thrice removed from ideas, Plato wished to highlight the principle difference between a priori ideas and their sensual embodiments, fearing that the latter might merit equal standing. Aristotle, on the other hand, by simply defining art as imitation, relegated the arts to the realm of second-order knowledge, without disparaging their standing within his overall theory of knowledge. Small wonder, then, that Aristotle's imitation became a guiding paradigm for those who wished to treat art's epistemic condition on its own terms. Moreover, it provided the yardstick with which to compare the arts and to measure their relative success. Thus imitation still constituted the point of departure for all of our treatises, even though

(CONT.)

PAINTING, having the *Eye* for its *Organ*, cannot be conceived to imitate, but thro' the Media of *visible* Objects. And farther, its Mode of imitating being always *motionless*, there must be subtracted from these the Medium of *Motion*. It remains then, that *Colour* and *Figure* are the only Media, thro' which Painting imitates.

MUSIC, passing to the Mind thro' the *Organ* of the *Ear*, can imitate only by *Sounds and Motions*.

POETRY, having the *Ear* also for its *Organ*, as far as *Words* are considered to be no more than *mere Sounds*, can go no farther in Imitating, than may be performed by *Sound* and *Motion*. But then, as *these its Sounds stand by Compact for the various Ideas with which the Mind is fraught*, it is enabled by this means to imitate, *as far as Language can express*; and that it is evident will, in a manner, include all things.

(CONT.)

the concept underwent continual refinements. The refinements, in their turn, eventually lead to deviations, which ultimately resulted in the deconstruction of 'imitation' into its conceptual components. Harris may serve as an instance of this transformation, though he does not go far enough. Still, using Locke the way he does grants Harris' imitation a more solid epistemological basis: Now that the senses are the source of all knowledge, the arts themselves are accorded a higher standing; their ideational footing, moreover, is guaranteed because of the newly conceived relationship between the sensual and the ideational. What Harris does not realize, of course, is that artistic ideas ought not to be confused with what he saw fit to term "natural" ideas.

The sensual aspects of the arts limit the number of senses employed by each, giving rise to, what Harris calls, their "media" — motion, sound, color and figure. Putting it this way immediately reveals the problems faced by the arts. Despite their "limitations" the arts pretend, nonetheless, to deal with the real world which they imitate. It also emphasizes the idea that not every subject matter is equally suitable for artistic treatment.

Listing the constraints under which art labors also provides insight into the processing and the productive capacities of the mind. Since the work of art is the source of knowledge, it enables the tracing of the working of the mind which controlled and guided its creation. As Vico puts it, man can know only that which he himself has created. Had Harris drawn the full conclusions of his own initial assessments, he might have arrived at a more subtle understanding of art, as well as of the uniqueness of each of the arts.

Now from hence may be seen, how these ARTS *agree*, and how they *differ*.

THEY *agree*, by being all MIMETIC, or IMITATIVE.

THEY *differ*, as they imitate by *different Media*; PAINTING by *Figure* and *Colour*; MUSIC, By *Sound* and *Motion*; PAINTING and MUSIC, by *Media which are Natural*; POETRY, for the greatest Part, by a *Medium which is Artificial* .c[4]

§3. As to that ART, which upon the whole is *most excellent of the three*; it must be observed, that among these various *Media* of imitating, some will naturally be *more* accurate, some *less*; some will *best* imitate one *Subject*; some, another. Again, among the Number of Subjects there will be naturally also a Difference, as to *Merit* and *Demerit*. There will be some *sublime*, and some *low*; some *copious*, and some *short*; some *pathetic*, and others *void of Passion*; some formed to *instruct*, and others *not capable* of it.

Now from these *two* Circumstances; that is to say, from the *Accuracy of the Imitation*, and the *Merit of the Subject imitated*,

---

c. A Figure painted, or a Composition of Musical Sounds have always a *natural Relation to that, of which they are intended to be the Resemblance.* But a Description in Words has rarely any such *natural Relation to the several Ideas, of which those Words are the Symbols. None* therefore understand the *Description*, but *those who speak the Language.* On the contrary, Musical and Picture-Imitations are *intelligible to all Men.*

WHY it is said that Poetry is *not universally*, but *only for the greater part* artificial, see below, Chapter the Third, where what *Natural Force* it has, is examined and estimated.

--------- ◈ ---------

4. The simple allocation of the various "media" to the three arts exposes Harris' conceptual inconsistencies. For artistic "media" to fit their corresponding "natural" senses, he must subtract motion and sound from painting, and figure and color from music and poetry. With regard to poetry, however, Harris breaks his theoretical frame and adds the "compact," an intervening symbol, different in nature from his sensual media. But, if symbolism is allowed to enter his artistic scheme, why limit it to poetry? Had his concern with artistic organization been more systematic, he might have discovered that each and every art has a "language" of its own, i.e. a symbolic system that requires acquaintance. That such central tenets eluded him may be attributed to his conception regarding natural language, which ignores the fact not recognize that language involves symbol-making. As a result even his analysis of poetry fails to take account of its structural unfolding or of the way it manipulates "sensate discourse."   Still, his later distinction between 'immediate' and 'non-immediate' artistic media will bear fruit, as will become most apparent in the case of Twining.

the Question concerning *which Art is most excellent*, must be tried and determined.

THIS however cannot be done, without a *Detail of Particulars*, that so there may be formed, on every part, just and accurate *Comparisons.* [5]

To begin therefore with Painting.

CHAP. II

On the Subjects which Painting imitates.——

On the Subjects which Music imitates.——

Comparison of Music with Painting.

THE FITTEST SUBJECTS FOR PAINTING, are all such THINGS, and INCIDENTS, *as are peculiarly characterised by* FIGURE *and* COLOUR.

OF this kind are the whole Mass[d] of *Things inanimate and vegetable;* such as Flowers, Fruits, Buildings, Landskips — The various Tribes of *Animal Figures;* such as Birds, Beasts, Herds, Flocks — the *Motions* and *Sounds peculiar* to each Animal Species, when accompanied with *Configurations,* which are *obvious* and *remarkable* [e] — The *Human Body* in all its

---

d. THE Reason is, that *these* things are almost *wholly* known to us by their *Colour* and *Figure*. Besides, they are as *motionless,* for the most part, in *Nature,* as in the *Imitation.*

e. INSTANCES of this kind are the Flying of Birds, the Galloping of Horses, the Roaring of Lions, and the Crowing of Cocks. And the Reason is, that though to paint Motion or Sound be *impossible,* yet the Motions and Sounds here mentioned having an *immediate and natural Connection with a certain visible* CONFIGURATION *of the Parts,* the Mind, from a Prospect of this *Configuration, conceives*

(CONT.)

---

5. Harris' aim, he tells us, is to examine the correspondences and the differences among the arts in order to establish their relative excellence. Ostensibly, the very question of priorities regarding the different arts seems anachronistic, a return to the "paragone" tradition. Yet Harris does not limit his question of "merit" solely to subject matter; and it applies to a larger scope than that. Since he deals with the cognitive aspects of imitation, he must similarly deal with the imitated subject. As already noted, the perception of the imitated subject is not limited to the two senses operative in the arts. Indeed, the compatibilities between art and its subjects may reveal the "limits" as well as the kinds of overcoming peculiar to each of the arts, including their different degree of "success."

Appearances (as Male, Female; Young, Old; Handsome, Ugly;) and in all its *Attitudes,* (as Laying, Sitting, Standing, &c.) —— The *Natural Sounds peculiar* to the *Human* Species, (such as Crying, Laughing, Hollowing, &c.)[f] — All *Energies, Passions,* and *Affections,* of the *Soul,* being in any degree *more intense* or *violent* than ordinary[g]— All *Actions and Events,* whose *Integrity* or *Wholeness* depends upon a *short and self-evident* Succession of Incidents[h] — Or if the Succession be extended, then *such Actions* at least, whose *Incidents are all along, during that Succession, similar*[i] — All *Actions* which being qualified as *above,* open themselves into a *large* Variety of Circumstances, *concurring all in the same Point of Time*[j]. — *All Actions* which

---

(CONT.)

insensibly that which is concomitant; and hence it is that, by a sort of *Fallacy,* the SOUNDS and MOTIONS *appear to be painted also.* On the contrary, not so in *such* Motions, as the Swimming of many kinds of Fish; or in *such* Sounds, as the Purring of a Cat; because *here* is no such *special Configuration* to be perceived. — *Homer* in his Shield describing the Picture of a Bull seized by two Lions, says of the Bull — ὁ δὲ μακρὰ μεμυκὼς "Ελκετο — *He, bellowing loudly, was drag'd along.* Where *Eustathius,* in commenting on this Bellowing, says, ὡς ἐδήλου τῷ χήματι (sic), as he (the Bull) *made manifest* (in the Picture) *by his Figure or Attitude.* Eust. in **J. Σ** p. 1224.

f. The Reason is of the *same* kind, as that given in the Note immediately preceding; and by the *same* Rule, the Observation must be confined to *natural Sounds only.* In *Language,* few of the Speakers know the *Configurations,* which attend it.

g. THE Reason is still of the *same* kind, *viz.* from their *Visible* Effects on the Body. They naturally produce either to the *Countenance* a particular *Redness* or *Paleness;* or a particular *Modification of its Muscles;* or else to the *Limbs,* a particular *Attitude.* Now all these Effects are *soley referable* to COLOUR and FIGURE, the two grand sensible Media, *peculiar* to Painting. See *Raphael's* Cartoons of St. *Paul* at *Athens,* and of his Striking the Sorcerer *Elymas* blind:
See also the Crucifixion of *Polycrates,* and the Sufferings of the Consul *Regulus,* both by *Salvator Rosa.**

h. For of *necessity* every Picture is a *Punctum Temporis or* INSTANT.

i. SUCH, for instance, as a Storm at Sea; whose *Incidents of Vision* may be nearly all included in foaming Waves, a dark Sky, Ships out of their erect Posture, and Men hanging upon the Ropes. —— Or as a Battle; which from Beginning to End presents nothing else, than Blood, Fire, Smoak, and Disorder. Now such *Events* may be well imitated *all at once;* for how long soever they last, they are but *Repetitions of the same* — *Nicias,* the Painter, recommended much the same Subjects, viz. a Seafight or a Land-battle of Cavalry. His reasons too are much the same with those mentioned in Note (g). He concludes with a Maxim, (little regarded by his Successors, however important,) that the Subject itself is as much a Part of the Painter's Art, as the Poet's Fable is a Part of Poetry. See *Demetrius* Phal. p. 53. Edit. *Ox.*

j. FOR PAINTING is not bounded in EXTENSION, as it is in DURATION. Besides, it seems true in *every Species of Composition,* that, as far as *Perplexity* and *Confusion* may be avoided, and the *Wholeness* of the Piece may be preserved *clear and intelligible,* the more ample the *Magnitude,* and the greater the *Variety,* the greater also, in proportion, the *Beauty* and *Perfection.* Noble instances of this are the Pictures above-mentioned in Note *(d).* See *Aristot. Poet.* cap. 7. Ὁ δὲ καθ᾽ αὑτὴν φύσιν τοῦ πράγματος ὅρος, ἀεὶ μὲν, [But as for the natural limit of the action... Arist. Poet. VII.12] &c. See also *Characteristicks,* V. I. p. 143. and *Boffu,* B.L. cap. 16. *L'Achille d'Homére est si grand, &c.*

* **See plates no 1-4 below.**

1. Raphael: St. Paul Preaching at Athens

2. Raphael: The Blinding of Elymous

The Seven Tapestry Cartoons by Raphael (at the Victoria and E. Albert Museum) are some of the most important surviving examples of High Renaissance art. They are part of a set of ten commissioned by Pope Leo X for tapestries destined for the Sistine Chapel in the Vatican. *The Blinding of Elymous* (Acts XII, 6-12) and *St. Paul Preaching at Athens* (Acts, XVII, 19-34) are part of this set. (For a history, description, and analysis of the cartoons see *The Raphael Cartoons*, introduced by John Pope-Hennessy [1966].)

3. Salvator Rosa: The Death of Atilius Regulus

Salvator Rosa's etchings were unusual in seventeenth-century art in that they rivaled the artists' paintings in seriousness of purpose. They were intended by the artist to proclaim both his artistic as well as his philosophical attitudes. Rosa (1615-1673) wished to be known as a 'free agent" (independent of patronage), through the wide circulation of the relatively cheap prints, and a fight for moral causes, through the subject matters he dealt with. *The Death of Atilius Regulus* portrays the Roman consul who refused to plea for his life after having been captured by the Carthaginians. It served as an example of Stoic qualities—courage, honesty, and calm acceptance of misfortune.

4. Salvator Rosa: The Crucifixion of Polycrates

The Crucifixion of Polycrates was intended to be companion to the Death of Regulus. It portrays the cruel, greedy and unscrupulous tyrant of Samas who was powerful and successful until fortune had its revenge and brought him to a cruel end, unrelieved by virtue.

are *known,* and known *universally,* rather than Actions *newly invented* or *known but to few* [k] .

AND thus much as to the Subjects of Painting.[6]

§2. IN MUSIC THE FITTEST SUBJECTS of IMITATION are all such THINGS and INCIDENTS, *as are most eminently characterised by* MOTION *and* SOUND.

MOTION may be either *slow* or *swift, even* or *uneven, broken* or *continuous.* — SOUND may be either *soft* or *loud, high* or *low.*

(CONT.)

------

k. THE Reason is, that a Picture being (as has been said) but a *Point* or *Instant,* in a Story *well known* the Spectator's Memory will supply the *previous* and the *subsequent.* But this cannot be done, *where such Knowledge is wanting.* And therefore it may be justly questioned, whether the most celebrated Subjects, borrowed by Painting from History, would have been any of them intelligible *thro' the Medium of Painting only,* supposing History to have been silent, and to have given *no additional Information.*

------ ∽ ------

6. In ch. I, as we have seen, Harris identifies sight and hearing as the only senses relevant to the arts. He further identifies four "media" — motion, sound, color and figure — as capable of being perceived by the senses. He thereby circumscribes the boundaries and limits of the several arts, which, he suspects, constrain each of them differently with regard to the choice of subject matter. On the level of "immediacy," we are told, figure and color pertain more readily to painting, whereas motion and sound pertain to both music and poetry. In ch. II, Harris makes an attempt to divide subjects according to their compatibilities with these two sets of "media." Beginning with figure and color, he presents us with an extended list of possible subjects following a certain logic, moving from the commonsensical to the less obvious through three stages. Starting with still-life, he moves to 1) bodies capable of movement, whose changing positions may be recognized as "instances" of movement. Continuing with recognizable instances of external movement he turns to 2) internal movement, which may likewise be represented through visible and recognizable instances. From continuity recognized by visible instances, he turns to 3) instances themselves—"successions of events"—whose implied continuity may be clinched and represented through a single visible instance.

With his extended list, Harris tried to show that painting, though static, is able to tackle subjects which contain dynamic elements, provided that we are fortified with prior knowledge which makes us recognize the referent through the reference. Harris' treatment of reference, however, falls short of dealing with dynamic elements contained within painting itself. Indeed, treating the dynamic elements by "static" artistic means, requires a level other than the immediate, prior knowledge which relates, for example, to moving bodies. Harris himself opens up a way to deal with these, since his willingness to entertain the relevance of prior knowledge to the perception of what is seen, challenges his theory of immediacy.

Wherever therefore any of these Species of *Motion* or *Sound* may be found in an *eminent* (not a *moderate* or *mean*) *degree,* there will be room for MUSICAL IMITATION.

THUS, in the *Natural* or *Inanimate World,* MUSIC may imitate the Glidings, Murmurings, Tossings, Roarings, and other *Accidents of Water,* as perceived in Fountains, Cataracts, Rivers, Seas, &c. — The same of Thunder — the same of Winds, as well the stormy as the gentle. — In the *Animal World,* it may imitate the *Voice* of some Animals, but *chiefly* that of singing Birds — it may also *faintly copy* some of their *Motions.* — In the *Human Kind,* it can also imitate some *Motions* [1] and *Sounds;* [m] and of Sounds those *most perfectly,* which are expressive of *Grief* and *Anguish.*[n]

AND thus much as to the Subjects, which Music imitates.

§3. IT remains then, that we *compare these two* ARTS together. And here indeed, as to *Musical Imitation in general,* it must be confessed that — as it can, from its Genius, imitate *only* Sounds and Motions — as there are not *many* Motions either in the *Animal* or in the *Inanimate* World, which are *exclusively peculiar* even to any *Species* and scarcely any to an *Individual* — as there are no *Natural* Sounds, which characterise at least *lower*

(CONT.)

It may be here added, that *Horace,* conformably to this Reasoning, recommends even to *Poetic* Imitation a *known* Story, before an *unknown.*

> ——*Tuque*
> *Rectius* Illiacum carmen *deducis in actus,*
> *Quam si proferres* ignota, indictaque primus.

Art. Poet. v. 128.

[You're better off telling the story of Troy in five acts
Than being the first to foist something new and untried
On the world.]

AND indeed as *the being understood to others,* either Hearers or Spectators, seems to be a *common Requisite* to *all Mimetic* Arts whatever; (for to those, who understand them not, they are in Fact no Mimetic Arts) it follows, that *Perspicuity* must be *Essential* to them *all;* and that no prudent Artist would neglect, if it were possible, any just Advantage to obtain this End. Now there can be no Advantage greater, than the *Notoriety of the Subject imitated.*

l. As the *Walk* of the Giant *Polypheme,* in the Pastoral of *Acis* and *Galatea.* — *See what ample Strides he takes,* &c.

m. As the *Shouts* of a Multitude, in the Coronation Anthem of, *God save the King,* &c.

n. THE Reason is, that *this Species* of Musical Imitation *most nearly* approaches Nature. For *Grief,* in most Animals, declares itself by *Sounds,* which are not unlike to *long Notes in the Chromatic System.* Of this kind is the Chorus of *Baal's* Priests in the Oratorio of *Deborah, Doleful Tidings, How ye wound,* &c.

than a Species (for the *Natural* Sounds of *Individuals* are in
every Species the *same)* — farther, as Music does but *imperfectly* imitate even these Sounds and Motions° — On the contrary,
as Figures, Postures of Figures, and Colours characterise not only
every sensible Species, but even *every Individual;* and for the most
part also the *various Energies* and *Passions* of every Individual —
and farther, as Painting is able, *with the highest Accuracy and
Exactness,* to imitate all these Colours and Figures; and while
Musical Imitation pretends at *most* to no more, than the raising
of Ideas *similar,* itself aspires to raise Ideas the very same — in
a word, as Painting, in respect of *its Subjects,* is equal to the
noblest Part of Imitation, *the imitating regular Actions consisting
of a Whole and Parts;* and of *such* Imitation, Music is *utterly incapable* — FROM ALL THIS it must be confessed, that MUSICAL IMITA-
TION IS GREATLY BELOW THAT OF PAINTING, and that *at best* it is but
an imperfect thing.

As to the *Efficacy* therefore of MUSIC, it must be derived from
another Source, which must be left for the present, to be considered of hereafter.[7]

THERE remains to be mentioned Imitation by Poetry.

O. THE Reason is from the *Dissimilitude* between the Sounds and Motions of *Nature,* and those of
Music. Musical Sounds are all produced from *even* Vibration, most *Natural* from *Uneven; Musical
Motions* are chiefly *Definite* in their Measure, most *Natural* are *Indefinite.*

---

7. Harris' treatment of imitation in music differs from its treatment in painting in three
interrelated aspects. First, he does not merely indicate the relevant artistic "media"
(sound and motion) but creates within them further distinctions, related to pairs of
opposites — slow-swift, high-low etc. Secondly, he insists that only when these inner
distinctions are saliently revealed by the imitated object that imitation in music may be
said to occur. Thirdly, he implies that the relation between the imitation and the imitated in music is literal (sound imitating sound) thus narrowing the scope of imitated
objects to those which are directly related to the particular sense operative in the art.
The rendering of passions in music, though it requires further inferences, is treated by
Harris in the same literal fashion. In other words, Harris finds no way to enlarge the
scope of musical imitation by the kinds of mental exercises he employes in the case
of painting.

(CONT.)

CHAP. III.

On the Subjects which Poetry imitates, but imitates only thro' natural *Media, or* mere *Sounds* —— *Comparison of Poetry in this Capacity, first with Painting, then with Music.*

POETIC IMITATION *includes every thing in it, which is performed either by* PICTURE-IMITATION *or* MUSICAL; *for its Materials* are *Words,* and Words are *Symbols by Compact of all Ideas.*

FARTHER as *Words,* beside their being *Symbols* by Compact, are also *Sounds variously distinguished* by their Aptness to be *rapidly* or *slowly* pronounced, and by the respective Prevalence of *Mutes, Liquids,* or *Vowels* in their Composition; it will follow that, beside their *Compact-Relation,* they will have likewise a *Natural Relation* to all such Things, between which and themselves there is any *Natural Resemblance.* Thus, for instance, there is *Natural* Resemblance between all forts of *harsh* and *grating* Sounds. There is Therefore (exclusive of its Signification) a *Natural*

———— ♫ ————

(CONT.)

Unfortunately, Harris, again, does not draw the full conclusions from his own arguments. On the surface, it seems that his distinctions with regard to musical qualities mark a willingness to deal with artistic organization within the art. However, since he is invariably guided by readily noticeable external differentiations, he fails, unlike Webb, to recognize the crucial symbolic significance of the contraries he observes in music. Moreover, if the visual "media" suffice for *clear* and *specific* imitation in the case of painting, but do not in the case of music, he should have entertained their possible *symbolic* functions. This, in itself, might have exposed the *cognitive* dubiousness of musical imitation, not to mention its artistic limitations and shortcomings. Harris was aware of some of these aspects, but at the cost of degrading the communicative ability of music. Yet the main challenge to Harris' argument lies in what he tries to hide in a footnote, i.e., the claim that the "language" of music is not a part of the natural world, and that it has no perceptual standing outside its own sphere. Had he drawn the full conclusion from this observation, he might have felt the need to change his basic assumption with regard to the epistemological structure of art (see fn. 2-3). Though he did ultimately exclude music from imitation, he missed the opportunity to enlist the arguments, which he had himself unwittingly provided, in order to explain the reasons for this exclusion.

Relation between the Sound of a vile Hautboy, and of that Verse
in *Virgil,*

> *Stridenti miserum stipula disperdere Carmen.*

Ecl. 3. ver. 27

[To murder a sorry tune on a scrannel straw.]

or of that other in *Milton.*

> *Grate on their Scrannel Pipes of wretched Straw.*

Lycidas

So also between the *smooth swift* Gliding of a River, and of that
verse in *Horace,*

> — *at ille*
>
> *Labitur, & labetur in omne volubilis aevum.*

Epist. 2. I. ver. 42, 43.

[Meanwhile, it flows, forever flows on and rolls by.]

AND thus in part even *Poetic* Imitation has its Foundation in
Nature. But then this Imitation goes not far; and taken without
the *Meaning* derived to the Sounds from *Compact,* is but little
intelligible, however perfect and elaborate.

§2. If therefore POETRY be *compared* with PAINTING, in respect of
this its *merely Natural and Inartificial* Resemblance, it may be
justly said that — In as much as of *this sort* of Resemblance,
Poetry (like Music) has no other Sources, than *those two of Sound*
and *Motion* — in as much as it often wants these Sources *themselves* (for Numbers of Words neither *have,* nor *can have* any
Resemblance to those *Ideas,* of which they are the *Symbols)* —
in as much as *Natural* Sounds and Motions, which Poetry thus
imitates, are themselves but *loose* and *indefinite Accidents* of
those *Subjects,* to which they belong, and consequently do but
loosely and *indefinitely* characterise them — lastly, in as much
as *Poetic* Sounds and Motions do but *faintly* resemble those of
Nature, which are *themselves* confessed to be so *imperfect* and
vague.— FROM ALL THIS it will follow (as it has *already* followed
of Music) that — POETIC IMITATION FOUNDED IN MERE NATURAL
RESEMBLANCE IS MUCH INFERIOR TO THAT OF PAINTING, and *at best*
but very *imperfect.*

§3. As to the Preference, which such POETIC IMITATION may claim before MUSICAL, or MUSICAL IMITATION before THAT; the Merits on each Side may appear perhaps *equal*. They both fetch their Imitations from *Sound* and *Motion*. Now MUSIC seems to imitate *Nature* better as to *Motion,* and POETRY as to *Sound*. The Reason is, that in *Motions* P *Music* has a *greater Variety;* and in *Sounds,* those of *Poetry* approach nearer to *Nature* .q[8]

IF therefore in *Sound* the *one* have the Preference, in *Motion* the *other,* and the *Merit* of Sound and Motion be supposed nearly *equal,* it will follow, that THE MERIT OF THE TWO IMITATIONS WILL BE NEARLY EQUAL ALSO.

------

p. MUSIC has no less than *five different Lengths of Notes* in ordinary use, reckoning from the Semi-brief to the Semi-quaver; all which may be *infinitely compounded,* even in any *one* Time, or Measure — POETRY, on the other hand, has but *two Lengths* or *Quantities,* a *long* Syllable and a *short,* (which is its Half) and *all the Variety of Verse* arises from such Feet and Metres, as these *two Species* of Syllables, *by being compounded,* can be made produce.

q. MUSICAL Sounds are produced by *even* Vibrations, which *scarcely any Natural* Sounds are — on the contrary, *Words* are the Product of *uneven* Vibration, and so are *most Natural* Sounds —Add to this, that *Words* are far more *numerous,* than *Musical Sounds.* So that Poetry, as to imitation by *Sound,* seems to exceed Music, not only in *nearness of Resemblance,* but even in *Variety also.*

——————— ⰻ ———————

8. Harris clearly differentiates between what he calls natural resemblance and resemblance through symbols. He presents the two as though they were mutually exclusive, rather than interdependent or growing one from the other. Hence he is inconsistent and does not employ the same yardsticks for all three arts as noted in our fn. 4. With regard to painting and music, imitation is judged on "natural" grounds, i.e., in terms of their "immediacy," whereas with regard to poetry Harris is willing to entertain the idea of a symbolic level as well. The insufficiency of poetry, as far as natural resemblance is concerned, does not perturb him, nor is he aware of the interrelationship between the "natural" musical aspects of language and the way they function on a symbolic level contextually, contributing to the overall artistic import.

Harris' comparison of music and poetry regarding their "natural" imitative powers, is interesting, for it reveals differences in the use of the parameters employed. He thus observes that the time element is more open to manipulation in music, whereas timbre is more variable in poetry. These issues will be discussed thoroughly by other writers during the century, in line with the long standing English tradition of dealing with the musical parameters of poetry. At any rate, what eludes Harris is that a "switch" in the roles of parameters may be the result of their different functions in their respective symbolic systems.

CHAP. IV.

On the Subjects which Poetry imitates, not by mere Sounds *or nat-ural* Media, *but by* Words *significant: the Subjects at the same time being such, to which the Genius of each of the other two Arts is* most perfectly *adapted — Its Comparison in these Subjects, first with Painting, then with Music.*

THE *Mimetic* Art of POETRY has been hitherto considered, as fetching its Imitation from mere *Natural* Resemblance. In this it has been shewn much *inferior* to PAINTING, and nearly *equal* to MUSIC.

It remains to be considered, what its Merits are, when it imitates not by mere *Natural* Sound, but by Sound *significant;* by Words, the *compact Symbols* of all kinds of Ideas. From hence depends its genuine Force. And here, as it is able to find Sounds expressive of *every* Idea, so is there *no Subject* either of Picture-Imitation, or Musical, to which it does not aspire; all Things and Incidents whatever being, in a manner, to be described by Words.

WHETHER *therefore* POETRY, *in this its proper sphere, be equal to the Imitation of the other two* ARTS, is the question at present, which comes in order to be discussed.

Now as *Subjects* are *infinite,* and the other two Arts are *not equally adapted* to imitate *all;* it is proposed, first to *compare* POETRY *with them in such* SUBJECTS, *to which they are most perfectly adapted.*

§2. To begin therefore with PAINTING. A SUBJECT, in which the Power of this Art may be *most fully* exerted, (whether it be taken from the *Inanimate,* or the *Animal,* or the *Moral* World) must be a SUBJECT, *which is principally and eminently characterised by certain Colours, Figures, and Postures of Figures — whose Comprehension depends not on a Succession of Events; or at least, if on a Succession, on a short and self-evident one — which admits a large Variety of such Circumstances, as all concur in the same individual Point of Time, and relate all to one principal Action.*

As to such a Subject therefore — In as much as POETRY is forced
to pass thro' the medium of *Compact*, while PAINTING applies
immediately thro' the Medium of *Nature;* the one being understood to all, the other to the Speakers of a certain Language only
— in as much as *Natural* Operations must needs be more *affecting,* than *Artificial* — in as much as Painting helps *our own rude*
Ideas by *its own,* which are *consummate* and are wrought up to
the Perfection of Art; while Poetry can raise *no other* ᵣ than what
every Mind is furnished with *before* — in as much as Painting
shews all the *minute and various concurrent Circumstances* of
the Event in the *same* individual Point of Time, as they appear
in *Nature;* while Poetry is forced to *want* this Circumstance of
Intelligibility, by being ever obliged to enter into some degree of
Detail — in as much as this Detail creates often the Dilemma of
either becoming *tedious,* to be *clear;* or if *not tedious,* then
obscure — lastly, in as much as all Imitations more *similar,* more
immediate, and more *intelligible,* are preferable to those which
are *less* so; and for the Reasons above, the Imitations of *Poetry*
are less *similar,* less *immediate,* and less *intelligible* than those
of *Painting* — From ALL THIS it will follow, that — IN ALL SUBJECTS
WHERE PAINTING CAN FULLY EXERT ITSELF, THE IMITATIONS OF PAINTING
ARE SUPERIOR TO THOSE OF POETRY, AND CONSEQUENTLY IN ALL SUCH
SUBJECTS THAT PAINTING HAS THE PREFERENCE.[9]

---

r. WHEN we read in MILTON of EVE, that
    Grace was in all her Steps, Heav'n in her Eye,
    In ev'ry Gesture Dignity and Love;
we have an Image *not* of that EVE, which MILTON conceived, but of *such an* EVE *only,* as every one,
by his own proper Genius, is able to represent, from reflecting on those *Ideas,* which he has annexed
to these several *Sounds.* The greater Part, in the mean time, have never perhaps bestowed one accurate Thought upon what *Grace, Heaven, Love,* and *Dignity* mean; or ever enriched the Mind with
Ideas of Beauty, or asked *whence* they are to be acquired, and by what *Proportions* they are *constituted.* On the contrary, when we view EVE as painted by an *able Painter,* we labour under no such
Difficulty; because we have exhibited before us the *better Conceptions of an* ARTIST, the *genuine*

--------- ᴜᴿ ---------

9. Harris' discussion of the ability of poetry to render "picture-imitations" reveals in
another way what he understands by natural vs. artificial imitation and why he considers the first to be preferable. Here, too, 'immediacy' relates to agreed upon *intelligibility.* Compared to this direct relationship, artificial imitation is related to a kind of
translation, which has to overcome its indirectness. In any event, it entails a loss of
(CONT.)

§3. AND now to compare POETRY with MUSIC, allowing to *Music* the same Advantage of a *well-adapted* Subject, which has already been allowed to *Painting* in the Comparison just preceding.

WHAT such a SUBJECT is, has already been described. And as to *Preference*, it must be confessed, that — In as much as MUSICAL IMITATIONS, tho' *Natural*, aspire not to raise the *same* Ideas, but only Ideas *similar* and analogous; while POETIC IMITATION, tho' *Artificial*, raises Ideas the very *same* — in as much as the *Definite* and *Certain* is ever preferable to the *Indefinite* and *Uncertain*; and that more especially in *Imitations*, where the principal⁵ Delight is *in recognizing the Thing imitated* — it will follow *from hence* that — EVEN IN SUBJECTS THE BEST ADAPTED TO

Ideas of perhaps a TITIAN or a RAPHAEL.

s. THAT there is an eminent Delight in *this very* RECOGNITION *itself*, abstract from any thing pleasing in *the Subject recognized*, is evident from hence — that, in all the Mimetic Arts, we can be *highly charmed* with *Imitations*, at whose *Originals* in Nature we are *shocked* and *terrified*. Such, for instance, as Dead Bodies, Wild Beasts, and the like.

THE Cause, assigned for this, seems to be of the following kind. We have a Joy, not only in the *Sanity* and *Perfection*, but also *in the just and natural Energies* of our several *Limbs* and *Faculties*. And hence, among others, the *Joy* in REASONING; as being the *Energy of that principal Faculty*, our INTELLECT *or* UNDERSTANDING. This Joy extends, not only to the Wise, but to the Multitude. For all Men have an *Aversion to Ignorance and Error*, and in some degree, however moderate, are glad to *learn* and to *inform* themselves.

HENCE therefore the *Delight, arising* from these *Imitations; as* we are enabled, in each of them, to *exercise the* REASONING FACULTY; and, by *comparing* the *Copy* with the *Archetype* in our Minds, to INFER that THIS is SUCH a THING; and, THAT, ANOTHER; a Fact remarkable among Children, even in their first and earliest Days.

Τὸ, τε γὰρ μιμεῖσθαι, σύμφυτον τοῖς ἀνθρώποις ἐκ παίδων ἐστὶ, καὶ τούτῳ διαφέρουσι τῶν ἄλλων ζώων, ὅτι μιμητικώτατόν ἐστι, καὶ τὰς μαθήσεις ποιεῖται διὰ μιμήσεως τὰς πρώτας· καὶ τὸ χαίρειν τοῖς μιμήμασι πάντας. Σημεῖον δὲ τούτου τὸ συμβαῖνον ἐπὶ τῶν ἔργων. Ἅ γὰρ αὐτὰ λυπηρῶς ὁρῶμεν, τούτων τὰς εἰκόνας τάς μάλιστα ἠκριβωμένας, χαίρομεν θεωροῦντες οἷον θηρίων τε μορφὰς τῶν ἀγριωτάτων, καὶ νεκρῶν. Ἅιτιον δὲ καὶ τούτου, ὅτι μανθάνεν οὐ μόνον τοῖς φιλοσόφοις ἥδισ-

(CONT.)

(CONT.)

control over the unambiguity and the "oneness" of understanding. Whereas the poet is free to give vent to his imagination, he does not control the imagination of others. This explains, in part, Harris' own commitment to "immediacy." Given similar premises, however, there are other ways to deal with these issues. Jacob, for example, realized that even painting must leave something unstated in order to activate the imagination of the beholder and enable him to render the picture complete. The artist does not stand to lose control thereby; on the contrary, he gains control, guiding the imagination of others. The recognition that art may set off the imagination in ways other than those entertained by Harris, will be recognized later and approved as desirable.

MUSICAL IMITATION, THE IMITATION OF POETRY WILL BE STILL MORE EXCELLENT.[10]

(CONT.)

τον, ἀλλὰ καὶ τοῖς ἄλλοις ὁμοίως· ἀλλ᾽ ἐπὶ βραχὺ κοινωνοῦσιν αὐτοῦ. Διὰ γὰρ τοῦτο χαίρουσι τὰς εἰκόνας ὁρῶντες, ὅτι συμβαίνει θεωροῦντας μανθάνειν καὶ συλλογίζεσθαι, τί ἕκαστον· οἷον, ὅτι οὗτος ἐκεῖνος.

Arist. Poet. c. 4.

[From childhood men have an instinct for representation, and in this respect man differs from the other animals that he is far more imitative and learns his first lessons by representing things. And then there is the enjoyment people always get from the representations. What happens in actual experience proves this, for we enjoy looking at accurate likenesses of things which are themselves painful to see, obscene beasts, for instance, and corpses. The reason is this. Learning things gives great pleasure not only to philosophers but also in the same way to all other men, though they share this pleasure only to a small degree. The reason why we enjoy seeing likenesses is that, as we look, we learn and infer

10. Whereas in the previous section Harris dealt with the content of imitation, here he deals with kinds of *reference* to the subject matter. In order to be able to differentiate among them, he introduces gradations into his concept of "immediacy," invoking degrees of "obviousness," in Twining's sense. Accordingly, both immediacy and obviousness are guaranteed in the case of painting. Music, by contrast, fulfills only the first condition, whereas poetry, notwithstanding its musical aspects, fulfils the second. Given the absence of the first or the second, Harris prefers the second. Again, Harris' judgment is guided by the assumption that the definite is aesthetically preferable. Harris fully acknowledges his debt, in this respect, to the Aristotelian tradition, which attributes the *intellectual* pleasure accompanying imitation to the awareness of its being an illusion. Twining will raise similar arguments with regard to immediacy and obviousness, without, however, fixing their relative merit. Though Twining is more lucid and responsible in his assessments, it goes without saying that he is heavily indebted to Harris — a fact he himself acknowledges.

CHAP. V.

*On the Subjects which Poetry imitates by Words significant, being
at the same time* Subjects not adapted *to the Genius of either of the
other Arts — The* Nature *of those Subjects — The* Abilities of Poetry
to imitate them — Comparison of Poetry in these Subjects, *first
with Painting, then with Music.*

THE MIMETIC ART of POETRY has now been considered in
two Views — First, as imitating by *mere natural* MEDIA:
and in this it has been placed *on a level* with MUSIC, but
much inferior to PAINTING — It has been since considered as imitating thro' *Sounds significant by Compact,* and that in *such*
Subjects respectively, where PAINTING and MUSIC have the *fullest
Power* to exert themselves. *Here* to Painting it has been held *inferior,* but to Music it has been *preferred.*

IT remains to be considered — what *other Subjects* Poetry has
left, to which the Genius of the other two Arts is less *perfectly
adapted* —How far Poetry is *able* to imitate them —and whether
from the *Perfection* of its Imitation, and the *Nature* of the
Subjects themselves, it ought to be called no more than *equal* to
its Sister Arts; or whether, on the whole, it should not rather be
called *superior.*

§2. To begin, in the first place, by comparing it with Painting.

THE *Subjects of Poetry,* to which the Genius of *Painting* is *not
adapted,* are — all Actions, whose[t] *Whole* is of so *lengthened* a
Duration, that *no Point of Time,* in any part of that Whole, can
be given *fit for Painting;* neither in its *Beginning,* which will
teach what is *Subsequent;* nor in its *End,* which will teach what
is *Previous;* nor in its *Middle,* which will declare both the
Previous and the *Subsequent.* — Also all Subjects so framed, as
to lay open the *internal Constitution of Man,* and give us an

---

what each is, for instance, "that is so and so."   Arist. Poet. IV.2-5]
t. FOR a just and accurate Description of *Wholeness* and *Unity,* see *Arist. Poet.* Ch. 7 & 8. and *Bossu,*

Insight into^u*Characters, Manners, Passions,* and *Sentiments.*[11]

THE *Merit* of these Subjects is obvious. They must necessarily of all be the most *affecting*; the most *improving*; and such of which the Mind has the *strongest Comprehension.*

FOR as to the *affecting Part* — if it be true, that all *Events* more or less *affect* us, as the *Subjects,* which they respect, are more or less nearly *related* to us; then surely those *Events* must needs be *most affecting,* to whose *Subjects* we are of all the *most intimately related.* Now such is the Relation, which we bear to *Mankind;* and Men and Human Actions are the Subjects, here proposed for Imitation.

---

his best Interpreter, in his Treatise on the *Epic Poem.* B. II. ch. 9, 10, 11.

u. FOR a description of CHARACTER, see below, Note *(w)* of this Chapter.

As for MANNERS, it may be said in general, that a *certain System of them* makes a *Character;* and that as these Systems, by being *differently compounded,* make each a *different* Character, so is it that *one* Man *truly differs* from *another.*

PASSIONS are obvious; *Pity, Fear, Anger, &c.*

SENTIMENTS are discoverable in all those Things, which are the *proper Business and end of* SPEECH *or* DISCOURSE. The chief Branches of this *End* are to *Assert* and *Prove;* to *Solve* and *Refute;* to express or excite *Passions;* to *amplify* Incidents, and to *diminish* them. It is in these things therefore, that we must look for *Sentiment.* See *Arist. Poet.* c. 19. — ἔστι δὲ κατὰ τὴν Διάνοιαν ταῦτα ὅσα ὑπὸ τοῦ λόγου δεῖ παρασκευασθῆναι. Μέρη δὲ τούτων, τό, τε ἀποκεικνῦναι, καὶ τὸ λύειν, καὶ τὸ πάθη παρασκευάζειν, —— καὶ ἔτι μέγεθος, καὶ σμικρότητα.

[Under the head of Thought come all the effects to be produced by the language. Some of these are proof and refutation, the arousing of feelings like pity, fear, anger, and so on, and then again exaggeration and depreciation. Arist. Poet. XIX.3-4]

          ↄ

11. Harris' explication concerning the ability of poetry to manage the kind of continuity which painting is unable to wield, even when manipulated, does not result from the fact that actions cannot be summarized in a single instance. For as he himself already told us, they clearly can. The case with which he is presently dealing involves the *dynamics* of the unfolding. Such dynamics portray processes whose features may constitute that which one wishes to call special attention to. His example of drama, is only one of many such examples in which the nature of the internal unfolding conveys the major message. The case of human character is an instance of a different kind, its "oneness" requires and depends on a mental record of a number of things, leading to a unique summation. Sentiment and mood in poetry are not markedly different from the delineation of character; they too are summations of constituents of an unfolding. It is of interest that in the case of sentiment Harris turns to rhetoric to exemplify his point. As discussed in volume I, it is the communicative capacity of rhetoric that was used by musical theorists to shed light on their own more ambiguous domain.

As to *Improvement* — there can be none surely (to *Man* at least) so great, as that which is derived from a just and decent Representation of *Human Manners*, and *Sentiments*. For what can more contribute to give us that *Master-Knowledge,* v without which, *all other* Knowledge will prove of little or no Utility.

As to our *Comprehension* — there is nothing certainly, of which we have so *strong* Ideas, as of that which happens in the *Moral* or *Human* World. For as to the *Internal Part,* or *Active Principle* of the *Vegetable,* we know it but *obscurely;* because there we can discover neither *Passion,* nor *Sensation.* In the *Animal* World indeed this *Principle* is more seen, and that from the *Passions* and *Sensations* which *there* declare themselves. Yet all still rests upon the mere Evidence of *Sense;* upon the Force only of *external* and *unassisted Experience.* But in the *Moral* or *Human* World, as we have a Medium of *Knowledge* far more *accurate* than this; so from hence it is, that we can comprehend *accordingly.*

---

v. ΓΝΩΘΙ ΣΑΥΤΟΝ [know thyself]. But farther, besides obtaining this *moral Science* from the Contemplation of Human Life; an End *common* both to Epic, Tragic, and Comic Poetry; there is a *peculiar* End to *Tragedy,* that of eradicating the Passions of *Pity* and *Fear.* Ἔστιν οὖν τραγῳδία μίμησις πράξεως σπουδαίας καὶ τελείας —— δι' ἐλέου καὶ φόβου περαίνουσα τὴν τῶν τοιούτων παθημάτων κάθαρσιν.   (Arist. Poet. IV.2) Arist. Poet. c. 6. TRAGEDY *is the Imitation of an Action important and perfect, thro'* PITY *and* FEAR *working the* PURGATION *of* SUCH-LIKE PASSIONS.
THERE are none, it is evident, so devoid of these two *Passions,* as those *perpetually conversant,* where the *Occasions* of them are most *frequent;* such, for instance, as the *Military* Men, the Professors of *Medicine, Chirurgery,* and the like. Their Minds by this Intercourse, become as it were *callous;* gaining an *Apathy* by *Experience,* which no *Theory* can ever teach them.
Now that, which is wrought in *these* Men by the *real Disasters of Life,* may be supposed wrought in others by the *Fictions of Tragedy,* yet with this happy Circumstance in favour of Tragedy, that, without the Disasters being *real,* it can obtain the *same* End.
IT must however, for all this, be confessed, that an Effect of this kind cannot reasonably be expected, except among Nations, like the *Athenians* of old, who lived in a perpetual Attendance upon these Theatrical Representations. For it is not a *single* or *occasional* Application to these Passions, but a *constant* and *uninterrupted,* by which alone they may be lessened or removed.
IT would be improper to conclude this Note, without observing, that the Philosopher in this place by PITY means not PHILANTHROPY, *Natural Affection a Readiness to relieve others in their Calamities and Distress;* but, by *Pity,* he means that SENSELESS EFFEMINATE CONSTERNATION, *which seizes weak Minds, on the sudden Prospect of any thing Disastrous;* which, in its more violent Effects, is seen in *Shriekings, Swoonings, &c..* a Passion, so far from laudable, or from operating to the Good of others, that it is certain to deprive the Party, who labours under its Influence, of all Capacity *to do the least good Office.*

WITH regard therefore to the various *Events* which happen *here*, and the various *Causes*, by which they are produced — in other Words, of all Characters, Manners, Human Passions, and Sentiments; besides the Evidence of *Sense*, we have the *highest Evidence additional*, in having an express *Consciousness* of something *similar within*; of something *homogeneous* in the Recesses of our own *Minds*; in that, which constitutes to each of us *his true and real Self.*

THESE therefore being the Subjects, *not adapted to the Genius of Painting*, it comes next to be considered, *how far Poetry can imitate them.*

AND here, that it has *Abilities* clearly *equal*, cannot be doubted; as it has *that* for the *Medium* of its Imitation, through which *Nature* declares herself in the *same* Subjects. For the *Sentiments* in *real Life* are only known by Men's *Discourse*. And the *Characters, Manners,* and *Passions* of Men being the *prompters* to what they *say*; it must needs follow, that their *Discourse* will be a *constant Specimen* of those *Characters, Manners,* and *Passions.*

> *Format enim Natura prius nos intus ad omnem*
>
> *Fortunarum habitum; juvat, aut impellit ad iram:*
>
> *Post* effert Animi Motus, INTERPRETE LINGUA.
>
> *Hor. de Arte Poet.* vers. 108.
>
> [Nature shapes our inner thoughts in advance to every state of fortune; she cheers us or impels us to wrath, or brings us to the ground and tortures us with grievous sorrow; later, she expresses our emotions, interpreting them with the tongue.]

Not only therefore *Language* is an *adequate* Medium of Imitation, but in *Sentiments* it is the *only* Medium; and in *Manners* and *Passions* there is no other, which can exhibit them to us after that *clear, precise,* and *definite Way*, as they in *Nature* stand allotted to the various sorts of Men, and are found to constitute the *several Characters* of each.[w][12]

§3. To *compare* therefore *Poetry,* in *these Subjects,* with *Painting* — In as much as no Subjects of Painting are *wholly superior* to Poetry; while the Subjects, here described, *far exceed the Power of Painting* — in as much as they are of *all* Subjects the most *affecting,* and *improving,* and such of which we have the *strongest Comprehension* — further, in as much as Poetry can *most accurately* imitate them — in as much as, besides all imitation, there is a *Charm* in Poetry, arising from its very

---

w. IT is true indeed that (besides what is done by *Poetry*) there is some Idea of *Character,* which even *Painting* can communicate. Thus there is no doubt, but that such a *Countenance* may be found by *Painters* for *Aeneas,* as would convey upon view a *mild, humane,* and yet a *brave* Disposition. But then this Idea would be *vague* and *general.* It would be concluded, only in the gross, that the Hero was *Good.* As to that System of Qualities *peculiar to Aeneas* only, and which alone *properly constitutes his true and real Character,* this would still remain a Secret, and be no way discoverable. For how deduce it from the mere *Lineaments* of a Countenance? Or, if it were deducible, how few Spectators would there be found so sagacious? It is here, therefore, that Recourse must be had, not to *Painting,* but to *Poetry.* So *accurate* a Conception of Character can be gathered only from a *Succession of various, and yet consistent Actions*; a Succession, *enabling us to conjecture,* what the Person of the Drama will do in the *future,* from what already he has done in the *past.* Now to such an Imitation, Poetry only is *equal*; because it is not *bounded, like Painting,* to *short,* and as it were, *instant* Events, but may imitate Subjects of *any Duration whatever.* See *Arist. Poet.* cap. 6. Ἔστιν δὲ ἦθος μὲν τὸ τοιοῦτον, ὃ δηλοῖ τὴν προαίρεσιν ὁποία τις ἐστὶν, ἐν οἷς οὐκ ἔστι δῆλον, εἰ προαιρεῖ-ται ἢ φεύγει ὁ λέγων. [Character is that which reveals choice, shows what sort of thing a man chooses or avoids in circumstances where the choice is not obvious, so those speeches convey no character in which there is nothing whatever which the speaker chooses or avoids. Arist. Poet. VI.24] See also the ingenious and learned *Bossu,* Book 4. ch. 4.

ഗ

---

12. Harris' argument concerning poetry's merit can be summarized in the following manner: First he identifies artistic merit with three main factors, partly derived from the classical tradition — affection (related to the "intimate"), improvement (related to "manners") and comprehension (related to "accuracy"). Then he tells us that these are most relevant to human action, which concerns us most and of which we have first-hand knowledge. This knowledge, Harris claims, is available to man only through language. Thus poetry, which employs language, rates as the highest among the arts.

There is nothing surprising in his argument, for again Harris ignores the particular import of internal artistic organization, depending only on antecedent knowledge; no wonder that ordinary comprehension turns out to be a prerequisite for affection and improvement. Harris in fact implies that there is only one kind of knowledge, i.e., knowledge unaffected by the manner in which it is arrived at, thereby depriving the different symbolic systems of their role in creating their own unique worlds.

Numbers[x]; whereas Painting has Pretence to no Charm, except that of Imitation only — lastly, (which will soon be shewn) in as much as Poetry is able to *associate Music*, as a most powerful Ally; of which Assistance, Painting is utterly incapable — FROM ALL THIS it may be fairly concluded, that — POETRY *is not only Equal, but that it is in fact* FAR SUPERIOR TO ITS SISTER ART OF PAINTING.[14]

§4. BUT if it exceed *Painting* in *Subjects*, to which Painting is *not adapted*; no doubt *will it exceed* MUSIC in *subjects* to Music *not adapted*. For *here* it has been *preferred*, even in those Subjects, which have been held *adapted the best of all.*

§5. POETRY IS THEREFORE, ON THE WHOLE MUCH SUPERIOR TO EITHER OF THE OTHER MIMETIC ARTS; *it having been shewn to be equally excellent* IN THE ACCURACY OF ITS IMITATION; *and to imitate* SUBJECTS, WHICH FAR SURPASS, AS WELL IN UTILITY, AS IN DIGNITY.

---

x. That there is a *Charm* in *Poetry*, arising from its *Numbers* only, may be made evident from the five or six first Lines of the *Paradise Lost;* where, without any Pomp of Phrase, Sublimity of Sentiment, or the *least Degree of Imitation*, every Reader must find himself to be sensibly delighted; and that, only from the graceful and simple *Cadence* of the *Numbers*, and that artful *Variation* of the *Caesura* or *Pause*, so essential to the Harmony of every good Poem.

An *English Heroic* Verse consists of ten *Semipeds*, or Half-feet. Now in the Lines above-mentioned the *Pauses* are varied upon *different* Semipeds in the Order, which follows; as may be seen by any, who will be at the Pains to examine.

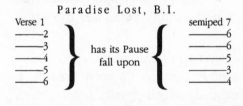

Paradise Lost, B.I.

Verse 1		semiped 7
2	} has its Pause {	6
3	fall upon	6
4		5
5		3
6		4

---

13. Harris deviates again from his conceptual scheme by introducing "charm" as an additional quality. This forces him to include elements which are not directly related to 'imitation' as he understands the concept. He might have introduced the subject earlier, in connection with painting, especially since it was quite prominent ever since Vasari and some of his contemporaries. Nonetheless, his treatment of charm in connection with poetry marks a new approach to prosody, i.e., to the preference of irregularity within given prosodic patterns, for which Milton was famous. Harris, we may recall, viewed music as rhythmically more varied than poetry, whereas poetry's strength resides in its variety of sound. By identifying "charm" with rhythmic variety, Harris, in fact, musicalizes poetry, lending it aesthetic significance.

CHAP. VI

On Music considered not as an Imitation, but as deriving its
Efficacy from another *Source. — On its joint Operation by this*
means with Poetry. — An Objection to Music solved. — The
Advantage arising to it, as well as to Poetry, from their being unit-
ed. — Conclusion.

◯N the above Discourse, MUSIC has been mentioned as an
Ally to Poetry. It has also been said to derive its *Efficacy*
from *another Source,* than *Imitation.* It remains, therefore,
that these things be explained.[14]

NOW, in order to this, it is first to be observed, that there are various *Affections,* which may be raised by the Power of *Music.*
There are Sounds to make us *chearful,* or *sad; martial,* or *ten-*
der; and so of almost every other Affection, which we feel.

IT is also further observable, that there is a *reciprocal Operation*
between our *Affections,* and our *Ideas;* so that, by a sort of *nat-*
ural Sympathy, certain *Ideas* necessarily tend to raise in us certain *Affections;* and those *Affections,* by a sort of Counter-
Operation, to raise the *same Ideas.* Thus *Ideas* derived from
Funerals, Tortures, Murders, and the like, naturally generate the
Affection of *Melancholy.* And when, by any *Physical Causes,* that
Affection happens to prevail, it as naturally generates the same
doleful Ideas.

AND hence it is, that *Ideas,* derived from *external* Causes, have
at *different* times, upon the *same* Person, so *different* an Effect.
If they happen to suit the Affections, which *prevail within,* then
is their Impression *most sensible,* and their Effect *most lasting.* If
the contrary be true, then is the Effect contrary. Thus, for

———— ∽ ————

14. The power of music does not reside in imitation but elsewhere, Harris has told us
earlier. However, dealing with the subject, he does not provide any justification for
breaking his scheme. The treatment of music along these lines, would require more
than some minor additional details. Taking music's affective powers for granted, Harris
is probably guided by a belief in the natural human capacity for music, related to an
innate disposition of the mind. Needless to say, the subject will be of major concern
to later writers.

instance, a Funeral will much more affect the same Man, if he see it when melancholy, than if he see it when chearful.[15]

Now this being premised, it will follow, that whatever happens to be the *Affection* or *Disposition* of Mind, which ought naturally to result from the Genius of any *Poem*, the *same* probably it will be in the Power of some Species of *Music* to excite. But whenever the *proper Affection* prevails, it has been allowed that then *all kindred Ideas,* derived from external Causes, make the *most sensible Impression.* The Ideas therefore of Poetry must needs make the most sensible Impression, when the [y]Affections, peculiar to them, are already excited by the Music. For here a *double Force is made co-operate to one End.* A Poet, *thus assisted,* finds not an Audience in a Temper, averse to the Genius of his Poem, or perhaps at best under a cool *Indifference;* but by the Preludes, the Symphonies, and *concurrent Operation* of the

---

y. QUINTILIAN elegantly, and exactly apposite to this Reasoning, says of *Music* — *Namque & voce & modulatione grandia elate, jucunda dulciter, moderata leniter canit, totaque arte* consentit cum eorum, quae dicuntur, AFFECTIBUS. *Inst. Orator.* l. 1. cap. 10. [But eloquence does vary both tone and rhythm, expressing sublime thoughts with elevation, pleasing thoughts with sweetness, and ordinary with gentle utterance, and in every expression of its art is in sympathy with the emotions of which it is the mouth-piece.]

——— ∽ ———

15. In the last sections it becomes clear that Harris is one of those who believe that music can activate *specific* passions. He orders these passions, as he did with regard to the musical parameters, in pairs of opposites — cheerful-sad, martial-tender. Harris, however, does not draw any conclusion from this parallelism. Later thinkers, especially Webb, will not miss its significance in their attempt to explain what Harris has taken for granted — the relation between sound and sentiment.

Nevertheless, the reciprocity Harris observes between Affections and Ideas is of importance with regard to his claim that music can raise specific passions. This observation is also central to Hume's theory of mind according to which affects lend color and direction to ideas, which, in turn, lend specificity to the passions. However, Harris enlists this argument only with regard to the desired relationship between music and poetry. Previously he has told us that an art-work which clearly directs one to an intended message is preferable to one which leads to free associations. To this he now adds two more conditions: 1) the directive act should be realized effectively and 2) the message should endure. By granting music the ability to fulfill the first condition, he also grants music a kind of *immediacy,* which he has not entertained previously. On the other hand, by identifying poetry with the second, he opens the scheme of poetry again, introducing yet another aesthetic desideratum.

Music in all its parts, rouzed into *those very Affections,* which he would most desire.

AN Audience, so disposed, not only embrace with Pleasure the Ideas of the Poet, when exhibited; but, in a manner, even *anticipate* them in their several Imaginations. The Superstitious have not a more previous Tendency to be frightened at the sight of Spectres, or a Lover to fall into Raptures at the sight of his Mistress; than a Mind, thus tempered by the Power of Music, to enjoy all Ideas, which are suitable to that Temper.

AND hence the *genuine* Charm of Music, and the *Wonders* which it works, thro' its great Professors.^z A Power, which consists not in Imitations, and the raising *Ideas*; but in the raising *Affections,* to which Ideas may correspond. There are few to be found so insensible, I may even say so inhumane, as when GOOD POETRY IS JUSTLY SET TO MUSIC, not in some degree to feel the Force of so *amiable an Union.* But to the Muses Friends it is a Force *irresistible,* and penetrates into the deepest Recesses of the Soul.[16]

> — *Pectus inaniter angit,*
> *Irritat, mulcat, falsis terroribus implet.*

[It tortures the soul in vain,

irritates it, maltreats it and fills it with false anxieties.]

---

z. SUCH, above all, is *George Frederick Handel;* whose Genius, having been cultivated by continued Exercise, and being itself far the sublimest and most universal now known, has justly placed him without an Equal, or a Second. This transient Testimony could not be denied so excellent an Artist, from whom this Treatise has borrowed such eminent Examples, to justify its Assertions in what it has offered concerning Music.

ᔕ
---

16. Harris' theory of "reciprocity" is now enlisted to justify the union of music and poetry, a subject which still raised considerable repercussions in eighteenth-century England. Indeed, Harris' rhapsody on the subject reminds one of verses from Shakespeare, Milton and others who praise the union and denigrate those who are "deaf" to its marvels. Music and poetry combined, indeed answer Harris' criteria of merit.

§2. Now this is *that Source*, from whence music was said formerly *to derive its greatest Efficacy*. And here indeed, not in ªImitation, ought it to be chiefly cultivated. On this account also it has been called a *powerful Ally* to Poetry. And farther, it is by the help of this Reasoning, that the *Objection* is solved, which is raised against the *Singing of Poetry* (as in Opera's, Oratorio's, etc.) from the want of *Probability* and *Resemblance to Nature*. To one indeed, who has no musical Ear, this Objection may have Weight. It may even perplex a Lover of Music, if it happen to surprise him in his Hours of *Indifference*. But when he is feeling the Charm of Poetry *so accompanied*, let him be angry (if he can) with that which serves only to interest him *more feelingly* in the Subject, and support him in a *stronger* and *more earnest* Attention; which enforces, by its Aid, the several Ideas of the Poem, and gives them to his Imagination with unusual Strength and Grandeur. He cannot surely but confess, that he is a *Gainer in the Exchange*, when he *barters* the want of a single Probability, that of *Pronunciation* (a thing merely arbitrary and every where different) for a *noble Heightening of Affections* which are suitable to the Occasion, and enable him to enter into the Subject with double *Energy* and *Enjoyment*.[17]

§3. FROM what has been said it is evident, that these two Arts can never be so powerful *singly*, as when they are *properly united*. For *Poetry*, when alone, must be necessarily forced to *waste* many of its richest *Ideas*, in the mere raising of Affections, when, to have been properly relished, it should have *found* those Affections in their highest energy. And *Music*, when alone, can only raise *Affections*, which soon *languish* and *decay*, if not maintained and fed by the nutritive Images of Poetry. Yet must

---

a. FOR the *narrow* Extent and *little* Efficacy of MUSIC, considered as MIMETIC or IMITATIVE art, see Ch. II. §3.

———— ∽ ————

17. With his argument concerning the reciprocal relationship between music and poetry, Harris enters the hot debate over opera. He attacks people like Addison who rejected opera for its irrationality, namely, for using song as its natural speech. Though Harris had previously advocated reasoning as the only important cognitive factor in art, he is now willing to recognize imagination, attention, and affectivity. Unfortunately he neither elaborates those points, nor does he give reasons for this new preference.

it be remembered, in this Union, that *Poetry* ever have the *Precedence;* its *Utility,* as well as *Dignity,* being by far the more considerable.[18]

§4. AND thus much, for the present, as to MUSIC, PAINTING, and POETRY, the Circumstances, in which they *agree,* and in which they *differ;* and the PREFERENCE, DUE TO ONE OF THEM ABOVE THE OTHER TWO.

The E N D .

---

18. It is here that Harris tries to explain the different capabilities of music and poetry, as far as their affective powers are concerned. The affections music raises, he explains, soon "languish and decay" because they are not "fed by imagery." Thus, music, according to Harris, does not raise images, in particular not of the kind that persist. The affectivity of music comes, therefore to a halt as the result of its evanescence. This argument is not entirely wrong, but it calls for corrections and qualifications which Harris does not supply.

Charles Avison
(1710-1770)

After Jacob, the man-of-letters, and Harris, the philosopher, Avison the musician joins our group. Like the others, Avison was by no means aware of belonging to a group which would eventually come to be identified with the turn to the so-called "*ut musica poesis.*" The group he "naturally" belonged to centered around music, but unlike earlier writers on the subject he was neither engaged in metaphysical speculation nor in scientific or technical deliberation. Rather, he saw his mission in explaining music in terms understandable to the layman — those who enjoyed the art but could not account for their experience and assess its value. It is this undertaking that led him to "correspondences": Through analogies with the familiar, i.e. painting, he sought to elucidate the unfamiliar, i.e. music, which had hitherto been burdened by "dark dialect and jargon," as Roger North put it (North, 1959: v as cited by Lipking 1970: 216). Indeed, in the hands of Avison, painting turned into a kind of explanatory model which helped expose musical aspects which had received but secondary attention.

Avison was well-versed for the job: He received his musical education in Italy, and upon his return to England became a pupil of Geminiani. In 1736, he was appointed organist of St. Nicholas at Newcastle, where he remained until his death. He composed several sets of sonatas and concertos which gained popularity, and participated in the editing of the eight volumes of psalms by Marcello — a composer he adored. Apart from his musical activities, Avison had the reputation of "a man of great culture and polish," and like Mizler and Scheibe in Germany, he was surrounded by a small circle of musical amateurs who were devoted to his views.

The discourse in Avison's essay grows from a specific assumption concerning music, according to which the harmonizing and reconciling powers of music make it (and the musician by extension) serve society, first and foremost. This Shaftesburian opting for the "public good" is felt throughout his essay, especially in his identification of music's beauty with the moral good. The Shaftesburian influence is also reflected in his reliance on a musical "inner sense" — "taste" or "nature" — as the ultimate judge of value. This philosophical legacy made him view the aesthetic in music as related to coherence, organicity and synthetic wholes. It explains how he could dispense with musical imitation, which, to his mind, offends some principle aesthetic values.

Unlike Hutcheson who advocated similar values, Avison put 'expression' at the center of his theory, integrating it with the Shaftesburian framework. Lipking might object, but the content Avison lent to 'expression,' though much of it remained vague, is of central importance (Lipking 1970: 223). Whereas traditional musical thought, since Galilei via Mersenne and the so called "*Affektenlehre*" group, identified 'expression' with specific musical *causes* (i.e. certain musical constituents) Avison conceptualized it primarily in terms of *effects*, as responses to combinations, not previously specified, between music's two basic components — melody and harmony. '*Espression*' as '*effect*,' as Lipking rightly observed (*ibid.*) is related to the principle of *je ne sais quoi*. This principle, heralded by late seventeenth century French thinkers in reaction to Neo-Classical dogmas, emphasized the ambiguity surrounding aesthetic judgement (Borgerhoff 1950: 174-245). However, as argued in Vol. I such criticism, paradoxically, contributed to the development of an independent epistemological framework concerning aesthetic queries. Though largely unaware of that development, Avison was related to it in various ways; moreover, his ideas were later integrated into that framework by thinkers of a more philosophical bent. Expression thus became part and parcel of the aesthetic in music not unlike the function of effects in Hanslik's *Vom musikalisch-Schönen*. The Le Brunians, Rogerson rightly observed, would have been greatly offended (Rogerson 1945: 85), but this shift in understanding not only contributed to the reconciliation of contemporary debates concerning the preference of melody over harmony; by calling melody "invention" and harmony "technique," it also gave new vent to composition. This kind of wedding of 'imagination' and 'discipline' had interesting implications for later theories.

It is not clear whether it was the eclectic nature of the treatise or its erudite appearance, uncommon among musicians of the time, that raised suspicion over Avison's authorial claim. Of course, whether Avison wrote the treatise himself or whether someone helped him write it, is irrelevant as far as the growth of ideas are concerned. At any rate, later thinkers unequivocally identified him as the author. Moreover, Avison became *the* musical authority for later thinkers and his ideas served some of them as starting points for further aesthetic excursions into music and its correspondences. To be sure, many took issue with his musical preferences (e.g. his criticism of Handel) and there was a certain Dr. Hayes who argued against Avison's views on the advantages of Ancient over Modern music. Though it was considered that Hayes had the better argument, Avison included Hayes' letter, together with his own reply, in later editions of the Essay. Whatever the interest of these debates, it should be reiterated that Avison's importance resides in his theory of expression. Despite its deficiencies, this theory constituted a real challenge to those in the British Isles and elsewhere (his treatise was soon to be translated into German) who still toyed with Aristotle's theory of imitation in their attempt to construct a more comprehensive aesthetic theory of music.

AN

E S S A Y

ON

MUSICAL EXPRESSION

PART I.

SECT. I.

On the Force and Effects of MUSIC.

As the public Inclination for Music seems every Day advancing, it may not be amiss, at this Time, to offer a few Observations on that delightful Art; such Observations, I mean, as may be chiefly applicable to the present Times: such as may tend to correct any Errors that have arisen, either in the Composition, or the Practice of Music.[1]

IF we view this Art in it's Foundations, we shall find, that by the Constitution of Man it is of mighty Efficacy in working both

—————— ◊ ——————

1. Avison confirms what we know from other sources about a steady increase in the amateur public for the arts in the eighteenth century, especially in England. In his treatise he tries to meet the needs of such a public, without overly engaging in technical matters. An aesthetic approach, based on comparisons among the arts, is again enlisted in order to communicate on a level intelligible to those who wish to understand what they already enjoy. Avison's approach has led to other kinds of discourses related to the understanding of music, such as Burney's and Hawkins' historical treatises, whose aim was, likewise, to enlighten the amateur, as Lipking has pointed out (1970: 211-324).

on his Imagination and his Passions. The Force of *Harmony*, or
Melody alone, is wonderful on the Imagination. *A full Chord*
struck, or a beautiful Succession of *single Sounds* produced, is no
less ravishing to the Ear, than just Symmetry or exquisite Colours
to the Eye.[2]

THE Capacity of receiving Pleasure from these musical Sounds,
is, in Fact, a peculiar and internal Sense; but of a much more
refined Nature than the external Senses: for in the Pleasures arising from our internal Sense of Harmony, there is no prior
Uneasiness necessary, in order to our tasting them in their full
Perfection; neither is the Enjoyment of them attended either with
Languor or Disgust. It is their peculiar and essential Property, to
divest the Soul of every unquiet Passion, to pour in upon the
Mind, a silent and serene Joy, beyond the Power of Words to
express, and to fix the Heart in a rational, benevolent, and happy
Tranquility.[3]

BUT, though this be the natural Effect of *Melody* or *Harmony*
on the Imagination, when simply considered; yet when to these

——————— ✍ ———————

2. At the beginning of the seventeenth century, Bacon had already pointed out some
kinesthetic relationships, referring to basic perceptual constituents (Bacon 1963: 388).
Avison seems to allude to the same idea, emphasizing not the constituents but their
resulting effects. Thus, by referring to an effect as "ravishing," he reveals the root of
metaphor while exemplifying its bridging role in the arts. Indeed, metaphor served as
a major tool in philosophical treatments which attempted to understand the arts
through comparisons among them. Nowadays, serious attempts are made to better
understand the connection between metaphor and its psychological effects in order to
gain insight into the problem of creative thought altogether (Miall 1987; Hausman
1989).

3. The idea that the capacity for aesthetic pleasure depends on a peculiar internal
sense—on a certain power of the mind to recognize what raises certain kinds of
ideas—is undoubtedly derived from Hutcheson. Hutcheson, in turn, based his argument partially on Shaftesbury's conception of harmony, which excluded imitation from
aesthetic discussion. Hence, it is not surprising that Avison, whose major concerns center on the activity of music making, adopts this basic Platonistic approach. Given the
fact that the musician is invariably concerned with integrating distinct components into
coherent forms, partially using acquired techniques and partially relying on his sensi-
bilities, Avison was in no need of the kind of arguments which Harris raised concerning imitation. However, the lesson learned from the aesthetic approach which relies
on the "real" senses, like that of Harris, could have supplied him with the *perceptual*
conditions under which the "inner" sense operates in its various manifestations.

is added the Force of *musical Expression*, the Effect is greatly increased; for then they assume the Power of exciting all the most agreeable Passions of the Soul. The force of Sound in alarming the Passions is prodigious. Thus, the Noise of Thunder, the Shouts of War, the Uproar of an enraged Ocean, strike us with Terror: so again, there are certain Sounds natural to Joy, others to Grief, or Despondency, others to Tenderness and Love; and by hearing *these*, we naturally sympathize with those who either *enjoy* or *suffer*. Thus Music, either by imitating these various Sounds in due Subordination to the Laws or *Air* and *Harmony*, or by any other Method of Association, bringing the Objects of our Passions before us (especially when those Objects are determined, and made as it were visibly, and intimately present to the Imagination by the Help of Words) does naturally raise a Variety of Passions in the human Breast, similar to the Sounds which are expressed: and thus, by the Musician's Art, we are often carried into the Fury of a Battle, or a Tempest, we are by turns elated with Joy, or sunk in pleasing Sorrow, roused to Courage, or quelled by grateful Terrors, melted into Pity, Tenderness, and Love, or transported to the Regions of Bliss, in an Extacy of divine Praise.[4]

But beyond this, I think we may venture to assert, that it is the peculiar Quality of Music to raise the *sociable and happy Passions*, and to *subdue* the *contrary ones*. I know it has been generally believed and affirmed, that it's Power extends alike to every Affection of the Mind. But I would offer it to the Consideration of the Public, whether this is not a general and fundamental Error. I would appeal to any Man, whether ever he found himself urged to acts of selfishness, Cruelty, Treachery, Revenge, or Malevolence by the Power of musical Sounds? Or if

——————— ☙ ———————

4. Here again Avison relies on an argument which he owes Hutcheson. Hutcheson speaks of "another source of beauty in music, related to expression" which he primarily associates with "sympathy," i.e., with the readiness of the mind to relate emotionally to that which it encounters. This readiness, which is related to the capacity to activate the passions, is also treated as a natural given, preventing Avison from inquiring into the processes it involves, whether with regard to the receptive soul or their implications in the arts.

he ever found Jealousy, Suspicion, or Ingratitude engendered in his Breast, either from Harmony or Discord? I believe no Instance of this Nature can be alledged with Truth. It must be owned, indeed, that the Force of Music may urge the *Passions* to an Excess, or it may fix them on false and improper Objects, and may thus be pernicious in it's Effects: but still the Passions which it Raises, though they may be misled or *excessive*, are of the benevolent and social Kind, and in their Intent at least are disinterested and noble.[a]

As I take this to be the Truth of the Case, so it seems to me no difficult Matter to assign a sufficient Reason for it: We have already seen that it is the natural Effect of air or Harmony to throw the Mind into a pleasurable State: And when it hath obtained this State, it will of course exert those Powers, and be susceptible of those Passions which are the most natural and agreeable to it. Now these are altogether of the benevolent Species; inasmuch as we know that the contrary Affections, such as Anger, Revenge, Jealousy, and Hatred, are always attended with Anxiety and Pain: Whereas all the various Modifications of Love, whether human or divine, are but so many kinds of immediate Happiness. From this View of Things therefore it necessarily follows, that every Species of musical Sound must tend to dispel the malevolent Passions, because they are *painful*; and nourish those which are benevolent, because they are *pleasing*.[5]

---

a. Lest the two Passions above-mentioned, of *Terror* and *Grief*, should be thought an Exception to this Rule, it may not be improper to remark as to the first, that the *Terror* raised by *Musical Expression*, is always of that grateful Kind, which arises from an Impression of something terrible to the Imagination, but which is immediately dissipated, by a subsequent Conviction, that the Danger is entirely imaginary: Of the same Kind is the Terror raised in us, when we stand near the Edge of a Precipice, or in sight of a tempestuous Ocean, or, are present at a tragical Representation on the Stage: In all these Cases, as in that of musical Expression, the sense of our *Security* mixes itself with the terrible Impressions, and melts them into a very sensible Delight. As to the second Instance, that of Grief, it will be sufficient to observe, that as it always has something of the social Kind for it's Foundation, so it is often attended with a Kind of Sensation, which may with Truth be called *pleasing*.

--------- *心* ---------

5. Avison's argument that music raises only "the sociable and happy passions" rests on his earlier assumption that melody and harmony "throw the mind into a pleasurable state." All the passions connected with malevolence are thus excluded by definition

(CONT.)

THE most general and striking Instance of the Power of Music, perhaps, that we know of, is that related of the *Arcadians* by POLYBIUS, in the fourth Book of his History; which, as it expressly coincides with the Subject in Question, I shall venture to give the Reader entire.

THIS judicious Historian, speaking of the Cruelties exercised upon the *Cynaethians* by the *Aetolians*, and the little Compassion that their Neighbours had shewn them; after having described the Calamities of this People, abhorred by all *Greece*, adds the following Remarks:

"As the *Arcadians* are esteemed by the *Greeks*, not only for the Gentleness of their Manners, their Beneficence and Humanity toward Strangers, but also for their Piety to the Gods; it may not be amiss to examine, in few Words, with Regard to the Ferocity of the *Cynaethians*, how it is possible, being incontestible *Arcadians* from their Origin, they are become so much distinguished by their Cruelty, and all Manner of Crimes, from the other *Greeks* of this Time. I believe, it can only be imputed to their having been the first and sole People of all the *Arcadians*, who were estranged from the laudable Institutions of their Ancestors, founded upon the natural Wants of those who inhabit *Arcadia*.

"THE Study of Music (I mean that which is worthy the Name) has its Utility every-where; but it is absolutely necessary among the *Arcadians*. For we must not adopt the Sentiment of *Ephorus*, who, in the Beginning of his Writings, advances this Proposition unworthy of him: *That Music is introduced amongst Men, as a Kind of Inchantment, only to deceive and mislead them.* Neither should we imagine that it is without Reason, that the ancient People of *Crete* and *Lacedemon* have preferred the Use of soft

―――――― *un* ――――――

(CONT.)

from the sphere of music. All this, as noted earlier, harks back to Shaftesbury. Nonetheless, Avison believes that music can be misused when applied to improper objects (hence acknowledging music's designative powers) or when it urges the passions to excess. Thus he agrees with the Greek view according to which music should be employed with care, without, however, blaming the content of music for its possible undesirable effects. The "benevolence" Avison ascribed to music reverberates in the writings of the entire group we are dealing with, though later thinkers tried to explicate some of its underlying assumptions and implications more systematically.

Music in War, to that of the Trumpet; or, that the *Arcadians*, in establishing their Republic, although in other Respects extremely austere in their Manner of Living, have shewn to Music so high a Regard, that they not only teach this art to their Children, but even compel their Youth to a Study of it to the Age of Thirty. These Facts are notoriously Known. It is also known, that the *Arcadians* are almost the only People, among whom their Youth, in obedience to the Laws, habituate themselves from their Infancy, to sing *Hymns* and *Peans*, as is usual among them, to the Honour of the Gods and Heroes of their Country. They are likewise taught the Airs of *Philoxenus* and *Timotheus*; after which, every Year during the Feasts of *Bacchus*, this Youth are divided into two Bands, the one consisting of Boys, the other of their young Men, who, to the Music of Flutes, dance in their Theatres with great Emulation, celebrating those Games which take their Names from each Troop. Even in their Assemblies and Parties of Pleasure, the *Arcadians* divert themselves less in Conversation, or relating of Stories, than in singing by Turns, and inviting each other reciprocally to this Exercise. It is no disgrace with Them, to own their Ignorance of other Arts: But they cannot deny their Ability in Singing, because, at all Events, they are necessitated to acquire this Talent; nor, in confessing their Skill, can they exempt themselves from giving Proofs of it, as that would be deemed amongst them a particular Infamy. Besides this, at the Care and Expence of the Public, their Youth are trained in Dancing and military Exercises, which they perform to the Music of Flutes; and every Year give Proof of their Abilities in the Presence of their Fellow-Citizens.

"Now it seems to me, that the first Legislators, in forming such kind of Establishments, have not had any Design of introducing Luxury and Effeminacy; but that they have chiefly had in view the Way of Living among the *Arcadians*, which their manual and toilsome Exercises rendered extremely laborious and severe; and the austere Manners of this People, to which the Coldness and Severity of the air in almost every Part of *Arcadia*, did greatly contribute.

"FOR it is natural to partake of the Quality of this Element. Thence it is, that different People, in Proportion to the Distance which separates them, differ from each other, not only in their exterior Form and Colour, but also in their Customs and Employments. The Legislators, therefore, willing to soften and temper this Ferocity and Ruggedness of the *Arcadians*, made all those Regulations which I have here mentioned, and instituted besides these, various Assemblies and Sacrifices, as well for the Men, as for the Women; and also Dances for their Children of both Sexes. In a Word, they contrived all Kinds of Expedients to soften and asswage, by this Culture of their Manners, the natural Rudeness and Barbarity of the *Arcadians.*

"BUT the *Cynaethians*, who inhabit the most rude and savage Parts of *Arcadia*, having neglected all those Helps, of which, on that Account, they had so much the more Occasion; and being, on the contrary, subject to mutual Divisions and Contests, they are, at length, become so fierce and barbarous, that there is not a City in *Greece*, where such frequent and enormous Crimes are committed, as in That of *Cynaethe.*

"AN Instance of the unhappy State of this People, and of the Aversion of all the *Arcadians* to their Form of Government, is the Treatment that was shewn to their Deputies which they sent to the *Lacedemonians* after the horrible Massacre in *Cynaethe.* In all the Towns of *Arcadia* which these Deputies entered, immediate Notice was give by an Herald, that they should instantly depart. But the Inhabitants of *Mantinea*, after the Departure of these Envoys, went so far, as to purify themselves by expiatory Sacrifices, and to carry the Victims round the City and it's Territories, to purify both the one and the other.

"WE have related all these things; First, that other Cities may be prevented from censuring in general the Customs of the *Arcadians*; or, lest some of the People of *Arcadia* themselves, upon false Prejudices, that the Study of Music is permitted them only as a superficial Amusement, should be prevailed upon to neglect this Part of their Discipline: in the second Place, to engage the *Cynaethians*, if the Gods should permit, to humanize and soften their Tempers, by an Application to the liberal Arts, and especially to Music. For this is the only Means, by which, they can ever be dispossessed of that Ferocity which they have contracted."[b6]

STILL farther to confirm what is here advanced on the Power of Music in raising the social and nobler Passions only, I will transcribe a Passage from the celebrated *Baron de* MONTESQUIEU

THIS learned and sensible Writer, animadverting on the severe Institutions of the Ancients in regard to Manners, having referred to several Authorities among the *Greeks* on this Head, particularly to the Relation of POLIBIUS above quoted, proceeds thus—"In the *Greek* Republics the Magistrates were extremely embarrassed. They would not have the Citizens apply themselves to Trade, to Agriculture, or to the Arts; and yet they would not have them idle. They found therefore, Employment for them in Gymnastic and military Exercises, and none else were allowed by their Institution. Hence the *Greeks* must be considered as a society of Wrestlers and Boxers. Now these exercises having a natural Tendency to render People hardy and fierce, there was a Necessity for tempering them with others that might soften their Manners. For this Purpose, Music, which influences the Mind by means of corporeal Organs, was extremely Proper. It is a kind of Medium between the bodily Exercises that render Men fierce and hardy, and speculative Sciences that render them unsociable and sour. It cannot be said that Music inspired Virtue, for this would

---

b. See *Dissertation où l'on fait voir, que les merveilleux effets, attribuez à la Musique des Anciens, ne prouvent point qu'elle fût aussi parfaite que la nôtre. Par M.* Burette. *Memoirs de Litterature, tirez des Registres de L'Academie Royale des Inscriptions & Belles Lettres. Tom. septieme,* whence the above Fragment of POLYBIUS is translated.
In the fifth, seventh, and eleventh Vols. of the *Holland* Edition of this Collection, the Reader will find several entertaining and curious Tracts on the Subject of Music.

6. Avison's example of the Arcadians as members of a civilized society brings to the fore the role of culture. Using the liberal arts, especially music, as socializing agents, guarantees proper manners and inhibits anti-social behavior. Avison differs from the Greek view concerning musical education not in content but in emphasis; he emphasizes the social benefits of music and its value for the society more than its character-forming contribution to the individual. For the Greeks, the value of music was strongly related to metaphysical assumptions of world harmony. Though relying on the Greeks, Avison, like so many of his century, dispensed with their metaphysics, even in its soft Shaftesburian version, ushering in cognitive and sociological arguments instead.

be inconceivable: But it prevented the Effects of a savage Institution, and inabled the Soul to have such a Share in the Education, as it could never have had without the Assistance of Harmony.

"LET us suppose among ourselves a Society of Men, so passionately fond of Hunting, as to make it their sole Employment; these People would doubtless contract a kind of Rusticity and Fierceness. But if they happened to receive a Taste for Music, we should quickly perceive a sensible Difference in their Customs and Manners. In short, the Exercises used by the *Greeks* excited only one Kind of Passions, *viz.* Fierceness, Anger, and Cruelty. But Music excites them all; it is able to inspire the Soul with a Sense of Pity, Lenity, Tenderness, and Love. Our moral Writers, who declaim so vehemently against the Stage, sufficiently demonstrate the Power of Music over the Soul.

"If the Society above-mentioned were to have no other Music than that of Drums and the Sound of the Trumpet, would it not be more difficult to accomplish this End, than by the more melting Tones of softer Harmony? The Antients were therefore in the Right, when under particular Circumstances they preferred one Mode to another in regard to Manners.

"But some will ask, why should Music be pitched upon preferable to any other Entertainment? It is, because of all sensible Pleasures there is none that less corrupt the Soul."[c]

THE Fact the Baron speaks of, seems to confirm what is here said on the Power of Music: for we see that Music was applied by the *Greeks* to awaken the nobler Passions only, such as Pity, Lenity, Tenderness, and Love. But should a State apply Music to give a Roughness of Manners, or inspire the contrary Passions of Hardheartedness, Anger, and Cruelty, it would certainly miss it's Aim; notwithstanding that the Baron seems to suppose the contrary. For he hath not alledged any Instance, or any Kind of Proof in Support of his Supposition. It is true, as he observes in the second Paragraph, that the Sound of Drums or Trumpets, would

---

c. Spirit of Laws, Vol. 1. p. 56.

have a different Effect from the more melting Tones of softer Harmony: Yet still, the Passions raised by these martial Sounds are of the *social* Kind: They may excite Courage and Contempt of Death, but never Hatred or Cruelty.[7]

S E C T I I.

On the Analogies between MUSIC and PAINTING.

From this short Theory we should now proceed to offer a few Observations relating to Composition.

But as musical Composition is known to very few besides the Professors and Composers of Music themselves; and as there are several Resemblances, or Analogies between this Art and that of *Painting*, which is an Art much more Obvious in its Principles, and therefore more generally known; it may not be amiss to draw out some of the most striking of these Analogies; and by this Means, in some Degree at least, give the common Reader an idea of musical Composition.[8]

——————— ◡ ———————

7. Avison's emphasis on the social aspects of music is not surprising in a century busy defining culture and the role of culture in different societies. An awareness that there is a variety of civilizations, opened the road to epistemological questions not entertained before. Avison enlists Montesquieu since the latter was undoubtedly one of the most prominent political theorists to tackle both the social and cultural issues at the time. Indeed, Montesquieu's views became central to Avison's argument: (1) He regarded music (and the liberal arts by extension) as a social mediator between the asocial activities of either the body or the mind (working separately). He seems to refer to the sharedness of musical experience. (2) He correlated the harmony of music, in its artistic sense, with that of social harmony, which stands in opposition to savage behavior. He seems to have entertained the possibility of transferring structures from one domain to another. And last but not least, (3) he viewed music as partaking in the customs and manners which effect the differences among societies and cultures. Avison clearly was in tune with all of these views, differing on only one minor point: Even the martial music of drums and trumpets, Avison believed, was of a positive, "social kind," though it can be abused through improper activation.

8. See fn. 1. It is interesting that Avison enlists painting rather than poetry to elucidate music. Painting, as far as he is concerned, is "more obvious in its principles." This argument is of the same kind as the ones we have encountered in Jacob and Harris with regard to 'universality' and 'immediacy' (Harris fn. 8). As already noted, in the course of the century it will become clear that painting is not as obvious as they

(CONT.)

The chief Analogies or Resemblances that I have observed between these two noble Arts are as follow:

I*st*, THEY are both founded in Geometry, and have Proportion for their Subject. And though the Undulations of Air, which are the immediate Cause of Sound, be of so subtile a Nature, as to escape our Examination; yet the Vibrations of musical *Strings* or *Chords*, from whence these Undulations proceed, are as capable of Mensuration, as any of those visible Objects about which Painting is conversant.

2*dly*, As the Excellence of a Picture depends on three Circumstances, *Design, Colouring*, and *Expression*; so in Music, the Perfection of Composition arises from *Melody, Harmony*, and *Expression*. Melody, or Air, is the Work of Invention, and therefore the Foundation of the other two, and directly analagous to *Design* in Painting. Harmony gives Beauty and Strength to the established Melodies, in the same Manner as Colouring adds Life to a just Design. And, in both Cases, the Expression arises from a Combination of the other two, and is no more than a strong and proper Application of them to the intended Subject.[d]

3*rdly*, As the proper Mixture of Light and Shade (called by the *Italians Chiaro-Oscuro*) has a noble Effect in Painting, and is,

---

d. *Melody* thus distinguished as the Foundation of a musical Composition, and compared to *Design* in Painting, hath been thought by some a vague and indeterminate Analogy; because *Harmony*, rather than *Melody*, ought to be esteemed the highest Excellence of every musical Work: yet, though this be admitted, it may still justly be said, that *Melody* is, in Reality, the *Ground-Work*, as it is the *first Principle* which engages the Composer's Attention

(CONT.)

——— ♫ ———

(CONT.)

thought it to be. The comparison between music and painting seems to be suggestive from another aspect: the fact that the two arts do not share any "literal" constituents — as does music with poetry — turns the comparison into a more clear-cut analogy. One of the first to utilize a comparison between music and painting was Zarlino. Arguing for variety of consonances, he says that "just as the sight of a picture is more delightful to the eye when it is painted with various colors than when it is painted with one color only, so the ear takes more pleasure and delight in the varied consonances which the more diligent composer puts into compositions, than in the simple and unvaried." (Strunk, vol. ii, p. 45). Notice that it is again the *immediate* perceptual values that are at stake in this comparison, pointing again to some kind of synaesthetic relation.

indeed, Essential to the Composition of a good Picture; so the judicious Mixture of Concords and Discords is equally essential to a musical Composition: as Shades are necessary to relieve the Eye, which is soon tired and digusted (sic) with a level Glare of Light; so discords are necessary to relieve the Ear, which is otherwise immediately satiated with a continued and unvaried Strain of Harmony. We may add (for the Sake of those who are in any Degree acquainted with the Theory of Music) that the *Preparations* and *Resolutions* of Discords, resemble the soft Gradations from Light to Shade, or from Shade to Light in Painting.

4*thly,* As in Painting there are three various Degrees of Distances established, *viz.* the *Fore-Ground,* the *intermediate Part,* and the *Off-Skip;* so in Music there are three different Parts strictly similar to these, *viz.* the Bass (or Fore-Ground), the Tenor (or intermediate), and the Treble (or Off-Skip). In Consequence of this, a musical Composition without its Bass, is like a Landscape without its Fore-Ground; without its Tenor it Resembles a Landscape deprived of its intermediate Part; without its Treble, it is analagous to a Landscape deprived of its Distance, or Off-Skip. We know how imperfect a Picture is, when deprived of any of these Parts; and hence we may form a Judgment of those who determine on the Excellence of any musical Composition, without seeing or hearing it in all it's Parts, and understanding their Relation to each other.

5*thly,* As in Painting, especially in the nobler Branches of it, and particularly in History-Painting, there is a principal Figure which is most remarkable and conspicuous, and to which all the other Figures are referred and subordinate; so, in the greater Kinds of musical Composition, there is a principal or leading *Subject,* or Succession of Notes, which ought to prevail, and be

(CONT.)

Thus, to strike out a *musical Subject,* and to carry it into *various Melodies,* may be compared to the *first Sketches* or *Out-Lines* in a Picture; (*this, I conceive, is what the Painters call Design*) and thence these *leading Principles* may be called the *Foundation* of every finished Piece in either of the Arts.

Therefore, wherever I speak of Harmony, in the Course of this Essay, I do not consider it as the first, but most important Circumstance which adorns, and supports the whole Performance.

heard through the whole Composition; and to which, both the Air and Harmony of the other Parts ought to be in like Manner referred and subordinate.

6thly, So again, as in Painting a Groupe of Figures, Care is to be had, that there be no Deficiency in it; but that a certain Fulness or Roundness be preserved, such as *Titian* beautifully compared to a Bunch of Grapes; so, in the nobler Kinds of musical Composition, there are several inferior Subjects, which depend on the Principal: And here the several Subjects (as in Painting the Figures do) are, as it were, to *sustain* and *support* each other: And it is certain, that if any one of these be taken away from a skillful Composition, there will be found a Deficiency highly disagreeable to an experienced Ear. Yet this does not hinder, but there may be perfect Composition two, three, four, or more Parts, in the same Manner as a Groupe may be perfect, though consisting of a smaller, or greater number of Figures. In both Cases, the Painter or Musician varies his Disposition according to the Number of Parts or Figures, which he includes in his Plan.

7thly, As in viewing a Picture, you ought to be removed to a certain Distance, called the Point of Sight, at which all its Parts are seen in their just Proportions; so, in a Concert, there is a certain Distance, at which the Sounds are melted into each other, and the various Parts strike the Ear in their proper Strength and Symmetry. To stand close by a Bassoon, or Double-Bass, when you hear a Concert, is just as if you should plant your Eye close to the Fore-Ground when you view a Picture; or, as if in surveying a spacious Edifice, you should place yourself at the Foot of a Pillar that supports it.

Lastly, THE various *Styles* in Painting —the grand—the terrible—the graceful—the tender—the passionate—the joyous—have all their respective Analogies in Music. — And we may add, in consequence of this, that as the Manner of Handling differs in Painting, according as the Subject varies; so, in Music, there are various Instruments suited to the different Kinds of musical Compositions, and particularly adapted to, and expressive of its several Varieties. Thus, as the rough handling is proper for Battles, Sieges, and whatever is great or terrible; and, on the contrary, the softer handling, and more finished Touches, are expressive of Love, Tenderness, or Beauty: So, in Music, the Trumpet, Horn, or Kettle-Drum, are most properly employed on the first of these Subjects, the Lute or Harp on the last. There is a short Story in the TATLER,[e] which illustrates this Analogy very prettily. Several eminent Painters are there represented in Picture as Musicians, with those Instruments in their Hands which most aptly represent their respective Manner in Painting.[9]

---

e. No. 153.

--- ♫ ---

9. Section I discusses Avison's theory concerning the "agreeable benevolence" of music. The theory provides the basis for section II in which he tries to teach uninformed music lovers in "eight easy lessons" something about the mysterious intricacies of music. Like a good teacher, he utilizes what his students either already know or are likely to grasp easily, in order to impart, by analogy, something that would require much more knowledge were it handled unto itself. His aim is to demystify his students, not to turn them into knowledgeable musicians; he hopes to buttress their appreciation for music by a general aesthetic conception of the working of the art.

Thus "Proportion," in lesson i, replaces the loaded concept of 'Harmony,' providing the common foundation for both arts — painting and music. Proportion in art, in lesson ii, is achieved through a perfect construction initiated by "invention" (design/melody) supported by technique (color/harmony) and resulting (in both music and painting) in the desired expression. "Perfection," lesson three teaches, may be highlighted through antitheses, which contrary to expectations, serves to reinforce the thesis, i.e., perfection.

Whereas lesson ii dealt with the constructive stages of the work of art, lesson iv discusses the artistic layers to be discerned in the finished work — from the immediate to the hidden, from the frontal to that in the background — adding a spatial dimension to the finished work. Lesson iv, in fact, exposes the major strategy which enables the creation of both artistic focal points (discussed in lesson v), as well as the relative weight of each of the various artistic elements in its contribution to the work as a whole (discussed in lesson vi). The "point of sight," (discussed in lesson vii), is a point of distance, at which the various factors, previously discussed, fuse. At this point, the elements of sound (by analogy) "melt into each other," making the constructive seams unnoticeable, thus allowing for an unimpaired impact of the construction as a whole. Lesson viii, which discusses the variety of styles, highlights the compatibilities between artistic "manner" and subject matter anchored, as they are in cultural convention.

Though Avison's comparisons are mostly oversimplified and even at times forced, he manages to impart an awareness of important aesthetic issues to his readers. Moreover, he creates a venue for metaphorical interactions among the arts by noting a similarity between functions, e.g. the functions of color in painting and harmony in music, of

(CONT.)

. . .

SECT. III.

On MUSICAL EXPRESSION, so far as it relates to the COMPOSER.

So much concerning the two Branches of Music, Air and *Harmony.* LET us now consider the third Circumstance, which is *Expression.* This, as hath been already observed, "arises from a Combination of the other two; and is no other than a strong and proper Application of them to the intended Subject."

FROM this Definition it will plainly appear, that Air and Harmony, are never to be deserted for the Sake of Expression: Because Expression is founded on them. And if we should attempt any Thing in defiance of these, it would cease to be *Musical Expression.* Still less can the horrid Dissonance of Cat-

——————— ♫ ———————

(CONT.)

space in paintings and sonoric layers in music . As far as music is concerned, Avison indeed succeeds in enabling us to conceptualize musical phenomena aesthetically, rather than as part of a practice. Altogether, the mapping of pictorial relationships on musical compositions, highlights both their immediate as well as their overall perceptual ingredients. The perceptual aspects, related to the process of hearing, remain outside the "picture," awaiting an analogy of a different kind.

It is pointless to argue with Avison over each and every one of the ideas expressed in his eight lessons. We would like to call attention, however, to one point, which reflects an important historical moment as far as music making is concerned. This moment, noted in our introduction to Avison, pertains to the debate concerning the precedence of melody over harmony, or vice versa, in the eighteenth century. Avison is clearly on the side of melody, otherwise why would he assign to melody the task of "design"? (See his fn d.)

It is interesting to note that Rousseau in his extended debate with Rameau, raised the same argument. In his *Essai sur l'orgine des langues* (pub. 1764) he added an important point, emphasizing that both melody and pictorial design (i.e. drawing) are the prime constituents of *meaning* in each of the arts respectively. However, this claim was strongly related, in his theory, to the idea of imitation, which Avison, as noted above, tried to dispense with.

Later in the treatise Avison explicitly advocates compositions in which melody reigns supreme. Still, the issue of melody vs. harmony gets confused, as the reader may well have noticed, in the discussion of the "fore-ground" vs. the "off-skip," relating the part of the bass to the former and that of the treble to the latter. At any rate, his position, whatever it was, did not prevent him from being a great admirer of Rameau.

Calls deserve this Appellation, though the Expression or Imitation be ever so strong and natural.

AND, as Dissonance and shocking Sounds cannot be called musical Expression; so neither do I think, can mere Imitation of several other Things be entitled to this Name, which, however, among the generality of Mankind hath often obtained it. Thus the gradual rising or falling of the Notes in a long Succession, is often used to denote Ascent or Descent, broken Intervals, to denote an interrupted Motion, a number of quick Divisions, to describe Swiftness or Flying, Sounds resembling Laughter, to describe Laughter; with a Number of other Contrivances of a parallel Kind, which it is needless here to mention. Now all these I should chuse to stile Imitation, rather than Expression; because, it seems to me, that their Tendency is rather to fix the Hearers attention on the Similitude between the Sounds and the Things which they describe, and thereby to excite a reflex Act of the understanding, than to affect the Heart and raise the Passions of the Soul.

HERE then we see a Defect or Impropriety, similar to those which have been above observed to arise from a too particular Attachment either to the *Modulation* or *Harmony*. For as in the first case, the Master often attaches himself so strongly to the Beauty of *Air* or Modulation, as to neglect the *Harmony*; and in the second Case, pursues his Harmony or Fugues so as to destroy the beauty of Modulation; so in this third Case, for the sake of a forced, and (if I may so speak) an unmeaning Imitation, he neglects both Air and Harmony, on which alone true musical Expression can be founded.[10]

———— ⳗ ————

10. In the last two paragraphs, Avison makes an interesting distinction between 'similitude' and 'expression,' challenging the theory of imitation. While similitude, Avison tells us, aims at a "reflex act of understanding" through the likeness "between the sounds and the things which they describe," musical expression, based on "air and harmony," aspires to "raise the passions of the soul." The role of music, Avison insists, is therefore not that of a passive designator causing the mind to recognize what it already knows, but that of an active agent—a mover of the passions of the soul.

There is nothing new in this assertion about the power of music. Members of the camerata, for example, more than a century earlier, were already insightful enough to sug-

(CONT.)

THIS Distinction seems more worthy our Notice at Present, because some very eminent Composers have attached themselves chiefly to the Method here mentioned; and seem to think they have exhausted all the Depths of Expression, by a dextrous Imitation of the Meaning of a few particular Words, that occur in the Hymns or Songs which they set to Music. Thus, were one of these Gentlemen to express the following Words of *Milton*,

——Their Songs
Divide the Night, and lift our Thoughts to Heav'n

It is highly probable, that upon the Word *divide*, he would run a *Division* of half a Dozen Bars; and on the subsequent Part of

———— ℘ ————

(CONT.)

gest that even the passions reside in the mind.(see Vol. I, Chapter 1) Still, what is new in Avison's treatise is the context in which it appears. In sections II of part I Avison tells us that air (melody) is an invention lending "design" to a musical composition, whereas harmony brings out its particular "coloring." Musical expression, in other words, resides in *bringing* about that perfect match between invention and a particular kind of "doing." An interesting equation results from this argument: In fn. 9 we saw that it is *proportion* achieved through the same relations, implying that for Avison 'proportion' and 'expression' are synonymous! Remember that Jacob transferred harmony from music to poetry and painting as a "*Lucina*"—the goddess of birth who assists the creative act. This assistance consisted of an ideal of coherence, according to which the artist molds his artistic materials. That proportion should function as a synonym for harmony is more readily understood than its functioning as a synonym for expression. By identifying proportion with expression one replaces a property related to the *object* with a property related to the *mind*.

Avison, it seems, was perhaps the first among the British (later thinkers repeated his arguments time and again) to maintain that simple musical imitation—"madrigalism" in its pejorative sense—is unartistic. Though Avison reinforces Vincenzo Galilei's arguments, he ironically related expression to an artistic ideal which Galilei attacked, i.e., harmony. Unlike Galilei, who recommended the transfer of some *practical* expressive techniques from the theatre to music, Avison utilizes extra-musical fields for *theoretical* needs only; the expressive in music, as far as Avison is concerned belongs exclusively to the realm of music.

As we have argued in Vol. I, it is because of the peculiar position of music in the theory of imitation that the whole notion of art residing in the making came to the fore. Avison's argument provides an example of the further development of that argument which eventually caused a shift of emphasis in the examination of art — from the relationship between Art and the objective world to a relationship between the different arts and their correlative perceptions.

the Sentence, he would not think he had done the Poet Justice, or *risen* to that *Height* of Sublimity which he ought to express, till he had climbed up to the very Top of his Instrument, or at least as far as a human Voice could follow him. And this would pass with a great Part of Mankind for musical Expression, instead of that noble Mixture of solemn Airs and various Harmony, which *indeed* elevates our Thoughts, and gives that exquisite Pleasure, which none but true Lovers of Harmony can feel.[11]

WERE it necessary, I might easily prove, upon general Principles, that what I now advance concerning Musical Imitation is strictly just; both, because Music as an imitative Art has *very confined Powers* , and because, when it is an ally to Poetry (which it ought always to be when it exerts its mimetic Faculty) it obtains its End *by raising correspondent Affections* in the Soul with those which ought to result from the Genius of the Poem. But this has been already shewn, by[f] a judicious Writer, with that Precision and Accuracy which distinguishes his Writings. To his excellent Treatise I shall, therefore, refer my Reader, and content Myself, in this Place, with adding two or three practical Observations by way of Corollary to his Theory.

1*st*, As *Music* passing to the Mind through the Organ of the Ear, can imitate only by[g] *Sounds and Motions*, it seems reasonable, that when *Sounds* only are the Objects of Imitation, the Composer ought to throw the mimetic Part entirely amongst the accompanying *Instruments*; because, it is probable, that the Imitation will be too powerful in the *Voice* which ought to be engaged in *Expression* alone; or, in other Words, in raising corre-

---

f. Vide three Treatises of *J.H.* the second concerning Poetry, Painting and Music.
g. Vide Page 57 in the above Treatise.

---

11. In line with his view concerning musical expression, Avison is bound to reject whatever might suggest that music is a kind of aggregate of sounds rather than a synthesis. Music works synthetically, Avison tells us, and only as such is music able to "lift our thoughts to Heav'n," i.e., to create the empathy that does justice to the words of poets.

spondent Affections with the Part.[h] Indeed, in some Cases, Expression will coincide with Imitation, and may then be admitted universally: as in such *Chromatic Strains* as are mimetic of the Grief and Anguish of the human Voice.[i] But to the Imitation of Sounds in the *natural* or *inanimate* World,[j] this, I believe, may be applied as a general Rule.

2*dly*, WHEN Music imitates *Motions*, the Rythm, and Cast of the Air, will generally require, that both the vocal and instrumental Parts coincide in their Imitation. But then, be it observed, that the Composer ought always to be more cautious and reserved when he applies this Faculty of Music to *Motion*, than when he applies it to Sound, and the Reason is obvious; the Intervals in Music are not so strictly similar to animate or inanimate Motions, as its Tones are to animate or inanimate Sounds. Notes ascending or descending by large Intervals, are not so like the stalking of a Giant,[k] as a Flow of even Notes are to the murmuring of a

---

h. I cannot bring a finer Illustration of my Meaning, than from the old Song in *Acis* and *Galatea*.

> Hush ye pretty warbling Quire,
> Your thrilling Strains
> Awake my Pains,
> And kindle soft Desire, &c.

Here the great Composer has very judiciously employed the vocal Part in the nobler Office of expressing, with Pathos, the plaintive Turn of the Words, while the Symphony and Accompanyment very chearfully imitates the Singing of *the warbling Quire*. But had Mr HANDEL admitted this *Imitation of Sound* into the vocal Part, and made it imitate the *thrilling Strains of the Birds* by *warbling Divisions*, it is manifest the Expression would have been injured; whereas, according to his Management of it, the *Imitation* greatly assists the Expression.

i. As to take Mr *H's* own example, the chorus of Baal's Priests in Deborah. *Doleful tidings how ye wound.*

j. Such as the Noise of Animals, the Roar of Thunder, Ocean, &c. The Murmur of Streams.

k. Mr *H.* has himself quoted a Passage in *Acis* and *Galatea*, *"See what ample strides he takes,"* as imitative of the *Walk* of *Polypheme*; but, I apprehend, the Majesty of that Air rather affected him by an *Association of Ideas*, than any great Similiarity in the Imitation.. An Association of this Kind, seems to have struck the Author of the *Paralele des Italiens et des François en ce qui regarde la Musique* "Pour la conformité (says he) de l'Air, avec le sens des paroles, je n'ay jamais rien entendu, en matiére de Symphonies, de comparable à celle qui fut exécutée à Rome, à l'oratoire de S. Jerôme de la Charité, le jour de la Saint Martin de l'année 1697, sur ces deux mots, *mille faette, mille flêches*: c'etoit un Air dont les Notes etoient pointées à la manière des Gigues; le caractère de cet Air imprimoit si vivement dans l'ame l'idée de fleche; et la force de cette idée seduisoit tellement l'Imagination, que chaque violon paroissoit être un arc; & tous les Archets, autant de flêches décochées, dont les pointes sembloient darder la Symphonie de toutes Parts; on ne sauroit entendre rien de plus ingenieux & de plus heureusement exprimé."

(CONT.)

Stream,[1] and little jiggish Slurrs are less like the Nod of *Alexander*,[m] than certain Shakes and Trills are to the Voice of the Nightingale.[n]

3dly, As Music can only imitate Motions and Sounds, and the *Motions* only imperfectly; it will follow, that musical Imitation ought never to be employed in representing Objects, of which

---

(CONT.)

We may learn from this, how far *musical Imitation,* simply considered, may amuse the Fancy of many who are less susceptible of the more delicate and refined Beauties of *Expression.* — The particular Felicity of the *Frenchman,* in the musical Performance here described, seems to have depended on this Similitude, *viz.* that every *Violin* appeared as a *Bow,* and all the *Bows,* like so many *Arrows shot off,* the *Points* of which, seemed to *dart* the Symphony through all it parts. Perhaps, so far as *Imitation* was necessary, his Observation might be just. But were this an Argument, that the business of *Imitation* was superior to every other in musical Composition, it would reduce the noblest Species of it, still lower than the *extravaganzi* of the instrumental Performances which we have noted in the Chapter on Modulation.

l. Here let me quote with Pleasure, the Air which Mr HANDEL has adapted to those charming Words of MILTON.
> Hide me from Day's garish Eye,
> While thee Bee, with honied Thigh,
> At her flow'ry Work does sing,
> And the Waters murmuring;
> With such Concert as they keep,
> Entice the dewy-feather'd Sleep.
> And let some strange mysterious Dream,
> Wave at his Wings in airy Stream
> Of lively Portraiture display'd,
> Softly on my Eyelids laid.
> Then, as I wake, sweet Music breath,
> Above, about, and underneath;
> Sent by some Spirit, to Mortals good,
> Or th'unseen Genius of the Wood.

Here the Air and the Symphony delightfully imitate the Humming of the Bees, the Murmuring of the Waters, and express the Ideas of Quiet and Slumber; but what, above all, demands this Eulogium, is the Master-stroke of accompanying the Voice with Trebles and Tenors, only till he comes to these Words, "Then, as I wake, sweet Music breath," where *the Bass begins* with an Effect that can be felt only, and not expressed.

I have chosen to give all my Illustrations on this Matter from the Works of Mr HANDEL, because no one has exercised this Talent more universally, and because these Instances must also be most universally understood.

m.   With ravish'd Ears,
>   The Monarch hears,
>   Assumes the God,
>   Affects to nod,
>   And seems to shake the Spheres.

In which air I am sorry to observe, that the *Affectation* of imitating this Nod, has reduced the Music as much below the Dignity of the Words, as *Alexander's* Nod was beneath that of *Homer's Jupiter.*

n. Vide il Penseroso.
>   Sweet Bird that shuns the Noise of Folly,
>   Most musical, most melancholy.

Motion or Sound are not the principal Constituents. thus, to Light, or Lightning, we annex the Property of Celerity of Motion; yet, it will not follow from thence, that an extremely swift Progression of Notes will raise the Idea of either one or the other; because, as we said, the Imitation must be, in these Cases, very partial.[o] Again, it is one Property of Frost to make Persons shake and tremble; yet, a tremulous Movement of Semitones, will never give the true Idea of Frost: though, perhaps, they may of a trembling Person.

4*thly*, As the Aim of Music is to affect the Passions in a pleasing Manner, and as it uses Melody and Harmony to obtain that End, its Imitation must never be employed on *ungraceful Motions*, or *disagreeable Sounds*; because, in the one Case, it must injure the *Melody* of the Air, and in the other, the *Harmony* of the Accompanyment; and in both Cases, must lose its Intent of affecting the Passions *pleasingly*.

5*thly*, As Imitation is only so far of use in Music, as when it aids the Expression; as it is only analogous to poetic Imitation, *when Poetry imitates* through mere natural Media,[p] so it should only be employed in the same Manner. To make the Sound eccho to the Sense in descriptive Lyric, and, perhaps, in the cooler Parts or epic Poetry is often a great Beauty; but, should the tragic Poet labour at shewing this Art in his most distressful Speeches; I suppose he would rather flatten than inspirit his Drama: In like Manner, the musical Composer, who catches at every particular[q] Epithet or Metaphor that the Part affords him, to shew his imitative Power, will never fail to hurt the true Aim of his Composition, and will always prove the more difficient in Proportion as his Author is more pathetic or sublime.[12]

---

o. What shall we say to excuse this same great Composer, who, in his Oratorio of *Joshua*, condescended to amuse the vulgar Part of his Audience by letting them *hear the Sun stand still*.

p. *H's* Treatises, p. 70.

q. To give but one Instance, how many Composers hath the single Epithet, WARBLING, misled from the true Road of Expression, like an *ignis fatuus*, and bemired them in a *Pun*?

---

12. In agreeing that music, as an imitative art, has "confined powers," Avison acknowledges his indebtedness to Harris. Moreover, both believe that to the extent that music exerts its mimetic powers, beyond the mere imitation of "sound by sound," it can only

(CONT.)

WHAT then is the Composer, who would aim at true musical Expression, to perform? I answer, he is to blend such an happy Mixture of Air and Harmony, as will affect us most strongly with the Passions or Affections which the Poet intends to raise: and

(CONT.) —————— ♍ ——————

raise *correspondent* affections. However, it should have already occurred to Harris that not only the passions which music is likely to raise require theoretical clarification, but the process which creates correspondences needs to be explained as well. In his five "practical observations" Avison makes an attempt in this direction. In observation 1 he appeals to his distinction between 'similitude' and 'expression' in the following way: Since similitude aims to be literal, it should be related to instruments. Expression, which aims to create a *correspondence*, should employ the human voice. As we shall see, Beattie and Smith repeat this argument but they understand it within a *symbolic* framework, attaching to each component different functions in the creation of the persuasive whole. Moreover, relying on Rousseau, Smith argues (not unlike Cone nowadays), that the accompaniment may function metaphorically as well, especially as the provider of a contextual atmosphere for the expressive agent.

From observation 2 it becomes clear that Avison is aware of the fact that correspondencies are effected through an "association of ideas" of the kind we would call metaphorical. Music, for example can only imitate "animate or inanimate sounds," says Avison, but not motion itself, for even motion requires the "association of ideas." Moreover, the effect thus created, can only be felt and not expressed. Now that he has revealed the "imperfection" of the imitation of motion, and since he has already (earlier in the treatise), discarded similitude from musical expression, it is hardly surprising that Avison should also reject in his third observation, objects which neither include motion nor sound as part of their *principle* constituents. (Twining will eventually explicate this point philosophically.) At any rate, observation 4 reminds us that music does not relate, altogether, to the objective world, for it affects the passions and this it should do without injuring either the melody or the harmony, i.e. the totality of the musical expression. In order to succeed, we are told in observation 5, music should aim to "echo the sense" of the words of the *entire* message, (an enterprise which Pope attributed to poetical rhyme in "Essay on Criticism," line 365) and not of *specific* words.

To summarize Avison's observations, we may draw a line which connects musical expressions to correspondent affections via the "association of ideas" — through the echoing relationship of sense, i.e., through the "general drift" of their communicative intent. Thus, the whole notion of correspondent musical affections amounts to a process whereby music — the general, benevolent, pleasant art — acquires specific meaning. Avison does not forget his previous contention and is ready to insist that musical meaning is circumscribed, for it should invariably strengthen rather than weaken the overall impact. How music goes about acquiring meanings — whether general or particular — is a complicated and highly important topic; it is to receive later on the full attention it deserves. Still, Avison's modest attempt is a contribution in the "right" direction (given hindsight) to this enormous topic.

that, on this Account, he is not principally to dwell on particular Words in the way of Imitation, but to comprehend the Poet's general Drift or Intention, and on this to form his Airs and Harmony, either by Imitation (so far as Imitation may be proper to this End) or by any other Means. But this I must still add, that if he attempts to raise the Passions by Imitation, it must be such a temperate and chastised Imitation, as rather brings the Object before the Hearer, than such a one as induces him to form a Comparison between the Object and the Sound. For, in this last Case, his Attention will be turned entirely on the Composer's art, which must effectually check the Passion. The Power of Music is, in this Respect, parallel to the Power of Eloquence: if it works at all, it must work in a secret and unsuspected Manner. In either Case, a pompous Display of Art will destroy its own Intentions: on which Account, one of the best general Rules, perhaps, that can be given for musical Expression, is that which gives Rise to the Pathetic in every other Art, *an unaffected Strain of Nature and Simplicity.*[r13]

THERE is no Doubt but many Rules may be deduced, both from the Compositions of the best Masters, and from Experience, in observing the Effects which various Sounds have upon the Imagination and Affections. And I don't know, whether the same Propriety, in regard to the Part of Expression in *Poetry,* may not

---

r. Whatever the State of Music may have been among the ancient *Greeks, &c.* or whether it was actually capable of producing those wonderful Effects related of it, we cannot absolutely determine; seeing all the uses of their *Enharmonic Scale* are totally lost; and of their musical Characters, which should have conveyed to us their Art, slender Traces any where to be found. From the Structure of their Instrument, we cannot form any vast Ideas of their Powers: ^AThey seem to have been far inferior to those in Use at present: but which, indeed, being capable of as much Execution as Expression, are only rendered more
(CONT.)

^ACALMET'S Dissertation sur la Musique des Anciens.

———— ᘓ ————

13. The composer's art is to elicit the "power of music," i.e. to create the desired musical expression. Once completed, however, the work should be free of the traces of the composer's labor in order to fulfill its function. To help his readers understand, Avison, the teacher, again resorts to an analogy—the power of eloquence. As we observed in Vol. I, rhetoric was still a widely held tradition in the eighteenth century and Avison could count on his readers to understand his concern with *acts of persuasion* which must conceal their "manipulative tricks" in order to succeed. His readers might have even noticed his allusion to Addison's identification of music's persuasive powers with "unsuspected eloquence":
(CONT.)

(CONT.)

liable to be abused. Thus, the too great Compass of our modern Instruments, tempting as well the Composer as Performer, to exceed the natural Bounds of Harmony, may be one reason why some Authors have so warmly espoused the Cause of the ancient Music, and run down that of the modern.[B]

I believe we may justly conclude, that the Force and Beauties of the ancient Music, did not consist so much in artful Compositions, or in any Superiority of Execution in the Performance: as in the pure Simplicity of its Melody; which being performed in Unisons, by their vast Chorusses of Voices and Instruments, no wonder the most prodigious Effects were produced.[C] Since the Time of GUIDO ARETINO,[D] the Laws and Principles of Harmony have been considerably enlarged, and by rendering this Art more intricate and complex, have deprived it of those plain, though striking Beauties, which, probably, almost every Hearer could distinguish and admire. And, I don't know whether this will not go some way, towards determining the Dispute concerning the superior Excellency of ancient

(CONT.)

[B]SIR WILLIAM TEMPLE'S, 1st Vol. Fol. p. 162.
[C] BONET, Histoire de la Musique.
[D]ARETINO lived in the eleventh century.

(CONT.)   ─────── ∽ ───────

Music can noble hints impart,
Engender fury kindle love;
With unsuspected eloquence can move,
and manage all the man with secret art.

["A Song for St. Cecilia Day" (in Addison 1914: 22)]

Avison, of course, was not the last among the British to utilize the analogy between music and rhetoric. In comparison to the Germans, however, the eighteenth-century British did not engage in particular analogies in the field of tropes and figures, an exercise that partially occupied them in the seventeenth century.]

Avison also objects to "pompous display" which should not be confused with musical expression. The latter may even be destroyed by such displays, for musical expression should at all times seem "unaffected." (This unaffectedness is related to the Renaissance principle of *facilità*, See Vol. I: 15) This point leads Avison to discuss some of the causes which, he believes, explain the "wonderful effects attributed to ancient Greek music (see his fn.). His argument proceeds as follows: Given the inferiority of their instruments and the absence of harmony, the Greeks must have performed their melodies in unison. Avison attributes the effects of Greek music, therefore, to the simplicity of its construction and to its weddedness to another art—poetry. The perfection of Greek music, in other words, was not solely its own. Music has in fact *progressed* since those distant days both in musical instruments as well as in musical means, e.g. harmony. Moreover, it has progressed from an adjunct status to a fully independent one, i.e., to the point of being able to create its own "perfection" without having to resort to external assistance. Despite music's progress, Avison, like Jacob, is cautious not to identify perfection with aesthetic value. Though music attached to language still largely dominates the scene in the eighteenth century, it is this century that witnessed the rise of pure instrumental music which incorporated "effects," both dramatic and lyrical. In fact, it is this independence which made possible the comparison of music to the other arts, contributing to the fruitfulness of aesthetic discussions.

as well be applied to *Musical Expression*; since there are discordant and harmonious Inflections of musical Sounds when united, and various Modes, or Keys, (besides the various Instruments themselves) which, like particular Words, or Sentences in writing, are very expressive of the different Passions, which are so powerfully excited by the Numbers of Poetry.[s][14]

(CONT.)

and modern Music. It is to be observed, that the Ancients, when they speak of its marvellous Effects, generally consider it as an adjunct to Poetry. Now, an Art in its Progress to its own absolute Perfection, may arrive at some intermediate Point, which is its Point of Perfection, considered as an Art joined to another Art; but not to its own, when taken separately. If the Ancients, therefore, carried Melody to its highest Perfection, it is probable they pushed the musical Art as far as it would go, considered as an Adjunct to Poetry: but Harmony is the Perfection of Music, as a single Science. Hence then we may determine the specific Difference between the ancient and modern Compositions, and consequently their Excellency.

s. "Soft is the Strain when *zephyr* gently Blows,
And the smooth Stream in smoother numbers Flows;
But when loud Surges lash the sounding Shore,
The hoarse, rough Verse should like the Torrent roar.
When Ajax strives some Rock's vast Weight to throw,
The Line too labours, and the Words move slow;
Not so, when swift Camilla scours the Plain,
Flies o'er the unbending Corn, and skims along the Main.
Hear how Timotheus vary'd Lays surprise,
And bid alternate Passions fall and rise!
While, at each Change, the Son of Libyan Jove,
Now burns with Glory, and then melts with Love:
Now his fierce Eyes with sparkling Fury glow,
Now sighs steal out, and Tears begin to flow:
Persians and Greeks like Turns of Nature found,
And the World's Victor stood subdu'd by Sound!
The Power of Music all our Hearts allow;
And what Timotheus was, is Dryden now.

Essay on Criticism

Perhaps, the Powers of Passion and Verse were never so happily exerted, for the Purpose of Music, as in this Ode: and, as happily hath the *Genius* of the *Composer*[A] been united with *That* of the *Poet.*

[A]Alexander's Feast, set to music by G.F. Handel.

———— ℆ ————

14. Like Jacob and Harris, Avison believes that the composer's art can be improved through practice of the art and the study of the works of great masters. Avison, however, also calls for an empirical observation of the "effects which various sounds have upon the imagination and affections." Moving from the art itself to its perception, enables Avison to entertain the possibility of a common dominator for expression in poetry and in music. What should be compared, in other words, is not poetry and music but the perception of their effects and their causes. Avison, thus, moves one step further towards an overall aesthetic theory. More particularly, Avison suggests in these paragraphs—in line with his former conception regarding the symbolic value of the chromatic scale—to view music "semantically," as a language capable of expressing the *different* passions.

Thus the *sharp* or *flat Key;* slow or lively Movements; the *Staccato;* the *Sostenute,* or smooth-drawn Bow; the striking *Diesis;*[t] all the Variety of Intervals, from a Semitone to a Tenth, &c; the various Mixtures of Harmonies, the Preparation of Discords, and their Resolution into Concords, the sweet Succession of Melodies; and several other Circumstances besides these, do all tend to give that Variety of Expression which elevates the Soul to Joy or Courage, melts it into Tenderness or Pity, fixes it in a rational Serenity, or raises it to the Raptures of Devotion.[15]

WHEN we consider the Fulness of Harmony, and Variety of Air which may be included in the Art of Composing *Fugues,* we may pronounce this Species of Composition, of all others, the most noble and diffusive; and which, like History-Painting, does not only contain the chief Excellencies of all the other Species, but is likewise capable of admitting many other Beauties of a superior Nature. But here, in the term *Fugue,* I do not include alone, those confined Compositions, which proceed by regular Answers, according to the stated Laws of Modulation, but chiefly, such as admit of a Variety of Subjects, particularly for Voices and Instruments united; and which, with their *Imitations, Reverses,* and other relative Passages, are conducted throughout the whole, in Subordination to their *Principal;* and, as the lesser Beauties or Decorations in Poetry, are subservient to the Fable of a Tragedy, or heroic Poem, so are these different, though kindred Airs, in the same Movement, in like Manner, subservient to some one principal Design and productive of all the

---

t. Or *Quarter Tone,* or less, if performed by the Voice or Violin, being an Interval in the *Enharmonic Scale* of the Ancients, and amazingly powerful in rousing the Passions.
This Interval is equally capable, in judicious Hands, of exciting Terror, Grief, Despondency, or the contrary Passions, in their Extremes; and the very wide Difference, in this Case, is chiefly produced from their different Accompanyments, and the particular Modulations in which they are employed.

———— ℘ ————

15. Avison now provides a series of examples of musical procedures which, when properly mixed, create the variety of musical expressions. It is to *these* that he attributes the power to "elevate the soul." Thus, at one and the same time, Avison manages to demystify the notion of the "powers" of music as well as to elevate the composer's art to the kind of "doing" which music involves.

Grandeur, Beauty, and Propriety, that can be expected from the most extensive Plan in the whole Range of musical Composition.[16]

BY a Diversity of Harmonies, the Chain and Progression of Melodies is also finely supported, and thence, a greater Variety of Expression will be found in the Construction of full Music: In this Case, the Composer hath the Advantage of throwing his tender and delicate Passages into the *Solo*, or those of a bolder Expression into the *Chorus*; and as there are oftentimes a Kind of *neutral* Airs, if I may so call them, which, by the Performer's Art, may be made expressive of very different Passions; or, as the same Words, by a Change in their Accent, convey a different Sense; so this musical Expression may be varied in such a Manner, that the same Passage, which has been heard alone, if repeated, may also be formed into *Chorus*; and *è contra*, the *Chorus* into *Solo*. In like Manner may be disposed the *Forte* and *Piano*.

WE may also here remark, that in ranging different Movements, in the same *Concerto*, or in other Suites of different Airs, the confined Order of keeping, in the Sequel of these, to one or two *Keys*, at most, produces but an irksome Monotony of Sounds: for it is not sufficient, that different Movements are of different Species; their Changes should also appear, as well in their *Keys*, as in their *Air:* and the Composer of Taste, will shew his Art in the Arangement of these *different Pieces*, as well as in his Variety of Modulation, or other Contrivances, in the *same Piece*.[u]

---

u. Such are the beautiful *Cantatas* of BATTISTA PERGOLESE, printed at *Naples* in the Year 1738. They are, perhaps, the most elegant Performances, in this Species of Composition, that have yet appeared.   (CONT.)

———— ⚘ ————

16. Avison distinguishes here between two different kinds of subordination. The first pertains to compositional techniques, e.g., fugal procedures, which follow their own rules of relative dominance and subservience. The second pertains to aesthetic considerations, which involve the subordination of the first to "the most extensive plan" of the musical composition. Like Jacob and Harris, Avison maintains that the different parts of a composition do not simply "add up" to create the whole; rather it is the *overall design* which dictates the hierarchical relations between the parts and determines their relative standing with regard to the composition as a whole. Avison's organic view of musical compositions is consistent with his synthetic view of musical expression (see fn. 11).

AND, as *Discords*, when judiciously managed, give their succeeding *Concords* a yet more pleasing Harmony; in like Manner some happy Contrivance in changing the Key of separate Movements, whether from *Flat* to *Sharp*, or *vice versa*, will still, in a higher degree, afford Relief and Pleasure to the hearer: many Alterations of this Kind may surely be affected without the least disagreeable Surprise; since we are not always delighted when the Modulation follows, as we naturally expect it, nor always shocked when *that* Expectation is disappointed.

THUS, by Contrivances of this Nature, we are charmed with an agreeable Variety, and which, perhaps, equally to the most striking *Air*, commands the Admiration of many Lovers of Music, who yet can no otherwise account for the Preference they may give to a fine Composition, than purely from the Pleasure it affords them. In fine, it is this masterly Taste and Method of Ranging, in beautiful Order, the distinguished Parts of a Composition, which gives the highest Delight to those who can enter into the real Merits of this Art: —A Circumstance, the musical Student would do well to consider, before he engages in any Trial of his Talent that Way. But, as Example is of much greater Force than any Rule or Precept whatever; I would recommend to him, a constant Perusal of the best Compositions in *Score*, where he will find all the Information he can desire on this Head.[v]

(CONT.)

The *Cantatas* of GIOVANNI BONOCINI, published in *London*, by Subscription, above thirty Years ago, are also very fine, and may still be called modern; though many Performers, who hear and see no farther than the most perishable Part of a Composition, have given them up to an exploded Taste: nevertheless, I shall venture to say, that the *Airs* of BONICINI are natural, and the *accompanied Recitative* masterly, and finely imagined in their Progression to the *Tempo-Giusto*, or regular Movement. I don't know any Method of Accompanyment with the Voice, more delicate and affecting than this, in which, the *Italians*, especially the two great Masters here noted, are peculiarly happy.

PORPORA'S *Cantatas* deserve also a particular Mention in this Place. The most agreeable Changes in Modulation, from one Movement to another, may be found in many of these, his Master-Pieces. The *Adagios* are generally, indeed, too much lengthened; by which Means, they are rather tedious when repeated from the *Da Capo*; and, notwithstanding I have thought the Subjects in them pleasing, and have heard them very finely performed; yet could I never be convinced, that their Author had learned the Art of knowing when he had done enough.

v. The musical student being here supposed to have some previous knowledge in the rudiments of harmony, it might not be amiss, before he attempts the more finished parts, to take a particular survey of RAMEAU'S *Principles of Composition*, now translated into

(CONT.)

AFTER all that has been, or can be said, the Energy and Grace of *Musical Expression* is of too delicate a Nature to be fixed by Words: it is a Matter of Taste, rather than of reasoning, and is, therefore, much better understood by Example than by Precept. It is in the Works of the great Masters, that we must look for the Rules and full Union of *Air, Harmony,* and *Expression*. Would modern Composers condescend to Repair to these Fountains of Knowledge, the public Ear would neither be offended or misled by those shallow and unconnected Compositions, which have of late so much abounded, especially those insipid Efforts that are daily made to set to Music that Flood of Nonsense which is let in upon us since the Commencement of our summer Entertainments, and which, in the Manner they are conducted, cannot possibly prove of any Advantage to Music: trifling Essays in Poetry, must depress, instead of raising the Genius of the Composer; who vainly attempts, instead of giving Aid to Sense (Music's noble Prerogative) to harmonise Nonsense, and make Dulness pleasing.[17]

(CONT.)

English; for, however prevailing a good ear may be found in the practice of composition, yet the rules of this art, as in all other arts, are founded in nature, and, therefore, must afford great assistance, even to those who may think but slightly of them. As the works of art without genius, though masterly, and studied in their construction, are often defective of spirit and taste; so are those of genius without art, very far from perfection: but when these are united, when the powers of nature, and the researches of art, are fully exerted, it is then only we may expect the noblest productions.

17. From these last paragraphs we learn that it behooves the composer to sustain the interest of his listeners and to merit their approval "professionally." Both of these objectives may be achieved by simple means, which however, require "taste," i.e., judicial handling. In fact, it involves no less than the satisfactory resolution of contraries— 1) the creation of "unity amidst variety" (see Hutcheson), 2) the use of expectation so as to neither shock nor become obvious, and 3) giving vent to the spirit of the artist, which abides by the rules of the art (see his last fn.). These are tall orders: the novice composer may, indeed, stand to gain a great deal from consulting the scores of his illustrious predecessors, those known for their "good taste," i.e., judgement and measure. Taste, in this broadened aesthetic-cultural sense, may be cultivated or even rest on cultivation, yet it enables, at one and the same time, the further development of a musical culture. Thus Avison, who strongly believes that the hidden rules of the art can be shown and explicated, is also willing to entertain the notion that aesthetic merit cannot be fully demystified.

THUS, it fares with Music, as it fares with her sister Poetry; for it must be owned, that the Compositions last mentioned, are generally upon a Level with the Words they are set to: their Fate too is generally the same; these *Insect* Productions seldom out-living the *Season* that gives them Birth.[18]

IT has been justly enough alledged,[w] with regard to the *Italian* Operas, that there are also many Improprieties in these, which offend even the most common Observer; particularly that egregious Absurdity of repeating, and finishing many Songs with the first Part; when it often happens, after the Passions of Anger and Revenge have been sufficiently Expressed, that Reconcilement and Love are the Subjects of the second, and, therefore, should conclude the Performance. But, as if it were unnatural to leave the Mind in this tranquil State, the Performer, or Actor, must relapse into all that Tempest and Fury, with which he began, and leave his Hearers in the Midst of it.

I have just hinted this unaccountable Conduct of the *Italian* Composers, by way of Contrast to a Conduct as remarkably ridiculous in our own; I mean, our Manner of setting one single trifling Air, repeated to many Verses, and all of them, perhaps, expressive of very different Sentiments or Affections, than which, a greater Absurdity cannot possibly be imagined, in the Construction of any musical Composition whatsoever.

WHAT may farther be observed in the Composition of these little Airs, is the general Method of repeating the same Thought in the *Ritornello*, which is heard in the Song. By this means, the Burthen of the Tune, be it ever so common, must incessantly Jingle in the Ear, and produce Nothing but some wretched Alternations between the Instrument and Voice.

ON the Contrary, if Subject of the Song was relieved by different Passages in the instrumental Part, but of a similar Air with the

---

w. TOSI on the florid song. p. 91.

———— ✍ ————

18. In fn. 14 we drew attention to what Avison calls "propriety of expression" (see fn. 14). He wishes to stress that both music and poetry must reveal a "propriety of expression" independent of each other, if the union between the two is to yield satisfactory results.

Vocal; this kind of Variety might support the Repetition of the whole, with somewhat more Spirit.[19]

AMONG the many excellent Ballads which our Language affords, I shall mention that of *Black-ey'd Susan*, wrote by Mr. GAY; and propose it as a Specimen, to shew by what Methods a Composer might handle this Genus of the lyric Poem: and which, indeed, is no other than to treat them, as the *Italians* have generally managed those little Love-Stories, which are the Subject of their *Serenatas*: —A kind of musical Production, extremely elegant, and proper for this Purpose. Therefore, I would recommend to our vocal Composers, some such Method of Setting to Music, the best *English* Songs, and which, in like Manner, will admit of various *Airs* and *Duetts*, with their *Recitative*, or musical Narratives, properly interspersed, to relieve and embellish the whole.

THUS one good Ballad may supply a fruitful Genius with a Variety of Incidents, wherein he will have sufficient Scope to display his Imagination, and to shew a Judgment and Contrivance in adapting his several Airs to the different Subjects of the Poetry. By this Means, not only a genteel and consistent Performance might be produced, but also fewer good Masters would lavish their musical Thoughts on Subjects so far beneath them: nor, on this Account, would there be any Dearth of those agreeable and familiar Airs, which might properly be calculated for those entertainments, where the public Ear should be always consulted; and of which, I have so good an Opinion, that, were this difference

---

19. Avison criticizes the da capo aria, since it clearly violates the logic of his "reconcilement" theory, according to which the repetition in the da capo scheme is not only superfluous, but ruins the unity that has already been achieved. Avison applies the same logic to strophic songs, opting in favor of through-compositions. *Ritornelli*, too, should convey the alteration between different passages, rather than emphasize the repetition. Whether Avison is right or wrong is arguable; he himself was rebutted by later British thinkers. [Adam Smith's and the painter John Brown's discussion of the Baroque aria are prime examples in this connection; see discussion in Vol. 1 and also Vol. II, in Smith's text.] However important, we shall not engage in argumentation here. Yet we wish to point out, that Avison tries, nonetheless, to be consistent both with his own aesthetic suppositions as well as with "English taste," which has opted, at the time, for the commonsensical and the realistic (See Vol. I).

between a just, or false taste, but fairly submitted to its decision, I should not dispute, but the Composition which was most natural and pleasing, would bid fairest for the general Approbation.

YET, so long as our Composers prosecute their Studies without the least Knowledge of any Works, but such as are on a Level with their own, they must never expect to advance in the Esteem of their Judges. For, as the striking Beauties in a fine Composition, elevate and enliven the Fancy; so is it depressed and vitiated by too great a Familiarity with whatever is mean and trifling. He, therefore, that is blessed with happy Talents for this art, let him shun all the Means of catching the common Air, which so strangely infects and possesses too many Composers; but, unless he has the Virtue of the *Bee*, who,

> "————With Taste so subtly true,
> From poisonous Herbs extracts the healing Dew,"

I fear, he must banish himself from almost every Place of public Resort, and fly, perhaps, to Monasteries and Cells, where the genuine Charms of Harmony may often, indeed, be found, for Stores to grace his future Productions.

OUR Church Music is equally capable of Improvements from the same sources of Taste and Knowledge. We seem, at present, almost to have forgot, that Devotion is the original and proper End of it. Hence that ill-timed Levity of Air, in our modern Anthems, that foolish Pride of Execution in our Voluntaries, which disgusts every rational Hearer, and dissipates, instead of heightning true Devotion.[20]

---------- ఴ ----------

20. At the beginning of his treatise, Avison defines music as a "socially benevolent" art. In line with his definition and with the English tradition of which he is part, Avison is more willing to rely on public judgement than on the "contrivances" of self-absorbed musicians. The latter seem to communicate more with themselves than with those whom they are expected to serve. Sensitivity to the public ear, Avison clarifies, does not necessarily mean degeneration into the "common and trifling." One should never lose sight of the functions music is called upon to serve, he adds, citing, for example, the heightening of true devotion in the case of church music.

From here till the end of section three of part II, Avison proceeds to discuss the works of composers which, to his mind, set the proper examples to be emulated. As we have noted in the introduction, Avison's musical criticism has elicited great polemics. Undoubtedly such polemics contributed to the musical life in England.

James Beattie

(1735-1803)

"Is there a heart that music cannot melt?
Ah me! How is that rugged heart forlorn!
Is there who ne'er those mystic transports felt
Of solitude and melancholy born?
He needs not woo the muse; he is her scorn.
The sophist's rope of cobweb he shall twine;

Mope o'er the schoolman's peevish page; or mourn,
And delve for life, in Mammon's dirty mine;
Sneak with the scoundrel fox, or grant with glutton swine."

(Beattie, The *Minstrel* LVI)

Born in Laurencekirk, a village in Kincardinshire, Scotland, James Beattie distinguished himself as a student at Marischal College, Aberdeen. From 1760 to the end of his life Beattie held the Chair of Moral Philosophy and Logic at that institution. Between the years 1760 and 1770 he published several essays and some poems, including the *Essay on Truth* (1770). In 1770 he obtained a pension of £200 and the University of Oxford granted him the honorary degree of LL.D. From 1790 to 1799 he was in a most precarious state of health and died in 1803.

In Aberdeen, Beattie belonged to a group of scholars centered around the philosopher Thomas Reid, whose main concern was to refute Hume's skepticism (see Vol. I: 227). In contradistinction to Hume who based his theory of knowledge on the subjectivity of perceptions, Reid believed in a necessary connection between sensations and objects and in the immediacy with which the mind reacts to that with which it is presented. He connected both beliefs via 'common sense' — which he related to common experience and natural laws pertaining to the mind, to self-evident truth and to generally agreed upon opinions. Not unlike Hutcheson, he conceived of consciousness, perception, memory, taste and other faculties as natural propensities (Bryson 1945/1968). While his theory of knowledge was attacked by philosophers, his contribution to aesthetics and criticism was and still is considered substantial. To mention just one relevant example, Reid's belief in the substantiality of secondary qualities enabled him to maintain that aesthetic qualities inhere in the artistic object: "When I hear an air in music that pleases me, I say it is fine, it is excellent. This excellence is not in me, it is in the music" (Kivy 1976: 165). The commitment to the ontological status of aesthetic qualities sheds light on what Beattie will eventually argue with regard to "secondary" *aesthetic* qualities, related to allied meanings. At any rate, for both Reid and Beattie, music still exemplified "natural," inherent beauty.

Defending Reid's theory of knowledge (to which he devoted his essay) Beattie unfortunately propagates the criticism hurled against his master. As for his own *aesthetic* ideas, it seems that his colleagues played a constructive role in their final formation, as Beattie informs the reader in the introductory remark to his essay on music and poetry. In any case, the spirit of the 'Common Sense' School is largely felt throughout the essay. The belief regarding the necessary connections between the rational and the natural, between the pleasurable and the instructive, are among the cornerstones of the essay, and so is his view of the laws underlying artistic phenomena. Despite these beliefs, however, Hume's skepticism finds a way into the essay and is felt in its most insightful and original parts. Philosophical rigor notwithstanding, Beattie's awareness of cognitive matters is already implied in the essay's title, effecting changes in the beliefs and opinions concerning the reception of art.

Pleasure, as the major objective of all art, should relate to the dictates of the medium , maintains Beattie. Ends and means, he adds, are closely related in generic and stylistic matters. Perception, however immediate, insists Beattie, issues in associations, which reinforcement turns into entrenched conventions. Conventions, in turn, delimit the credibility of the probable. Mimesis at large, and the fictive in particular, are thus anchored in systems of expectations, related to culture — dependent on time and place. Tradition, as manifest in culture, argues Beattie, is thus crucial for both art making and for its understanding. Nonetheless, imagination plays a major role in the creation of new works, involving a great variety of "probable" causal connections.

Most of the above ideas are developed in the chapters which deal with literary writings of sorts. Distinguishing between literary and historical writings, Beattie concentrates on the rising novel, which also called for clarification at the time, with regard to the relationship between ends and means. To the *shaping* of the author's point of view and the *unfolding* of parts in relationship to ensuing wholes, Beattie seems to employ aspects which will eventually loom large in the comparison between literature and music.

To be sure, the problem of the unfolding of music is still peripheral in Beattie's discussion of this art; yet it is closely connected with his main argument concerning imitation in music. Clearly, dealing with the referent of music engages the self-evident epistemological base of the mimetic theory. As far as extra-musical meanings are concerned, Beattie points to their "associative basis," which depends on modes of designation and habituation. Altogether, Beattie denies that music is innate meanings and dissociates its value from its import. Nevertheless, music's susceptibility to the creation of affect constitutes one of its major attributes. Though he does not directly explicate this thesis, he emphasizes, 1) the "synthetic" nature of music, 2) its ability to circumscribe the ambiguity of the emotions with which it is associated, and 3) its anchorage in a unique propensity (Reid's "musical ear"; see Kivy 1976) which is cultivated through exposure. No wonder that he accepts instrumental music as a legitimate and powerful medium. If Beattie still adheres to the "benevolence" of music, it is because of its perceived relationship to the general principle of the pleasurable in art.

Beattie's influence on eighteenth-century thinkers in England and in Germany was considerable.

Advertisement

THE following Essays (which were read in a private literary society many years ago), having been seen and approved of by some learned persons in England, are now published at their desire. In writing them out for the press, considerable amendments were made, and new observations added; and hence some slight anachronisms have arisen, which, as they hurt not the sense, it was not thought necessary to guard against.

AN

E S S A Y

ON

POETRY AND MUSIC,

AS THEY AFFECT THE MIND

HE rules of every useful art may be divided into two
kinds. Some are necessary to the accomplishment of the
end proposed by the artist, and are therefore denominated Essential Rules; while others, called Ornamental or
Mechanical, have no better foundation than the practice of some
great performer, whom it has become the fashion to imitate. The
latter are to be learned from the communications of the artist, or
by observing his work: the former may be investigated upon the
principles of reason and philosophy.

These two classes of rules, however different, have often been
confounded by critical writers, without any material injury to art,
or any great inconvenience, either to the artist or to his disciple.
For frequently it happens, that fashion and philosophy coincide;
and that an artist gives the law in his profession, whose principles are as just as his performance is excellent. Such has been
the fate of POETRY in particular. Homer, whom we consider as
the founder of this art, because we have none more ancient to
refer to, appears, in the structure of his two poems, to have proceeded upon a view of things equally comprehensive and rational: nor had Aristotle, in laying down the philosophy of the art,

any thing more to do, than to trace out the principles of his contrivance. What the great critic has left on this subject, proves Homer to have been no less admirable as a philosopher than as a poet; possessed not only of unbounded imagination, and all the powers of language, but also of a most exact judgment, which could at once propose a noble end, and devise the very best means of attaining it.

An art, thus founded on reason, could not fail to be durable. The propriety of the Homeric mode of invention has been acknowledged by the learned in all ages; every real improvement which particular branches of it may have received since his time, has been conducted upon his principles; and poets, who never heard of this name, have, merely by their own good sense, been prompted to tread the path, which he, guided by the same internal monitor, had trod before them. And hence, notwithstanding its apparent licentiousness, true Poetry is a thing perfectly rational and regular; and nothing can be more strictly philosophical, than that part of criticism may and ought to be, which unfolds the general characters that distinguish it from other kinds of composition.

Whether the following discourse will in any degree justify this last remark, is submitted to the reader. It aspires to little other praise, than that of plain language and familiar illustration; disclaiming all paradoxical opinions and refined theories, which are indeed showy in the appearance, and not of difficult invention, but have no tendency to diffuse knowledge, or enlighten the human mind; and which, in matters of taste that have been canvassed by mankind these two thousand years, would seem to be peculiarly incongruous.

The train of thought that led me into this inquiry was suggested by a conversation many years ago, in which I had taken the freedom to offer an opinion different from what was maintained by the company, but warranted, as I then thought, and still think, by the greatest authorities and the best reasons. It was pleaded against me, that taste is capricious, and criticism variable; and that the rules of Aristotle's Poetics, being founded in the practice of Sophocles and Homer, ought not to be applied to the poems of other ages and nations. I admitted the plea, as far as these rules are local and temporary; but asserted, that many of them, being founded in nature, were indispensable, and could not be violated without such impropriety, as, though overlooked by some, would always be offensive to the greater part of readers, and obstruct the general end of poetical composition: and that it would be no less absurd, for a poet to violate the *essential* rules of his art, and justify himself by an appeal from the tribunal of Aristotle, than for a mechanic to construct an engine on principles inconsistent with the laws of motion, and excuse himself by disclaiming the authority of Sir Isaac Newton.

The characters that distinguish poetry from other works of literature, belong either to the SUBJECT, or to the LANGUAGE: so that this discourse naturally resolves itself into two parts. — What we have to say on Music will be found to belong to the first.[1]

---

1. In his introductory remarks, Beattie makes the distinction between art as a phenomenon and the exemplifications of art. Whereas the latter tolerate changes of style and a variety of tastes, the former has its own dictates which manifest themselves in the differences among the various arts. If the two are confused, Beattie argues, it is due to the fact that great artists are not oblivious to the dictates of the medium in which they are active. Like other thinkers with whom we have dealt, Beattie recognizes both the interrelationship between the two in practice and the need to distinguish between them theoretically. The essentials of the medium, he maintains, are akin to natural laws. Since by essentials he means all factors relating to basic dictates of the mind, he considers it possible to grant aesthetic principles a more rigorous epistemological status.

ᴘART I.

POETRY *considered with respect to its*
MATTER *or* SUBJECT.

HEN we affirm, that every art or contrivance which has a meaning must have an end, we only repeat an identical proposition: and when we say, that the essential or indispensable rules of an art are those that direct to the accomplishment of the end proposed by the artist, we repeat a definition whereof it would be captious to controvert the propriety. And therefore, before we can determine any thing in regard to the essential rules of this art, we must form an idea of its END or DESTINATION.[2]

CHAP. I.

Of the end of Poetical Composition.

THAT one end of Poetry, in its first institution, and in every period of its progress, must have been, TO GIVE PLEASURE, will hardly admit of any doubt. If men first employed it to express their adoration of superior and invisible beings, their gratitude to the benefactors of mankind, their admiration of moral, intellectual, or corporeal excellence, or, in general, their love of what was agreeable in their own species, or in other parts of Nature; they must be supposed to have endeavored to make their poetry *pleasing*; because, otherwise, it would have been unsuitable

─────── ᴥ ───────

2. By arguing that ends and means are intimately related in art, Beattie implies that the former are determined by the very means which art employs, such as the creation of virtual images, for example. This observation, which is made immediately after his remark about scientific and aesthetic laws, highlights the difference between the two, for normative considerations never enter into the factors related to natural phenomena. In this respect, art resembles scientific theory more than it resembles nature itself.

to the occasion that gave it birth, and to the sentiments it was intended to enliven. Or if, with Horace, we were to believe, that it was first used as a vehicle to convey into savage minds the principles of government and civility;[a] still we must allow, that one chief thing attended to in its composition must have been, to give it charms sufficient to engage the ear and captivate the heart of an unthinking audience. In latter times, the true poet, though in chusing materials he never lost sight of utility, yet in giving them form (and it is the *form* chiefly that distinguishes poetry from other writings), has always made the entertainment of mankind his principal concern. Indeed, we cannot conceive, that, independently on this consideration, men would ever have applied themselves to arts so little necessary to life, and withal so difficult, as music, painting, and poetry. Certain it is, that a poem, containing the most important truths, would meet with a cold reception, if destitute of those graces of sound, invention, and language, whereof the sole end and aim is to give pleasure.[3]

But is it not the end of this art, *to instruct*, as well as *to please?* Verses, that give pleasure only, without profit, — what are they but chiming trifles? And if a poem were to please, and at the same time, instead of improving, to corrupt the mind, would it not deserve to be considered as a poison rendered doubly dan-

---

a. The honour of civilizing mankind, is by the poets ascribed to poetry (*Hor. Ar. Poet. vers. 391*); — by the orator, to oratory, (*Cicero, de Orat. lib.* I. § 33.) — and by others to philosophy. (*Cicero, de Orat. lib.* I. § 36, 37.; and *Tusc. Quest. lib.* 5. § 5.) — It is probably a gradual thing, the effect of many co-operating causes; and proceeding rather from favourable accidents, or the special appointment of Heaven, than from the art and contrivance of men.

--------- ⟪⟫ ---------

3. Having discussed the relationship between "ends" and "essentials," Beattie tells us that one of the ends of Poetry is to give pleasure. This he bases on two major assumptions: 1) that poetry came into being in order to express pleasure through "adoration" or through "gratitude" and 2) that the expression itself must have been compatible with the sentiment it was "intended to enliven." Linking the ends with the essentials, i.e. the useful with the aesthetic, enables Beattie to explain, on the one hand, why man has applied himself to the arts, and on the other, why he has persisted in doing so. The arts, as it turns out, "though not necessary to life" (as Harris had stated before him) seem to perform an important cultural as well as a psychological function, by embodying and conveying, a reaction to life.

gerous and detestable by its alluring qualities? — All this is true: and yet pleasure is undoubtedly the immediate aim of all those artifices by which poetry is distinguished from other composi- tions, — of the harmony, the rhythm, the ornamented language, the compact and diversified fable: for I believe it will be allowed, that a plain treatise, destitute of all these beauties, might be made to convey more instruction than any poem in the world. As writ- ing is more excellent than painting, and speech than music, on account of its superior usefulness; so a discourse, containing profitable information even in a rude style, may be more excel- lent, because more useful, than any thing in Homer or Virgil: but such a discourse partakes no more of the nature of poetry, than language does of melody, or a manuscript of a picture; whereas an agreeable piece of writing may be poetical, though it yield lit- tle or no instruction. To instruct, is an end common to all good writing, to all poetry, all history, all sound philosophy. But of these last the principal end is to instruct; and if this single end be accomplished, the philosopher and the historian will be allowed to have acquitted themselves well: but the poet must do a great deal for the sake of pleasure only; and if he fail to please, he may indeed deserve praise on other accounts, but as a poet he has done nothing. — But do not historians and philosophers, as well as poets, make it their study to please their readers? They generally do: but the former please, that they may instruct; the latter instruct, that they may the more effectually please. Pleasing, though un-instructive, poetry may gratify a light mind; and what tends even to corrupt the heart may gratify profligates: but the true poet addresses his work, not to the giddy, nor to the worthless, nor to any party, but to mankind; and, if he means to please the *general* taste, *must* often employ instruction as one of the arts that minister to this kind of pleasure.

The necessity of this arises from a circumstance in human nature, which is to man (as Erasmus in Pope's opinion was to the priesthood) "at once his glory and his shame," namely, that the human mind, unless when debased by passion or prejudice, never fails to take the side to truth and virtue: — a sad reflection, when it leads us to consider the debasing influence of passion and prejudice; but a most comfortable one, when it directs our view to the original dignity and rectitude of the human soul. To favour virtue, and speak truth, and take pleasure in those who do so, is natural to man; to act otherwise, requires an effort, does violence to nature, and always implies some evil purpose in the agent.[4]

. . .

Let it be remarked too, that though we distinguish our internal powers by different names, because otherwise we could not speak of them so as to be understood, they are all but so many energies of the same individual mind; and therefore it is not to be supposed, that what contradicts any one leading faculty should yield permanent delight to the rest. That cannot be agreeable to reason, which conscience disapproves; nor can that gratify imagination which is repugnant to reason. — Besides, belief and acquiescence of mind are pleasant, as distrust and disbelief are painful; and therefore, that only can give solid and general satisfaction, which has something of plausibility in it; something which we conceive it possible for a rational being to believe. But no rational being can acquiesce in what is obviously contrary to nature, or implies palpable absurdity.[5]

---------- ᘏ ----------

4. This is another important assumption which enables Beattie to adhere to his previous premise about the pleasing function of poetry, in the face of the ostensibly competing end of instruction. To favor virtue and truth, he tells us in a true Shaftesburian spirit, is natural to man. If poetry also instructs, it is due to the fact that instruction, as such, also pleases. He is thus able, like Hutcheson, to attentuate the difference between enlightening and delighting — so basic to the Horatian poetic view which he seems to adopt — by rendering them both compatible with human nature. It is only a difference in emphasis, he tells us, that separates historians and philosophers from poets. However, since his interest is in the latter, his remaining task is to explicate, in both theory and practice, how the difference in emphasis which characterizes poetry is brought about.

5. Since the "same individual mind" presides over the various faculties, Beattie rightly assumes that they must all submit to some overriding principles whereby each becomes plausible. This unity of the mind he calls "rationality" — viewed from the perspective of the mind's products. Whether or not rationality can be considered as governing the operations of the mind depends, of course, on the definition of the concept itself.

Poetry, therefore, and indeed every art whose end is to please, must be natural; and if so, must exhibit real matter of fact, or something like it; that is, in other words, must be, either according to truth, or according to verisimilitude.

And though every part of the material universe abounds in objects of pleasurable contemplation, yet nothing in nature so powerfully touches our hearts, or gives so great variety of exercise to our moral and intellectual faculties, as man. Human affairs and human feelings are universally interesting. There are many who have no great relish for the poetry that delineates only irrational or inanimate beings; but to that which exhibits the fortunes, the characters, and the conduct of men, there is hardly any person who does not listen with sympathy and delight. And hence, to imitate human action, is considered by Aristotle as essential to this art; and is indeed essential to the most pleasing and most instructive part of it, I mean to epic and dramatic composition. Mere descriptions, however beautiful, and moral reflections, however just, become tiresome, where our passions are not occasionally awakened by some event that concerns our fellow-men. Do not all readers of taste receive peculiar pleasure from those little tales or episodes, with which Thomson's descriptive poem on the Seasons is here and there enlivened? and are they not sensible, that the thunder-storm would not have been half so interesting without the tale of the two lovers[b]; nor the harvest-scene, without that of Palemon and Lavinia[c]; nor the driving snows, without that exquisite picture of a man perishing among them?[d] It is much to be regretted, that Young did not employ the same artifice to animate his Night-Thoughts. Sentiments and descriptions may be regarded as the pilasters, carvings, gildings, and other decorations of the poetical fabric; but human actions are the columns and the rafters, that give it stability and elevation. Or, changing the metaphor, we may con-

---

b. Summer, vers. 1171.
c. Autumn, vers. 177.
d. Winter, vers. 276.

sider these as the soul which informs the lovely frame; while those are little more than the ornaments of the body.[6]

Whether the pleasure we take in things natural, and our dislike to what is the reverse, be the effect of habit or of constitution, is not a material inquiry. There is nothing absurd in supposing, that between the soul, in its first formation, and the rest of nature, a mutual harmony and sympathy may have been established, which experience may indeed confirm, but no perverse habits could entirely subdue. As no sort of education could make man believe the contrary of a self-evident axiom, or reconcile him to a life of perfect solitude; so I should imagine, that our love of nature and regularity might still remain with us in some degree, though we had been born and bred in the Sicilian villa above mentioned, and never heard any thing applauded but what deserved censure, nor censured but what merited applause.[7] Yet habit must be allowed to have a powerful influence over the sentiments and feelings of mankind. Objects to which we have been long accustomed, we are apt to contract a fondness for; we conceive them readily, and contemplate them with pleasure; nor do we quit our old tracts of speculation or practice, without reluctance and pain. Hence in part arises our attachment to our own professions, our old acquaintance, our native soil, our homes, and to the very hills, streams, and rocks in our neighbourhood. It would therefore be strange, if man, accustomed as he is from his earliest days to the regularity of nature, did not contract a liking to her productions, and principles of operation.

———— ฌ ————

6. From the last paragraph, we may infer that for Beattie "rationality" is related to "naturalness," which in the case of art is identified with "truth" or "verisimilitude." Taken together, they stand for Beattie's further inference that human affairs serve better as objects of artistic imitation than do objects of "pleasurable contemplation," for they relate to sentiments, morality, as well as to the intellectual capacity which constitutes man's rationality.

7. In a quasi-Platonic way, Beattie asserts that there must be some "mutual harmony" between human nature and the rest of nature from their "first formation"; hence his identification of rationality with naturalness. Thus, before commencing a discussion of the factors which influence sentiments and feelings, Beattie seems to set their limits.

Yet we neither expect nor desire, that every human invention, where the end is only to please, should be an exact transcript of real existence. It is enough, that the mind acquiesce in it as probable, or plausible, or such as we think might happen without any direct opposition to the laws of Nature: — or, to speak more accurately, it is enough, that it be consistent, either, first, with general experience; or, secondly, with popular opinion; or, thirdly, that it be consistent with itself, and connected with probable circumstances.[8]

First: If a human invention be consistent with *general* experience, we acquiesce in it as sufficiently probable. *Particular* experiences, however, there may be, so uncommon and so little expected, that we should not admit their probability, if we did not know them to be true. No man of sense believes, that he has any likelihood of being enriched by the discovery of hidden treasure; or thinks it probable, on purchasing a lottery-ticket, that he shall get the first prize; and yet great wealth has actually been acquired by such good fortune. But we should look upon these as poor expedients in a play or romance for bringing about a happy catastrophe. We expect that fiction should be more consonant to the *general* tenor of human affairs; in a word, that not possibility, but probability, should be the standard of poetical invention.[9]

———— ⚓ ————

8. Habit, according to Beattie, breeds sympathy, and acquaintance leads to attachment. Mimesis, Beattie implies, is related to habituation — entrenched ways of looking at the world. Man enjoys what he recognizes, and he recognizes that which he is able to perceive. Though Beattie is unaware of the overall philosophical implications of his suggestion, he nevertheless introduces a turn in the very concept of verisimilitude. Accordingly, he is able to maintain that art need not render "exact transcripts of real existence" in order to please; it is sufficient if the imitation relates in some form or another to the habits of the mind, i.e., if the mind, "acquiesces in it as probable." While Beattie does not altogether drop mimesis thereby, he seems to enlarge its theoretical scope so as to include "fancy" as well.

9. A fictive world based on what one has learned to expect, we are told, is more persuasive than an unexpected genuine possibility. Thus, the 'suspension of disbelief' rests on reality already experienced. If the fictive may turn real when expected, whereas the real may appear fictitious if unsuspected, that which raises expectations indeed deserves special attention.

Secondly: Fiction is admitted as conformable to this standard, when it accords with received opinions. These may be erroneous, but are not often *apparently* repugnant to nature. On this account, and because they are familiar to us from our infancy, the mind readily acquiesces in them, or at least yields them that degree of credit which is necessary to render them pleasing. Hence the fairies, ghosts, and witches of Shakespeare, are admitted as probable beings; and angels obtain a place in religious pictures, though they do not now appear in the scenery of real life. Even when a popular opinion has long been exploded, and has become repugnant to universal belief, the fictions built upon it are still admitted as natural, because they were accounted such by the people to whom they were first addressed; whose sentiments and views of things we are willing to adopt, when, by the power of pleasing description, we are introduced into their scenes, and made acquainted with their manners. Hence we admit the theology of the ancient poets, their Elysium and Tartarus, Scylla and Charybdis, Cyclops and Circe, and the rest of those "beautiful wonders" (as Horace calls them) which were believed in the heroic ages; as well as the demons and enchantments of Tasso, which may be supposed to have obtained no small degree of credit among the Italians of the sixteenth century, and are suitable enough to the notions that prevailed universally in Europe not long before.[e] In fact, when Poetry is in other respects true; when it gives an accurate display of those parts of nature about which we know that men in all ages must have entertained the same opinion, I mean those appearances in the visible creation, and those feelings and workings of the human mind, which are obvious to all mankind; — when Poetry, I say, is thus far according to nature, we are very willing to be indulgent to what is fictitious in it, and to grant a temporary allowance

---

e. In the fourteenth century, the common people of Italy believed, that the poet Dante actually went down to hell, that the *Inferno* was a true account of what he saw there; and that his sallow complexion, and stunted beard (which seemed by its growth and colour to have been too near the fire), were the consequences of his passing so much time in that hot and smoky region. *See Vicende della litteratura del Sig. C. Denina, cap 4.* — Sir John Mandeville's Book of Travels, written not long after, was not only ratified by the Pope, after having been compared with the *Mappa Mundi* of that time, but, what is more strange, seems to have been seriously believed by that adventurous knight himself, though a man of considerable learning, and no despicable taste.

to any system of fable which the author pleases to adopt; provided that he lay the scene in a distant country, or fix the date to
a remote period. This is no unreasonable complaisance: we owe
it both to the poet and to ourselves; for without it we should neither form a right estimate of his genius, nor receive from his
works that pleasure which they were intended to impart. Let him,
however, take care, that his system of fable be such, as his countrymen and contemporaries (to whom his work is immediately
addressed) might be supposed capable of yielding their assent
to; for otherwise we should not believe him to be in earnest: and
let him connect it as much as he can with probable circumstances, and make it appear in a series of events consistent with
itself.[10]

For (thirdly) if this be the case, we shall admit his story as
probable, or at least as natural, and consequently be interested
in it, even though it be not warranted by general experience, and
derive but slender authority from popular opinion. Calyban, in
the Tempest, would have shocked the mind as an improbability,
if we had not been made acquainted with his origin, and seen
his character displayed in a series of consistent behaviour. But
when we are told, that he sprung from a witch and a demon, a
connection not contrary to the laws of Nature, as they were
understood in Shakespeare's time, and find his manners con-

———— ⟋ ————

10. Using expectation as a cognitive criterion, the Aristotelian principle of probability
becomes applicable also to that which to begin with is fictitious, i.e. that which represents nothing in reality. Such fictive inventions depend on socialization which
reflects a consensus formed by a living tradition. Thus, even that which was once considered true but is no longer believed to be so, may enter into "make believe."
Nevertheless, fictive elements should be contextually anchored in what the people to
whom the work of art is addressed believe to be universally true as far as the human
mind is concerned. The mind which performs these operations enjoys and employs
cultural capital as shared currency. Yet even this is better served if some distance is
created (setting the scene in a remote country) in order to avoid a cognitive dissonance. (Magicians and gods, Pirrotta tells us, fared better in song — opera's unnatural speech — than did ordinary characters, see Pirrotta 1969/1982.) The credibility we
grant the work, Beattie concludes, depends on our belief that the author assumed that
his audience may have believed that which he had caused them to believe by means
of a "system of fables" he constructed.

formable to his descent, we are easily reconciled to the fiction. In the same sense, the Lilliputians of Swift may pass for probable beings; not so much because we know that a belief in pygmies was once current in the world (for the true ancient pygmy was at least thrice as tall as those whom Gulliver visited), but because we find, that every circumstance relating to them accords with itself, and with their supposed character. It is not the size of the people only that is diminutive; their country, seas, ships, and towns, are all in exact proportion; their theological and political principles, their passions, manners, customs, and all the parts of their conduct, betray a levity and littleness perfectly suitable: and so simple is the whole narration, and apparently so artless and sincere, that I should not much wonder, if it had imposed (as I have been told it has) upon some persons of no contemptible understanding. The same degree of credit may perhaps for the same reasons be due to his giants. But when he grounds his narrative upon a contradiction to nature; when he presents us with rational brutes, and irrational men; when he tells us of horses building houses for habitation, milking cows for food, riding in carriages, and holding conversations on the laws and politics of Europe; not all his genius (and he there exerts it to the utmost) is able to reconcile us to so monstrous a fiction: we may smile at some of his absurd exaggerations; we may be pleased with the energy of style, and accuracy of description, in particular places; and a malevolent heart may triumph in the satire; but we can never relish it as a fable, because it is at once unnatural and self-contradictory.[11]

------------ *un* ------------

11. Beattie's last observation does not add much to his previous observations, save for the insistence on internal consistency within fictive worlds. One may well ask what creates contradiction within a fictive world. From Beattie's examples it appears that the same laws by which we understand the real world govern the unity of fictive worlds, excluding their fictitious premise. Thus, for example, in the minuscule dimensions of Lilliput, proportions must be maintained in order not to destroy the desired illusion.

Baumgarten's transfer of the Leibnizian "possible worlds" into the context of the fictitious engages this epistemological problem. Less a philosopher than a literary critic, Beattie exemplifies how theoretical observations concerning the bringing about of works of art enrich literary criticism.

. . .

If we were to prosecute this subject any further, it would be proper to remark, that in some kinds of poetical invention a stricter probability is required than in others: — that, for instance, Comedy, whether Dramatic or Narrative,[f] must seldom deviate from the ordinary course of human affairs, because it exhibits the manners of real, and even of familiar life; — that the Tragic poet, because he imitates characters more exalted, and generally refers to events little known, or long since past, may be allowed a wider range; but must never attempt the marvellous fictions of the Epic Muse, because he addresses his work, not only to the passions and imagination of mankind, but also to their eyes and ears, which are not easily imposed on, and refuse to be gratified with any representation that does not come very near the truth; — that the Epic Poem may claim still ampler privileges, because its fictions are not subject to the scrutiny of any outward sense, and because it conveys information in regard both to the highest human characters, and the most important and wonderful events, and also to the affairs of unseen worlds, and superior beings. Nor would it be improper to observe, that the several species of Comic, of Tragic, of Epic composition, are not confined to the same degree of probability; for that Farce may be allowed to be less probable than the regular Comedy; the Masque, than the regular Tragedy; and the Mixed Epic, such as The Fairy Queen, and Orlando Furioso, than the pure Epopee of Homer, Virgil, and Milton. — But this part of the subject seems not to require further illustration. Enough has been said, to show, that nothing unnatural can please; and that therefore Poetry, whose end is to please, must be ACCORDING TO NATURE.[12]

---

f. Fielding's *Tom Jones, Amelia,* and *Joseph Andrews,* are examples of what I call the Epic or Narrative Comedy: perhaps *the Comic Epopee* is a more proper term.

--------- ✍ ---------

12. Leaving behind the problem of the fictive versus the real, Beattie now proposes a certain subdivision within the fictive. However, it turns out that the various literary genres have to be judged according to the same principles he formulated for assessing the distinction between the real and the fictive. Their essentials, too, have to be evaluated

(CONT.)

CHAP. III

Poetry exhibits a system of nature somewhat different from the reality of things.

TO exhibit *real nature* is the business of the historian; who, if he were strictly to confine himself to his own sphere, would never record even the minutest circumstance of any speech, event, or description, which was not warranted by sufficient authority. It has been the language of critics in every age, that the historian ought to relate nothing as true which is false or dubious, and to conceal nothing material which he knows to be true. But I doubt whether any writer of profane history has ever been so scrupulous. Thucydides himself, who began his history when that war began which he records, and who set down every event soon after it happened, according to the most authentic information, seems however to have indulged his fancy not a little in his harangues and descriptions, particularly that of the plague of Athens: And the same thing has been practised, with greater latitude, by Livy and Tacitus, and more or less by all the best historians, both ancient and modern. Nor do I blame them for it. By these improved or invented speeches, and by the heightenings thus given to their description, their work becomes more interesting, and more useful; nobody is deceived, and historical truth is not materially affected. ... But the fictitious part of history, or of story-telling, ought never to take up much room; and must be highly blameable when it leads into any mistake either of facts or of characters.

(CONT.)   ———— ⚭ ————

according to the objectives they aim to achieve. These relations between essentials and ends is what Beattie means by "according to nature." His major contribution to literary theory is his preoccupation with persuasive ways of doing, and not with ideal types like those which concerned the Neo-Classicists. Thus, his list of genres easily finds room for the upcoming novel (which had not yet even been "christened," as we learn from his footnote), since knowledge of its means leaves no doubt regarding its ends.

Now, why do historians take the liberty to embellish their works in this manner? One reason, no doubt, is, that they may display their talents in oratory and narration: But the chief reason, as hinted already, is, to render their composition more agreeable. It would seem, then, that something more pleasing than real nature, or something which shall add to the pleasing qualities or real nature, may be devised by human fancy. And this may certainly be done. And this it is the poet's business to do. And when this is in any degree done by the historian, his narrative becomes in that degree poetical.

The possibility of thus improving upon nature must be obvious to every one. When we look at a landscape, we can fancy a thousand additional embellishments. Mountains loftier and more picturesque; rivers more copious, more limpid, and more beautifully winding; smoother and wider lawns; vallies more richly diversified; caverns and rocks more gloomy and more stupendous; ruins more majestic; buildings more magnificent; oceans more varied with islands, more splendid with shipping, or more agitated by storm, than any we have ever seen, it is easy for human imagination to conceive. Many things in art and nature exceed expectation; but nothing sensible transcends, or equals the capacity of thought: — a striking evidence of the dignity of the human soul! The finest woman in the world appears to every eye susceptible of improvement, except perhaps to that of her lover. No wonder, then, if in poetry events can be exhibited more compact, and of more pleasing variety, than those delineated by the historian, and scenes of inanimate nature more dreadful or more lovely, and human characters more sublime and more exquisite both in good and evil. Yet still let nature supply the ground-work and materials, as well as the standard, of poetical fiction. The most expert painters use a layman, or other visible figure, to direct their hand and regulate their fancy. Homer himself founds his two poems on authentic tradition; and Tragic as well as Epic poets have followed the example. The writers of romance too are ambitious to interweave true adventures with their fables; and, when it can be conveniently done, to take the outlines of their plan from real life. Thus the tale of Robinson

Crusoe is founded on an incident that actually befel one Alexander Selkirk, a sea-faring man, who lived several years alone in the island of Juan Fernandes; Smollet is thought to have given us some of his own adventures in the history of Roderick Random; and the chief characters in Tom Jones, Joseph Andrews, and Pamela, are said to have been copied from real originals. — Dramatic Comedy, indeed, is for the most part purely fictitious; for if it were to exhibit real events as well as present manners, it would become too personal to be endured by a well-bred audience, and degenerate into downright abuse; which appears to have been the case with the *old comedy* of the Greeks.[g] But, in general, hints taken from real existence will be found to give no little grace and stability to fiction, even in the most fanciful poems. Those hints, however, may be improved by the poet's imagination, and set off with every probable ornament that can be devised, consistently with the design and genius of the work; — or, in other words, with the sympathies that the poet means to awaken in the mind of his reader. For mere poetical ornament, when it fails to interest the affections, is not only useless but improper; all true poetry being addressed to the heart, and intended to give pleasure by raising or soothing the passions; — the only effectual way of pleasing a rational and moral creature. And therefore I would take Horace's maxim to be universal in poetry; "Non satis est, pulchra esse poemata; *dulcia* sunto;" "It is not enough that poems be beautiful; let them also be *affecting*." — for that this is the meaning of the word *dulcia*, is admitted by the best interpreters, and is evident from the context.[h] [13]

g. Compare Hor. lib. I. sat. 4. vers. 1. — 5. with Ar. Poet vers. 281–285.
h. Hor. Ar. Poet. vers. 95 — 100.

———— ↄ ————

13. Against the background of the rise of the novel in the eighteenth century, Beattie is preoccupied with the question of 'realism' as related to the boundaries between historical and literary writing (see fn. 4). Though his discussion still engages in a sort of Renaissance rhetoric, especially as far as ideal nature vs. nature-as-given is concerned, he extracts some basic principles which guide rather than circumscribe the styles he deals with. Historical accounts, he tells us, require poetical features to render them more interesting; literary works, on the other hand, resort to reality in order to achieve

(CONT.)

. . .

Every thing in nature is complex in itself, and bears innumerable relations to other things; and may therefore be viewed in an endless variety of lights, and consequently described in an endless variety of ways. Some descriptions are good, and others bad. An historical description, that enumerates all the qualities of any object, is certainly good, because it is true; but may be as unaffecting as a logical definition. In poetry no unaffecting description is good, however conformable to truth; for here we expect not a complete enumeration of qualities (the chief end of the art being to please), but only such an enumeration as may give a lively and interesting idea. It is not memory, or the knowledge of rules, that can qualify a poet for this sort of description; but a peculiar liveliness of fancy and sensibility of heart, the nature whereof we may explain by its effects, though we cannot lay down rules of the attainment of it.[14]

When our mind is occupied by any emotion, we naturally use words, and meditate on things, that are suitable to it, and tend to encourage it. If a man were to write a letter when he is very angry, there would probably be something of vehemence or bitterness in the style, even though the person to whom he wrote were not the object of his anger. The same thing holds true of every other strong passion or emotion: — while it predominates in the mind, it gives a peculiarity to our thoughts, as well as to our voice, gesture, and countenance: and hence we expect, that

(CONT.)   ———— ℩ℜ ————

credibility. To be effective, it turns out, requires the understanding both of affectivity and reality in terms of ends and means, with regard to the medium in question. In the final analysis, it is the mixture of the two, rather than clear-cut dichotomies, which marks the borders between different types of narrative. Once the desired mixture is determined, the role of each of its components, is effected (as Beattie implies with reference to ornamentation).

14. On the basis of his earlier observations, Beattie is able to distinguish between different kinds of 'wholes' — logical, factual and poetical. Whereas the first two lend themselves to objective assessments, the third, which deals with qualities, is defined less by clear-cut rules. What turns a poetical work into a persuasive whole, is a matter of the "sensibility of heart." What he means by this phrase is elaborated in the paragraphs which follow.

every personage introduced in poetry should see things through the medium of his ruling passion, and that his thoughts and language should be tinctured accordingly. A melancholy man walking in a grove, attends to those things that suit and encourage his melancholy; the sighing of the wind in the trees, the murmuring of waters, the darkness and solitude of the shades: a chearful man in the same place, finds many subjects of chearful meditation, in the singing of birds, the brisk motions of the babling stream, and the liveliness and variety of the verdure. Persons of different characters, contemplating the same thing, a Roman triumph, for instance, feel different emotions, and turn their view to different objects. One is filled with wonder at such a display of wealth and power; another exults in the idea of conquest, and pants for military renown; a third, stunned with clamour, and harassed with confusion, wishes for silence, security, and solitude; one melts with pity to the vanquished, and makes many a sad reflection upon the insignificance of worldly grandeur, and the uncertainty of human things; while the buffoon, and perhaps the philosopher, considers the whole as a vain piece of pageantry, which, by its solemn procedure, and by the admiration of so many people, is only rendered the more ridiculous: — and each of these persons would describe it in a way suitable to his own feelings, and tending to raise the same in others. We see in Milton's Allegro and Penseroso, how a different cast of mind produces a variety in the manner of conceiving and contemplating the same rural scenery. In the former of these excellent poems, the author personates a chearful man, and takes notice of those things in external nature that are suitable to chearful thoughts, and tends to encourage them; in the latter, every object described is serious and solemn, and productive of calm reflection and tender melancholy: and I should not be easily persuaded, that Milton wrote the first under the influence of sorrow, or the second under that of gladness. — We often see an author's character in his works; and if every author were in earnest when he writes, we should oftener see it. Thomson was a man of piety and benevolence, and a warm admirer of the beauties of nature; and every description in his delightful poem on the Seasons tend to raise the same laudable affections in his reader. The parts of nature that attract his notice are those which an impious or hard-hearted man would neither attend to nor be affected with, at least in the same manner. In Swift we see a turn of mind very different from that of the amiable Thomson; little relish for the sublime or beautiful, and a perpetual succession of violent emotions. All his pictures of human life seem to show, that deformity and meanness were the favourite objects of his attention, and that his soul was a constant prey to indignation,[i] disgust, and other gloomy passions arising from such a view of things. And it is the tendency of almost all his writings (though it was not always the author's design) to communicate same passions to his reader: insomuch, that, notwithstanding his erudition, and knowledge of the world, his abilities as a popular orator and man of business, the energy of his style, the elegance of some of his verses, and his extraordinary talents in wit and humour, there is reason to doubt, whether by studying his works any person was ever much improved in piety or benevolence.

And thus we see, how the compositions of an ingenious author may operate upon the heart, whatever be the subject. The affections that prevail in the author himself direct his attention to objects congenial, and give a peculiar bias to his inventive powers, and a peculiar colour to his language. Hence his work, as well as face, if Nature is permitted to exert herself freely in it, will exhibit a picture of his mind, and awaken correspondent sympathies in the reader. When these are favourable to virtue, which they always ought to be, the work will have that *sweet pathos* which Horace alludes to in the passage above mentioned; and which we so highly admire, and so warmly approve, even in those parts of the Georgic that describe inanimate nature.

Horace's account of the matter in question differs not from what is here given, "It is not enough," says he, "that poems be beautiful; let them be affecting, and agitate the mind with whatever passions the poet wishes to impart. The human counte-

---

i. For part of this remark we have his own authority, often in his letters, and very explicitly in the Latin Epitaph which he composed for himself: — "ubi saeva indignatio ulterius cor lacerare nequit." *See his last will and testament.*

nance, as it smiles on those who smile, accompanies also with sympathetic tears those who mourn. If you would have me weep, you must first weep yourself; then, and not before, shall I be touched with your misfortunes. — For nature *first* makes the emotions of our mind correspond with our circumstances, infusing real joy, sorrow, or resentment, according to the occasion; and *afterwards* gives the true pathetic utterance to the voice and language."[j] — This doctrine, which concerns the orator and the player no less than the poet, is strictly philosophical, and equally applicable to dramatic, to descriptive, and indeed to every species of interesting poetry. The poet's sensibility must first of all engage him warmly in his subject, and in every part of it; otherwise he will labour in vain to interest the reader. If he would paint external nature, as Virgil and Thomson have done, so as to make her amiable to others, he must first be enamoured of her himself; if he would have his heroes and heroines speak the language of love or sorrow, devotion or courage, ambition or anger, benevolence or pity, his heart must be susceptible of those emotions, and in some degree feel them, as long at least as he employs himself in framing words for them; being assured that

He best shall paint them who can feel them most.[k]

The true poet, therefore, must not only study nature, and know the reality of things; but must also possess fancy, to invent additional decorations; judgment, to direct him in the choice of such as accord with verisimilitude; and sensibility, to enter with ardent emotions into every part of his subject, so as to transfuse into his work a pathos and energy sufficient to raise corresponding emotions in the reader.[15]

j. Ar. Poet. vers. 99. — 101.
k. Pope's Eloisa, vers. 366.

——————— *ᴜᴫ* ———————

15. Beattie connects the concept of the "sensibility of heart" to the concept of sympathy so common in eighteenth-century England. This concept derives from the Horatian doctrine, according to which the affective reaction of the artist to nature, and its consequent embodiment in certain artistic configurations, is reflected in a reverse order in

(CONT.)

"The historian and the poet," says Aristotle, "differ in this, that
the former exhibits things as they are, the latter as they might
be:"[1] — I suppose he means, in that state of perfection which is
consistent with probability, and in which, for the sake of our
own gratification, we wish to find them. If the poet, after all the
liberties he is allowed to take with the truth, can produce nothing more exquisite than is commonly to be met with in history,
his reader will be disappointed and dissatisfied. Poetical representations must therefore be framed after a pattern of the highest probable perfection that the genius of the work will admit: —
external nature must in them be more picturesque than in reality; action more animated; sentiments more expressive of the feelings and character, and more suitable to the circumstances of the
speaker; personages better accomplished in those qualities that
raise admiration, pity, terror, and other ardent emotions; and
events, more compact, more clearly connected with causes and
consequences, and unfolded in an order more flattering to the
fancy, and more interesting to the passions. But where, it may be
said, is this pattern of perfection to be found? Not in real nature;
otherwise history, which delineates real nature, would also delin-
eate this pattern of perfection. It is to be found only in the mind

---

1. Poetic. sect. 9.

(CONT.)   ———— ◡◠ ————

the reaction of the recipient. A correspondence is thus created between passions
imparted and passions felt. By interpolating his concept of sensibility, Beattie somewhat softens the simplistic assumption on which his theory is based, emphasizing the
possibility that the same aspects in nature can call forth different reactions. This implies
the notion of the "point of view," which, according to Beattie, is the message of his
work, embodied in its non-semantic features. However, Beattie understates his own
observation, for the process he so well describes need not stop with the reaction of
the artist but may also activate the reception of the point of view embedded in the art-
work.

Interpretation, not mechanical sympathy, connects the work of art, the world it represents and its artistic significance, as will be explicated later.

of the poet; and it is imagination, regulated by knowledge, that enables him to form it.[16]

In the beginning of life, and while experience is confined to a small circle, we admire every thing, and are pleased with very moderate excellence. A peasant thinks the hall of his landlord the finest apartment in the universe, listens with rapture to the strolling ballad-singer, and wonders at the rude wooden cuts that adorn his ruder compositions. A child looks upon his native village as a town; upon the brook that runs by, as a river; and upon the meadows and hills in the neighbourhood, as the most spacious and beautiful that can be. But when, after long absence, he returns in his declining years, to visit, once before he die, the dear spot that gave him birth, and those scenes whereof he remembers rather the original charms than the exact proportions, how is he disappointed to find every thing so debased, and so diminished! The hills seem to have sunk into the ground, the brook to be dried up, and the village to be forsaken of its people; the parish-church, stripped of all its fancied magnificence, is become low, gloomy, and narrow, and the fields are now only the miniature of what they were. Had he never left this spot, his notions might have remained the same as at first; and had he travelled but a little way from it, they would not perhaps have received any material enlargement. It seems then to be from observation of many things of the same of similar kinds, that we acquire the talent of forming ideas more perfect than the real objects that lie immediately around us: and these ideas we may

---------- ඟ ----------

16. Even though this paragraph refers to poetical representations as compared to historical renditions, Beattie is in fact dealing with the query concerning the role of art. Whereas art, as we have learned in the previous sections, is also related to reality, it treats reality both as point of departure and of reference. Art's main objective is to isolate the qualities with which it deals, rendering them more perfect than the way we know them from real life: more picturesque, more expressive, more animated, more compact: in short, "more clearly connected with cause and consequences." For Beattie, patterns of perfection — so essential in eighteenth-century thought — are intensifications which only "the imagination, regulated by knowledge" is able to form. Thus, the artistic is invariably wedded to the imagination, while its communicative aspects derive from shared knowledge.

improve gradually more and more, according to the vivacity of
our mind, and extent of our experience, till at last we come to
raise them to a degree of perfection superior to any thing to be
found in real life. There cannot, sure, be any mystery in this doctrine; for we think and speak to the same purpose every day.
Thus nothing is more common than to say, that such an artist
excels all we have ever known in his profession, and yet that we
can still conceive a superior performance. A moralist, by bringing together into one view the separate virtues of many persons,
is enabled to lay down a system of duty more perfect than any
he has ever seen exemplified in human conduct. Whatever be
the emotion the poet intends to raise in his reader, whether
admiration or terror, joy or sorrow; and whatever be the object
he would exhibit, whether Venus or Tisiphone, Achilles or
Thersites, a palace or a pile of ruins, a dance or a battle; he generally copies an idea of his own imagination; considering each
quality as it is found to exist in several individuals of a species,
and thence forming an assemblage more or less perfect in its
kind, according to the purpose to which he means to apply it.[17]

Hence it would appear, that the ideas of Poetry are rather general than singular; rather collected from the examination of a
species or class of things, than copied from an individual. And
this, according to Aristotle, is in fact the case, at least for the most
part; whence that critic determines, that Poetry is something
more exquisite and more philosophical than history.[m] The historian may describe Bucephalus, but the poet delineates a
warhorse; the former must have seen the animal he speaks of, or

---

m. Poetic. sect. 9.

--------- ✍ ---------

17. Again Beattie resorts to the Renaissance notion of an ideal nature, though adding
an important qualification. Whereas the Renaissance thinker regarded 'ideal nature' as
a kind of assemblage of exquisite qualities, for Beattie this assemblage rests on observations and experience which cultivate the sensitivity for excellence. Comparative
evaluation of degrees of excellence is thus necessary for the excellence imagined.
Judgement thus becomes an integral part of artistic creation which truly fulfills its role,
i.e. creates perfection. Beattie implies that one has first to cultivate oneself in order
be able to add to culture.

received authentic information concerning it, if he mean to describe it historically; for the latter it is enough that he has seen several animals of that sort. The former tells us, what Alcibiades actually did and said; the latter, what such a species of human character as that which bears the name of Achilles would probably do or say in certain given circumstances.[18]

CHAP. V.

Further Illustrations. Of Poetical Arrangement.

IT was formerly remarked, that the *events* of Poetry must be "more compact, more clearly connected with causes and consequences, and unfolded in an order more flattering to the imagination, and more interesting to the passions," than the events of history commonly are. This may seem to demand some illustration.

I. Some parts of history interest us much; but others so little, that, if it were not for their use in the connection of events, we should be inclined to overlook them altogether. But all the parts of a poem must be interesting: — Great, to raise admiration or terror; unexpected, to give surprise; pathetic, to draw forth our tender affections; important, from their tendency to the elucidation of the fable, or to the display of human character; amusing, from the agreeable pictures of nature they present us with; or of peculiar efficacy in promoting our moral improvement. And therefore, in forming an Epic or Dramatic Fable, from history or tradition, the poet must omit every event that cannot be improved by one or other of these purposes.

———— ⚘ ————

18. Beattie agrees with Aristotle that artistic ideas are generalities, related to classes of objects. Every artistic expression is but an exemplification of the class to which it belongs. The art object, itself a particular manifestation, thus symbolizes the general rather than derives from it. Although an advocate of the rising realistic novel, Beattie avoids the trap of believing that the characters in the novel have a one-to-one relationship to *real* characters. On the whole, philosophy and art, more than art and history, share the attempt to delve into essences, as idealistic philosophy will eventually maintain. Authors such as Coleridge and Goethe will claim that the particular in art creates the general through its symbolic function, rather than simply exemplify it.

II. Some events are recorded in history, merely because they are true; though their consequences be of no moment, and their causes unknown. But of all poetical events, the causes ought to be manifest, for the sake of probability; and the effects considerable, to give them importance.

III. A history may be as long as you please; for, while it is instructive and true, it is still a good history. But a poem must not be too long: — first, because to write good poetry is exceedingly difficult, so that a very long poem would be too extensive a work for human life, and too laborious for human ability; — secondly, because, if you would be suitably affected with the poet's art, you must have a distinct remembrance of the whole fable, which could not be, if the fable were very long;[n] and, thirdly, because poetry is addressed to the imagination and passions, which cannot long be kept in violent exercise, without working the mind into a disagreeable state, and even impairing the health of the body. — That, by these three peculiarities of the poetical art, its powers of pleasing are heightened, and consequently its end promoted, is too obvious to require proof.

IV. The strength of a passion depends in part on the vivacity of the impression made by its object. Distress which we see, we are more affected with than what we only hear of; and, of several descriptions of an affecting object, we are most moved by that which is most lively. Every thing in poetry, being intended to operate on the passions, must be displayed in lively colours, and set as it were before the eyes: And therefore the poet must attend to many minute, though picturesque circumstances, that may, or perhaps must, be overlooked by the historian. Achilles putting on his armour, is described by Homer with a degree of minuteness, which, if it were the poet's business simply to *relate* facts, might appear tedious or impertinent; but which in reality answers a good purpose, that of giving us a distinct image of this dreadful warrior: it being the end of poetical description, not

---

n. Aristot. Poet. § 7.

only to *relate* facts, but to *paint* them;° not merely to inform the judgement, and enrich the memory, but to awaken the passions, and captivate the imagination.[19]

---

o. Homer's poetry is always picturesque. Algarotti, after Lucian, calls him the prince of painters. He sets before us the whole visible appearance of the object he describes, so that the painter would have nothing to do but to work after his model. He has more epithets expressive of colour than any other poet I am acquainted with: *black* earth, *wine-coloured* ocean, and even *white* milk, &c. This to the imagination of those readers who study the various colourings of nature is not a little amusing, however offensive it may be to the delicacy of certain critics; — whose rules for the use of epithets if we were to adopt, we should take the palm of poetry from Homer, Virgil, and Milton, and bestow it on those simple rhymers, who, because they have no other merit, must be admired for barrenness of fancy, and poverty of language. — An improper use of epithets is indeed a grievous fault. — And epithets become improper: — 1, when they add nothing to the sense; or to the picture; — and still more, when, 2. they seem rather to take something away from it; — 3. when by their colloquial meanness they debase the subject. — These three faults are all exemplified in the following lines:

> The chariot of the King of kings,
>> Which *active* troops of angels drew,
> On a strong tempest's *rapid* wings,
>> With *most amazing* swiftness flew.   *Tate and Brady.*

--------- ᥊ ---------

19. Having discussed the difference between poetry and history, Beattie now draws some basic conclusions with regard to poetry, which serve, at the same time, as instructions for poets. Poetry, we have learned from the previous discussion, treats "probabilities." Though anchored in experience, probabilities address the imagination. Hence, all parts of a poem must be interesting enough to capture the imagination. Moreover, poems must be so conceived as to sustain the memory of their parts and the passions which they evoke, if they are to be perceived as organic units. The strength of the passions evoked, Beattie argues, depends on the "vivacity" of the impressions imparted. Given all of this, Beattie contends that the length of poems must be circumscribed and the handling of their materials prescribed. The fictitious, in short, must be credible so that the probabilities may thrive in the imagination.

Beattie's reference to the degree of "minuteness" with which Homer describes Achilles putting on his armor, calls to mind Auerbach's brilliant analysis of "Odysseus' Fear" (1953). Both writers are concerned with the "end" of poetic description; both maintain that the text does not intend merely to relate facts, but rather to captivate the imagination. Yet Auerbach goes a step further, arguing that the minuteness of the description also characterizes Homer's particular style. The latter, we are told, intends to leave nothing it mentions unexternalized in terms perceptible to the senses. The representation, thus, embodies a specific kind of reality: through its uniform "illumination" in which all events take place in the "foreground," meanings are unmistakably displayed. This kind of representation contrasts sharply with another basic kind — "biblical" representation, which brings certain parts into relief, while passing over others, suggestive of the "unexpressed." Creating a "background" quality, with a multiplicity of mean-

(CONT.)

. . .

V. The origin of nations, and the beginnings of great events, are little known, and seldom interesting ; whence the first part of every history, compared with the sequel, is somewhat dry and tedious. But a poet must, even in the beginning of his work, interest the readers, and raise high expectation; not by any pomp of style, far less by ample promises or bold professions; but by setting immediately before them some incident, striking enough to raise curiosity, in regard both to its causes and to its consequences. He must therefore take up his story, not at the beginning, but in the middle; or rather, to prevent the work from being too long, as near the end as possible: And afterwards take some proper opportunity to inform us of the preceding events, in the way of narrative, or by the conversation of the persons introduced, or by short and natural digressions.[20]

. . .

VI. If a work have no determinate end, it has no meaning; and if it have many ends, it will distract, by its multiplicity. Unity of design, therefore, belongs in some measure to all compositions, whether in verse or prose. But to some it is more essential than to others; and to none so much as to the higher poetry. In certain kinds of history, there is unity sufficient, if all the events recorded be referred to one person; in others, if to one period of time, or to one people, or even to the inhabitants of one and the

(CONT.) ——————— ℳ ———————

ings, invites interpretation. Auerbach, most interestingly, suggests that these two basic styles have exercised a determining influence on the representation of reality in European culture.

Refining the theory of imitation, as we have seen, has led in many directions; one entailed the examination of different of modes of representation. These, in turn, reintroduced questions regarding what was being represented.

20. Engaging the reader from the outset of a poem, raising his expectations from the start, Beattie tells us, is more important than a proper chronology. The latter may be supplied, if necessary, "in retrospect." A work of art should never lose sight of its ends, it must channel all else in order to highlight and heighten the desired aims. A poem, in other words, is not governed by a linear sequence, but by a gravitational center which bestows equilibrium on its parts.

same planet. But it is not enough, that the subject of a poetical fable be the exploits of one *person*; for these may be of various and even of opposite sorts and tendencies, and take up longer time, than the nature of poetry can admit: — far less can a regular poem comprehend the affairs of *one period*, or of *one people*: — it must be limited to some *one great action or event*, to the illustration of which all the subordinate events must contribute; and these must be so connected with one another, as well as with the poet's general purpose, that one cannot be changed, transposed, or taken away, without affecting the consistence and stability of the whole.[p] In itself an incident may be interesting, a character well drawn, a description beautiful; and yet, if it disfigure the general plan, or if it obstruct or incumber, instead of helping forward the main action, a correct artist would consider it as but a gaudy superfluity or splendid deformity; like a piece of scarlet cloth sowed upon a garment of a different colour.[q] Not that all the parts of the fable either are, or can be, equally essential. Many descriptions and thoughts, of little consequence to the plan, may be admitted for the sake of variety; and the poet may, as well as the historian and philosopher, drop his subject for a time, in order to take up an affecting or instructive digression.

The doctrine of poetical digressions and episodes has been largely treated by the critics. I shall only remark, that, in estimating their propriety, three things are to be attended to: — their connection with the fable or subject; — their own peculiar excellence; — and their subserviency to the poet's design.

I. Those digressions, that both arise from and terminate in the subject; like the episode of the angel Raphael in Paradise Lost, and the transition to the death of Cesar and the civil wars in the first book of the Georgic; are the most artful, and if suitably executed claim the highest praise: — those that arise from, but do not terminate in the subject, are perhaps second in the order of merit; like the story of Dido in the Eneid, and the encomium on

p. Aristot. Poet. § 8.
q. Hor. Ar. Poet. vers. 15, &c.

a country-life in the second book of the Georgic: — those come
next, that terminate in, but do not rise from the fable; of which
there are several in the third book of the Eneid, and in the
Odyssey: — and those, that neither terminate in the fable, nor
rise from it, are the least artful; and if they be long, cannot escape
censure, unless their beauty be very great.

But, 2. we are willing to excuse a beautiful episode, at whatever expence to the subject it may be introduced. They who can
blame Virgil for obtruding upon them the charming tale of
Orpheus and Eurydice in the fourth Georgic, or Milton for the
apostrophe to light in the beginning of his third book, ought to
forfeit all title to the perusal of good poetry; for of such divine
strains one would rather be the author, than of all the books of
criticism in the world. Yet still it is better, that an episode possess
the beauty of connection, together with its own intrinsic elegance, than this without the other.

Moreover, in judging of the propriety of episodes, and other
similar contrivances, it may be expedient to attend, 3. to the
design of the poet, as distinguished from the fable or subject of
the poem. The great design, for example, of Virgil, was to interest his countrymen in a poem written with a view to reconcile
them to the person and government of Augustus. Whatever,
therefore, in the poem tends to promote this design, even though
it should, in some degree, hurt the contexture of the fable, is
really a proof of the poet's judgment. and may be not only
allowed but applauded.[21]

———————— ⟋♫⟍ ————————

21. Beattie's extended comparison of literature and history culminates in his discussion
of the unity of design. He connects Shaftesbury's concern with unity and Hutcheson's
concern with design, which presuppose "unity amidst variety." Unlike Hutcheson who
links the origin of design to the supernatural, Beattie redeems the discussion of its theological context and turns it into an aesthetic issue. It is not inspiration, it turns out,
which guarantees the perfection of a work of art but rather an understanding of the
way it is constructed, planning it accordingly and abiding by its dictates. The artificial
in art gains more attention than the artistic in nature.

Beattie also adds a novel notion to the concept of unity. For the first time, perhaps, he
tries to apply this concept to something in the process of becoming. He implies that a

(CONT.)

. . .

The more poetry improves nature, by copying after general ideas collected from extensive observation, the more it partakes (according to Aristotle) of the nature of philosophy; the greater stretch of fancy and of observation it requires in the artist, and the better chance it has to be universally agreeable. An ordinary painter can give a portrait of a beautiful face: but from a number of such faces to collect a general idea of beauty more perfect than is to be found in any individual, and then to give existence to that idea, by drawing it upon canvas (as Zeuxis is said to have done when he made a famous picture of Helen[r]), is a work which one must possess invention and judgment, as well as dexterity, to be able to execute. For it is not by copying the eyes of one lady, the lips of another, and the nose of a third, that such a picture is to be formed; — a medley of this kind would probably be ridiculous, as a certain form of feature may suit one face, which would not suit another: — but it is by comparing together several beautiful mouths (for example), remarking the peculiar charm of each; and then conceiving an idea of that feature, different perhaps from all, and more perfect than any: and thus proceeding through the several features, with a view, not only to the colour, shape, and proportion, of each part, but also to the harmony of the whole.[22]

---

r. Plin. Hist. Natur, lib. 35. [p. 105]

(CONT.   *ɯℛ*

harmonious relationship, as a constructive concept, partially affects the way a whole is created and perceived, for such "wholes" have parts which only reveal themselves successively. Given this new emphasis, it is not surprising that Beattie rejects the idea of multiplicity of ends in the artistic work, calling for a clear focus. His insistence that digressions require "justifications" tends to reinforce his major premise, for he calls at all times for a connectedness with the main aim of the work (though it may only be revealed in retrospect). His demand that digressions should also be treated artfully and should, in that respect, perhaps, even exceed the rest, grows from the belief that they should be experienced as belonging to the overall design — by the author's guiding hand.

22. We have already seen that Beattie uses the Renaissance dictum concerning the improvement on nature in two other connections: the one relating to the idea of art as

(CONT.)

. . .

Poets may refine upon nature too much, as well as too little;
for affectation and rusticity are equally remote from true elegance. — The style and sentiments of comedy should no doubt
be more correct and more pointed than those of the most polite
conversation: but to make every footman a wit, and every gentleman and lady an epigrammatist, as Congreve has done, is an
excessive and faulty refinement. The proper medium has been
hit by Menander and Terence, by Shakespeare in his happier
scenes, and by Garrick, Cumberland, and some others of late
renown. — To describe the passion of love with as little delicacy as some men speak of it, would be unpardonable; but to
transform it into mere platonic adoration, is to run into another
extreme, less criminal indeed, but too remote from universal
truth to be universally interesting. To the former extreme Ovid
inclines; and Petrarch, and his imitators, to the latter. Virgil has
happily avoided both: but Milton has painted this passion, as distinct from all others, with such peculiar truth and beauty, that we
cannot think Voltaire's encomium too high, when he says, that
love in all other poetry seems a weakness, but in Paradise Lost a
virtue. — There are many good strokes of nature in Ramsay's
Gentle Shepherd; but the author's passion of the *Rus verum*
betrays him into some indelicacies:[s] a censure that falls with
greater weight upon Theocritus, who is often absolutely inde-

---

s. The language of this poem has been blamed, on account of its vulgarity. The Scotch dialect is sufficiently rustic, even in its most improved state: but in the Gentle Shepherd it is often debased by a
phraseology not to be met with, except among the most illiterate people. Writers on pastoral have
not always been careful to distinguish between coarseness and simplicity; and yet a plain suit of
cloaths and a bundle of rags are not more different.

(CONT.)   ———— 𝔰 ————

an intensification of that which it imitates and the other relating to a principle of selection based on experience (fn. 16, 17). Here Beattie combines the two to highlight the
compositional aspect with which he is concerned in the last sections. It is not that the
most beautiful lips should be combined with the most beautiful nose, but that each
should be selected with a view of the other. The most beautiful combination — "the
harmony of the whole" — results from an understanding of a kind of combinatorics.
The individual item thus results from a coordination which takes into account a variety of constraints.

cent. The Italian pastoral of Tasso and Guarini, and the French of Fontenelle, run into the opposite extreme (though in some parts beautifully simple), and display a system of rural manners, so quaint and affected as to outrage all probability. I should oppose several great names, if I were to say, that Virgil has given us the pastoral poem in its most perfect state; and yet I cannot help being of this opinion, though I have not time at present to specify my reasons. — In fact, though mediocrity of execution in poetry be allowed to deserve the doom pronounced upon it by Horace;[t] yet it is true, notwithstanding, that in this art, as in many other good things, the point of excellence lies in a middle between two extremes; and has been reached by those only who fought to improve nature as far as the genius of their work would permit, keeping at an equal distance from rusticity on the one hand, and affected elegance on the other.[23]

CHAP. VI
Remarks on Music

SECT. I.
Of Imitation. Is Music an Imitative Art?

MAN from his birth is prone to imitation, and takes great pleasure in it. At a time when he is too young to understand or attend to rules, he learns, by imitating others, to speak, and walk, and do many other things equally requisite to life and happiness.

---

t. Hor. Ar. Poet. vers. 373

------ *ฟ* ------

23. Beattie has argued all along that the function of poetry is not to render nature as it is, but rather nature idealized, so as to fall within the boundaries of the probable, i.e. remain credible. "Refining" nature, he now tells us, must avoid extremes, for extremes yield "diminishing returns," not with regard to credibility of contents but rather with regard to the *manner* of its presentation. Elegance is a midpoint between *"affectation"* and *"rusticity,"* he tells us, not a high point on a linear scale of gradation; carefully balanced, it depends on a proper mixture. In short, elegance, excellence etc. are not clearly-defined independent qualities but rather *values* contextually determined.

Most of the sports of children are imitative, and many of them
dramatical. Mimickry occasions laughter; and a just imitation of
human life upon the stage is highly delightful to persons of all
ranks, conditions, and capacities.

Our natural propensity to imitation may in part account for the
pleasure it yields: for that is always pleasing which gratifies natural propensity; nay, to please, and to gratify, are almost synonymous terms. Yet the peculiar charm of imitation may also be
accounted for upon other principles. To compare a copy with the
original, and trace out the particulars wherein they differ and
wherein they resemble, is in itself a pleasing exercise to the
mind; and, when accompanied with admiration of the object imitated, and of the genius of the imitator, conveys a most intense
delight; which may be rendered still more intense by the agreeable qualities of the *instrument* of imitation, — by the beauty of
the colours in painting, by the harmony of the language in poetry; and in music, by the sweetness, mellowness, pathos, and
other pleasing varieties of vocal and instrumental sound. And if
to all this there be added the merit of a moral design, Imitation
will then shine forth in her most amiable form, and the enraptured heart acknowledge her powers of pleasing to be irresistible.[24]

24. The merit of imitation functions, as we shall see, as a point of reference for Beattie's
inquiry into the aesthetics of music. His use of the Aristotelian framework is typical of
most of the British thinkers, particularly of Twining and Smith, who, following Beattie,
further qualify Aristotle's ideas. Despite his own "imitation" of the revered philosopher,
a "tracing out of the particulars" wherein Beattie differs from Aristotle, may reveal the
new awareness of the centrality of the mind and its operations. Beattie identifies the
merit of imitation 1) as a natural propensity (a concept not unlkie that of "faculties"
used by other eighteenth-century thinkers), which may be easily observed and is
immediate and within the scope of everybody's experience, and 2) as an intellectual
exercise of the mind, which requires awareness and judgement. The difference
between the two, already noticed by Hutcheson, will be further explicated by Smith.
Though they differ, they are equally natural, Beattie implies, as far as the ability to
please is concerned; the quest for pleasure, as we have already learned from
Shaftesbury and Hutcheson, is basic to man qua man.

. . .

Since Imitation is so plentiful a source of pleasure, we need not wonder, that the imitative arts of poetry and painting should have been greatly esteemed in every enlightened age. The imitation itself, which is the work of the artist, is agreeable; the thing imitated, which is nature, is also agreeable; and is not the same thing true of the instrument of imitation? Or does any one doubt, whether harmonious language be pleasing to the ear; or certain arrangements of colour beautiful to the eye?

Shall I apply these, and the preceding reasonings, to the musical Art also, which I have elsewhere called, and which is generally understood to be, Imitative? Shall I say, that some melodies please, because they imitate nature, and that others, which do not imitate nature, are therefore unpleasing? — that an air expressive of devotion, for example, is agreeable, because it presents us with an imitation of those sounds by which devotion does naturally express itself? — Such an affirmation would hardly pass upon the reader; notwithstanding the plausibility it might seem to derive from that analogy which all the fine arts are supposed to bear to one another. He would ask, What is the natural sound of devotion? Where is it to be heard? When was it heard? What resemblance is there between Handel's *Te Deum*, and the tone of voice natural to a person expressing, by articulate sound, his veneration of the Divine Character and Providence? — In fact, I apprehend, that critics have erred a little in their determinations upon this subject, from an opinion, that Music, Painting, and Poetry, are all imitative arts. I hope at least I may say, without offence, that while this was my opinion, I was always conscious of some unaccountable confusions of thought, whenever I attempted to explain it in the way of detail to others.

But while I thus insinuate, that Music is not an imitative art, I mean no disrespect to Aristotle, who seems in the beginning of his Poetics to declare the contrary. It is not the whole, but *the greater part* of music, which that philosopher calls Imitative; and I agree with him so far as to allow this property to some music, though not to all. But he speaks of the ancient music, and I of the modern; and to one who considers how very little we know of the former, it will not appear a contradiction to say, that the one might have been imitative, though the other is not.

Nor do I mean any disrespect to music, when I would strike it off the list of imitative arts. I allow it to be a fine art, and to have great influence on the human soul: I grant, that, by its power of raising a variety of agreeable emotions in the hearer, it proves its relation to poetry, and that it never appears to the best advantage but with poetry for its interpreter: and I am satisfied, that though musical genius may subsist without poetical taste, and poetical genius without musical taste; yet these two talents united might accomplish nobler effects than either could do singly. I acknowledge too, that the principles and essential rules of this art are as really founded in nature, as those of poetry and painting. But when I am asked, What part of nature is imitated in any good picture or poem, I find I can give a definite answer: whereas, when I am asked, What part of nature is imitated in Handel's *Water-music*, for instance, or in Corelli's *eighth concerto*, or in any particular English song or Scotch tune, I find I can give no definite answer: — though no doubt I might say some plausible things; or perhaps, after much refinement, be able to show, that music may, by one shift or other, be made an imitative art, provided you allow me to give any meaning I please to the word *imitative*.[25]

———— ∽ ————

25. On the basis of his propositions concerning imitation (which we have partially omitted), Beattie is now ready to posit the major question which will occupy his discussion of music: What is the referent of music? The theory of mimesis assumed the existence of a copy and an original, that the two are related, and that the relationship is recognized. By posing the question in the way he does, Beattie in fact challenges some of the basic assumptions of the theory. To begin with, he isolates the concept of reference, questioning how something refers, and eventually entertains the possibility that art needs no original at all. (Interestingly, Beattie's immediate predecessors managed to avoid the question, as far as music is concerned. Thus, for example, Harris simply lowers the status of music as an art, for he accepts imitation as a normative factor, whereas Avison treats the whole question as irrelevant, considering expression to be internal to works of art.)

(CONT.)

Music is imitative, when it readily puts one in mind of the thing imitated. If an explanation be necessary; and if, after all, we find it difficult to recognise any exact similitude, I would not call such music an imitation of nature; but consider it as upon a footing, in point of likeness, with those pictures, wherein the action cannot be known but by a label proceeding from the mouth of the agent, nor the species of animal ascertained without a name written under it. But between imitation in music and imitation in painting, there is this one essential difference: — a bad picture is always a bad imitation of nature, and a good picture is necessarily a good imitation; but music may be exactly imitative, and yet intolerably bad; or not at all imitative, and yet be perfectly good. I have heard, that the *Pastorale* in the eighth of Corelli's *Concertos* * (which appears by the inscription to have been composed for the night of the Nativity) was intended for an imitation of the song of angels hovering above the fields of Bethlehem, and gradually soaring up to heaven. The music, however, is not such as would of itself convey this idea: and, even with the help of the commentary, it requires a lively fancy to connect the various movements and melodies of the piece with the motions and evolutions of the heavenly host; as sometimes flying off, and sometimes returning; singing sometimes in one quarter of the sky, and sometimes in another; now in one or two parts, and now in full chorus. It is not clear, that the author intended any imitation; and whether he did or not, is a matter of no consequence; for the music will continue to please, when the tradition is no more remembered. The harmonies of this *pastorale* are indeed so uncommon, and so ravishingly sweet, that it is almost

(CONT.)   ——— ♫ ———

That music should prove essential to the clarification of these crucial questions is not surprising, since attempts to subject music to the assumptions underlying imitation have never fared well. Beattie may be ready to forgo 'imitation' as an all-encompassing artistic theory, because he is aware of cultural changes which also entail new criteria for the organization of knowledge. Respectful as he is of Aristotle, he is not ready to grant him prophetic powers, for he is aware that theories of art are intimately related to the state of the arts themselves.

* See example II 1.

Example II-1

Corelli, Concerto no.8, op. VI (*Fatto per la notte di Natale*) 2nd Movement

Example II-2

A Cantata: "In harmony would you excell"

From: W.H. Gratton Flood, "Eighteenth Century Essayist on Poetry and Music", *Musical Quarterly 2*, 1916: 191-86

Example II-2 (cont.)

(2)

Example II-2 (cont.)

(3)

Trolloping lolloping galloping trolloping. Lolloping galloping trol—lop.

Lolloping trolloping galloping lolloping. Trolloping galloping lol—lop.

Now creep sweep. Sweep sweep the deep See see Ce li a

Ce lia dies dies dies dies dies dies dies dies

While true lo-vers eyes Weeping sleep Sleeping weep Wee ping sleep

fast

Bo peep. bo peep. bo peep. bo peep peep. bo bo peep.

Example II-2 (cont.)

(4)

impossible not to think of heaven when one hears them. I would not call them imitative; but I believe they are finer than any imitative music in the world.[26]

Sounds in themselves can imitate nothing directly but sounds, no in their motions any thing but motions. But the natural sounds and motions that music is allowed to imitate, are but few. For, first, they must all be consistent with the fundamental principles of the art, and not repugnant either to melody or to harmony. Now the foundation of all true music, and the most perfect of all musical instruments, is the human voice; which is therefore the prototype of the musical scale, and a standard of musical sound. Noises, therefore, and inharmonious notes of every kind, which a good voice cannot utter without straining, ought to be excluded from this pleasing art: for it is impossible, that those vocal sounds which require any unnatural efforts, either of the singer or speaker, should ever give permanent gratification to the hearer. I say, permanent gratification; for I deny not, that the preternatural screams of an Italian singer may occasion surprise, and momentary amusement, but those screams are not music; they are admired, not for their propriety or pathos, but, like rope-dancing, and the eating of fire, merely because they are uncommon and difficult. — Besides, the end of all genuine music is, to introduce into the human mind certain affections, or susceptibilities of affection. Now, all the affections, over which music has any power, are of the agreeable kind. And therefore, in this art, no imitations of natural sound or motion, but such as tend to inspire agreeable affections, ought ever to find a place. The song of certain birds, the murmur of a stream, the shouts of multi-

———— ⚓ ————

26. Though Beattie is willing to forgo imitation as an intrinsic principle for the intelligibility of art, he is aware of an array of possibilities with which music might become associated, "if one puts one's mind to it." In other words, meaning is external to music; it has to be informed and formed either by designative texts, or through association or habituation. In any case, Beattie is aware of the function of culture and tradition in elucidating that which does not contain what is attributed to it, despite professed intentions. He is also prepared to maintain that the aesthetic significance of music does not depend on the meaning which is ascribed to it. What, then, are the "essentials" of music?

tudes, the tumult of a storm, the roar of thunder, or a chime of bells, are sounds connected with agreeable or sublime affections, and reconcileable both with melody and with harmony; and may therefore be imitated, when the artist has occasion for them: but the crowing of cocks, the barking of dogs, the mewing of cats, the grunting of swine, the gabbling of geese, the cackling of a hen, the braying of an ass, the creaking of a saw, or the rumbling of a cart-wheel, would render the best music ridiculous. The movement of a dance may be imitated, or the stately pace of an embattled legion; but the hobble of a trotting horse would be intolerable.[27]

There is another sort of imitation by sound, which ought never to be heard, or seen, in music. To express the local elevation of objects by what *we* call *high* notes, and their depression by *low* or *deep* notes, has no more propriety in it, than any other pun. *We* call notes *high* or *low*, in respect of their situation in the written scale. There would have been no absurdity in expressing the highest notes by characters placed at the bottom of the scale or musical line, and the lowest notes by characters placed at the top of it, if custom had so determined. And there is reason to think, that something like this actually obtained in the musical scale of the ancients. At least it is probable, that the deepest or gravest sound was called *Summa* by the Romans, and the shrillest or acutest *Ima*; which might be owing to the construction of their instruments; the string that sounded the former being perhaps

———— ☙ ————

27. Harris had already pointed out that in simple imitative music, sound imitates sound, i.e. no translation from original to medium takes place. Despite the apparent directability this "imitation" enjoys, Harris alludes to the ambiguous reference achieved thereby, a point which will be clarified by Twining. Harris is also aware of 'motion' as an element harboring imitative possibilities. Webb, as we shall see, applies both criteria ingeniously in his essay on the origin of language. Beattie combines these notions of musical imitation with Avison's notion of music's normative "agreeability." Thus, he adds a further constraint to the copy, to abide by music's own artistic dictates. In addition to subserving means to desired ends, Beattie would also submit all possible ends to an end which is "genuine" to music, namely its susceptibility to the creation of affect. How is the list of means related to the end which he singles out is brilliantly treated by Webb.

highest in place, and that which sounded the latter lowest. — Yet
some people would think a song faulty, if the word *heaven* was
set to what we call a *low* note, or the word *hell* to what we call
a *high* one.[28]

All these sorts of illicit imitation have been practised, and by
those too from whom better things were expected. This abuse of
a noble art did not escape the satire of Swift; who, though deaf
to the charms of music, was not blind to the absurdity of musicians. He recommended it to Dr. Ecclin, an ingenious gentleman
of Ireland, to compose a *Cantata* in ridicule of this puerile mimicry.* Here we have *motions* imitated, which are the most inharmonious, and the least connected with human affections; as the
trotting, ambling, and *galloping,* of Pegasus; and *sounds* the
most unmusical, as *crackling* and *sniveling,* and *rough roystering
rustic roaring strains*: the words *high* and *deep* have high and
deep notes set to them; a series of short notes of equal lengths
are introduced, to imitate *shivering* and *shaking*; an irregular rant
of quick sounds, to express *rambling*; a sudden rise of the voice,
from a low to a high pitch, to denote *flying above the sky*; a
ridiculous run of chromatic divisions on the words *Celia dies*;
with other droll contrivances of a like nature. In a word, Swift's
Cantata alone may convince any person, that music uniformaly
imitative would be ridiculous. — I just observe in passing, that
the satire of this piece is levelled, not at absurd imitation only,
but also at some other musical improprieties; such as the idle

———————— ⟂ ————————

28. The subject of "madrigalism" recurs time and again among the British writers. They
all seem to follow Galilei's attack on the assumption that music works analytically
rather than synthetically. Aware of cultural conventions and their making, Beattie goes
one step further, showing that the entire exercise of madrigalism is built upon the
working of metaphors: for example, he says that entrenched metaphors (high notes as
"high" etc.) are indeed received as "truths"; therein lies their credibility but not their
affectivity. (The reader may recall that Beattie made use of the distinction between credibility and affectivity in his discussion of history vs. poetry, see fn. 13.) Affectivity is thus
something that has to be made and remade anew. Indeed, the entire system of 'alle-
gorism in music' (so called by Bukofzer 1939–1940), is attributed to the acquisition of
meaning and not to intrinsic musical powers.

*See example II 2.

repetition of the same words, the running of long extravagant divisions upon one syllable, and the setting of words to music that have no meaning.

If I were entitled to suggest any rules in this art, I would humbly propose (and a great musician and ingenious writer seems to be of the same mind[u]), that no imitation should ever be introduced into music purely instrumental. Of vocal melody the expression is, or ought to be, ascertained by the poetry; but the expression of the best instrumental music is ambiguous. In this, therefore, there is nothing to lead the mind of the hearer to recognise the imitation, which, though both legitimate and accurate, would run the risk of being overlooked and lost. If, again, it were so very exact, as to lead our thoughts instantly to the thing imitated, we should be apt to attend to the imitation only, so as to remain insensible to the general effect of the piece.[29]

. . .

In vocal music, truly such, the words render the expression determinate, and fix the hearer's attention upon it. Here therefore legitimate imitations may be employed; both because the subject of the song will render them intelligible, and because the attention of the hearer is in no danger of being seduced from the principal air. Yet even here, these imitations must be laid upon the instrumental accompaniment, and by no means attempted by the singer, unless they are expressive, and musical, and may be easily managed by the voice. In the song, which is the principle

---

u. Avison on Musical Expression, p. 57.

29. Contrary to shared opinion in the operatic age, which derided instrumental music for its "ambiguity," Beattie, following Avison, agrees that music is ambiguous as far as meaning is concerned, but since he no longer views meaning as intrinsic to the art, he has no problem accepting instrumental music for what it is. Moreover, preoccupation with meaning, argues Beattie, risks overlooking the general effect of a piece of music. It seems that Beattie, too, is aware of the fact that music works synthetically and not analytically. With Twining and Smith, the "ambiguity" of instrumental music will even become a merit, as we shall see.

part, expression should be predominant, and imitations never used at all, except to assist the expression. Besides, the tones of the human voice, though the most pathetic of all sounds, are not suited to the quirks of imitative melody, which will generally appear to best advantage on an instrument. In the first part of that excellent song, "Hide me from day's gairish eye, "While the bee with honey'd thigh " At her flowery work does sing, "And the waters deep murmuring, "With such concert as they keep, "Intice the dewy feather'd sleep." — Handel imitates the murmur of groves and waters by the accompaniment of tenors:* in another song of the same *Oratorio,* "On a plat of rising ground, "I hear the far-off curfew sound, "Over some wide-water'd shore, "Swinging slow with sullen roar," — he makes the bass imitate the evening-bell:* in another fine song, "Hush, ye pretty warbling choir," — he accompanies the voice with a flageolet that imitates the singing of birds:* in the "Sweet bird that shun'st the noise of folly," the chief accompaniment is a German flute imitating occasionally the notes of the nightingale.* — Sometimes, where expression and imitation happen to coincide, and the latter is easily managed by the voice, he makes the song itself imitative. Thus, in that song, "Let the merry bells ring round, "And the jocund rebecks sound, "To many a youth and many a maid, "Dancing in the chequer'd shade," — he makes the voice in the beginning imitate the *sound* of a chime of bells, and in the end the *motion* and gaiety of a dance.*

Of these imitations no body will question the propriety.[30] But Handel, notwithstanding his inexhaustible invention, and won-

---

30. Beattie, following hints of Avison, relegates expression and imitation to the voice and to the instrumental accompaniment respectively. Whereas imitation may relate to the object it imitates in a literal fashion, expression, as we have seen, does not have an object which it can resemble. In other words, all the parts of a work of art may be said to refer, but their modes of reference may differ, as Twining will further elucidate. The attribution of different roles to accompaniment and voice, in the construction of the overall illusion, is in itself an important contribution to the understanding of the working of symbols. Nonetheless, Beattie's is still a rudimentary formulation of this important topic.

*See examples II 3, 4, 5.

Example II-3

"Hide Me From Day's Garish Eye"

From *L'allegro, Il Pensoroso, ed Il Moderato* (1740), The German Handel Society, Leipzig 1859.

Example II-3 (cont.)

Example II-4

"Oft On A Plat of Rising Ground"

From *L'allegro, Il Pensoroso, ed Il Moderato* (1740), The German Handel Society, Leipzig 1859.

Example II-5

"Hush Ye Pretty Warbling Choir!"

From *Acis And Galatea* (1718), in Hallische Handel-Ausgabe, heraus. von Wolfram Winezus, G. F. Handel Gesellschaft, Bd. 9/1, 1991.

Example II-5 (cont.)

derful talents in the sublime and pathetic, is subject to fits of trifling, and frequently errs in the application of his imitative contrivances. In that song "What passion cannot music raise and
quell," when he comes to the words, "His listening brethen stood
around, "And wondering on their faces *fell*," — the accompanying violoncello falls suddenly from a quick and *high* movement
to a very slow and low *movement*.

. . .

One of the most affecting styles in music is the *Pastoral*. Some
airs put us in mind of the country, of "rural sights and rural
sounds," and dispose the heart to that chearful tranquillity, that
pleasing melody, that "vernal delight," which groves and streams,
flocks and herds, hills and vallies, inspire. But of what are these
pastoral airs imitative? Is it of the murmur of waters, the warbling
of groves, the lowing of herds, the bleating of flocks, or the echo
of vales and mountains? Many airs are pastoral, which imitate
none of these things. What then do they imitate? — the songs of
ploughmen, milkmaids, and shepherds? yes: they are such, as we
think we have heard, or might have heard, sung by the inhabitants of the country. Then they must *resemble* country-songs; and
if so, these songs must also be in the pastoral style. Of what then
are these country-songs, the supposed archetypes of pastoral
music, imitative? Is it of other country-songs? This shifts the difficulty a step backward, but does not take it away. Is it of rural
sounds, proceeding from things animated, or from things inanimate? or of rural motions of men, beasts, or birds? of winds,
woods, or waters? — In a word, an air may be pastoral, and in
the highest degree pleasing, which imitates neither sound nor
motion, nor any thing else whatever.

After all, it must be acknowledged, that there is some relation at
least, or analogy, if not similitude, between certain musical
sounds, and mental affections. Soft music may be considered as
analogous to gentle emotions; and loud music, if the tones are
sweet and not too rapid, to sublime ones; and a quick succession of noisy notes, like those we hear from a drum, seems to

have some relation to hurry and impetuosity of passion. Sometimes, too, there is from nature, and sometimes there comes to be from custom, a connection between certain musical instruments, and certain places and occasions. Thus a flute, hautboy, or bagpipe, is better adapted to the purposes of rural music, than a fiddle, organ, or harpsichord, because more portable, and less liable to injury from the weather: thus an organ, on account both of its size and loudness, requires to be placed in a church, or some large apartment: thus violins and violoncellos, to which any degree of damp may prove hurtful, are naturally adapted to domestic use; while drums and trumpets, fifes and french-horns, are better suited to the service of the field. Hence it happens, that particular tones and modes of music acquire such a connection with particular places, occasions, and sentiments, that by hearing the former we are put in mind of the latter, so as to be affected with them more or less, according to the circumstances. The sound of an organ, for example, puts one in mind of a church, and of the affections suitable to that place; military music, of military ideas; and flutes and hautboys, of the thoughts and images peculiar to rural life. This may serve in part to account for musical expressiveness or efficacy; that is, to explain how it comes to pass, that certain passions are raised, or certain ideas suggested, by certain kinds of music: but this does not prove music to be an imitative art, in the same sense in which painting and poetry are called imitative. For between a picture and its original, between the ideas suggested by a poetical description and the objects described, there is a strict similitude: but between soft music and a calm temper there is no strict similitude; and between the sound of a drum or of an organ and the affection of courage or of devotion, between the music of flutes and a pastoral life, between a concert of violins and a chearful company, there is only an accidental connection, formed by custom, and founded rather on the nature of the instruments, than on that of the music.[31]

———— ♫ ————

31. Searching for the "roots of reference" of affective music, Beattie introduces a new distinction, i.e. between analogy and resemblance. He further divides analogy into

(CONT.)

. . .

Music, therefore, is pleasing, not because it is imitative, but because certain melodies and harmonies have *an aptitude* to raise certain passions, affections, and sentiments in the soul. And, consequently, the pleasures we derive from melody and harmony are seldom or never resolvable into that delight which the human mind receives from the imitation of nature.

All this, it may be said, is but a dispute about a word. Be it so: but it is, notwithstanding, a dispute somewhat material both to art and to science. It is material, in science, that philosophers have a determined meaning to their words, and that things be referred to their proper classes, And it is of importance to every art, that its design and end be rightly understood, and that artists be not taught to believe that to be essential to it, which is only adventitious, often impertinent, for the most part unnecessary, and at best but ornamental.[32]

(CONT.)

———— ⚏ ————

"natural" and "by custom." It is the latter which explains why imitation in music is assumed. Indeed, habituation, as he has already pointed out, may work wonders; learned and acquired conventions are often believed to be "natural." Moreover, what is "natural" is very limited. The roots of the analogies created are often to be found in circumstances irrelevant to the association which they come to bear, as his discussion of the meaning ascribed to certain instruments exemplifies. In any case, the origins of reference are often forgotten, as a genre (e.g. the pastoral) becomes crystallized and identified as such. Hence the power of intertextuality in art, which often functions as a substitute for external reference.

32. Beattie concludes this section in the way he began the entire treatise, namely, by submitting his particular investigation to a general view of knowledge. Whereas at the beginning of the treatise he emphasizes the scientific standing of aesthetic inquiries, here he stresses its philosophical underpinnings. Defining major concepts in aesthetics, we learn, is not arbitrary, nor does it relate to that vocabulary which describes the various arts. Terms employed should reveal a system in which their application as well as their meaning is mutually circumscribed. This not only facilitates communication among those who try to define and understand art but also helps those who create works of art. Artists may improve their vocation through insight into the implications of their artistic applications. It should be borne in mind that Beattie himself was a poet.

SECT. II.

How are the pleasures we derive from Music to be accounted for?

IT was said, that certain melodies and harmonies have *an aptitude* to raise certain passions, affections, and sentiments, in the human soul. Let us now enquire a little into the nature of this *aptitude*; by endeavouring, from acknowledged principles of the human constitution, to explain the cause of that pleasure which mankind derive from music. I am well aware of the delicacy of the argument, and of my inability to do it justice; and therefore I promise no complete investigation, nor indeed any thing more than a few cursory remarks. As I have no theory to support, and as this topic, though it may amuse, is not of any great utility, I shall be neither positive in my assertions, nor abstruse in my reasoning.

The vulgar distinguish between the sense of hearing, and that faculty by which we receive pleasure from music, and which is commonly called *a musical ear*. Every body knows, that to hear, and to have a relish for melody, are two different things; and that many persons have the first in perfection, who are destitute of the last. The last is indeed, like the first, a gift of nature.

II . . .

A man unskilled in music might imagine, that the most agreeable harmony[v] must be made up of the sweetest concords, without any mixture of discord: and in like manner, a child might fancy, that a feast of sweet-meats would prove the most delicious banquet. But both would be mistaken. The same concord may be more or less pleasing, according to its position; and the sweeter concords often produce their best effect, when they are introduced by the harsher ones, or even by discords; for then they are most agreeable, because they give the greatest relief to the ear: even as health is doubly delightful after sickness, liberty after confinement, and a sweet taste when preceded by a bitter. Dissonance, therefore, is necessary to the perfection of harmony. But consonance predominates; and to such a degree, that, except

---

v. *Melody*, in the language of art, is the agreeable effect of a single series of musical tones: *Harmony* is the agreeable effect of two or more series of musical tones founded at the same time.

on rare occasions, and by a nice ear, the discord in itself is hardly perceptible.

Musicians have taken pains to discover the principles on which concords and discords are to be so arranged as to produce the best effect; and have thus brought the whole art of harmony within the compass of a certain number of rules, some of which are more, and others less indispensable. These rules admit not of demonstrative proof: for though some of them may be inferred by rational deduction from the very nature of sound; yet the supreme judge of their propriety is the human ear. They are, however, founded on observation so accurate and so just, that no artist ever thought of calling them in question. Rousseau indeed somewhere insinuates, that habit and education might give us an equal relish for a different system of harmony; a sentiment which I should not have expected from an author, who for the most part recommends an implicit confidence in our natural feelings, and who certainly understands human nature well, and music better than any other philosopher. That a bass of *sevenths*, or *fourths*, or even *fifths*, should ever become so agreeable to any human ear, as one constructed according to the system, is to me as inconceivable, as that Virgil, turned into rugged prose, would be read and admired as much as ever. Rousseau could not mean to extend this remark to the whole system, but only to some of its mechanical rules: and indeed it must be allowed, that in this, as well as in other arts, there are rules which have no better foundation than fashion, or the practice of some eminent composer.[33]

---

33. Beattie seems well versed in the literature which discusses music, though he does not always name his sources. For example, the distinction between hearing and musical hearing is an Aristoxenian one, which Beattie may have known about directly or indirectly. Beattie attaches this notion to the dispute over Rameau's writings, concerning the status of the rules which he has unveiled. Though attributing a great deal to conventions, as we have seen, Beattie stands between Rameau and Rousseau, for he attributes to the musical ear a natural standing. The musical ear, he implies, can neither be reduced to inflexible rules, nor can its special fitness for music be ignored. According to Beattie, there are rules which are anchored in nature and others which are anchored in convention. The musical ear is thus a kind of content-free propensity, well-qualified to learn and develop the combinations of the natural and the conventional.

Natural sensibility is not taste, though it be necessary to it. A painter discovers both blemishes and beauties in a picture, in which an ordinary eye can perceive neither. In poetical language, and in the arrangement and choice of words, there are many niceties, whereof they only are conscious who have practised versification, as well as studied the works of poets, and the rules of the art. In like manner, harmony must be studied a little in its principles by every person who would acquire a true relish for it; and nothing but practice will ever give that quickness to his ear which is necessary to enable him to enter with adequate satisfaction, or rational dislike, into the merits or demerits of a musical performance. When once he can attend to the progress, relations, and dependencies, of the several parts; and remember the past, and anticipate the future, at the same time he perceives the present; so as to be sensible of the skill of the composer, and dexterity of the performer; — a regular concerto, well executed, will yield him high entertainment, even though its regularity be its principal recommendation. The pleasure which an untutored hearer derives from it, is far inferior: and yet there is something in harmony that pleases, and in dissonance that offends, every ear; and were a piece to be played consisting wholly of discords, or put together without any regard to rule, I believe no person whatever would listen to it without great disgust.

After what has been briefly said of the agreeable qualities of musical notes, it will not seem strange, that a piece, either of melody or of harmony, of little or no expression, should, when elegantly performed, give some delight; not only to adepts, who can trace out the various contrivances of the composer, but even to those who have little or no skill in this art, and must therefore look upon the whole piece as nothing more than a combination of pleasing sounds.[34]

———— ♫ ————

34. A strong believer in the kind of clarification that rests on introducing distinctions, Beattie introduces a further distinction which emerges from the previous paragraphs, namely, that between natural sensibility and musical taste. Like Shaftesbury, Jacob, and

(CONT.)

III . . .

Music, however, would not have recommended itself so effectually to general esteem, if it had always been merely instrumental. For, if I mistake not, the expression of music without
poetry is vague and ambiguous; and hence it is, that the same
air may sometimes be repeated to every stanza of a long ode or
ballad. The change of the poet's ideas, provided the subject continue nearly the same, does not always require a change of the
music: and if critics have ever determined otherwise, they were
led into the mistake, by supposing, what every musician knows
to be absurd, that, in fitting verses to a tune, or a tune to verses, it is more necessary, that *particular words* should have *particular notes* adapted to them, than that the *general tenor* of the
music should accord with the *general nature* of the sentiments.

It is true, that to a favourite air, even when unaccompanied
with words, we do commonly annex certain ideas, which may
have come to be related to it in consequence of some accidental associations: and sometimes we imagine a resemblance
(which however is merely imaginary) between certain melodies
and certain thoughts or objects. Thus a Scotchman may fancy,
that there is some sort of likeness between that charming air
which he calls *Tweedside*, and the scenery of a fine pastoral
country: and to the same air, even when only played on an
instrument, he may annex the ideas of romantic love and rural
tranquillity; because these form the subject of a pretty little ode,
which he has often heard sung to that air. But all this is the effect
of habit. A foreigner who hears that tune for the first time, entertains no such fancy. The utmost we can expect from him is, to
acknowledge the air to be sweet and simple. He would smile, if
we were to ask him, whether it bears any resemblance to the

(CONT.) ———— ∽ ————

others, he believes that taste rests on cultivation and that cultivation is a process
whereby one learns to identify the inner workings of a piece of art, the functions of
its parts and their interdependencies. Taste, in contradistinction to "natural sensibility,"
is a kind of literacy which may turn into a second nature, as it were. Improving upon
the "untutored" ear, it increases the pleasure derived from music.

hills, groves, and meadows, adjoining to a beautiful river, nor would he perhaps think it more expressive of romantic love, than of conjugal, parental, or filial affection, tender melancholy, moderate joy, or any other gentle passion. Certain it is, that on any one of these topics an ode might be composed, which would suit the air most perfectly. So ambiguous is musical expression.

It is likewise true, that music merely instrumental does often derive significancy from external circumstances. When an army in battle-array is advancing to meet the enemy, words are not necessary to give meaning to the military music. And a solemn air on the organ, introducing or dividing the church-service, may not only elevate the mind, and banish impertinent thoughts, but also, deriving energy from the surrounding scene, may promote religious meditation.

Nor can it be denied, that instrumental music may both quicken our sensibility, and give a direction to it; that is, may both prepare the mind for being affected, and determine it to one set of affections rather than another; — to melancholy, for instance, rather than merriment, composure rather than agitation, devotion rather than levity, and contrariwise. Certain tunes, too, there are, which having been always connected with certain actions, do, merely from the power of habit, dispose men to those actions. Such are the tunes commonly used to regulate the motions of dancing.[35]

———— ⚬ ————

35. Beattie now interrelates three major points, which have been alluded to earlier. To begin with, he re-emphasizes the "general nature" of music, i.e. that music works synthetically and not in an atomized fashion. If music can be made to relate to words, it is not the meaning of particular words which it conveys but rather their general sentiment. Then, following Descartes, Beattie reminds us that the relationship between music and its meaning is not an inherent one but a consequence of habituated associations. Unlike Descartes, however, Beattie believes that such associations are not altogether arbitrary; indeed, they might even explain the "powers" of music. Beattie understands what Webb explicates at length, that different affections fall into classes (for example, "tender melancholy" to "moderate joy" may constitute a single class) and that these relate to different kinds of music, which likewise lend themselves to division into classes. In other words, it is precisely circumscribed ambiguity that is at the

(CONT.)

Yet it is in general true, that poetry is the most immediate and most accurate interpreter of Music. Without this auxiliary, a piece of the best music, heard for the first time, might be said to mean something, but we should not be able to say what. It might incline the heart to sensibility: but poetry, or language, would be necessary to improve that sensibility into a real emotion, by fixing the mind upon some definite and affecting ideas. A fine instrumental symphony well performed, is like an oration delivered with propriety, but in an unknown tongue; it may affect us a little, but conveys no determinate feeling; we are alarmed, perhaps, or melted, or soothed, but it is very imperfectly, because we know not why: — the singer, by taking up the same air, and applying words to it, immediately translates the oration into our own language; then all uncertainty vanishes, the fancy is filled with determinate ideas, and determinate emotions take possession of the heart.

A great part of our fashionable music seems intended rather to tickle and astonish the hearers, than to inspire them with any permanent emotions. And if that be the end of the art, then, to be sure, this fashionable music is just what it should be, and the simpler strains of former ages are good for nothing. Nor am I now at leisure to inquire, whether it be better for an audience to be thus tickled and astonished, than to have their fancy impressed with beautiful images, and their hearts melted with tender passions, or elevated with sublime ones. But if you grant me this one point, that music is more or less perfect, in proportion as it has more or less power over the heart, it will follow, that all music merely instrumental, and which does not derive

(CONT.) ———— ♫ ————

heart of the expressive powers of music. Given the associations to which certain musical configurations (style, genres etc.) have come to adhere, Beattie is now able to explain what Harris has taken for granted, i.e. why music is able to "both prepare the mind for being affected, and determine it to one set of affections rather than another." Preparation and determination, which the ancients called the "tuning of the soul," differs from supplying the mind with "food for thought," as Harris has already pointed out. Beattie's arguments, as a whole, lend support to this last point as well.

significancy from any of the associations, habits, or outward circumstances, above mentioned, is to a certain degree imperfect; and that, while the rules hinted at in the following queries are overlooked by composers and performers, vocal music, though it may astonish mankind, or afford them a slight gratification, will never be attended with those important effects that we know it produced of old in the days of simplicity and true taste.[36]

. . .

Every thing in art, nature, or common life, must give delight, which communicates delightful passions to the human mind. And because all the passions that music can inspire are of the agreeable kind, it follows, that all pathetic or expressive music must be agreeable. Music may inspire devotion, fortitude, compassion, benevolence, tranquility; it may infuse a gentle sorrow that softens, without wounding, the heart, or a sublime horror that expands, and elevates, while it astonishes, the imagination: but music has no expression for impiety, cowardice, cruelty, hatred, or discontent. For every essential rule of the art tends to produce pleasing combinations of sound; and it is difficult to conceive, how from these any painful or criminal affections should arise. I believe, however, it might be practicable, by means of harsh tones, irregular rhythm, and continual dissonance, to work the mind into a disagreeable state, and to produce horrible thoughts, and criminal propensity, as well as painful sensations. But this would not be music; nor can it ever

---

36. In the last paragraphs, Beattie seems to reiterate eighteenth-century commonplaces concerning the contribution of poetry to the clarification of music on the one hand, and the superficiality of much of contemporary instrumental music on the other. Partly contradicting his earlier argument concerning the inner sufficiency of instrumental music, he now warns against the detachment of music from associations, habits, or outward circumstances, that is, from cultural embeddedness and the meanings which accompany it.

Paradoxically, it is the "embedded music" which may variegate musical expression, whereas the "detached music" may lead to stagnation, to a way of tantalizing the ear.

be for the interest of any society to put such a villanous art in practice.[37]

. . .

IV. Is there not reason to think, that variety and simplicity of structure may contribute something to the agreeableness of music, as well as of poetry and prose. Variety, kept within due bounds, is pleasing, because it refreshes the mind with novelty; and is therefore studiously sought after in all the arts, and in none of them more than in music. To give this character to his compositions, the poet varies his phraseology and syntax; and the feet, the pauses, and the sound of contiguous verses, as much as the subject, the language, and the laws of versification will permit: and the prose-writer combines longer with shorter sentences in the same paragraph, longer with shorter clauses in the same sentence, and even longer with shorter words in the same clause; terminates contiguous clauses and sentences by a different cadence, and constructs them by a different syntax; and in general avoids all monotony and similar sounds, except where they are unavoidable, or where they may contribute (as indeed they often do) to energy or perspicuity. The musician diversifies his *melody*, by changing his keys; by deferring or interrupting his cadences; by a mixture of slower and quicker, higher and lower, softer and louder notes; and, in pieces of length, by altering the rhythm, the movement, and the air: and his *harmony* he varies, by varying his concords and discords, by a change of modulation, by contrasting the ascent or slower motion of one part to the descent or quicker motion of another, by assigning different harmonies to the same melody, or different melodies to the same harmony, and by many other contrivances.

———— ♫ ————

37. Reiterating Avison and Webb regarding the benevolence of music, Beattie does see a possibility for music to be "sensational," i.e. to deviate from its postulated harmoniousness, though he disapproves of it. Indeed music can and did step out of the limits enforced on it by the naively enlightened eighteenth century, once other aesthetic ideals arose.

Simplicity makes music, as well as language, intelligible and
expressive. It is in every work of art a recommendatory quality.
In music it is indispensable; for we are never pleased with that
music which we cannot understand, or which seems to have no
meaning. Of the ancient music little more is known, than that it
was very affecting and very simple. All popular and favourite
airs; all that remains of the old national music in every country;
all military marches, church-tunes, and other compositions that
are more immediately addressed to the heart, and intended to
please the general taste; all proverbial maxims of morality and
prudence, and all those poetical phrases and lines, which every
body remembers, and is occasionally repeating, are remarkable
for simplicity. To which we may add, that language, while it
improves in simplicity, grows more and more perfect: and that,
as it loses this character, it declines in the same proportion from
the standard of elegance, and draws nearer and nearer to utter
depravation.[w] Without simplicity, the varieties of art, instead of
pleasing, would only bewilder the attention, and confound the
judgment.

Rhythm, or Number, is in music a copious source of both variety and uniformity. Not to enter into any nice speculation on the
nature of rhythm,[x] (for which this is not a proper place), I shall
only observe, that notes, as united in music, admit of the distinction of quick and slow, as well as of acute and grave; and
that on the former distinction depends what is here called
Rhythm. It is the only thing in a tune which the drum can imitate. And by that instrument, the rhythm of any tune may be imitated most perfectly, as well as by the sound of the feet in dancing: — only as the feet can hardly move so quick as the drum-
sticks, the dancer may be obliged to repeat his strokes at longer
intervals, by supposing the music divided into larger portions; to
give one stroke, for example, where the drummer might give two
or three, or two where the other would give four or six. For
every piece of regular music is supposed to be divided into small

w. See *Le Vicende della Litterature del. Sig. Carlo Denina*.
x. The nature of Rhythm, and the several divisions of it, are very accurately explained by the learned
author of *An Essay on the origin and progress of language*, vol, ii. p. 301.

portions (separated in writing by a cross line called a *bar*) which, whether they contain more or fewer notes, are all equal in respect of time. In this way, the rhythm is a source of *uniformity*, which pleases by suggesting the agreeable ideas of regularity and skill, and, still more, by rendering the music intelligible. It also pleases, by raising and gratifying expectation: for if the movement of the piece were governed by no rule; if what one hears of it during the present moment were in all respects unlike and incommensurable to what one was to hear the next, and had heard the last, the whole would be a mass of confusion; and the ear would either be bewildered, having nothing to rest upon, and nothing to anticipate; or, if it should expect any stated *ratio* between the motion and the time, would be disappointed when it found that there was none. — That rhythm is a source of very great *variety*, every person must be sensible, who knows only the names of the musical notes, with such of their divisions and subdivisions as relate to time; or who has attended to the manifold varieties of quick and slow motion, which the drum is capable of producing.

As order and proportion are always delightful, it is no wonder that mankind should be agreeably affected with the rhythm of music. That they are, the universal use of dancing, and of "the spirit-stirring drum," is a sufficient evidence. Nay, I have known a child imitate the rhythm of tunes before he could speak, and long before he could manage his voice so as to imitate their melody; — which is a proof, that human nature is susceptible of this delight previously to the acquirement of artificial habits.[38]

38. Variety "within due bounds," Beattie tells us, contributes to "agreeableness"; novelty is paramount in refreshing the mind, and in no art is it more sought after than in music. Yet variety should not be used at the expense of simplicity, for simplicity assures coherence, by preventing bewilderment and "compound judgement." Moreover, simplicity depends in no small measure on familiarity, according to Beattie. How then does music overcome what may seem at first glance contradictory requirements? Beattie's discussion of rhythm exemplifies how the two may be reconciled. Variety and uniformity can be made to cooperate in music by differentiating between

(CONT.)

V. I hinted at the power of accidental association in giving significancy to musical compositions. It may be remarked further,
that association contributes greatly to heighten their agreeable
effect. We have heard them performed, some time or other, in an
agreeable place perhaps, or by an agreeable person, or accompanied with words that describe agreeable ideas: or we have
heard them in our early years; a period of life, which we seldom
look back upon without pleasure, and of which Bacon recommends the frequent recollection as an expedient to preserve
health. Nor is it necessary, that such melodies or harmonies
should have much intrinsic merit, or that they should call up any
distinct remembrance of the agreeable ideas associated with
them. There are seasons, at which we are gratified with very
moderate excellence. In childhood, every tune is delightful to a
musical ear; in our advanced years, an indifferent tune will
please, when set off by the amiable qualities of the performer, or
by any other agreeable circumstance. — During the last war, the
Belleisle march was long a general favourite. It filled the minds
of our people with magnificent ideas of armies, and conquest,
and military splendor; for they believed it to be the tune that was
played by the French garrison when it marched out with the honours of war, and surrendered that fortress to the British troops.
— The flute of a shepherd heard at a distance, in a fine summer
day, amidst a beautiful scene of groves, hills, and waters, will
give rapture to the ear of the wanderer, though the tune, the
instrument, and the musician, be such as he could not endure in

(CONT.) ——————— ᴥ ———————

various levels with regard to the same parameter. For example, by differentiating
between the various levels of rhythm — beat, meter and rhythm — Beattie is able to
show how differences may be subsumed under similarities on a higher level, not
unlike the process which characterizes the nature of abstraction. Music thus follows a
process of "sense-making" which is intelligible, without having to resort to further
meanings. From a philosophical point of view, Hutcheson explicated the idea of "unity
amidst variety" in profounder terms. Nonetheless, via his musical example, Beattie
shows how this governing aesthetic principle is able to encompass entire systems as
well as continuous, perceptible processes. The importance of this kind of observation
is that it leads to further investigation into the hierarchical nature of music, in particular, as far as tonal relations are concerned.

any other place. — If a song, or piece of music, should call up only a faint remembrance, that we were happy the last time we heard it, nothing more would be needful to make us listen to it again with peculiar satisfaction.

It is an amiable prejudice that people generally entertain in favour of their national music. This lowest degree of patriotism in not without its merit: and that man must have a hard heart, or dull imagination, in whom, though endowed with musical sensibility, no sweet emotions would arise, on hearing, in his riper years, or in a foreign land, those strains that were the delight of his childhood. What though they be inferior to the Italian? What though they be even irregular and rude? It is not their merit, which in the case supposed would interest a native, but the charming ideas they would recal to his mind: — ideas of innocence, simplicity, and leisure, of romantic enterprise, and enthusiastic attachment; and of scenes, which, on recollection, we are inclined to think, that a brighter sun illuminated, a fresher verdure crowned, and purer skies and happier climes conspired to beautify, than are now to be seen in the dreary paths of care and disappointment, into which men, yielding to the passions peculiar to more advanced years, are tempted to wander. — There are couplets in Ogilvie's Translation of Virgil, which I could never read without emotions far more ardent than the merit of the numbers would justify. But it was that book which first taught me "the tale of Troy divine,"[y] and first made me acquainted with poetical sentiments; and though I read it when almost an infant, it conveyed to my heart some pleasing impressions, that remain there unimpaired to this day.[39]

---

y. Milton's Penseroso.

39. Beattie's last observation in this section deals with "accidental associations" which make significant certain kinds of music. Beginning with associations which an individual may attach to a certain composition and concluding with associations that a whole nation may share, Beattie emphasizes that such associations are independent of the intrinsic merit of the music. Once the music is so "possessed," it is able to evoke memories of the situation that gave rise to the association. Hence the tendency to

(CONT.)

. . .

SECT. III.

Conjectures on some peculiarities of National Music

THere is a certain style of melody peculiar to each musical
country, which the people of that country are apt to prefer to
every other style. That they should prefer their own, is not surprising; and that the melody of one people should differ from
that of another, is not more surprising, perhaps, than that the language of one people should differ from that of another. But there
is something not unworthy of notice in the particular expression
and style that characterise the music of one nation or province,
and distinguish it from every other sort of music. Of this diversity Scotland supplies a striking example. The native melody of the
highlands and western isles is as different from that of the southern part of the kingdom, as the Irish or Erse language is different from the English or Scotch. In the conclusion of a discourse
on music as it relates to the mind, it will not perhaps be impertinent to offer a conjecture on the cause of these peculiarities;
which, though it should not (and indeed I am satisfied that it will
not) fully account for any one of them, may however incline the
reader to think that they are not unaccountable, and may also
throw some faint light on this part of philosophy.

Every thought that partakes of the nature of passion, has a correspondent expression in the look and gesture: and so strict is
the union between the passion and its outward sign, that, where
the former is not in some degree felt, the latter can never be perfectly natural, but, if assumed, becomes aukward mimickry,
instead of that genuine imitation of nature, which draws forth the
sympathy of the beholder. If, therefore, there be, in the circum-

(CONT.) ———— *ın* ————

enlist music for political and national purposes; indeed, Beattie continues (in the following section) to deal with what he calls national music, trying to formulate some of
its peculiarities.

stances of particular nations or persons, any thing that gives a peculiarity to their passions and thoughts, it seems reasonable to expect, that they will also have something peculiar in the expression of their countenance, and even in the form of their features. Caius Marius, Jugurtha, Tamerlane, and some other great warriors, are celebrated for a peculiar ferocity of aspect, which they had no doubt contracted from a perpetual and unrestrained exertion of fortitude, contempt, and other violent emotions. These produced in the face their correspondent expressions, which being often repeated, became at last as habitual to the features, as the sentiments they arose from were to the heart. Savages, whose thoughts are little inured to controul, have more of this significancy of look, than those men, who, being born and bred in civilized nations, are accustomed from their childhood to suppress every emotion that tends to interrupt the peace of society. And while the bloom of youth lasts, and the smoothness of feature peculiar to that period, the human face is less marked with any strong character, than in old age: — a peevish or surly stripling may elude the eye of the physiognomist; but a wicked old man, whose visage does not betray the evil temperature of his heart, must have more cunning than it would be prudent for him to acknowledge. Even by the trade or profession the human countenance may be characterised. They who employ themselves in the nicer mechanic arts, that require the earnest attention of the artist, do generally contract a fixedness of feature suited to that one uniform sentiment which engrosses them while at work. Whereas, other artists, whose work requires less attention, and who may ply their trade and amuse themselves with conversation at the same time, have for the most part smoother and more unmeaning faces: their thoughts are more miscellaneous, and therefore their features are less fixed in one uniform configuration. A keen penetrating look indicates thoughtfulness and spirit; a dull torpid countenance is not often accompanied with great sagacity.

This, though there may be many an exception, is in general true of the visible signs of our passions; and it is no less true of the audible. A man habitually peevish, or passionate, or querulous, or imperious, may be known by the sound of his voice, as well as by his physiognomy. May we not go a step farther, and say, that if a man under the influence of any passion were to compose a discourse, or a poem, or a tune, his work would in some measure exhibit an image of his mind? I could not easily be persuaded, that Swift and Juvenal were men of sweet tempers; or that Thompson, Arbuthnot, and Prior were ill-natured. The airs of Felton are so uniformly mournful, that I cannot suppose him to have been a merry, or even a chearful man. If a musician, in deep affliction, were to attempt to compose a lively air, I believe he would not succeed: though I confess I do not well understand the nature of the connection that may take place between a mournful mind and a melancholy tune. It is easy to conceive, how a poet or an orator should transfuse his passions into his work: for every passion suggests ideas congenial to its own nature; and the composition of the poet, or of the orator, must necessarily consist of those ideas that occur at the time he is composing. But musical sounds are not the signs of ideas; rarely are they even the imitations of natural sounds: so that I am at a loss to conceive how it should happen, that a musician, overwhelmed with sorrow, for example, should put together a series of notes, whose expression is contrary to that of another series which he had put together when elevated with joy. But of the fact I am not doubtful; though I have not sagacity, or knowledge of music, enough to be able to explain it. And my opinion in this matter is warranted by that of a more competent judge; who says, speaking of church-voluntaries, that if the Organist "do not feel in himself the divine energy of devotion, he will labour in vain to raise it in others. Nor can he hope to throw out those happy instantaneous thoughts, which sometimes far exceed the best concerted compositions, and which the enraptured performer would gladly secure to his future use and pleasure, did they not as fleetly escape as they rise."[z] A man who has made music the study of his life, and is well acquainted with all the best examples of style and expression that are to be found

---

z. Avison on Musical Expression, page 88, 89 [in the original edition, not included here].

in the works of former masters, may, by memory and music practice, attain a sort of mechanical dexterity in contriving music suitable to any given passion; but such music would, I presume, be
vulgar and spiritless, compared to what an artist of genius throws
out, when under the power of any ardent emotion. It is recorded of Lulli, that, once when his imagination was all on fire with
some verses descriptive of terrible ideas, which he had been
reading in a French tragedy, he ran to his harpsichord, and struck
off such a combination of sounds, that the company felt their hair
stand on end with horror.

Let us therefore suppose it proved, or, if you please, take it for
granted, that different sentiments in the mind of the musician will
give different and peculiar expressions to his music; — and upon
this principle, it will not perhaps be impossible to account for
some of the phenomena of a national ear.[40]

———— ♏ ————

40. The increased awareness of other nations and cultures, which characterizes the
eighteenth century, is well represented in Beattie's introduction to his discussion of
national music. His anthropological theory, though elementary and undeveloped, contains some interesting distinctions which stem from his previous observations on the
working of the mind. Thus, he proposes a system of interrelated factors which com-
bine to allow for identification and differentiation of cultures. Circumstances, says
Beattie, give rise to sentiments, and sentiments find expression in outward signs — in
kinds of gestures which, when repeated, become crystallized and fixed, as Condillac
proposed. Such "physiognomy" is easily identified and identifies its carriers. Since
musical sounds are not signs of ideas, as we have already learned from Beattie's discussion of music's ambiguity, most of his examples are not musical. Music presents, he
believes, a special case for Beattie, as we have learned from his discussion of the
process whereby music may be possessed by ideas. Hence, what he ascribes to other
gestures applies to music as well. Once possessed, music's power to evoke sentiments
makes it the agent par excellence through which identities are created and decoded.
Indeed, soon such an awareness gave rise to the so called "national schools" of music
and eventually also to the field of comparative musicology.

* * *

In Part II of his treatise, Beattie deals with the Language of Poetry, the "instrument" by
means of which poetry "affects the mind." Beattie's discussion is too long and diffuse
to be presented here; however, some of the points he raises have a direct bearing on
our discussion. Beattie divides this part into two major chapters: the first discusses "natural language" in broad terms with regard to tropes and figures; the second discusses
the "elements of sound."

"Natural language," Beattie observes, is usually defined in terms of tones, attitudes and configurations "which are universal to mankind and everywhere understood." Aware of the conventionalized nature of most of human expression, Beattie rejects this eighteenth-century cliché, attempting to bestow upon the old principle of "decorum" (which advocates the matching of the linguistic expression of protagonists to their age, sex, status, psychological and dramatic situation) a cognitive standing. In contradistinction to the "determinate and absolute" criteria of "good language" (related to grammatical rules etc.), Beattie argues that "natural language" is relative and "can be estimated by those only, who have studied men as well as books; and who attend to the real or supposed character of the speaker as well as to the import of what is spoken" (p. 197). Experience, intuition and psychological sophistication are necessary for the creation of natural speech, Beattie implies (not unlike Galilei's requirements in his deliberation concerning affective expression in music).

Aware of the "essential" role of genres and media in achieving desired artistic "ends," Beattie turns to justify digressions from the outcome of principle he himself formulated. For example, in epic poetry an elevated and uniform style is bestowed upon each of the personae, being indirectly quoted by a narrator, whose "assumed character and pretensions are higher than those of the historian and philosopher" (p. 204). An implied author, (e.g. the narrator in Æneid), Beattie suggests, is distinct from his maker (e.g. Virgil); enjoying a fictive status, his utterances are perceived as "natural" despite their outward artificiality. Beattie's observation is of course related to the increasing awareness of the cognitive role which an implied point of view may have; the implication of this awareness of opera is of interest as well as of importance.

Beattie's discussion of tropes and figures derives from traditional rhetoric, which never lacked cognitive awareness. Focusing on the centrality of "figures of thought" for poetry, he identifies their function as filling lacunae in the current vocabulary. Whether permanent figures (e.g. in synaesthetic transference) or momentary ones, they contribute to the semantic and prosodic aspects of poetry and their theoretical considerations. "Tropes and figures," Beattie observes, "promote brevity; and brevity, united with perspicuity, is always agreeable. Sentiments thus delivered, and imagery thus painted, are readily apprehended by the mind, make a strong impression upon the fancy, and remain long in the memory." Unfortunately, Beattie, does not go beyond this "perspicuity," and "brief" description of the role of figures; like so many others of his time he left the more profound philosophical and cognitive problems which figurative language raises to later thinkers, primarily to those of the twentieth century.

Beattie also relates figures to the traditional *enargeia*, i.e. to verbal pictures which appeal to the imagination. This, he notes, is of special importance to the "language of passion," for appropriate figures may "direct the fancy to objects congenial to their own nature." An angry man, for example, is prone to use hyperboles, "conceiving his injury greater than it really is" (p. 251). The link between metaphors and passions is indeed significant, as contemporary psychological research tries to show.

In addition to hyperbole, Beattie also considers *prosopopeia* and *apostrophe* as most passionate figures. The first, *prosopopeia*, i.e. personification, is conceived as "natural" when "things inanimate make a strong impression" upon the speaker, or when a con-

tinuous affection makes him fancy that all nature sympathizes with him. "Our affections," observes Beattie, "are indeed the medium through which we may be said to
survey ourselves, and every thing else; and whatever be our inward frame, we are apt
to perceive a wonderful congeniality in the world without us" (p. 255). Hence the
effective power of all demonic creatures in literature, observes Beattie; hence, we may
add, their "natural" participation in the most passionate of all discourses — music.
Turning to *apostrophe* — "a sudden diversion or speech from one person to another
person or thing" — Beattie argues, necessitates proper preparation of the mind. A sudden address to the dead, for example, will be considered natural only in very passionate circumstances which are well founded. "Figurative language," Beattie concludes, is especially suited to the supposed condition of the poet, because figures are
suggested by the fancy and the "fancy of him who composes poetry is more employed
than that of any other author" (p. 265). Altogether, the vital link Beattie forges between
figurative language on the one hand and imagination and passions on the other, is
always subjugated to the cognitive constraints of genre, style and cultural norms.

Beattie's treatment of poetical sound coheres with his overall approach. Pleasure is
considered the prime criterion for all "musical" considerations, subjecting both timbre
(phonetics) and time (measure). As we have already seen, "poetical license" allows this
rule to be satisfied via tropes, whenever proper names are "offensive." Continuing in
the same vein, Beattie implies a parallelism between versification (related to measure)
and tropes, for when successful they, too, render "the connection of things obvious to
the understanding... and enliven every emotion the poet intends to raise in the reader..." (p. 276; see our discussion of this point in Vol. I: 87-92). Typical of Beattie is also
his tolerance of the use of rhyme, and his observation that "against custom in these
matters it is vain to argue." This again shows his sensitivity to the weight of entrenched
artistic procedures. Beattie does not miss the chance to point out how the variety of
poetic versification enables us to render "natural" each poetic genre. He elegantly connects this conception to a shortened version of the "coincidence" theory related to the
proper match between poetical and emotional movement. Although musical disso-
nances are allowed, these, too, (like all Beattie's theoretical components), are, in the
final analysis, subordinated to dominating cognitive consonances.

Daniel Webb
⸙
(1735-1803)

Born in 1719 in Maidstown, Daniel Webb received a classical education at Oxford. Webb wrote 3 treatises:

An Inquiry into the Beauties of Painting (and into the Merits of the Most Celebrated Painters, Ancient and Moderns), London, 1760, *Remarks on the Beauties of Poetry*, London 1762, and *Observations on the Correspondence between Poetry and Music*, London, 1769.

The relation between taste and science is the overarching problem, which concerned Webb in his three essays. In the opening of his *Inquiry into the Beauties of Painting* (1760), Webb tells us that "the source of taste is feeling, so is it of judgement," he continues, "which is nothing more than this same sensibility, improved by the study of its proper objects, and brought to a just point of certainty and correctness" (1760: 8). Issues of taste, we have seen, received a major thrust with the growing awareness of the middle-class of the impact exerted by its economic power on matters related to aesthetic preferences. Rejecting the conservative and aristocratic aesthetic criteria, the up and coming bourgeoisie opted for a more subjective attitude, one less based on academic judgement. It was, however, the third Earl of Shaftesbury who encouraged such a development by considering taste as well as judgment to be grounded in feeling — a special "sense" responsible for both. But, as the reader may recall, Shaftesbury related both to the concept of "perfection," which he viewed, like Baumgarten, as a guiding force in decision-making in moral and other spiritual domains. As noted in Vol. I, 'beauty' thus acquired an esteemed position in man's striving for perfectibility.

In line with this tradition, Webb felt obliged to reexamine some aesthetic assumptions critically, considering himself responsible for the cultivation of the young. These two tasks are well reflected in Webb's treatises, and complement each other. Whereas the *Inquiry* is primarily concerned with advising the young with regard to taste in the visual arts, it also reopens on several theoretical issues which are examined closely. By contrast, Webb's other two treatises begin more theoretically and proceed to offer valuable advice to poets, amounting to no less than a reform in English poetry.

It is not altogether surprising, therefore, that Webb should refuse artists the status of critics, while retaining a full appreciation of their technical knowledge. Neither does he deny the artist's creative powers; in fact he considered himself as dependent on them. He believed that the understanding of the *nature* of artistic creation does not necessarily constitute a part of the artist's domain, arguing that criticism is itself a different kind of creative act, gaining momentum with increased refinement. Webb's criticism rested on a vast knowledge of classical as well modern literary and philosophical sources, drawing mainly on concepts and arguments employed by the empiricists. He added his own good commonsense, using, for example, his own experience of poetic delivery as empirical data for the unveiling of its effect. By analogy, he also enlisted poetic rhetoric as a model of the effects of music for which he had less ready evidence. Indeed, analogies served Webb to sift out his arguments. Unlike some of his contemporaries, however, he was well aware that simple analogies won't do, and one of his main concerns was to bridge the different incommensurable phenomena via factors they held in common.

The present treatise attempts to specify that which constitutes the relationship between sound and sentiment — known empirically but not well understood theoretically — and illustrates Webb's procedure. It should be viewed as part of an overall conception according to which the "polite arts" consist of "different means of addressing the same passions." As such, Webb tells us, the arts "are the most effectual and ready method of conveying our ideas" (1760: 10). The correspondences among the arts, which he sought, consist of the relationship between the perceptual constituents of each artistic medium and that which characterizes the passions. Characterizing the perceptual infrastructure peculiar to each art, Webb employs empiricist terminology to give exactitude and depth to contentions held from the days of Jacob. Of central importance is his differentiation between 'succession of ideas' and 'succession of impressions' which he applies to poetry and music, respectively. In his treatment of passion he is aware of the shortcomings of the seventeenth-century approach, and tries to adopt a more persuasive one. This treatment, we believe, resulted in a genuine theoretical breakthrough, in which four *classes* of emotions ("love," "pride," "anger" and "sorrow") seem to share a common theoretical space and in which "mixed" emotions may find their specific location. For our own argument, it should be borne in mind that this view was conceived in an attempt to solve an *aesthetic* problem. It is 'movement,' or "coincidence of movement" by means of which Webb bridges the two incommensurable subjects, poetry and music, for it is movement which constitutes their unified, theoretical space. Although Webb demonstrated the centrality of movement for each of the arts, he did not leave it at that, but, rather, connected each through a third factor — the "vibrations" they both cause. The coincidence which occurs is associative — a "natural" association between the musical movement and the emotional "locus" to which it relates.

Combined with poetry, music acquires further specificity, due to the "label" which poetry bestows upon it, a label related to a certain emotion in the given class (e.g. "courage" and "indignation" in the case of "anger"). In the interaction between the two, poetry gains as well. While poetry "lends music sentiments," i.e. specific emotions, it "borrows movement" and flexibility, which supply nuances to emotions. This may be achieved in poetry only when constraints of language are reduced, as is the case of monosyllabic poetry, the units of which are liable to result in manifold successions, according to the nature of the desired movement. The units themselves, in such a case, Webb argues, consist of a "succession of impressions", preserving the nature of a primitive state of expression, in which combinations of sounds and movements imitate, directly or metaphorically, external and internal objects.

Webb's analysis of prosodical procedures, including his attack on sanctioned Greek prosody, closes a circle opened by Jacob a generation earlier. Unlike Jacob, Webb not only differentiated between musicalized and painterly poetry, but unequivocally put at the service of the former his major persuasive powers. Whereas this preference reflects a change in taste, it also demonstrates Webb's ability to delve deep into the secrets — technical as well as perceptual — of the artistic illusion. In fact, this provided Webb with the ability to assess changing tastes and artistic value, and to consider the kinds of interactions and correspondences among the arts, existing as well as desired.

OBSERVATIONS
ON THE
CORRESPONDENCE
BETWEEN

POETRY and MUSIC

By the AUTHOR of

AN ENQUIRY into the BEAUTIES of

PAINTING

Concordant carmina nervis.
Ovid. Metam.
["the lyre responds in harmony to song"]

Carminis suavitas, numerique, non solum ad aurium
delectationem compositi, sed ad res ipsas exprimen-
das, omnemque animi motum concitandum efficaces.
Lowth de Sacr. Poet. Hebræorum.

[The pleasantness of the poem and the metre is composed not only in
order to delight the ears, but is capable also to express the content and to
stir up every motion in the soul.]

LONDON
Printed for J. DODSLEY, in Pall-mall.

M DCC LXIX.

To his GRACE

The D U K E

OF

G R A F T O N,

First Lord of the Treasury, &c. &c.

MY LORD,

THE beauty of order in the disposition of visible objects, the powerful effects of arrangement in the succession of our ideas, of measure and proportion in the successions of sounds, are but different modifications of one common principle. The *lucidas ordo* of Horace marks how much he thought the second connected with the first; the design of the following essay is to prove, how intimately the third is connected with both: to point out the origin, and to lay open the advantages of a musical elocution.[1] We who have no other merit than to feel these advantages are under a natural subjection to those who exert them: the Critic, my Lord Duke, is but a dependent on the Orator. It is under

———— ✧ ————

1. From the first innocent sentences of his dedicatory remarks to Lord Grafton, one can learn a great deal about Webb's position and intentions concerning the present essay. Webb, like the former members of our group, considered painting, poetry and music the major constituents of the fine arts. As noted in our introduction, Webb dealt with poetry and painting before he undertook the present study. In these essays as well as in the present one, Webb differs from previous writers by taking the commonality of the three arts as a starting point for subsequent arguments, rather than as a point to arrive at.

From the outset it is clear that when he talks about commonality in the arts he recognizes two crucial elements: the first refers to order and arrangement — properties to be found in the art object — and the second refers to their effect on the percipients. He reminds us that Horace connected the two in his *lucidus ordo;* but we might add that Horace did not realize that the concept divides into two distinct theoretical propositions, related to cause and effect.

Webb differs also from the Neoplatonic approach which held that the various arts convey similar ideas even though they are differently clad. His emphasis on organization and effect leaves room for differences among the arts as far as properties, contents and perceptual aspects are concerned. In other words, his theory does not contradict Lessing's approach concerning the "limits" of the individual arts, it only identifies their commonality with a general cognitive principle, whereby different kinds of organization both address as well as elicit different kinds of mental effects. In short he makes room for a Lessing within a Hutchesonian framework which he then attempts to subsume. In his *Remarks on the Beauties of Poetry* Webb expressed his commitment to the sanction of this dependence, that I presume to engage your Grace's attention; and to claim a part of that time which you so happily employ to the noblest purposes. [2]

I have the honour to be

   Your GRACE'S

      Most humble, and

         Obedient servant,

         DANIEL WEBB.

———— ℒ ————

the Shaftesburian legacy, to which he adds an interesting notion: "It is probable," he reflects there, "that all the powers which produce these refined pleasures spring from one common principle, as it is evident they tend to one common end: for there is such an intercourse among them, that while we perfect our sensations in any one of them, we acquire a general aptness for them all." The "common principle" — that of harmony and proportion — when cultivated with regard to one sensual domain, Webb tells us, is thus usable in other domains as well, acting, as it were, like an overall 'sense.' Regardless of its empirical validity, this notion contributed to the *actual* formation of connections among the arts.

What are the actual connections among the arts? Webb, it seems, never confuses perceptual processes with general aesthetic qualifiers. This distinction goes a long way to establish the uniqueness of each artistic domain, enabling Webb to go beyond Lessing's "limits," i.e. to entertain possible ways of completing each other.

2. Webb's humble talk should not mislead us. Though he claims both dependence on the artist and subjugation to his lord, he stands to lose nothing thereby. By allowing himself to impose on the attention of his lord, he makes a major claim for the worthwhile nature of criticism and its independent standing. More than his predecessors in the group, Webb recognizes criticism as an area of knowledge with which he can identify, and which he can represent, and contribute to. Of course, this is in line with the ascendancy of criticism in the eighteenth century, and complies, in the main, with views expressed by Webb in the *Remarks on the Beauty of Poetry*.

In the Remarks Webb distinguishes between 'genius,' on the one hand, and 'taste' and 'sensibility,' on the other, identifying the former with the ability to discover a "just and beautiful relation between two ideas," and the latter with the disposition to feel the "merit of that invention." While assailing the "vanity of the critics...who are continually insinuating to us that they partake, in some measure, of that divinity which they attribute to the poets," Webb does not hesitate to stress that "in Poetry, as in Philosophy, new relations are struck out, new influences discovered, and every superior genius moves in a world of his own." Criticism, according to Webb, is thus marked by its own creativity, not essentially different from that of the artistic brand, and yet not identical with it either. Indeed, Webb moves in a world of his own in the present treatise; the discovery of new relations that build a new theoretical edifice is what concerns him most.

OBSERVATIONS

ON THE

CORRESPONDENCE

BETWEEN

POETRY and MUSIC.

*T*HOUGH the influence of music over our passions is very generally felt and acknowledged; though its laws are universally the same, its effects in many instances constant and uniform; yet we find ourselves embarrassed in our attempts to reason on this subject, by the difficulty which attends the forming a clear idea of any natural relation between sound and sentiment.[3]

------- ⓦ -------

3. What is interesting about these opening remarks of Webb is the scientific attitude which he adopts. Webb distinguishes between the recognition of the existence of certain relations among phenomena (sound and sentiment) and the understanding of that which constitutes such relations. Departing from Harris and Avison who took these relations for granted, Webb implies that serious criticism, seeking lawfulness ("natural relations" as he calls it), labors under scientific constraints. Indeed, as Kepler argued in his debate with Fludd, the relation between sound and sentiment involves a serious theoretical problem, for the two are incommensurable. Whether Webb was aware of that debate, is unclear, though Fludd's writings, from the beginning, were quite known among British thinkers, as is apparent from Hawkins' history of music published in 1776 (Hawkins 1776). Indeed, the present treatise reveals that Webb was well versed in seventeenth-century Latin treatises dealing with music, whether speculative or more

(CONT.)

SOME have thought to elude this difficulty, by supposing, that the influence of sound on passion may arise from the habit of associating certain ideas with certain sounds. It cannot be necessary to enter into a formal examination of such a principle as this, since it must fall of course on the discovery of a better.

I HAVE observed a child to cry violently on hearing the sound of a trumpet, who, some minutes after, hath fallen asleep to the soft notes of a lute. Here we have evident marks of the spirits being thrown into opposite movements, independently of any possible association of ideas. This striking opposition in the effects of musical impressions seems to indicate the regular operation of a general and powerful principle.[4]

ALL musical sounds are divided into acute and grave: the acute spring from strong, the grave from weaker vibrations. No sound, therefore, can act as a single impression, since we cannot have a feeling of it but in consequence of a succession of impressions:
(CONT.)

practical, whether of British origin or not. At any rate, he seemed to be fully aware of the "embarrassment" involved in the enterprise of bridging physics and psychology, and was cautious in the methodology he adopted for that purpose.

4. As discussed in Vol. I (36–44), Descartes was perhaps the first to view the relationship between sound and passion as determined by "habits of association." This is why he was willing to relinquish his entire project concerning the affective nature of music. However, the doctrine of the "association of ideas" that flourished among the British, revealed that such associations are not simple and might be related to basic epistemological and cognitive matters. Even Hume's well-known skepticism, expressed in his relegation of scientific, causal relations to habits of mind, is an offspring of this doctrine, and paradoxically implies the belief that associations are themselves lawful, and might harbor some basic operations that are not immediately apparent. Interestingly, literary critics exploited "associations" expressly for providing "scientific" explications of matters such as the power of imagination, the mystery of genius and the concepts of the beauty and the sublime. Webb was undoubtedly influenced by these explications, for he, too, in his essay on poetry, considered the beauty of painting as stemming primarily from a special kind of association of ideas — the creation of new and unexpected metaphors. In the present essay, though he rejects arbitrary or even cultural or poetic aspects, he pursues a kind of mechanism of association, in line with the scientific orientation he adopted (see fn. 3, above): interested in immediate impact, he shares the belief that this mechanism is related to a "regular operation of a general powerful principle."

should it appear, that our passions act in like manner by successive impressions, or, that they affect us on a principle similar to that which is deduced from the analysis of sounds, we might then hope to become masters of the desired secret, and to discover, so far as such things are discoverable, the nature of the relation between sound and sentiment.[5]

As we have no direct nor immediate knowledge of the mechanical operations of the passions, we endeavour to form some conception of them from the manner in which we find ourselves affected by them: thus we say, that love softens, melts, insinuates; anger quickens, stimulates, inflames; pride expands, exalts; sorrow dejects, relaxes: of all which ideas we are to observe, that they are different modifications of motion, so

---

5. Webb here carefully avoids talking about 'ideas' in connection with either music or feeling. He resorts to the Humean terminology which mediates between 'sensations' and 'ideas' via impressions. Impressions, according to Hume, have a standing of their own; as sensations which are cognitively recognized but not yet signified by anything other than themselves, they are less durable than ideas but more immediately vital. Though single sounds seem to behave like impressions, Webb states that unless they are part of a succession, they make no musical sense at all. In other words, music depends on succession for its perceptual existence, thus implicating time, context and order.

To confirm and enlarge our interpretation of the Humean base of Webb's conception, we resort again to his *Reflections*. As may be expected, the essence of poetry is identified by Webb as a "succession of ideas," whereas painting does not enjoy such an advantage. All the beauties of poetry are ascribed to this basic property, and emphasis is put on the right succession of ideas which is necessary for the gradual emergence of images. Already in that essay music is presented as parallel to poetry, as consisting of a succession of impressions: keeping in mind the cognitive difference between the succession of ideas and the succession of impressions Webb will make use of the parallelism for both correspondences and connections between these two arts.

Webb does not yet qualify the nature of that succession of impressions as far as music is concerned, nor does he specify what distinguishes one succession from the other. He does tell us, however, that the desirable bridge between sound and sentiment can be established on this ground, for impressions, he assumes, are equally meaningful units in the emotional realm. Moreover, they may behave in similar manner, a fact which may explain the analogical connection between them, which the mind intuitively discerns. How the mind unknowingly establishes analogies is a major question in itself, in which Webb but partially engages.

applied, as best to correspond with our feelings of each particular passion.[6] From whence, as well as from their known and visible effects, there is just reason to presume, that the passions, according to their several natures, do produce certain proper and distinctive motions in the most refined and subtle parts of the human body.[a] What these parts are, where placed, or how fitted to receive and propagate these motions, are points which I shall not inquire into. It is sufficient for my purpose to have it admitted, that some such parts must exist in the human machine: however, as in our pursuits after knowledge, it is discouraging to be reminded every moment of our ignorance, I shall take advantage of the received opinion touching this matter, and assign the functions in question to the nerves and spirits. We are then to take it for granted, that the mind, under particular affections, excites certain vibrations in the nerves, and impresses certain movements on the animal spirits.[7]

a. Omnis enim motus animi suum quendam a natura habet vultum, et sonum, et gestum: et ejus omnis vultus, omnesque voces, ut nervi in fidibus, ita sonant, ut a motu animi quoque sunt pulsæ

Cicero de Oratore.

[For nature has assigned to every emotion a particular look and tone of voice and bearing of its own; and the whole of a person's frame and every look on his face and every utterance of his voice are like the strings of a harp, and sound according as they are struck by each successive emotion.]

6. Webb assumes that a relationship between music and passions can be found in a kind of "mechanical operation" of which he is ignorant. He, therefore, attempts to infer from the experience of affective states something about this mechanism. However, it is not the entire mechanism which interests him, only that part which is immediately related to experiences. In a rather crude introspective manner, therefore, he classifies certain emotions by the correlative movements which they imply. As we shall see, movement and the nature of movement will serve to establish the analogy which Webb is after. Moreover, it will also supply hints concerning their shared cognitive basis. Indeed, it is only the kind of experience which the two elicit, that will provide relevant hypothesis about the mechanism which they share.

7. Not only Cicero, but a number of significant figures in the course of the centuries, viewed the "animal spirits" as a vehicle for transmitting movement from and to the mind. In Vol. I we discussed Ficino's and Descartes' theories in this connection. We noted the partial irrelevance of such speculations to the examination of the process they tried to elucidate. By contrast, Webb is more aware of the theoretical standing of

(CONT.)

I SHALL suppose, that it is in the nature of music to excite similar vibrations, to communicate similar movements to the nerves
and spirits. For, if music owes its being to motion, and, if passion cannot well be conceived to exist without it, we have a right
to conclude, that the agreement of music with passion can have
no other origin than a coincidence of movements.[b] [8]

b. Si quis igitur ita harmoniam accommodare posset, ut spiritus eodem prorsus motu, quo harmoni-
ci numeri, moveretur, is intentum effectum produceret haud dubie, idem enim præstaret quod in
duobus polychordis exactissime concordatis sit; quorum alterutrum modulis harmonicis incitatum in
altero etiam intacto eandem omnino harmoniam producit. [Therefore if someone would be
able to accommodate the harmony so that the spirit would be moved by the
same movement of the harmonious metres, that man would undoubtedly produce an intense effect, for, the same thing which happens in two synchro-
nized/well-tuned strings — would then happen: one of the strings roused by
modulated harmonies produces entirely the same harmony in the other,
though untouched.] Kirch. Musur. I. vii.

WHETHER we account for the imitations of music in this manner, or call them, after Aristotle, the
ὁμοιώματα τῶν ἠθῶν καὶ παθῶν —simulacra morum et affectionum [likenesses of characters
(CONT.)   (CONT.)

each of the components he postulates. He clearly distinguishes between the theoretical need for certain assumptions, on the one hand, and their verifications, on the other.
It is evident that the explanation he seeks requires a mediator between the mind and
the bodily sensations both to transmit commands and to decipher sensations. The
mind, he suggests, "under particular affections excites certain vibrations in the nerves
and impresses certain movements on the animal spirits."

8. Since experience shows that there is an "influence of music over our passions" and
since passions, as we were told in the previous paragraph, excite vibrations in the
nerves, and since we know independently that music "owes its being to motion,"
Webb is willing to entertain the supposition that a similarity exists between the kinds
of vibrations that music and the passions excite — "a coincidence of movement."
Movement and kinds of movement provide the objective common denominator that
equates particular passions and certain kinds of music. Music and passion are not related to each other metaphysically, except through a neutral physicalistic third factor
which they hold in common. The notion of "coincidence" is thus a purely scientific
one, and therein lies its strength. Few qualifications to this explication are in place.
First, the movement Webb refers to relates to the level of effects rather than of causes, i.e. to that which music and passion bring about rather than to that which initiates
them. As far as passion is concerned, Webb is not interested in such causes, as he has
already told us. As for music, it will become clear in what follows, that he is willing to
entertain the idea that the "succession of impressions" is the source of that physical
reaction. Unlike Ficino who identified cause with effect on a pure physical basis
despite their avowed metaphysical import, Webb tries to avoid metaphysics and connects the physical to the cognitive. Without entering the complicated question of body
and soul, he assumes that certain bodily operations which are basic to man are enact-
ed by his mental activities.

WHEN, therefore, musical sounds produce in us the same sensations which accompany the impressions of any one particular passion, then the music is said to be in unison with that passion; and the mind must, from a similitude in their effects, have a lively feeling of an affinity in their operations.[10]

IN my Remarks on the Beauties of Poetry, I have observed,[11]

THAT, in music, we are *transported* by sudden transitions, by an impetuous reiteration of impressions.

THAT we are *delighted* by a placid succession of lengthened tones, which dwell on the sense, and insinuate themselves into our inmost feelings.

(CONT.)

and affections] —we have alike in view a principle of assimilation; with this difference, that, by establishing a mode of operation, whether real or imaginary, we are enabled to convey our ideas with greater clearness touching the several modes of *imitation.*[9]

9. Webb's footnote is a meta-theoretical one, and reinforces what we have said in our fn. 8 concerning the need for an objective common-denominator, which can bestow unity on the modes of imitation — the various kinds of musical expression. As will immediately be seen, his principle of the "coincidence of movement" serves well in this connection. Though Webb wants to believe that the vibrations in the case of both music and the passions are independently anchored in some reality, the nature of that reality, Webb tells us, is irrelevant to the functions which it serves. Mattheson also connected passions and music through vibrations, but he related the two to the very same process, making music into a factor not essentially different from any other emotional stimulant. By connecting the two through a neutral third factor, Webb avoids the arbitrariness of explanation while preserving the phenomenon under investigation. The aesthetic element does not get lost, neither does the uniqueness of the art.

10. Webb here introduces an additional concept — that of affinity. His argument is as follows: Since music and passion both cause vibrations, a similitude between the vibrations is recognized by the percipient, who then infers the affinity between music and passion with regard to their operations. A clear picture is thus obtained of that which has been experienced but could not be accounted for. What may sound like a circular argument, is in fact characteristic of the way man interacts with and becomes informed about the world he encounters.

11. The following sentences are taken almost literally from the *Remarks* (Hecht 1920: 96), except that in the present context Webb drops the former derogatory nuances with regard to music (see our fn. 13 below). As we noted in the introduction, the present essay may be considered a kind of elaboration and expansion of what Webb had to say about music. Part of the "inquiries" he made there, particularly those pertaining to the advantages of blank verse over couplets, serve here as data on which he elaborates.

THAT a growth or climax in sounds *exalts* and *dilates* the spirits, and is therefore a constant source of the *sublime*.

IF an ascent of notes be in accord with the sublime, then their descent must be in unison with those passions which *depress* the spirits.

ALL musical impressions, which have any correspondence with the passions, may, I think, be reduced under one or other of these four classes.

IF they agitate the nerves with violence, the spirits are hurried into the movements of anger, courage, indignation, and the like.

THE more gentle and placid vibrations shall be in unison with love, friendship, and benevolence.

IF the spirits are exalted or dilated, they rise into accord with pride, glory, and emulation.

IF the nerves are relaxed, the spirits subside into the languid movements of sorrow.[12]

FROM these observations it is evident, that music cannot, of itself, specify any particular passion, since the movements of every class must be in accord with all the passions of that class.

—— For instance, the tender and melting tones, which may be expressive of the passion of love, will be equally in unison with the collateral feelings of benevolence, friendship, and pity; and

12. Differences among versions of the "same" ideas of a given author often provide insights as to the transformation in his thought and to its guiding lines. Webb in the *Remarks* also listed only four kinds of passions, but saw fit to present them as contrasting binaries. Thus between the first kind and the second he introduced the words "on the contrary" which are omitted in the present treatise. Based on his earlier version we allow ourselves to read his list of passions in the present treatise, employing the same logic. Combining the two treatises it becomes clear that Webb was striving towards a system which includes two different kinds of binaries, one which creates a qualitative contrast and the other which can be ordered on a scale. Each of the passions contains both cause and effect related to succession of impressions and to the vibrations respectively, enabling their simultaneous scaling. Each pair of passions thus yields a single axis which bridges them (e.g. anger/hate — joy/love; glory/elation — degradation/depression). Between two such orthogonal axes it is possible to map a momentary recognition of the overall passion expressed in a given piece of music.

so on through the other classes. [13]

ON hearing an overture by Iomelli, or a concerto by
Geminiani, we are, in turn, transported, exalted, delighted; the
impetuous, the sublime, the tender, take possession of the sense
at the will of the composer. In these moments, it must be confessed, we have no determinate idea of any agreement or imitation; and the reason of this is, that we have no fixed idea of the
passion to which this agreement is to be referred. But, let eloquence co-operate with music, and specify the motive of each
particular impression, while we feel an agreement in the sound
and motion with the sentiment, song takes possession of the
soul, and general impressions become specific indications of the
manners and the passions.[14]

13. Starting with what seemed like "Semantic Differentials" with regard to the affects
(e.g. as "scales" to measure anger, courage and indignation), Webb arrived at a sort of
"factorial classification" of affects ("the movement of every class must be in accord with
all the passions of that class"). This may be considered a major breakthrough in the
deliberations concerning the passions, which were until then immersed in unsystem-
atized typologies. On the basis of this observation, Webb rightly concludes that music
is unable to be specific with regard to the passions. Interestingly, the same observation occurs already in a footnote in Webb's *Remarks*. There, however, it appears as part
of the traditional discussion of the relative merits of each of the arts as far as imitation
is concerned: "If painting be inferior to poetry, music, considered as imitative art, must
be greatly inferior to painting: for as music has no means of explaining the motives of
its various impressions, its imitations of the manners and passions must be extremely
vague and indecisive..." (p. 103). This awareness may have prompted Webb to look
into that "vagueness" and to reveal something about music, and through music, about
the nature of passions. It may explain why he omitted, in the present treatise, his previous ranking of the arts including that of music. Webb thus clearly departs from the
paragone tradition and the system of "the great chain of being" (Schueller 1953) to
which Harris and others still adhered.

14. In this paragraph Webb exemplifies how the indefinite in music might turn into a
definite feeling through a kind of labeling suggested by the text. The text and the
music, Goodman (1968) would have said, are "coextensive with a label." This does not
mean, according to Webb, that the music is coextensive with only one label; it is related to the entire class to which a given label is given. Webb's musical examples are of
course instrumental pieces of the kind which provoked debates over their aesthetic
standing (see Vol. I, Chapter 3). The arguments which Webb enlists, qualify some cognitive issues without losing sight of the "powers of music," i.e. music's capacity to emulate passions, by being vague with regard to its definition and specific with regard to
its dynamics.

IT is imagined by some, that verse hath no other object than to please the ear. If by this they understand, that verse cannot excite or imitate passion, they would do well to reflect on the nature of pleasure: at least, through this medium, were there no other, verse must have an influence over all those passions which are founded in pleasure. But verse is motion, and verse produceth pleasure, which is likewise motion.[c]

How then? hath nature struck out a correspondence between external and mental motion in one instance, to the exclusion of all others: provident, industrious, in establishing laws for an inferior purpose, would she stop short at the first opening of advantage, and contract her system at the very point where it called for enlargement? I do not wish to set out upon better ground than in direct opposition to such ideas as these.[15]

IT has been supposed, that the correspondence of music with passion springs from a coincidence of movements; and that these movements are reducible to four classes, distinguished by their accords with the passions of pride, sorrow, anger, and love. Should these principles hold good in verse, which is the music

c. Ὑποκείσθω δ' ἡμῖν εἶναι τὴν ἡδονήν, κίνησίν τινα τῆς ψυχῆς. Arist. Rhet. c. xi [Let it be assumed by us that pleasure is a certain movement of the soul,...].

ἡδονή, voluptas—huic verbo omnes duas res subjiciunt, lætitiam in animo, commotionem suavem jucunditatis in corpore.

Cicero de Finibus, l. ii.

[Every person in the world who knows Latin attaches to this word two ideas — that of gladness of mind, and that of a delightful excitation of agreeable feeling in the body.]

15. In the previous sections Webb tried to relate music to passion through a shared factor to which both are independently related, i.e., movement. He now applies the same procedure to the relationship between verse and passion. Since it cannot be shown how verse excites or imitates passions directly, Webb falls back on the pleasure that verse is known to produce, in order to establish their common denominator, i.e. motion. But since he had already established the relationship between passion and motion independently, the two — verse and passion — could now be related to each other through motion. He than proceeds to ask an interesting question which also contains an important assumption. His question pertains to the laws of nature with regard to the correspondence between an external and mental motion. He assumes that his particular findings reveal a more general law the nature of which allows for kinds of "enlargement" without defying its basic principles. This assumption in fact constitutes the heuristic base of his investigation.

of language, we shall have little reason to doubt of their extending to music in general.[16]

THE passion of love is soft and insinuating; it dwells with a fond delight upon its object:

> — Illum absens absentem auditque, videtque
>
> [He was away now, out of sight and hearing, but she still saw him and still heard his voice.]

> O fairest of creation, last and best
> Of all God's works. Creature in whom excell'd
> Whatever can to fight or thought be form'd
> Holy, divine, good, amiable, or sweet.[d]

And again:

> Awake,
> My fairest, my espous'd, my latest found,
> Heav'n's last best gift, my ever-new delight,
> Awake.[e]

THE expansion of pride is constant in its influence, and compels the measures into a corresponding movement. In the following lines, we have at once a description of the passion, and a proof of its effect:

> Op'ner mine eyes,
> Dim erst, dilated spirits, ampler heart
> And growing up to godhead.[e]

> Ast ego, quæ divum incedo regina, Jovisque
> Et soror, et conjux.[f]
> But I, who move supreme, heav'n's queen, of Jove
> The sister, the espous'd.

IT seems to me, that the pleasure which we receive from great and sublime images arises from their being productive of sensa-

d. Paradise Lost.
e. Paradise Lost.
f. Æneid. l. I.

16. What is interesting about Webb's new proposition is that he is about to show us how he proceeds to establish an "enlargement" by creating a new correspondence from the correspondences he has already established. The relationship between passion and verse on the one hand and passion and music on the other generates a new correspondence between the two relationships via movement, yielding a more encompassing relationship between music (including verse), and the passions.

tions similar to those which are excited by pride. Whether the sensation springs from a consciousness of superiority in ourselves, or from the contemplation of greatness in external objects, we feel the same enlargement of heart; our emotions are congenial, and their accords consonant:

> Thus far these beyond
> Compare of mortal prowess, yet observ'd
> Their dread commander: he above the rest
> In shape and gesture proudly eminent,
> Stood like a tow'r.[g]

THE movement the most opposed to pride must be in accord with sorrow. A descent of notes, if I mistake not, prevails through the following passage:

> Me miserable! which way shall I fly
> Infinite wrath, and infinite despair?
> Which way I fly is hell; myself am hell;
> And in the lowest deep a lower deep
> Still threat'ning to devour me opens wide.
> O then at last relent; is there no place
> Left for repentance; none for pardon left?[g]

IN general, a protracted sound, joined to a kind of languor or weakness in the movement, will be happily expressive of sorrow:

> Longas in fletum ducere voces.
>
> [Drawing out its lingering notes into a wail. Aenei IV 463.]
>
> Earth felt the wound, and nature from her seat
> Sighing, through all her works gave signs of woe
> That all was lost.[h]

ON comparing this passage with the following, we shall observe the difference between an imitation by movement, and an imitation by *sound* :

> Tellus et pronuba Juno
> Dant signum, fulsere ignes et conscius Æther
> Connubii, summoque ulularunt vertice nymphæ. [i]
>
> [Primaeval Earth and Juno, Mistress of the Marriage, gave their
> sign. The sky connived at the union; the lightning flared; on
> their mountain-peak nymphs raised their cry.]

g. Paradise Lost.

h. Paradise Lost.

i. Æneid, l. IV.

IN this second instance, the agreement depends on the force of a particular word or sound, as being imitative of a particular idea. In the former, the accord springs from an agreement of syllables or sounds no otherwise imitative than as they determine by their succession the nature of the movement. A distinction which must be carefully observed in the application of that general maxim,

The sound must seem an echo to the sense.[k]

IT cannot be expected, that the principles of imitation should operate in all similar cases with an equal happiness. There is a stubbornness in the nature of language, which often renders it unapt to fall into that order and succession to which the affection leads us. But the indulgence which the poet may claim from this consideration must not be extended so far as to encourage him to a total violation of the laws of harmony. When our passions are strongly engaged, we are impatient of opposition; and, in every such case, a counter-movement in measure hath much the same effect with a discord in music. Under the impression of these ideas, I cannot reconcile to my feelings that passage with which the Roman poet closes his mournful tale of the death of Priam:

Jacet ingens litore truncus,
Avulsumque humeris caput, ac sine nomine corpus.[l]
[His tall body was left lying headless on the shore, and by it the head hacked from his shoulders: a corpse without a name.]

THERE is a vigor in this movement that is at variance with the idea: it counter-acts our feelings, renders the nerves elastic, and sets the spirits on the spring.

IN the next example, a movement of *dejection* follows, and thereby marks more strongly the character of anger:

Ite,
Ferte citi flammas, date vela, impellite remos.
— *Infelix Dido!* [m]

[Quick! Bring some firebrands, hand out arms. Put your weight to the oars! ....Oh, poor, poor Dido,...]

k. Pope's Essay on Criticism.

l. Æneid, l. II.

m. Æneid, l. IV.

> Fly,
> Catch the quick flames, spring forward, crowd the sails —
> *Lost, lost Eliza!*

WHEN anger hath for its object a studied and distant revenge, its impetuosity gives place to a deliberate vehemence:

> No, let us rather chuse,
> Arm'd with hell-flames and fury, all at once
> O'er heav'n's high tow'rs to force resistless way,
> Turning our tortures into horrid arms
> Against the torturer; when to meet the noise
> Of his Almighty engine he shall hear
> Infernal thunder; and for lightning, see
> Black fire and horror shot with equal rage
> Among his angels.[n] [17]

IN the preceding arrangement of the passions and their accords, anger, pride, sorrow, and love, have been made to preside over, and govern, as it were, the simple movements of music; but as our passions in general are derived from these, or

---

n. Paradise Lost.

17. In his *Remarks,* Webb adopted Pope's statement that the "sound must seem an echo to the sense" though he qualified it. Having accepted Harris's and Avison's conception of the power of sound to imitate either through sound or through motion, he rejected, for poetry, the first kind of imitation in favor of the latter. "The music of the verse, he maintained, "should be governed by the idea" since "the nature of language will not admit... a constant correspondence." In the present treatise he provides the theoretical basis for this statement. Guided by the classification which he has already established, he provides a number of examples which show that different kinds of verse do fall, more or less, into the four classes he had established. It is no coincidence that Webb chooses blank verse, and Milton as its representative, since he has already established in his *Remarks* that blank verse is not constrained by a pre-established prosodic formula, thereby allowing for the pliability necessary for the creation of what he had called "sentimental harmony." Thus there is in his examples, to begin with, a correspondence between the sense of the text — the implicit "label" which it provides — and the movement which accompanies it. To be sure, his demonstrations fall short of providing proof of his claims, with regard to their prosodic aspects as well as their statistical manifestations. One should bear in mind, however, that he considered 'experience' in the way it was understood by the empiricist philosophers, and not the way it is understood nowadays, even in the humanities and the social sciences, as something itself requiring verification. In the final analysis he was after a theory to explain the artistic phenomena as he knew them, and as he assumed others experienced them.

partake, in some degree, of their nature, it should seem that we
may, by the various combinations of these primary movements,
attain to the expression of *almost* every passion. Thus, pity will
find its accord in an union of the movements of sorrow and love;
for there cannot be pity without benevolence; and benevolence
directed to a particular object is a mode of love:

> How art thou lost, how on a sudden lost,
> Defac'd, deflower'd, and now to death devote?[o]

JOY is a lively motion of the spirits in ascent, as partaking of
the nature of pride. For pleasure, according to the Stoics, is a
sublatio animi, [p] a lifting-up of the mind. The affinity between
pleasure and pride is thus happily marked by the poet:

> That now,
> As with new wine intoxicated both,
> They swim in mirth, and fancy that they feel
> Divinity within them breeding wings
> Wherewith to scorn the earth.[q]

BUT the expansion of joy differs from that of pride, as being
apt to break forth in prompt and lively sallies, flying in giddy rapture from one object to another:

> All Heav'n
> And happy constellations on that hour
> Shed their selectest influence; the earth
> Gave sing of gratulation, and each hill ——
> Joyous the birds, fresh gales and gentle airs
> Whisper'd it to the woods, and from their wings
> Flung rose, flung odours.[r]

TERROR is a perturbation of the spirits, connected with the sublime by the enlargement of its images, and the vehemence of its
impressions:

> What if the breath that kindled those grim fires
> Awak'd should blow them into sev'nfold rage
> And plunge us in the flames? or from above
> Should intermitted vengeance arm again
> His red right hand to plague us? what if all

---

o. Paradise Lost.

p. ἔπαρσις

q. Paradise Lost.

r. Paradise Lost.

Her stores were open'd, and this firmament
Of hell should spout her cataracts of fire
Impendent horrors?[r]

IN the following passage, the agitations of terror subside into movements of dejection: for fear hath its foundation in sorrow, and, as such, must have a tendency to conform with its principle:

> While we perhaps,
> Caught in a fiery tempest, shall be hurl'd
> Each on his rock transfix'd, the sport and prey
> Of wracking whirlwinds, or for ever sunk
> Under yon boiling ocean, wrapt in chains;
> "There to converse with everlasting groans,
> Unrespited, unpitied, unrepriev'd,
> Ages of hopeless end."[s]

INDIGNATION is a mixed affection, uniting the vehemence of anger with the expansion of pride:

> Heu furiis incensa feror, nunc augur Apollo,
> Nunc Lyciae fortes, nunc et Jove missus ab ipso
> Interpres divum fert horrida jussa per auras.[t]

[The Furies have me now, they burn, they drive...! So, now, it seems, he has his orders from Apollo's own Lycian oracle, and next even the Spokesman of the Gods is sent by Jove himself to deliver through the air to him the same ghastly command!]

> Fury distracts my brain; now Phœœbus warns,
> Now dreams, now oracles, now winged gods
> Bring the curs'd mandate.

FROM these we pass to movements of pure and unmixed pride:

> Scilicet is superis labor est, ea cura quietos
> Sollicitat! neque te teneo, neque dicto refello.[t]

[So I am to believe that the High Powers exercise their minds about such a matter and let concern for it disturb their calm! Oh, I am not holding you. I do not dispute your words.]

> Think we such toils, such cares, disturb the peace
> Of heav'n's blest habitants! alike I scorn
> Thy person and imposture.

How sudden is the return to anger?

> Fly, be gone,

s. Paradise Lost.

t. Æneid, l. IV.

Rush through the billows, brave the storm —[18]

IF there are passions which come not within the reach of musical expression, they must be such as are totally painful. Painting and sculpture, on whatever subjects employed, act simply, as imitative arts; they have no other means of affecting us than by their imitations. But music acts in the double character of an art of impression as well as of imitation: and if its impressions are necessarily, and, in all cases pleasing, I do not see how they can, by any modification, be brought to unite with ideas of absolute pain. I am confirmed in this opinion by observing, that shame, which is a sorrowful reflection on our own unworthiness, and therefore intirely painful, hath no unisons in music. But pity, which is a sorrow flowing from sympathy, and tempered with love, hath a tincture of pleasure. Hence the poet:

Dimn sadness did not spare,
That time, celestial visages; yet, mix'd
With pity, violated not their bliss.[u]

PITY, therefore, hath its unisons in music; so hath emulation, which is noble and animating, to the exclusion of envy, which is base and tormenting. The same distinction must extend to anger and hatred; for anger hath a mixture of pleasure, in that

u. Paradise Lost.

18. The four passions which he illustrated through the verse which he chose, are the ones which he previously claimed presided over the movement of music. Now he wishes to enlarge his scheme, trying to show its inclusiveness. In line with his basic procedure he tries to create new kinds of correspondences. He exemplifies these new possibilities by means of poetry rather than music, because poetry provides him with both ready labels and shared, available experience. The new labels, he shows us, consist of combinations of labels which are representatives of different classes; the movement, related to the mixed label, finds its place within the two hypothetical axes (see fn. 11) which by definition imply combinations. Adding what he has already told us about music consisting of a "succession of impressions," an additional axis is evoked, which can chart both the movement over time inclusive of its direction. Interestingly, modern psychology dealing with affect, has also arrived at a reduction of the great number of affects to three basic dimensions, allowing for the location of individual passions within that space (see Vol. I: 238-240;253-4).

it stimulates to revenge;[w] but hatred, having no such hope, works inward and preys upon itself.

THE number of the passions thus excluded from becoming the subjects of musical expression will not be very considerable, since, on a strict inquiry into those passions which are generally esteemed painful, we shall find that this very often depends on their motives and degrees. Thus terror, though in reality it be founded in pain, is yet in several of its modes attended with pleasure, as is evident in every instance where the means employed to excite it, either by the idea or the movement, have any connexion with the sublime. But terror, like many other passions, though it be not absolutely painful in its nature, may become so from its excess; for horror, as I conceive, is nothing more than fear worked up to an extremity:

> I could a tale unfold, whose lightest word
> Would harrow up thy soul.[x]

IT is on this same principle, that certain passions are found to add beauty or deformity to the countenance, according to the different degrees of force with which they act. A truth so well understood by capital painters, that they throw the extremes of passion into strong and charged features, while they reserve the finer expressions for the heightenings of beauty. Shakespear has touched on this last circumstance with his usual happiness:

> O what a deal of scorn looks beautiful
> In the contempt and anger of his lip.[y] [19]

w. Πάσῃ ὀργῇ ἕπεσθαί τινα ἡδονὴν τὴν ἀπὸ τῆς ἐλπίδος τοῦ τιμωρήσασθαι   [...anger is always accompanied by a certain pleasure, due to the hope of revenge to come.] Arist. Rhet. 1. II. c. ii.

x. Hamlet

y. Twelfth Night.

19. Though Webb has committed himself to the ability of music to treat the entire spectrum of passions, he does not overlook the limits of the medium. Unlike painting, he tells us, music combines imitation with impression; in order to become music, it operates in a synthetic fashion, uniting successions of impressions into wholes. Music involves the perceptual experience of perfectibility which, in turn, is identified with pleasure. Logically, therefore, music cannot treat passions which do not please. Webb manages to circumvent this problem by analyzing the painful as depending on "motives" which lie outside the emotional sensation itself, although, in the final analy-

(CONT.)

MR. Locke, considering the passions as modes of pleasure or pain, divides them into such as are absolutely pleasing, or absolutely painful, to the entire exclusion of all mixed affections. This division is too vague and general; it may save us the trouble of a minute investigation, but it will never lead us into a knowledge of the human heart. Thus, desire, according to this philosopher, is founded in uneasiness; but Aristotle will have its foundation to be in pleasure: whereas, in truth, it is a compound of both: of uneasiness through the want of an absent good; of pleasure from the hope of obtaining that good. I am tempted to convey my idea of this subject by an illustration borrowed from painting. Let us suppose the painful passions to be *shades*, the pleasing *lights*; we shall then find that many of our passions are composed of mid-tints, running more or less into light or shade, pleasure or pain, according to the nature, motive, or degree of the passion. For instance, if grief arises from the sufferings of others, it becomes pity, and is pleasing by its nature. If grief, proceeding from our own sufferings, be hopeless, and therefore excessive, it becomes misery or despair, and is painful from its degree.

LET grief be tempered with hope, it hath a tincture of pleasure:

> All these and more came flocking, but with looks
> Down-cast and damp; yet such wherein appear'd
> Obscure, some glimpse of joy, t'have found their chief.
> Not in despair.[z]

THE remembrance of that which was dear to us, though it causes grief, yet it gives to our sorrow a cast of pleasure, as it produces in the soul the movements of love. It is in this situation, particularly, that we are said to *indulge* our grief:

---

z. Paradise Lost.

(CONT.)

sis, he is willing to grant that certain passions are indeed excluded from becoming the subject of musical expression. Recent studies (e.g. Clynes 1980) show that music is indeed incapable of portraying the certain emotions like jealousy and guilt.

> Ask the faithful youth,
> Why the cold urn of her whom long he lov'd
> So often fills his arms.[a]

IF grief should spring from a consciousness of guilt, it is shame, and is painful from its motive; if attended with innocence, it may come within that beautiful description,

> She sat like patience on a monument,
> Smiling at grief.[b][20]

IN order to treat of the passions with precision, we should determine their several modes, and fix an unalienable sign on each particular feeling. To this end we should have a perfect intelligence of our own natures, and a consummate knowledge of every thing by which we can be affected: in short, we should have conceptions in all points adequate to their objects. Such knowledge would be intuitive. We should, in this case, want no comparisons of our ideas and sentiments; no illustration of one thing by its resemblance to another: thus every proposition would be reduced to a simple affirmation, the operations of the understanding would cease, and the beauties of the imagination could have no existence. Providence has judged better for us, and by limiting our powers has multiplied our enjoyments.[21]

a. Akenside, Pl. of Im.

b. Twelfth Night.

20. Webb tells us that Locke also tried to reduce the number of passions as much as possible without eliminating any one of them. If Webb takes issue with Locke it is not because of a difference over the number of passions but because Locke's scheme is dichotomous, imposing a categorical distinction which defies reality. Webb also kept passions within a dichotomous scheme, but did not separate them categorically, thus allowing for an endless number of combinations among his classes. Webb also differs from Locke by not admitting pain into one of his classes but relegating it in part to the mind which is also informed about "motives and degrees" which lie outside the felt sensation. Between that which is known and that which is sensed "midtints" are created that can be incorporated within his four classes.

21. Though man possesses intuition, Webb tells us, he is not guided by sheer instinct as far as his perceptions and emotions are concerned. His understanding is a product of transformations of the known to the unknown which he himself effects. Understanding, thus, is a kind of operation related to the imagination; it is not a given but something arrived at. Moreover, this process which man is engaged in, is an enjoy-

(CONT.)

THE wisdom so conspicuous in the abridgement of our perceptions, appears with equal evidence in the bounds prescribed
to those arts which were destined for our delight and improvement. It has been observed, that music can have no connexion
with those passions which are painful by their nature; neither can
it unite with our other passions when they become painful by
their excess; so that the movements of music being in a continued opposition to all those impressions which tend either to disorder or disgrace our nature, may we not reasonably presume,
that they were destined to act in aid of the moral sense, to regulate the measures and proportions of our affections; and, by
counter-acting the passions in their extremes, to render them the
instruments of virtue, and the embellishments of character.[22]

I NEED not profess, that, in forming my ideas of the passions,
I have trusted much more to poets than to philosophers: among
the latter, there have been some who would by no means have
admitted the distinction just now established between emulation
and envy. Hobbes hath, after his manner, given us the portraits
of these passions, but with such sister-like features, that it is no
easy matter to distinguish the one from the other. He has, with

(CONT.)

able creative act. Understanding, learning and creativity have thus a lot in common;
they create relations among separate things introducing novel entities to the mind. It
is amazing how modern Webb sounds; nowadays, perceptual, emotional and creative
processes are viewed more and more in terms of cognitive transformations, related to
comparisons, resemblances and metaphors (Miall 1987).

22. Here Webb connects two kinds of "limitations" which he discussed earlier, one is
related to the non-automatic nature of the understanding and the other to the restrictions that prevent music from arousing passions which are painful. It is this limitation
which enables music's "measured" nature to counteract the passions which music itself
cannot handle. It is the listener, according to Webb, who transfers the "measuredness"
of music to the unmeasured passion, thereby instantiating a kinship between the two.
If music serves as an instrument of virtue it is not because of natural cause and effect,
Webb implies. The venerable tradition concerning the powers of music seems here to
undergo a significant turn, not unlike Hume's revolution with regard to causal relations
in general: it is man's own associative power, conditioned by habits and imagination,
which creates new phenomena for which he seeks lawfulness (cf. fn. 4 above).

equal industry, and for the same purpose, excluded from pity and the sympathetic affections every idea of benevolence or of natural beauty; conceiving them, contrary to all true feelings, to be nothing more than the different workings of one and the same narrow and selfish principle. It may be considered as a happiness in our subject, that it exempts us from a dependence on the systems of philosophers, or the refinements by which they are supported. The process in which we are engaged obliges us to trace the passions by their internal movements, or their external signs; in the first, we have the musician for our guide; in the second, the painter; and the poet in both: it is the province of music to catch the movements of passion as they spring from the soul; painting waits until they rise into action, or determine in character; but poetry, as she possesses the advantages of both, so she enters at will into the province of either, and her imitations embrace at once the movement and the effect. How delightful, in this point of view, to contemplate the imitative arts; those sister-graces, distinguished yet depending on a social influence; the inspirers of elegant manners and affections; the favourites of that Venus, or nature, whose beauties it is their office to cultivate, and on whose steps it is their joy to attend![23]

AMONG the opinions which have prevailed touching the union of music with passion, the most general seems to be this —— That as melody is a thing pleasing in itself, it must naturally unite with those passions which are productive of pleasing sensations;

---

23. Webb is aware that his theory of the passions may disregard traditional philosophical constraints. As an empiricist, however, he is committed to experience and common sense without having to contradict them from the very start. If he chooses to make his point through the arts, it is because the arts have formulated these experiences in sound, shape and combinations thereof, permitting shared observations. Thus, music makes internal movement audible, painting employs signs to fixate the actions it causes, while poetry does both. Webb can afford to present the arts in the way he does, since he has already provided the cognitive substance for his claims.

Thirty years earlier Jacob divided the arts similarly (p. 86 above) and Webb's argument undoubtedly rests on that tradition. Yet, by adding that the passions are the common denominator against which all the arts are gauged, Webb introduces the kind of refinement which enables him to conceive exchanges and combinations among the arts without forgoing their basic boundaries.

in like manner as graceful action accords with a generous sentiment, or as a beautiful countenance gives advantage to an amiable idea. The proposition taken singly is vague and superficial;
but the illustrations by which it is supported penetrate deeper,
and give us an insight into the relation between the cause and
the effect: for in what manner can action become the representative of sentiment, unless it strikes us as springing from some
analogous movement in the soul? it is the same thing with regard
to beauty, which can give no advantage to sentiment, without
being thrown into motion; nor can this motion have any meaning or effect, unless it carries with it the idea of a corresponding
agitation in the mind.

IT was from a feeling of an imitative virtue in music, or of its
aptness to excite pathetic motions, that Shakespear attributes to
it the power of producing a kind of reverberation in the soul:

> Duke. How do'st thou like this tune?
> Viola. It gives a very echo to the feat
> Where love is throned.[c]

LET us apply this idea to the effects of the forté and piano in
music. Loudness is an increased velocity in the vibration, or a
greater vibration made in the same time.[d] Music therefore
becomes imitative, when it so proportions the enforcement or
diminution of sound to the force or weakness of the passion, that
the soul answers, as in an echo, to the just measure of the
impression. It is from a propensity in our nature to fall in with
these reciprocal or responsive vibrations, that, in expressing our
own sentiments, or in reciting those of others, the voice mechan-
ically borrows its tone from the affection; thus it rises into vigor

c. Twelfth Night.

d. HENCE it is, that those, who, through indelicacy of ear, are insensible to finer impressions, are
observed to be affected by loud music; because the increase of the impression forces the dull and
sluggish organ into responsive vibration.

IF to loudness be united a greater intenseness or weight of sound, as when music acts in full chorus,
the impression is still farther augmented; and the effects, though less exquisite, become more powerful.

BUT if the ear is so unhappily formed as that music can neither solicit nor compel the organ into unison, then the consequence will be, either that the impression shall produce weak and imperfect
movements, and like a constant monotonous murmur lull the hearer asleep, or it will excite strong
and irregular vibrations, in which case it acts like a repeated noise, sets the nerves on the fret, and
throws the spirits into a painful disorder.

with the bold, and subsides into softness with the gentler feelings. We may try the experiment on the following lines:

> Back from pursuit thy pow'rs with loud acclaim
> Thee only extoll'd, Son of thy Father's might,
> To execute fierce vengeance on his foes:
> Not so on man; "Him thro' their malice fall'n,
> Father of mercy and grace, thou did'st not doom
> So strictly, but much more to pity incline."[e]

THIS fall of notes, or weakness in the movement, is in the true spirit of musical imitation. The poet was so sensible of the happiness, that in the moment after he repeats the very same movement, and contrasts it by measures the most lofty and sonorous:

> No sooner did thy dear and only son
> Perceive thee purpos'd not to doom frail man
> So strictly, but much more to pity inclin'd ——
>
> Hail, Son of God, Saviour of men! thy name
> Shall be the copious matter of my song
> Henceforth, and never shall my harp thy praise
> Forget, nor from thy Father's praise disjoin.[f]

SOMEWHAT different from the transition in this last example is an even and continued swell from the piano into the forté: this, in music, is attended with a high degree of pleasure: on repeating the following passage, we discover the source of this pleasure, and find that it proceeds from the spirits being thrown into the same movement as when they rise from sorrow into pride, or from an humble into a sublime affection:

> If thou beest he: but O how fall'n, how chang'd
> From him, who in the happy realms of light
> Cloath'd with transcendent brightness didst outshine
> Myriads, though bright.[g]

A DESCENT of sound from the forté into the piano hath a no less pleasing effect, corresponding with the condition of the nerves, when from a state of exertion, which hath a mixture of pain, we feel the sweet relief of a gradual relaxation:

---

e. Paradise Lost.
f. Paradise Lost.
g. Paradise Lost.

> He stood
> With Atlantean shoulders, fit to bear
> The weight of mightiest monarchies; his look
> Drew audience and attention still as night
> Or summer's noon-tide air.[h]

FROM the tenor of these examples it appears, that pleasure is not, as some have imagined, the result of any fixed or permanent condition of the nerves and spirits, but springs from a succession of impressions, and is greatly augmented by sudden or gradual transitions from one kind or strain of vibrations to another. It appears further, that the correspondence between music and passion is most striking in those movements and transitions which in each are productive of the greatest pleasure; consequently the source of pleasure must be in both the same, and the foundation of their union can be no other than a common principle of motion.

What has been just remarked concerning the nature of pleasure, accounts for the observation that a motion in any degree tending towards grace is more pleasing than the most gracefule attitude. It is the nature of the imagination, in these occasions to conceive something more than can be executed; hence it is, that a finished action almost ever disappoints and falls short of our expectations, while, on the other hand, motion which just rises above the measure of simplicity, if happily design, commits as it were to our fancy the completion of the idea and prompts us to the exertion of our finest feelings.

It was the consequence of having made this observation, that Raphael, that pupil of the Graces, threw his figures much oftner into motions that attitudes: and it is on the same principle, that the simple graces of the minuet, which are always in progression, give us a more sensible pleasure than the highest display of attitude in theatrical dances.

If this observation holds good in the beautiful it must still have greater force in the pathetic. While an actor is in motion the

---

h. Paradise Lost.

mind of the spectator endeavors to keep pace with him; when the action is brought to a point, or determines in an attitude, the progress of the mind is at an end, and this, at a time, when the imagination would naturally carry it on through a succession of movements. It is contrary to the nature of passion to rest at any fixed point: there may be, perhaps, an exception from this rule in the case of extreme horror; but it must be of horror unutterable —— Vox faucibus hæsit [the voice clave to his throat (Aeneid II 774, III 48, IV 280, XII 868)]. —— From the moment that a passion falls within the compass of expression, we cannot even conceive it, much less can we represent it, so as to separate from it the idea of increase or diminution.   That action therefore which brings the mind to a full stop cannot be the representative of a mind in motion. The tortures of the Laocoon are most happily expressed by the efforts which he makes to support them, or by the degrees of action which the artist hath wisely kept in reserve.[24]

I HAVE remarked on a former occasion, that in the sublime, "such images as are in motion, and which, by a gradual enlargement, keep our senses in suspense, are more interesting than those which owe their power to a single impression, and are perfect at their first appearance." Where there can be no gradation in an object, its influence on the mind is too suddenly determined. Is it not from the force of progressive sensations that the

24. Having offered several examples, Webb summarizes them in more general terms. Up to now, Webb conceived of passion mainly as a common point of reference for the arts, i.e., as the one thing which the arts try to imitate. Here he views passion as a consequence of artistic doing, i.e, the aesthetic experience. Though his claim about passion, consisting of a kind of movement, holds equally with regard to aesthetic experience, he again resorts to actual observations in order to reinforce his claim. His initial definition of music as consisting of successions of impressions thus becomes a criterion for all the arts, not as far as their constitutive units are concerned, but as a kind of model of mental processing, as he exemplifies through painting. Thus, from this treatise of 1769 we are already forewarned that the condition of music will be posited as a desired state to be emulated by the other arts. Webb's argument contains another point, made earlier by Jacob (see above, p. 91), that the work of art must leave room for the imagination, in fact, the room it leaves is directly related to the intensity of the experience it invites.

vivacity of our conceptions seems, at times, to exalt us above ourselves? hence the enthusiastic raptures, the boasted inspiration of poets, when the imagination, hurried through a train of glowing impressions, kindles in her course, and wonders at a splendor of her own creating. It is curious to observe what a chain runs thro' our feelings. When the sensual Anacreon draws the portrait of his mistress, he cloaths the libertine with a cautious modesty: thus, after having described the beauties of her face and neck, he stops short ——

> A scarlet vest
> Shall hide beneath its folds the rest:
> Yet, let a little be reveal'd,
> A specimen of what's conceal'd.[i]

Si qua latent, meliora putat [If they are concealed, they are better, he reckons.]: —— But we have touched upon a subject in which the progress of the imagination may be too curiously pursued.[25]

IF we have discovered any one common principle by which our feelings are connected, our next care must be to observe how far the arts can affect us in virtue of this principle, and what relation they bear one to the other in their several operations. How extensive might be the influence of these ideas, were they to be enlarged into system, and traced by men of genius through all their consequences! Infinite are the advantages which may be derived from a diligent attention to the mechanical effects of passion; from an accurate investigation of the correspondent move-

---

i. Στόλισον τὸ λοιπὸν αὐτὴν
'Υποπορφύροισι πέπλοις,
Διαφαινέτω δὲ σαρκῶν
'Ολίγον, τὸ σῶμ' ἐλέγχον.

25. While in the preceding paragraph Webb emphasized the relation of expression to a representation that contains "increase or diminution" like that which exemplifies passion, here he enlists the "increase and diminution" as structuring elements of the object creating the experience of the sublime. The sublime, according to Webb, is evoked by constituents of a regular artistic experience brought to an extreme, resulting in self-reflection on the very experience. Viewing the halting moment of the sublime as experiencing the experience, is a novel approach to the concept of the sublime; it will receive further elaboration by subsequent writers.

ments of music, and   from the consequent application of the powers of verse to the support and enforcement of the pathos.

As to the last of these advantages, I am persuaded that our general neglect of it has been owing, for the most part, to the mean opinion we are taught to entertain of our native language. We cannot, it must be confessed, pretend to equal the sweetness of sound or dignity of motion in the Greek measures; but I do not think the comparison so much against us with regard to our musical accords in general; and the reason is this: What we lose through the poverty of our measures, is in some degree restored by the simplicity in the construction of our language, in which every idea is so distinct, unmixed, and complete in itself, that it not only suggests, but often creates its own accord: whereas the arbitrary transpositions in the Greek and Latin make such breaks in the thoughts, and throw them so much out of that order in which they rise up in the mind, that the correspondence between the movement and the idea must become less frequent than would naturally be the case were the construction more simple. We shall generally find, that wherever there is a striking beauty in the ancient poetry, there is at the same time a remarkable simplicity in the succession of the ideas. In the communication of a thought, our aim is to produce in the minds of others an image of what passes in our own: in proportion, therefore, as our feelings are thrown out of their natural order, the image is unfaithful, and the operations of our minds must lose a part of their influence. [26]

26. Webb turns here to a more detailed examination of the relation between arts and aesthetic experience. This leads him to the then much-discussed subject of the adaptability of modern language to poetry, which he will eventually discuss in detail. Viewing the problem from the point of view of the receptive mind rather than that of poetical considerations, he is free to entertain new ideas concerning language's effective powers. Like Condillac, he too considered Classical Greek as a richer language than modern English (French in the case of Condillac). However, both insist (it is very likely that Webb borrowed the idea from Condillac) that simplicity brings along its own advantages; it introduces distinctions which make for a clearer relationship between the signifier and the signified. Liable as it is to manipulation as far as ordering of words is concerned, it permits a more immediate correspondence between the unfolding of language and the movement of thought; moreover, it may produce in the mind of others what passes through the speaker's mind, by a sort of "sympathetic vibration."

IF an irregularity in the order of the impressions obstructs the genuine effect of the idea, we may easily imagine in what manner it must disturb the music of the verse. To instance in one particular: If, when the epithet is divided from its substantive, the intervening idea should have no immediate relation to either, it is evident that no accord can be perfectly preserved through such a confusion of impressions.

As thus:

> Infandum, | Regina, jubes renovare | dolorem.
> [Majesty, too terrible for speech is the pain which you ask me to revive,...]

BUT let the epithet be restored to its natural situation, and the ideas fall of themselves into an according movement, as in the very next line:

> Trojanas ut opes, et lamentabile regnum ——
> [...the greatness which was Troy and the Trojan Empire ever to be mourned.]

"It is the general quality of verse, says Quintilian, to reduce all ideas under the same laws."[k] Therefore, say our modern rhymers, verse hath no other object than to please the ear. It is unfair to draw from a general principle an inference which admits of no exception: and the principle in question, though true with respect to versification founded on an artificial prosody, and supported by the refinement of transposition, becomes less comprehensive when applied to verse, in which the quantities of syllables are determined by accent, and the accent by feeling; and where the ideas succeeding in their natural order must, if not impeded by counter-pursuits, communicate a part of their motion to the medium of their impressions. But, as I propose to resume this subject in another place, I shall confine myself, for the present, to matter of fact; and observe, that if our measures can ascend to the most exalted, and descend into the most depressed condition of the mind, they must necessarily include the accords of the intermediate affections. We may rest the proof of these powers on the following examples:

k. Versificandi genus est, unam legem omnibus sermonibus dare. l.IX. c. iv.

> Mean while inhabit lax, ye pow'rs of heav'n;
> And thou my Word, begotten Son, by thee
> This I perform: speak thou, and be it done:
> My over-shadowing spirit and might with thee
> I send along.[1]

SUCH is the effect of this last movement, that our spirits partake in the enlargement, the expansion, of the divine essence. How affecting is the contrast in these beautiful lines?

> So much I feel my genial spirits droop,
> My hopes all flat; nature within me seems
> In all her functions weary of herself.[m][27]

HAVING thus tried the foundation of our hypothesis by a variety of experiments, let us now proceed to examine how far these same principles may be found to agree with the history of Poetry and Music.

IN the first ages of the world, men's thoughts were altogether employed on their feelings; prompted by nature to the communication of those feelings, their words followed the motion of their sensations, and became rather the imitative than the arbitrary signs of their ideas. Hence it is, that original languages, or, which is the same thing, the original parts of mixed languages, are always the most expressive. Plato, after having suggested that language owed its origin to the deepest reflection, and the most consummate wisdom, was notwithstanding forced to acknowledge, that words expressive of their ideas abounded most in the

---

1. Paradise Lost.

m. Samson Agonistes.

27. Webb furthers his argument through a discussion of regularity and irregularity in verse. There is the kind of verse which is characterized by an immediately audible "sameness" (awareness of which is attributed here to Quintilian, which may not, however, correspond to the unfolding of the idea expressed. In line with his observations concerning the desired correspondence between the succession of impressions in music and the succession of ideas in poetry, the "Quintilian" regularity cannot sustain either. By contrast, irregular verse, i.e. blank verse, permits both. The number of syllables in blank verse is determined by accents, which in turn are dictated by underlying feelings. The latter function as a base for the unfolding of ideas as well. Neither is governed by external patterns nor are they necessarily subservient to them as Webb has elaborated at length in his *Remarks on the Beauty of Poetry* (see our discussion on this point in Vol. I: 87-92).

barbarous, or, as he otherwise calls them, the most ancient languages;[n] an inconsistency into which he was betrayed in consequence of his having set out on the investigation of language at the wrong end; for though compounds, in many instances, carry in them the marks of mature reflection, and great ingenuity, yet the signs of simple ideas, which were the first in order, and with which of course he should have begun, are of a very different character: these, most undoubtedly, like the ideas which they represent, were the off-spring of sensation; they were the result of reiterated attempts, by men of lively feelings, to excite conceptions in others by the happiest indications of their own.

WORDS are modifications of sound and motion; consequently they may become imitative of all those ideas which have any natural relation to either.[28]

---

n. In Cratylo.

28. The eighteenth century was extremely interested in the development of language. This interest arose partly from the discovery of exotic cultures and the differences among cultural systems. Already in the seventeenth century, the increasing awareness of the arbitrariness of linguistic signs created a discourse with regard to the relationship between such signs and thought. The increment added by the eighteenth century is evident in the attempts to fathom the development of languages and to compare them, in order to gain insights into their functioning, and into the relationship between their conventional and their cognitive elements. One should bear in mind, however, that the individuals who dealt with these questions differed from each other. Thus, Vico was interested in language as part of the making of culture, Condillac was interested in the cognitive development of the individual, and Rousseau emphasized its social implications. Nor should one forget someone like Monboddo, whose interests were more purely linguistic, though he arrived at his understanding of language through anthropological investigations.

Against this background, Webb's attempt was a more modest one, since he was, after all, primarily concerned with the kind of language related to feelings. His interest in the primitive origins of language was related primarily to his interest in musicalized poetry. Sharing Condillac's and Rousseau's belief that language tried at the beginning to emulate basic feelings, he sought in contemporary language those primordial and natural "gestures" that can be enlisted for expressive poetry. Indeed Webb's claim that passion is a sort of motion helps to explain Condillac. However, whereas Condillac's gestures are of a more general nature, functioning like inexplicit utterances, Webb's gestures are both atomized and specific, and are already part of a codal system. Anchoring the origin even of individual words in movement, as he explains in what follows, enables Webb to create an additional link between poetry and passion on the one hand, and poetry and music on the other.

IMITATIONS of sounds operate by a direct similitude in the words — groan, sigh, whine, hiss, shriek, howl, and the like. The imitations of motion are of the same kind in the words — cling, climb, swing, wind, glide, drive. These, tho' monosyllables, and therefore usually considered as single impressions, yet, being composed of several distinct elementary sounds, possess, in effect, the advantage of a succession of impressions: of this we shall be more sensible by comparing them with their opposites — flit, spring, skip, start, drop. In order to account for this remarkable difference, we should inquire into the mechanical formation of letters, or of the elementary sounds of which words are composed; but as this would be a dry and tedious discussion, I shall refer those who may desire to trace this subject minutely, to the philosophers and grammarians who have enlarged upon it.°

SOME imitations act with the united powers of sound and motion, as — sob, gulp, clap, thump, bounce, burst; in others, the organs of speech seem to undergo the very operation specified, as may be experienced in some of the examples already given, and still more forcibly, perhaps, in the words — grind, screw, lisp, yawn: nor is it at all an argument against the aim of imitation in these, that similar articulations are employed without any view to imitation in other instances; because the signs of all simple ideas which have no relation either to sound or motion must have been altogether arbitrary, and, as no attention to similitude could take place in their formation, might as well have

---

o. Vide Platonem in Cratylo. Dion. Hal. de Struct. Orat. Wallisii Gram. Ling. Ang.

---

29. This paragraph makes clear why Webb identified atomized words as gestures. The single word, he tells us, is in itself a "succession of impressions" due to its compound phonetic construction. Whereas in Condillac's theory, single words — their formations, not their location in the overall cognitive scheme — are of an arbitrary nature, Webb grants these formations an iconic status embracing an extra cognitive value. Indeed, Webb distinguishes between two kinds of "direct similitude," the one which refers to sound, and the other to motion. While the first, as a kind of onomatopoeia, presents a "token" of the thing itself, the second, which refers to meaning as expressed in motion, is a "type" of similitude. A third kind of direct imitation embraces sound and motion, token and type.   (CONT.)

been comprehended in one combination of sounds as another.[29]

I HAVE called the preceding imitations direct, to distinguish them from such as do not seem to have an immediate connexion with their object: thus we often borrow ideas from the touch or taste, and apply them metaphorically to sounds, as — soft, hard, smooth, rough, sweet, harsh, and their similars. In like manner the words — sharp, flat, so universally applied to musical sounds, owe the fitness of their application to their conveying different ideas of motion, the one being expressive of a quick, the other of a dull, or languid impression.[30]

THE last class of imitations is very extensive; it includes all those articulations, which, though they do not amount to a direct designation of the idea, are yet so constructed as to favour, in some degree, the imitation of the action intended, as in — smile, grin, frown, stare: Under this class likewise may be ranked all such approaches to the idea as seem formed to coincide with the changes and inflexions of the voice, to which we are prompted by a spirit of imitation, as in the following contrast — rise, fall; fret, sooth; cut, melt; and infinite others.[31]

THE imitations of sounds depend for the most part on vowels; they are obvious, simple, and accurate in their similitude. With

(CONT.)

The idea that the immediate imitative power of language consists of sound and motion, is not new, and was employed since Harris, as we have seen. However, whereas Harris and his followers identified motion with a prosodic unfolding in time, Webb's concern is also with motion related to basic phonetic aspects. Webb is not disturbed by the fact that imitation through motion and sound are neither necessary nor sufficient for the communicative act, for he opts to remain on the emotional level.

30. Whereas in the previous paragraphs Webb discussed direct similitude, in this paragraph he discusses indirect imitation. The latter, while it does not operate phonetically, is connected metaphorically to motion, via qualities borrowed from other senses, which serve the audible realm synaesthetically.

31. Webb's last class of imitation deals with a kind of adaptability of meaning and motion in words which refer neither to sound nor to motion directly, though they imply the latter. Interestingly, different terms related to voice inflections are included in this class.

regard to these, therefore, all primitive languages should resemble one another, allowance being made for the differences which might have arisen from organization, from the temperature of the air, or the degrees of sensibility in the first inventers.

THE imitations of motion depend mostly on consonants; these are far more numerous than the former, less perfect in their similitude, but more powerful by their impressions, because passion and sentiment find their accords in motion. Hence it is, that original languages abound in consonants.

THE representation of a sound is the (e)cho of that sound; such signs can no otherwise differ throughout the primitive languages than in their degrees of similitude. But the same modifications of motion may be represented by various articulations, or by sounds totally different: because the similitude is determined by the quality of the movement, and not by the nature of the sound. In this case, therefore, the representative, tho' it hath its origin in imitation, must owe its establishment, *in part*, to consent or agreement. Hence it follows, that a diversity in original languages, with regard to signs of this kind, cannot be brought as an argument against a common principle of imitation.[32]

FROM signs founded in imitation, and confirmed by consent, the transition was easy and natural to the institution of signs, which, having no relation to their ideas, must have owed their

32. In this short description of the development of language, Webb leads us from its primitive stage to its developed form. The beginning of language, as far as he is concerned, rests on the imitation of sounds through vowels, creating resemblance via similitude. The consonances later contribute to the variability and richness of language which is necessary for its own efficacy. From this stage onward, variability and its employment rest on social consent with respect to those combinations that make codification possible. Thus whereas languages differ from each other, their development shares some basic principles; they all start from impressions and move towards effective communication, subject to similar constraints. Webb's emphasis on key factors in the development of language is well taken, despite a number of inaccuracies concerning the relation between motion, consonances and vowels and the lack of distinction between, what nowadays, might be referred to as intonation (related to pitch) and wave-form (related to timbre). It adds to the general picture of the eighteenth century which portrayed language as a structured cultural system molded by society.

establishment solely and intirely to compact. In short, as we cannot conceive how compact could have taken place, had it not been suggested by some leading idea or experiment, and, as supernatural means are never admitted where there are natural adequate to the purpose, I see no reason why we should hesitate to embrace an hypothesis, which discovers the origin of the representative in the nature of the thing represented; and, by giving meaning to sound, and expression to motion, deduces the invention of language, in its first spring, from a simple and almost mechanical exertion of our faculties.[33]

WERE we to select from the monosyllables in our language any two signs expressive of very different ideas, and, by adding new sounds or syllables, to throw them into similar terminations and movements, we should, in great measure, dispossess them of their imitative virtue. It is, therefore, to the same spirit of imitation which prevailed in the formation of the signs themselves, that we owe their being governed in our language through their several declensions and conjugations by the preposition and auxiliary verb; as, by the use of these, each word still preserves, through every circumstance of case, mood, and tense, the same imitative force which it enjoyed by its original formation. Thus, what hath been imputed to simplicity or want of invention in our ancestors, becomes a proof of justness in their feelings, and of constancy in their natures: and, while we implicitly admire the superior ingenuity in the construction of the Greek and other languages, we do no more, in effect, than profess a preference of sweetness to force, or, of a general dignity of sound to the specific energy of imitation.

As the Greek language hath been the channel through which the knowledge of antiquity hath descended to us, it was natural that we should adopt the ideas, and proceed on the authority, of

33. Webb invokes a meta-theoretical consideration to justify his assumption that the "origin of the representative" in language is "in the nature of the thing represented," i.e. sound. Calling for demystification, he argues that mystification often raises issues which are not readily identified with the object in need of explaining. Economy in theoretical elements is the preferred strategy, he implies.

the Greek writers. And yet, a very little reflection might have taught us, that, with regard to the origin of language, they were, of all people, the least fitted to be our instructors. They wrote at a time when their language had been improved to a high degree of refinement; when it retained few or no traces of its primitive character, or of affinity with its rude original, the Phenician. Without examples or materials in their own language, they were too proud to borrow them from any other; destitute of true principles, they took up with the first that presented themselves to their imagination: thus, attributing to single letters or sounds what could only result from their combinations, they supposed the α to be expressive of greatness, the η of length: they went farther, and confounding the ideas of figure and sound, they conceived the O to be an audible representation of roundness: notions altogether fantastical, I had almost said, puerile; but trifles become venerable from certain characters, and we respect even the slumbers of the divine Plato.p[34]

IF imitation had so great a share in the formation of language, it must have acted with equal force in the government of modulation. Music, in its original purity, was used as a mode of conveying or enforcing sentiment; it was either the substitute or the support of language: might we follow the authority of Lucretius, we should acknowledge her for the elder sister, the tutoress of poetry:

---

p. In Cratylo.

34. Webb's interest in the elevation of English poetry leads him to challenge the accepted superiority of the Greek language. Like some of his contemporaries, Webb sees the Greeks as representative of a highly sophisticated culture that cannot serve as a model for the primitive state of man. Thus, for example, the lack in Greek, of special words for declensions, conjugations, prepositions, and auxiliary verbs mutilates the forceful imitations of feelings through sounds. On the other hand, Webb decries the Greek tendency to attribute symbolic power to single letters, because effective imitations are rooted in gestures, and gestures in sound are a compound phenomenon. A similar argument was raised much earlier by Vincenzo Galilei against the highly sophisticated musical culture of his day for the double misdemeanor of occupying itself with "sweet" combinations of sounds removed from the ideas which these sounds were supposed to evoke, and attributing symbolic significance to isolated details which cannot carry much meaning.

At liquidas avium voces imitarier ore
Ante fuit multo, quam lævia carmina cantu
Concelebrare homines possent, aureisque juvare.
[...to imitate with the mouth the liquid notes of the birds came long before men could delight their ears by warbling smooth carols in song.]

WERE this idea to be reduced within the terms of a simple proposition, it would amount to no more than this: — The natural preceded artificial language,q or, that sounds must have been imitative before they were made the signs of our ideas by compact.

MEASURE, according to Longinus, belongs to poetry, because it is the province of poetry to employ the passions.r Now that union of measure with passion is founded on the principle of an according movement. Lucretius felt the force of this principle in music; and seems to have inferred from it, that in the beginning of time, passion produced song; and, when language was invented, passion and song gave birth to measure.

WE are informed that the Chinese tongue consists of a few undeclined monosyllables, each word having many different significations, determined by the various modulations and accents with which it is accompanied. As the primitive parts of the languages reputed original are all monosyllables, this description of the Chinese may be considered as an image of every infant language: certainly it throw a happy light on the poet's conjecture, confirms the comment I have made on his idea, and brings an apparent flight of the imagination under the sober view of a philosophical progression.

THAT such an example of primitive simplicity should be found at this time in a language of so high antiquity as the Chinese,

q. Ergo, si varii sensus animalia cogunt,
Muta tamen cum sint varias emittere voces:
Quanto mortales magis æquum est tum potuisse
Dissimiles alia atque alia res voce notare? L.V.

[Therefore if different feelings compel animals, dumb though they are, to utter different sounds, how much more natural it is that mortal men should then have been able to mark different things with one sound of another!]
r. Μᾶλλον δὲ πρόσεστι τὸ Μέτρον τῷ Ποιητικῷ, πάθεσι πλείστοις χρωμένῳ· δι᾽ ὧν ἁρμονία κατασκευάζεται . [It is rather the measure that serves the poet, who uses a great many emotions, thereby producing harmony.]

would appear very extraordinary, were we not to reflect on the conduct of this people in dividing their language into vulgar and scientific; into a language of sounds and a language of characters; whence it has happened, that, intent solely on the improvement and multiplication of their characters, they have abandoned their oral language to its original poverty. Had no such division obtained, their musical signs or accented modulations would, as in other languages, have been gradually converted into fixed and decisive articulations. It is true, that the Ethiopians, Egyptians, and many other nations in imitation of them, divided their language into sacred and vulgar; but as the sacred consisted of vague and undecisive symbols, ill fitted to convey any useful or certain knowledge, they were under the necessity of attending to the cultivation of the vulgar tongue.[35]

IN our attempts to express our feelings by words significative of those feelings, we should find ourselves limited to a certain

35. By re-introducing music at this point, Webb attempts to lend additional support to his conception of the development of language. To be sure, music is not enlisted here as a full-fledged art, only in terms of its possibility of inflection — movement without measure. Webb thus adds another musical element to the imitative possibilities of language, i.e. the intonative aspect. This assumption carries with it an additional assumption with regard to poetry, namely, that poetry also contributed the important factor of measure to the development of language. Webb does not really explain the role of "modulation" in communication as did Condillac or Rousseau, though he could well have used their arguments to bolster his theory of the correspondence between movement and passion. Had he done that, he would have had to reconcile a theory of communication (related to intoning as a referential system) with a theory of expression (related to intoning as expressing an independent emotional curve). In any case, like Condillac and Rousseau, Webb too endorsed the idea of the inseparability of music and language at their initial stage. His account of Chinese as a tonal language teaches us that he also had in mind the idea of a later divergence of music from language. It stands to reason that he might have agreed with Condillac that language developed in the direction of the "scientific," while music progressed in the direction of the "emotional." His discussion of the divergence within the Chinese language of its tonal aspects from its signs, implies that the symbolic basis which suffices for music as an art, falls short of supplying the proper tools for language if it is to fulfill its communicative function. Whereas Mersenne and Leibniz confused the "scientific" with the "emotional" in discussing music's universal appeal, Webb understood, that music's linguistic capacities invariably relate to passion alone.

number of ideas; all those being necessarily excluded which have no relation to sound or motion: add to this, that a complex idea cannot be represented by any single image or impression. Where imitation fails, compact must take place. But the improvement of language by the multiplication of arbitrary signs, though necessary to the purposes of speculation, would ill correspond with the vivacity of our sensations, with that imitative spirit which had given being to language, and with the early and constant influence of an expressive modulation: We should therefore strike into collateral resources, and fall upon new sounds and movements, springing from certain arrangements of words, and successions of syllables:[s] the process is easily comprehended; with an imitative articulation would co-operate imitation by accent; accents determine the times in which successive syllables are pronounced; syllables of unequal quantities must, in the course of their successions, fall into metrical proportions:[t] and the ear, prompt to cultivate its own pleasure, would seize on every approach to a musical rhythmus.

AT this period, and under these circumstances, no man could be distinguished by his genius, without an ear for music, and a talent for versification; and, the principle of imitation being in both the same, the characters of poet and musician would of course be united in the same person. This union, with the principles which produced it, properly considered, we shall have no difficulty in conceiving, that the first improvements of eloquence should appear in verse,[u] and the earliest efforts of genius be conveyed in song.

---

s. Καὶ τὰς συλλαβὰς δὲ οἰκείως, οἷς ἂν βούλωνται παραστῆσαι πάθεσι, ποικίλως φιλοτεχνοῦσιν. [They adapt the very syllables and letters to the emotions which they wish to represent.] Dion. Hal. de Struct. Orat.

t. Λέξεως δὲ γενομένης αὐτὴ ἡ φύσις τὸ οἰκεῖον μέτρον εὗρε. [But once dialogue had been introduced, by its very nature it hit upon the right measure.] Arist. Poet. c. iv.

u. Ὡς δ' εἰπεῖν, ὁ πεζὸς λόγος ὅγε κατασκευασμένος μίμημα τοῦ ποιητικοῦ ἐστι· πρώτιστα γὰρ ἡ ποιητικὴ κατασκευὴ παρῆλθεν εἰς τὸ μέσον καὶ εὐδοκίμησεν· Εἶτα ἐκείνην μιμούμενοι, λύσαντες τὸ μέτρον, τ' ἄλλα (sic) δὲ φυλάξαντες τὰ ποιητικά, συνέγραψαν· [But prose discourse — I mean artistic prose — is, I may say, an imitation of poetic discourse; for poetry, as an art, first came upon the scene and was first to win approval. Then came... prose writings in which they imitated the poetic art, abandoning the use of metre but in other respects preserving the qualities of poetry.] Strabo I.1 (sic).

BUT, if every original language consisted for the most part of monosyllables; and, if measure, as hath been supposed, was the genuine and immediate result of feeling, it should seem, that there must have been some one simple and primitive mode of versification antecedent to all others, and similar in its mechanism throughout the several languages.

IT has been observed of rude and uncivilized nations, as it may of the rude and uncivilized of every nation, that in their common conversation they seem to sing. Let us imagine ourselves in a state not far removed from the origin of things. Let our voice follow freely the impulse of sentiment, and run uncontrouled into the natural variations of emphasis and accent. We have traced in these variations the origin of measure. But measures, simply as such, have no determined effect; in order to constitute verse, they must be brought to act in certain times and proportions; to this end we employ the pause:ʷ from the determination and division of the several movements in succession, springs a musical dependence of one movement on another. Such are the principles of the verse which we have received from our northern ancestors; such, perhaps, were the Hebrew and Oriental measures;ˣ and such, we may presume, was the οἰχεῖον μέτρον, [a proper meter] those artless and familiar numbers, to which, in the opinion of their master-critic, the Greeks were directed by a natural impulse.³⁶

w. Primum quia sensus omnis habet suum finem possidetque naturale intervallum, quo a sequentis initio dividatur: deinde, quod aures continuam vocem secutæ, ductæque velut prono decurrentis orationis flumine, tum magis judicant cum ille impetus stetit [...firstly because every group of connected thoughts has its natural limit and demands a reasonable interval to divide it from the commencement of what is to follow: Secondly because the ear, after following the unbroken flow of the voice and being carried along down the stream of oratory, finds its best opportunity of forming a sound judgement on what it has heard, when the rush of words comes to a halt..] — Hæc est sedes orationis, &c. [It is there that style has its citadel.]

Quint Inst. l. IX. c. iv.

x. Mensuræ quæ dependent a rebus ipsis. [Measures which depend on the things themselves.]   Lowth, de Sac. Poetr. Heb. p. 32. note 1.

36. In the previous note we commented on the insufficiency of the basic primitive constituents of language — its imitative aspects — for the performance of its communicative function. As far as Webb is concerned, it follows that poetry, which should adhere to a more direct mode of communication, has a problem. Poetry uses words for their

(CONT.)

The great simplicity of our measures seems to have brought
them too much into contempt with the zealous admirers of the
Greek and Latin. It is said, that we have no syllables of determined quantities. How then can we have a regular and supported rhythmus? all measures spring from the differences in the
quantities of successive syllables; the quantity of a syllable is the
time employed, or the force bestowed, by the voice on its pronunciation. Now, whether these quantities are governed by an
invariable prosody, or flow from the impression of the sense and
accent, the effects will be much the same in all parallel movements:

> Θέλω λέγειν 'Ατρείδας,
> Θέλω δὲ Κάδμον ᾄδειν
> I fain would praise the Atrides,
> I fain would sing of Cadmus.

THE simplest measures are those in which each foot, or metrical division, consists but of two syllables. If the accent rises on
the first syllable, and subsides in the second, the weaker vibration will produce a sound of shorter duration,^{y} and there will be
a transition in the sounds from acute to grave:

>   >   >
Sing, my I harp, of I God on   I high.

y. Syllaba acuta longius intervallum penetrat, et plures sui similes syllabas propagat in aëre; ideoque
et diutius vivit ejus imago audibilis, et a distantibus melius percipitur et majori intervallo repetitur ab
echo, quam syllaba gravis, aut syllabico accentu remisse prolata: non secus ac fit in chorda intensius
ducta, quam in ea quæ remissius: et hinc nimirum est, ut syllaba acuta videatur semper longior quam
gravis, spectata scilicet mora; non quia dum est in ore proferentis ipsi insistitur, sed quia ejus species
in aëre vivit. [A high-pitched syllable sets a longer interval and propagates many
more similar syllables in the air. Therefore its audible image lives longer and
is perceived better from a distance, and it is repeated by an echo at a greater
interval than a low syllable, or it is prolonged mildly by the syllabic accent,
similar to what happens when a string is stretched stronger in comparison to
one less taut; and as a result a high syllable seems always longer than a low
one, a pause being evidently observed — not because it is continued while it
is in the mouth of the utterer, but because its appearance lives in the air.]
Kirch.   Musur. 1. VIII. c. vii.

(CONT.)

denotative function, and their sound for expressive weight. But since the expressive
musical possibilities of language are limited, poetry must create new combinations that
abide by the original force of the old utterances. As far as he is concerned, the system
of blank versification which Webb had already recommended, fulfills both requirements
by adding an expressive dimension to the denotative function. Webb tries to show that
these constituted the underlying rules of Ancient poetry.

IF the accent[z] is thrown on the second syllable, and the voice touches lightly on the first, the duration of the sounds will be as the force of the vibrations, and the passage from grave to acute:

>   >   >   >
And on the wings of mighty winds.

BY this it appears, that men fell upon the use of measures on the very same principle by which they struck into a musical succession of notes. The learned Kircher had even gone so far, as to suppose music to have been the off-spring of accentuation — Vides igitur quo modo ex natura accentus paulatim musica excreverit — And, in fact, what is music in its simplest form, in recitative for instance, but a happy accommodation of the powers of accent and movement to the tones and proportions of our feelings? We have seen that the quantities of syllables are but the variations of accent; and that primitive measures were nothing more than transitions from acute sounds to grave, or from grave to acute. How is this? have the Greek and Teutonic poesy one common origin? do the cedar and the bramble spring from the same root? The language of the imagination is imposing; let us attend to that of common sense — Poema nemo dubitaverit ab imperito quodam initio fusum, et aurium mensura, et similiter decurrentium spatiorum observatione esse generatum; mox in eo repertos pedes.[a] [...poetry was originally the outcome of a natural impulse and was created by the instinctive feeling of the ear for quantity and the observation of time and rhythm, while the discovery of feet came later] — What the critic understood by the aurium mensura, &c. may be collected from a ludicrous passage in the Plutus of Aristophanes, where the sycophant, or informer, in the act of rejecting the stench of a sacrifice, completes a verse of six iambics by the mere play of accents, without the aid of prosody or articulation:

z. Let it be remembered, that, throughout this discourse, the word *accent* is made to denote an acute, or grave, sound; or, which is the same thing, an enforcement, or relaxation of the voice, on a single syllable.

a. Quint. de Inst. Orat. 1. IX. c. iv.

Within, in all their filth,
Are heaps of broil'd fish, and of greasy roast meat.
>   >   >   >   >   >
Hu hu, hu hu, hu hu, hu hu, hu hu, hu hu.[b]

As the most ingenious compounds, in language, are but artificial combinations of simple ideas, increasing with the improvements of the understanding; in like manner, the most artificial measures, in poesy, are nothing more than ingenious variations of the simple proportions of sounds, keeping pace with the refinements of taste and feeling: for the dactyle does but repeat the second stroke of the trochee, the anapæst the first of the iambic. Ut proinde rhythmus late sumptus nihil aliud fit, quam sonus quidam proportionatus, ex tardis et velocibus motibus, sive, quod idem est, ex variis acuminis et gravitatis gradibus compositus. [Accordingly, rhythm, taken broadly, is nothing other than a certain sound proportioned by slow and rapid movements, or, what is the same, composed of various degrees of "acuteness" and "graveness."][c]

THIS principle is not confined to regular and established measures; it governs the succession of our monosyllables even in common discourse, but much more when the occasion calls for a spirited and impassioned articulation. As to our words of two, three, or four syllables, we have borrowed them for the most part from other languages; but, in ours, they disown their vernacular accents; and, complying with the genius of our national pronunciation, fall with great regularity into iambic and trochaic movements. Upon the whole, the laws of musical and therefore of metrical proportions, however varied they may be in their modes, are universal in their influence; they obtain in all languages, and extend through every branch of elocution. Hence it is, that

---

b. Ἔνδον ἐστίν, ὦ μιαρωτάτω
    Πολὺ χρῆμα τεμαχῶν, καὶ κρεῶν ὠπτημένων.
    ὔυ, ὔυ, ὔυ, ὔυ, ὔυ, ὔυ.   Act. IV. Sc. iii.
[I remember numbers if I remember them as words.]
                                   —Numeros memini, si verba tenerem.
c. Kirch. Musur. 1. VIII. c. iii.

prose hath its rhythmus, as well as verse; that expression so much depends on the music of the voice; and that the finest strains of eloquence fall short of their effects, when delivered in equal tones, or with a lifeless and unaccented pronunciation.37

No language can be incapable of metre, unless the nature of its construction should be such, as that all its syllables must necessarily be pronounced in equal times. It was reserved for the spirit of modern criticism to conceive the existence of such a language: and to render the example still more remarkable, it hath been fixed upon the Jews; a people, who, to a natural heat of temper, united the most ardent enthusiasm, and were distinguished from every other nation on the earth, by the quickness of their feelings, and the vehemence of their passions. Let those who can insist on such a paradox reconcile it to history and to nature.

GARCILASSO de la Vega informs us,[d] that the poets of Peru used not rhimes, but a kind of loose verse consisting of long and short syllables; his meaning will be best understood by the specimens which he has given us of those measures. The first is a sonnet addressed to the Peruvian Isis, or Juno. The Latin translation of this piece is recommended by La Vega as a faithful copy of the original:

> Pulchra Nympha,   Fairest Goddess,

d. Comment. of Peru.

e. The bucket, or water-measure of the Egyptian Isis.

37. Among the numerous issues related to the relative merit of the Ancients vs. the Moderns, poetry raised the question of the advantage of qualitative over quantitative meters. Supporting the advantages of qualitative versification, Webb maintains that pattern is perceived irrespective of its origin, whether it is inherent in the words themselves (as in quantitative meters), or externally imposed upon them (as in qualitative meters). While quantitative and qualitative poetry may be equal from a perceptual point of view, quantitative poetry lacks affectivity, being unable to impose a regularly ordered succession on syllables independently of their length. Moreover, the given order of a certain kind of qualitative versification is what permits internal play without losing regularity. Taking into account that the majority of words used in English poetry consist of single syllables, as Webb noted, even greater possibilities of relating sense to accent are opened thereby. Webb is aware that accent may be related to different

(CONT.)

Frater tuus	Now thy brother
Urnam tuam[e]	Breaks thy urn, and
Nunc infringit;	Sends the tempest:
Cujus ictus[f]	At each blow, a
Tonat, fulget,	Sound tremendous
Fulminatque	Bursts from heav'n, and
Sed tu, Numpha,	Unremitting
Tuam lympham	Lightning flashes,
Fundens, pluis,	Thunder rattles.
Interdumque	But thou, nymph, thy
Grandinem feu	Clouds collecting,
Nivem mittis.[g]	Pour'st their waters;
Mundi factor	And commixing
Vinchoca	Hail and snow, in
Ad hoc munus	Storm descendest.
Te fullicit	Of the world the
Et præfecit.[h]	Great Creator
	To this function
	Thee appointed,
	Partner of his
	Pow'r, and glory.

---

f.   Cavum conversa cuspide montem
     Impulit in latus, ac venti, velut agmine facto,
     Qua data porta ruunt
[...he swung his trident round where the shell of the cliff was thin, and struck
home. The winds formed line, and charged through the outlet which he had
made. With tornado blasts they swept the earth.]
     Intonuere poli, et crebris micat ignibus æther.

[The thunder cracked in heaven's height, and in the air above a continuous
lightning flared.]
g.   Thus Juno:
     His ego nigrantem commistum grandine nimbum
     Desuper infundam.
[I shall set over them a black cloud charged with mingled rain and hail,...]
h.   Tibi divum pater
     Et mulcere dedit fluctus, et tollere.
[To you, my Lord Aeolus, he who is father of all gods and king of all men has
given authority to lull the waves or to rouse them.] Æn, 1. I.

(CONT.)

physical parameters — duration, volume or pitch — which by definition are universal.
The basic contrast between accented and unaccented syllables is considered as an initial qualifying communicative unit, which connects the musical non-semantic to the linguistic ideational. With this universal criterion Webb is able to bridge poetry and language and to assess their relationship across different cultures.

THE second specimen is part of a love-song, and runs thus in English:

> To the fair one
>   Go, my song;
> Say, at midnight
>   I shall come.

IT is to be observed in both these examples, that the first repose of the voice is on the fourth syllable; that, while the pause distinguishes, the sense connects the movements, producing an effect equivalent to a verse of eight, or of seven syllables. In this joint operation we discover the origin of our rhythmus, and have as it were in prospect all the consequent variations and improvements of our measures.

THE Hebrew or Oriental measures, for there could be no material difference in the verse of sister-dialects, are thus described by a modern critic[i] — Genus liberum — versus habens cum brevitate sonoros, musicis poeticisque pedibus constantes, qui tibiæ saltationibusque facile accommodentur, ut cantando, atque a saltantibus recitati perfectum carmen videri potuerint. [Free Style — has verses with short sounds, consistent with musical and poetical metres, which are accommodated easily to singing by flutes and dances, and while recited by the dancers seem to counstitute a perfect poem.] — This description expresses the genius of all primitive poetry; it is a portrait which finds its original under very meridian: the features are Oriental, American, Saxon; they unite under one common character the most distant regions, and afford the fairest proof of the universality of those laws by which measures have sprung out of a natural prosody.[38]

WE have seen, that the first enlargement of our verse grew out

---

i. Michaelis on Lowth, page 5.

38. We shall not take issue with Webb with regard to the particulars of his examples, because nowadays we know more about the languages he cites as well as about the nature of their prose and poetry. It is important, however, to restate the major argument which Webb tries to promote through these examples. The argument amounts to a claim that natural prosody gave rise to meters which are recognizable as cyclic patterns differentiated by two basic qualities — long vs. short, accented vs. unaccented.

of the reciprocal dependence of successive movements. But as a continual succession of equivalent impressions must fatigue the ear, a relief was sought to the monotony by diverting the movements from an immediate into an alternate dependence.

> To drive the deer with hound and horn
>   Earl Piercy took his way;
> The child may rue that is unborn
>   The hunting of that day.[k]

THE responses of the stanza set the genius of our rhythmus in the clearest light; and it is probable that rhimes were first employed as the marks of these responses. But an unvaried and uniform alternation was ill fitted to correct a monotonous harmony: it became expedient therefore to extend the scale of the rhythmus, to give it a more liberal flow, and, by introducing with greater freedom into the movements measures of unequal and even opposite effects, to throw them into new modes and degrees of dependence. Let us examine whether our pentameter be formed for the attainment of these ends, and how far it may be intitled to the flattering distinction of heroic verse.[39]

THE genuine measures of this verse are the trochee, the iambic, and the spondee;[l] but it runs with the greatest promptness and constancy into the iambic. From this very difference it

k. Chevy Chace.

l. Some are of opinion, that the dactyle may take place in the pentameter. This verse consists of five feet, or ten syllables; if, therefore, we appropriate three syllables to any one foot, then there must be in that verse a foot of one syllable: for instance,

> And vindicate the ways of God to man.

IF the word vindicate be considered as a dactyle, then the monosyllable *and* must be a compleat measure, which is absurd, and contrary to the nature of measure.

39. In these two paragraphs Webb claims that the recognizable cyclic patterns also allow for rhythmic variability. In fact, the pattern provides a stable point of reference against which the rhythm is pitted, breaking the monotony while retaining regularity. However, in the example which he cites, he shows that even the play between meter and rhyme can yield a new kind of pattern, albeit on a higher level, which may become equally monotonous. What interests Webb is the principle which permits the free play of versification, without committing it to any single pattern. The pentameter, related to blank verse, exemplifies for Webb the former while the Heroic verse exemplifies the latter.

is, that we derive the principal means of varying our measures; as in the passage from the trochee to the iambic, a movement, the most spirited and elastic:

>   >

Arms and the man I sing[m]

>   >

Stood like a tow'r.

WHEN an enforced or ascending accent strikes on a monosyllable, the vibrations continue, as in the chord of a musical instrument, after the impression or articulation hath ceased; especially when the stroke is succeeded by a pause, as in the last example. It has been before observed, that the structure of a monosyllable may be such as to render it equivalent to a succession of impressions. Where accent and structure co-operate, they may give a degree of duration to a single syllable, which it would be difficult to equal by a succession of syllables:

And, fled from the monarchs, St. John, *dwells* with thee.[n] [40]

BUT the point the most in favor of our versification is this, that, as accents are modes of expression, every advantage which they bestow on the signs of our ideas extends with greater force to the ideas themselves, and the sense receives a higher improvement than the sound. It should seem, that the mechanism of the Greek verse took its rise, and derived its advantages, from the opposite principle; a point of difference which is recommended to the consideration of those, who, governed rather by authority than feeling, exclaim against the barbarism of a monosyllabical

m. Dryden's Trans. of the Æn.

n. Pope's Essay on Man.

40. From fn. 1 it becomes clear that Webb views the single foot — the smallest unit of versification — as basically composed of an internal contrast. Viewed this way, makes it possible to arrive at different measures through effecting a shift in the alternation between the inner components of the foot (cf. fn. 38). This shift creates a kind of movement which may be enlisted in order to convey effectively the sense of the words. The overall frame provided by measure together with the possibility of shift, allow for pauses to obtain a temporal substance. Rhetorical pauses, even within a given poetic line, thus become possible, rendering additional affectivity.

rhythmus; and seem to estimate words more by the space which they fill, than by the effects which they produce.

IT is said, that monosyllables are fit to describe a slow and heavy motion; and may be happily employed to express languor and melancholy — What inference are we to draw from hence, should it appear, that monosyllables may be full as happily employed on the opposite motions and affections?

> No; fly me, fly me, far as pole from pole.
> Ah! come not, write not, think not once of me.
> Pant on thy lip, and to thy heart be press'd;
> Give all thou canst, and let me dream the rest.

IN our verse, it is the sense that gives vigor to the movement. Monosyllables bring our ideas into a closer order, and more immediate comparison; consequently their relations become more striking. The feeblest and heaviest lines in our language are those which are overcharged with polysyllables.

THE strong propensity in the pentameter to the iambic measure[o] is the cause that a counter-measure, as in the passage from the iambic to the trochee, produceth a kind of check or suspension of the movement:

$$> \quad >$$
Not to know me, argues thyself unknown.[p]

$$> \quad >$$
Hail, Son of God, Saviour of men.[p]

THERE is a singular dignity in this transition, when it springs, as in these examples, from an elevation in the sentiment; our minor poets employ it simply as a variation of the cadence.

---

o. This verse is never more musical than when it consists intirely of iambics: on the contrary, two trochees in succession, have an ill effect, as:

$$> \quad >$$
Gen'rous converse, a soul exempt from pride.
Essay on Crit.

p. Paradise Lost.

q. Acres, quæ ex brevibus ad longas insurgunt: leniores, quæ a longis in breves descendunt. [When a short syllable is followed by a long the effect is one of vigorous ascent, while a long followed by a short produces a gentler impression and suggests descent.] Quint. 1. IX. c. iv.

BUT the relaxation of the trochee may be so brought into q
contrast with the spring of the iambic as to produce effects
directly opposed to those which we have just experienced:

> The downy feather on the cordage hung

>   >
>   Moves not.[r]

WHERE no pause intervenes, and the succession is immediate,
the effect may be equivalent to *that* of a spondee:

> With easy course
> The vessels glide, unless their speed be stopp'd

>   >   >
>   By *dead calms* that oft' lie on those smooth seas.[s]

THE last foot in this verse is a perfect spondee; for, where the
accents fall with equal force on each syllable of a foot, their
quantities will be equal. As again, in the line which immediately
follows:

> While every Zephyr sleeps, then the shrouds drop.

THE laws of art, it is true, prescribe that our pentameter should
terminate in an iambic: but there are beauties of a rank to supersede laws, and the genius of our verse hath a dispensing power.

THE opposition in the prompt and elastic motion of the iambic
to the slow and dwelling step of the spondee is one of the happiest resources in our simple versification:

> So much I feel my genial spirits droop,
> My hopes all flat[t] ——

Let us hear the most artless and untutored of the British Muses.

---

r. The Fleece.
s. The Fleece.
t. Samson Agonistes.
u. Sternhold's Version of the Psalms.

> Great grief, O Lord, doth me assail,
> Some pity on me take,
> My eyes wax dim[u] ——

Thus nature and sentiment give existence to measures which art and reflection adopt for their own.[x][41]

I HAVE supposed that the rhythmus of our verse depends on the relative effects of successive movements: thus, should movements of equal force be divided by the pause into equal time, the balance will be exact, and the rhythmus perfect:

> Or seek to ruin — whom I seemed to raise.[y]

ON the contrary, should the structure of the verse be such, as that the ear cannot with facility make a division of the movements, nor reduce into any proportion their successive effects, then the rhythmus will be dissolved, and the movements become prosaic.

> And with a pale and yellow melancholy.[z]

The constant and even tenor of the couplet secures it from falling into such relaxations; a security, however, in which the poet hath little reason to triumph, while the perpetual returns of similar impressions lie like weights upon our spirits, and oppress the

---

x. Ante enim carmen ortum est quam observatio carminis. [For poetry originated before the laws which govern it.] Quint. Inst. Orat.

y. Ben. Johnson, Verses addressed to Shakespear.

z. Twelfth Night

a. Similitudine tædium ac satietatem creat: quodque est dulcius, magis perit: amittitque et fidem, et affectus, motusque omnes. Quint. Inst. Orat. L. ix. c. iv. [We should also weary and cloy our audience by the resulting monotony; the sweeter the rhythm, the sooner the orator who is detected in a studied adherence to its employment will cease to carry conviction or to stir the passions and emotions.]

41. This series of examples highlights the effective power of monosyllables with regard to the potential kinds of movement which they contain. They correspond to the four classes of passions listed in the first part of Webb's treatise and concludes his argument about the relationship between the nature of movement and certain classes of passion in the domain of poetry. A full definition of the theory relates to the correlation of cognitive constraints and the constraints which limit the artistic medium. This makes for compatibility of the nature of versification and of the nature of the affective sentiments which Webb explicated. Webb further argues that the province of the art is to exploit this basic compatibility effectively.

imagination.[a] Strong passions, the warm effusions of the soul, were never destined to creep through monotonous parallels; they call for a more liberal rhythmus; for movements, not balanced by rule, but measured by sentiment, and flowing in ever new yet musical proportions:

> O though, that with surpassing glory crown'd
> Look'st from thy sole dominion like the God
> Of this new world, at whose sight all the stars
> Hide their diminish'd heads, to thee I call;
> But with no friendly voice, and add thy name,
> O sun, to tell thee how I hate thy beams.[b][42]

THE vast accession to our language of foreign compounds and polysyllables hath opened new springs, and multiplied the means of varying our modulations. But under whatever form these variations appear, or however artfully they may be wrought, in imitation of a classical rhythmus, yet they still act in subjection to that simple and original principle, by which the accent governs the measure, while the sense, in conjunction with the laws of musical succession, governs the accent. It will likewise be found, that the sense in most cases determines the pause. And thus we prove, by an uniform and unaltered practice, what had been before inferred from the reason of the thing, that the origin of verse was from the impression of sentiment.

WHATEVER disputes may have arisen among the learned concerning the parent or primitive tongue, they perfectly agree as to its genius and character, and admit with one consent, that it must have been barren of words, rude of sound, of the simplest con-

b. Paradise Lost.

42. Though Webb classified the different passions and their relationships to characteristic movements, he does not deal explicitly with the variability of movement and its role. After discussing versification at length, including the monotonous types, he insists that passions do not "flow" monotonously; variability is inherent in the very difference between one sentiment and another even within a given class. Does a motion then move rhythmically? Whether one considers it metaphorically or otherwise, it remains essential that the nature of the movement is what qualifies the passage of time and that it is the passage of time that poetry versifies (cf. fn. 24).

struction, and abounding with monosyllables. The Greek language, therefore, whether derived or original, had its æra of rudeness and simplicity; and, if so, the simplest measures must have been the first in order.[c] The highest praise of human wit is, to have improved or refined on the hints given by nature; to act without such hints, would be to create.

IT may be asked in this place, what advantages did the Greeks derive from their improvements on the simplicity of their primitive measures? and, how far may the knowledge of these advantages be of use to us, or promote the refinement of our language and measures.

IT cannot be imagined that the Greeks could create any new mode of imitation: their great object seems to have been, by a gradual reformation of their language, to vary their measures, and multiply the resources of sound and motion; not so much in the view of improving the means of imitation, as of preserving to the ear the continual enjoyment of a regular dignity and sweetness of versification. It was in consequence of this general intention, that they bestowed the utmost dignity of sound and motion on the most familiar ideas, though they hereby deprived the

---

c. Certum quippe est linguas omnes, quæ monosyllabis constant, esse cæteris antiquiores. Multis abundavit monosyllabis antiqua Græca, cujus vestigia apud poetas, qui antiquitatem affectarunt, remansere non pauca. Salmasius, de re Hellecnistica. [It is indeed established that all languages which consist of monosyllbles are more ancient than the others. Ancient Greek abounded with monosyllables, not a few traces of which remained in the works of poets who aspired to antiquity.]

43. Even if these last paragraphs reiterate Webb's earlier statement with regard to the regularity of Greek poetry, his emphasis here is on aesthetic preferences as instances of cultural choice. Webb tells us that the Greeks forwent the "hints of nature" (concerning imitation) in favor of an "utmost dignity of sound and motion on the most familiar ideas." In other words, pleasant formulae were superimposed on ideas rather than emerge organically from sentiments. The English, says Webb, made the opposite choice. Though they adopted foreign compounds and polysyllables in the development of their language, these were not permitted to spoil the infrastructure of their poetry which organically wedded sense, measure and accent. Note how different is Webb's estimation of Greek culture, compared with Jacob's, who saw the Greeks as the epitome of all that is admirable in art: restraint, simplicity, expressiveness etc. (cf. Vol. II: 107-109).

more important of their just distinction and pre-eminence.[43]

THE music of the hexameter is noble, vigorous, sublime; but in this, as in our modern counterpoint, the specific impressions are sunk in the general effect.[d] All refinements have a tendency to efface the principles of the art into which they are introduced. Were the counterpoint to take intire possession of our music, we should lose every idea of its original destination, and the sole object of the art would be to flatter the ear.

To the second part of the question proposed, I answer, that, to make our language capable of a perfect polish, and classical rhythmus, we must cast it over again, purge and transmute it into a more ductile character. The first step towards such a reformation would be the most difficult; for we must disclaim the supports which we have borrowed from other tongues, and form our own compounds out of our primitive roots. In the management of this process, we must, after the example of the Greeks, reduce by every art our redundant consonants; soften and draw out by a happy mixture of vowels the rude but expressive monosyllable. We must reject the preposition and auxiliary verb, and supply their functions by adjunct sounds and varied terminations. In this pursuit, the habitual preference of sound to sense would extend from the signs of our ideas to their order, and transposition would necessarily become a part of the reformation. I say necessarily, because a construction perfectly simple would be inconsistent with the genius of a language abounding, like the Greek, with polysyllables. Ὦ ᾿Αθηναιοι ἄνδρες, εὔχομαι τοις πᾶσι καὶ πάσαις θεοις. How improved by inversion? Ὦ ἄνδρε" ᾿Αθηναιοι, τοις θεοις εὔχομαι πᾶσι καὶ πάσαις. We shall be still more sensible of the advantage in the change from Θεὰ ἄειδε

d. Il contrappunto, essendo composito di varie parti, l'una acuta, l'altera grave, questa di andamento presto, quella di tardo, che hanno tutte a trovarsi in sieme, e ferir l'orecchie ad un tempo, comme potrebbe egli muovere nell' animo nostro una tal determinata passioné, la quale di sua natura rechiede un determinato moto, e un determinato tuono. [The counterpoint, which consists of parts, one acute, the other grave, one which goes fast, the other slow, when all together strike the ear simultaneously, how are they able to move our soul in one determinate passion, the nature of which requires a single determinate motion and tone.] Algarotti, *Saggio sopra l'Opera in Musica*, p. 285.

οὐλομένην μῆνιν, to Μῆνιν ἄειδε θεὰ Οὐλομένην. [Athenians, I pray to all the gods and goddesses.] Thus the refinements of language, by multiplying its sounds, made it necessary to throw the ideas out of their natural order; and transposition, by varying the relations and proportions of those sounds, gave birth to artificial measures, and a fixed prosody.

IN a language consisting mostly of monosyllables, transposition is seldom used, or, when used, differs little from an absolute simplicity.   For instance, we hardly attend to   the difference between

>   My faith and truth, O Samson, prove.

And

>   O Samson, prove my faith and truth.

IN prose we are less tempted to violate the simplicity of our construction, because we are not under an equal necessity of supporting the movements.e It is true, that we have borrowed a great number of polysyllables from other languages; but we temper the precipitation or redundance of these sounds by the frequent interposition of our native monosyllables. It was on this principle, it should seem, that the Greeks continued to employ those monosyllabic particles which had been originally the signs of cases, though they had rendered them of no effect with regard

---

e. The movements of prose hold a middle course, between a total neglect, and an absolute strictness of measure:

>   Numerisque fertur
>
> Lege solutis.

Id quod Cicero optime videt, ac testatur frequenter, se quod numerosum sit quærere: ut magis non αρυθμον, quod esset inscitum et agreste, quam ευρυθμον, quod poeticum est, esse compositionem velit. [This fact is clearly understood by Cicero, who frequently shows that the sense in which he desires that prose should be rhythmical is rather that it should not lack rhythm.] Quint. Inst. 1. IX. c. iv.

44. In order to illustrate the degree of artificiality in Greek poetry, and to ridicule the idea that English poetry ought to be made to emulate to the Greek model, Webb details the changes that would have to be introduced into English in order to qualify. In the final analysis, he shows that such changes, were they introduced, would have resulted both in the "effacement" of the "principles of the art," and in a separation of poetry and music.

to the sense, from the moment that their functions had been supplied by termination.[44]

VARIOUS have been the conjectures of learned and ingenious men touching the causes of the separation of Music from Poetry. The greatest difficulty with me is, to comprehend how their union could have subsisted after the institution of measures founded on artificial quantities. We must take this subject a little higher.

MUSICAL pronunciation must depend on the laws of musical succession: accordingly, in the pronunciation of words of two syllables, music constantly throws its accent on the first: as in glóry, rúin; or on the second, as rejoíce, exúlt.[f] In words of three syllables, music takes no notice of quantities otherwise than by lengthening or shortening the duration of the middle syllable; as in émphasis, hármony, emphátic, harmónic. Words of four syllables are, in the language of music, nothing more than duplications of words of two; that is to say, they regularly fall, either into two iambics, as facílitáte, omnípoténce; or into two trochees, as únrelénting, únfrequénted. By this it appears, that the same principle, which throws our native monosyllables into measure, forms and directs the general pronunciation of our mixed language; with this difference, that, as the sense could have no part in determining the accents of polysyllables, the relative quantities of these syllables must have been decided intirely by the ear, and have fallen singly under the laws of musical accentuation: to which must be added, that these quantities are, by a regular and uniform pronunciation, become invariable; and so far partake of the advantage, while at the same time they point out the origin, of a fixed prosody.

THE constancy with which we have adhered to these laws, hath preserved the native character of our verse through every stage of its improvement. By repeating the first stroke of the iambic, and the second of the trochee, the ancients formed their anapæst and dactyle. By reducing their polysyllables under the

---

f. A word, therefore, of two syllables hath no advantage, in point of movement, over two monosyllables thrown into the same measure. But eight verses out of ten, throughout our best poems, have no other advantage than what they derive from the use of dissyllables. What do we mean when we exclaim against a monosyllabical rhythmus?

government of our musical accents, we have dispossessed them in some degree of their artificial advantages, and subdued them to the tenor of a monosyllabical rhythmus. The rhythmus of every language depends principally on the signs of simple ideas, as by these we more immediately express our feelings; these signs, in our language, are for the most part monosyllables. I need not repeat what hath been already observed concerning the construction of our languages. How absurdly have our ancestors been charged with a dull neglect of classical advantages, and a perverse predilection for their own rude measures and barbarous articulation!

IF from musical quantities we pass to the consideration of an artificial prosody, it will be difficult to conceive, that this change could have been made with a view, as some have imagined, to a more intimate and perfect union of Music with Poetry: since, should music observe the quantities by institution, she must abandon her own; should she neglect those quantities, the musical rhythmus would be at variance with the poetic.

THE artifice of contracted measures, and the variety resulting from these contrasts, are most unfavorable to music, because they disturb her in the government of her accents, and thwart her in the exertion of her natural powers. It is for this reason, that, from our simple measures, music ever selects the most simple. But the ancient lyric poesy abounds with the most varied measures, and embraces every mode of versification: true; it abounds likewise with the most picturesque images, and the boldest metaphors: are we therefore to conclude that these are the true objects of musical imitation? How long are we to be amused with

---

g. De Poematum Cantu et viribus Rhythmi. [About the melody of poems and the powers of rhythm.]

45. Isaac Vossius's treatise, mentioned in Webb's fn. g was published at Oxford in 1673. Consisting mainly of an advocacy of the music of the Ancients, it was ridiculed by contemporaries for its utter ignorance of modern music. Hawkins went so far as to refer to the book as "an unintelligible rhapsody...a futile and unsatisfactory disquisition." Webb apparently takes issue with Vossius's contention, in the present context, to rebut supposed opponents to his claim for the superiority of modern poetry (on Vossius see Schueller 1960; Lipking 1970: 213).

inferences drawn from an union which we do not comprehend, and from a practice of which we have not one decisive example?

VOSSIUS⁸ [45] asserts with great confidence, that the music of the ancients derived its excellence from the force of their poetic rhythmus: this force he makes to consist in the power of conveying just and lively images of the things represented. It seems intirely to have escaped him, that these images are confined to objects of sound or motion; and that, in the imitation of such, music must, from its nature, be superior to verse; so that the more powerful imitation must have borrowed its advantages from the more imperfect. From this notable proposition he concludes, that modern language and poesy are totally unqualified to unite with music. And yet, where measure flows from the laws of musical pronunciation, Poetry and Music have one common rhythmus: and, if sentiment takes a part in determining the measure, their union becomes still more happy and intimate: for music hath no expression but in virtue of her accents; nor have her accents any imitative force but what they derive from senti-

46. We understand from the last few paragraphs that Webb's argument about versification amounts to a challenge of a well entrenched belief that Greek poetry possessed overriding musical powers, and as such deserves to serve as a model for all other poetic attempts and their musical renderings. In fact, Webb endeavors to show that Greek poetry was unable, by definition, to create an effective union of music and poetry since it hampered music's possibility to assist in clinching sentiments. Restricted by "contracted" measures, music could not add its variegated flow to the verse.

This misunderstanding of the Ancients enables Webb to argue that the Greeks failed also in their understanding of the kind of poetical contents suitable for alignment with music. Thus they matched picturesque images and bold metaphors with music, overlooking the fact that only poems denoting sound, motion, and through them emotion, qualify. Sound and motion, as Webb told us earlier, are inherent to music imitation, and not the other way around, as was wrongly claimed by Vossius. This allows Webb to make his final statement: "music borrows sentiment from poetry and lends her movements, and consequently must prefer that mode of versification which leaves her most at liberty to consult her own genius."

How erroneous it must have seemed to Webb that the members of the Florentine Camerata should have hoped to retrieve music's powers through the Greek mode of alignment of music and text! History "proved" Webb right, for opera, luckily, used the text to label emotions and let music, unhampered by the dictates of prosody, articulate their motion. Webb, of course, lived to witness this development, which must have affected his aesthetic explication.

ment. The truth is, music borrows sentiments from poetry, and lends her movements, and consequently must prefer that mode of versification which leaves her most at liberty to consult her own genius.[46]

AFTER what hath been already observed of the nature and origin of these sister-arts, it cannot be thought necessary, in this place, to prove, that a dramatic spirit must be the common principle of their union. This spirit is not confined to the regular drama; it inspires the lover's address, the conqueror's triumph, the captive's lamentation; in short, it may govern every mode of composition in which the poet assumes a character, and speaks and acts in consequence of that character.[47]

To sentiments which spring from character and passion, the lyric poet should unite images productive of sentiment and passion. Objects in repose, or the beauties of still-life, fall not within the province of musical imitation; nor can music take a part in the colouring of language. Our modern lyric poesy is a school for painters, not for musicians. The form of invocation, the distinctions of the strophe, the antistrophe, and chorus, are mere pretensions. To what purpose do we solicit the genius of music, while we abandon, without reserve, the plectrum for the pencil, and cast aside the lyre, as a child doth its rattle, in the moment that we proclaim it to be the object of our preferences?

BUT it is said, that music, by its impressions on one sense, may excite affections similar to those which take their rise from another: and it has been inferred from hence, that the musician can, by a kind of enchantment, *paint* visible objects. To paint by movements would be enchantment indeed; but the wonder ceas-

h. Dict. de Musique, Art. IMITATION.

47. The relationship of poetry and music, Webb says, is via sentiment and movement. Sentiment, however, assumes a living subject — a feeling character. It is feelings, therefore, which may both be labeled as well as qualified by a joint venture with the sister arts; hence they need not be confined to "regular drama." What is implied by Webb is a "oneness," a quality the representation of which is a synthesis related to reactions that results from a multiplicity of actions. Leo Spitzer, in his own ingenious way, called this oneness — *"Stimmung"* (mood). Whereas Webb's argument no doubt reflects his awareness of melodrama, i.e., opera, it makes ample room for the Lied as it developed from the eighteenth century onward.

es when we are made to understand, that music hath no other means of representing a visible object, than by producing in the soul the same movements which we should naturally feel were that object present.[h]

THESE observations lead us to the necessary distinction of the image from its effect; of its beauty as a visible object, from its energy as a source of pathetic emotions. Thus we draw the line between painting and music: nor does the occasion call for a master-stroke; their separation will be marked in the choice of their objects:

> Long, pity, let the nations view
> Thy sky-worn robes of tenderest blue,
> And eyes of dewy light.[i]
> Deserted at his utmost need
> By those his former bounty fed,
> On the bare earth expos'd he lies
> With not a friend to close his eyes.[k]

IF, instead of expressing our own, we describe the feelings of others, and so enter into their condition as to excite a lively sense

---

i. Collins, Ode to Pity.
k. Dryden, Alexander's Feast.

48. In the opening remarks of his treatise, Jacob distinguished between two kinds of poetry, one related to painting through descriptions, and the other related to music through sentiments. The treatises that followed Jacob contributed to the substantiation of this distinction, but only with Webb has it run full circle. Having established the nature of sentiment and its relationship to movement and having showed how these are manifested in music and language, Webb is able to create distinctions within poetry as well as to specify the limits of the arts as well as their correspondences. Thus Webb is entitled to insist that "coloring" language will not contribute to the strengthening of its emotional effect.

In the contemporary debate concerning the standing of the *ut pictura poesis* he sides, of course, with those who wish to promote the kind of poetry which speaks the language of music. Thus his previous recommendation with regard to the musicalization of poetry assumes a major proportion; it amounts to no less than the replacement of "image" by "effect," i.e., *pictura* by *musica*. It is no coincidence that Webb cites Collins, in whose poetry this transition actually took place.

(CONT.)

of their several affections, we retain the spirit of the drama, tho'
we abandon the form. The most perfect poem of this kind, in
our language, is the Feast of Alexander, by Mr. Dryden. Here,
music unites with poetry in the character of a descriptive art; but
then the objects of her descriptions are her own impressions.[48]

IT was objected by Aristotle to the poets of his time, that they
were the principal speakers in their own poems; contrary to the
practice of Homer, who well knew, that, while the poet speaks,
the imitation or the drama ceases.[l] It is remarkable that this is
the very æra from which Plutarch dates the corruption of music.
When the poet ceased to write from the movements of the heart,
the musician began to sing from the caprice of the imagination.[49]

IN proportion as the spirit of expression declines, a taste for
description will, of course, prevail; we *express* the agitations and
affections of our minds; we *describe* the circumstances and qualities of external objects: the application of measure to either pur-

---

l. De Poet. c. xxiv.

m. Pope, Essay on Criticism.

(CONT.)

Webb's emphasis on the preference of "effect" to "image" does not altogether elimi-
nate descriptions, but circumscribes them to those which excite affections. Webb follows here Rousseau's argument, in which he claims that music deals with the "energy"
evoked by external forms rather than with the forms themselves. Smith, as we shall
see, will also enlist this argument in his attempt to highlight the uniqueness of opera's
artistic illusion.

49. From this paragraph we can readily learn how influential Aristotle was for Webb
(as he was for Twining and other members of the group), for in fact the previous pages
directly relate to Aristotle's distinction between the voice of the poet and that of the
characters he portrays. It should be clear that Aristotle is not referring to the narrator
as an "implicit persona" (to use Cone's [1974] term), which enriches the complexity of
the interacting forces in the overall mental state portrayed. On the contrary, Aristotle's
"principle speaker" deprives the protagonists of their "character" through his own presence, without regard to the fictive world he attempts to portray. Nonetheless, Webb's
use of Aristotle reflects the increasing awareness in the eighteenth century of the possibility of enlisting the narrator in molding the fictive world. However, Webb lacks the
new insights of several of his countrymen, whose experiments with the narrator's point
of view led to a new understanding of the fragility of the conditions of representation
and of the possibility of establishing new conditions, more akin to the rendering of
states of consciousness.

pose depends on the nature of the subject, or the genius of the writer. A single instance may suffice to set this idea in the clearest light:

> When Ajax strives some rock's vast weight to throw,
> The line too labours, and the works move slow.[m]

So will they in the expression of a deep and heavy affliction:

> And in this harsh world draw thy breath in pain.[n]

LIKE parallels may be continued thro' all the examples which have been given of pathetic accords. Now, though the imitations of verse may be applied to the purposes either of expression or of description, it is not the same thing with regard to music, the effects of which are so exquisite, so fitted by nature to move the passions, that we feel ourselves hurt and disappointed, when forced to reconcile our sensations to a simple and unaffecting coincidence of sound or motion.[50]

AGAIN, in descriptive poetry, the imitations often turn on the force of particular words, on the resemblance between the sign and the idea:

> *Jarring* sound
> Th' infernal doors, and on their hinges *grate*
> *Harsh* thunder.[o]

---

n. Hamlet.

o. Paradise Lost.

50. Webb's last remarks in his treatise draw conclusions from his previous attempts to assess the correspondences of poetry and music, or by way of analogy, to establish their individual uniqueness, from a perceptual-cognitive point of view. He begins by telling us that the application of measure — the musical aspect of poetry — depends on the nature of its subject, regardless of being descriptive or expressive. In other words, the music of poetry qualifies the kind of movement dictated by the text irrespective of its mode of symbolization. Not so with music. Music, because of its "exquisite" control over movement, is wasted if forced to a union with that which does not possess equal refinement, Webb's argument is an aesthetic one, reminiscent of all those arguments concerning the subservience of text to music because music to begin with has its own mode of symbolization, which the text is called upon to name. In other words, music dictates the choice of text to which it lends its powers. Whereas Webb does not develop this argument explicitly, given his other commitments, he seems nonetheless to imply it; this will indeed be verified in the following paragraphs.

IN this, and in every other instance where the resemblance is determined by sound, the characters of Poetry and Music are directly opposed; for, the nature of articulation strictly considered, it will appear, that in poetry, the imitations of harsh and rude sounds must be the most perfect; in music, it is just the reverse. It was for this reason, that our incomparable Milton, in his imitations of musical ideas, threw the force of the imitation, not on the sound, but on the movement:

> Save where silence yields
> To the night-warbling bird, that now awake
> Tunes sweetest his *love-labor'd* song.p

TASSO was not so judicious, or trusted too much to the sweetness of his language:

> Odi quello usignuolo,
> Che vá di ramo in ramo
> Cantando, Io amo, Io amo.q
> Hear that sweet nightingale,
> Who flies from grove to grove
> His song — I love, I love.

THESE imitations of musical ideas by articulate sounds have much the same effect with the imitations of the force of particular words by musical sounds.

Thus, Handel seldom fails to ascend with the word *rise*, and descend with the word *fall.* Purcell goes still farther, and accompanies every idea of *roundness* with an endless *rotation* of notes. But what shall we say to that musician, who disgraces the poet by realizing his metaphors, and, in downright earnest, makes the fields *laugh*, and the vallies *sing.* In music, it is better to have no ideas at all than to have false ones, and it will be safer to trust to the simple effects of impression than to the idle conceits of a forced imitation.

IN our attempts to reduce music into an union with descriptive poetry, we should do well to consider, that music can no otherwise imitate any particular sound, than by becoming the thing it imitates: it hath an equal facility in conforming with sim-

---

p. Paradise Lost.

q. Aminta.

ple ideas of motion. What effects can be expected from imitations, in which there is neither ingenuity in the execution nor importance in the object?

VERSE on the other hand, considered as motion, falls far short of the promptness and facility of music; nor can it, with respect to sounds, rise above a distant and vague assimilation: its imitations, therefore, in either case, may be attended with some degree of surprise and pleasure. The misfortune is , that our poets dwell too much on this trifling advantage, and pursue it, to an almost total neglect of the nobler purposes of imitation.[51]

I AM not so vain as to expect that my ideas on this subject should have much weight with the professors of either art, or influence them to a change of those principles and pursuits in which they are supported by an established practice. But this I will venture to affirm, that there cannot be a more certain proof of a corrupt taste, than to find the powers of imitation diverted from the more important to inferior purposes. I shall submit my sentiments on this point, as I have done on every other, to a fair examination. There is a passage in Virgil where he describes the heavy fall of an ox — Procumbit humi bos — I am not at all struck with this imitation, and the reason must be, that there is

---

51. Like in the section which footnote 50 refers to, Webb continues to impart advice based on aesthetic assumption. His distinction between impressions and ideas as far as music and poetry are concerned (see fn. 5), are now related to their imitated object, based on resemblance of cognitive content — i.e. between impressions and impressions and between ideas and ideas. Thus poetry is able to create both kinds of resemblances — between sign (which itself, according to the empiricist tradition is an idea) and the idea of a sound and between motion (i.e impressions) and a musical sensation. Music, on the other hand is better qualified for the latter, since she herself assumes the role of the imitated object, i.e. impressions. The reader may recall that Webb connected the idea of impressions in music to succession, implying thereby that music is synthetic in nature. Reiterating Galilei's claim against madrigalism, which contradicts the overall mood of the poem, he thus provides a more philosophical argument then Galileo did. And, like all abstractions, his argument too makes room for exceptions; a limited possibility of musical "descriptions" is feasible, Webb tells us, relying on historical examples which proved that expression and description may be congenial, to a certain extent. These examples indeed benefited from the tradition that Galilei gave rise too, while preserving in part that which he criticized.

nothing either pleasing or interesting in the object. But, let the
idea be of a nature to engage our attention, and we are no longer
indifferent to its accord:

> Scarce from his mould
> Behemoth, biggest-born of earth, upheav'd
> His vastness.[r]

THE effect still rises upon us with the interest which we take
in the object:

> Sic fatus senior, telumque imbelle sine ictu
> Conjecit.[s]
>
> [So said the aged king and he cast his spear.]

WHY is the feebleness in this movement so very affecting? Is it
not, that it corresponds with our pity of the poor old king, and
completes the image of his forlorn condition:

> Exhausted, spiritless, afflicted, fall'n.[t]

WHENCE is it then, that, in poetry, the most celebrated examples of imitation are such as are merely descriptive?

IN imitating the motions of external objects through their various modifications, as, of lightness, heaviness, rapidity,[u] slowness, force, weakness, and the like, the merit of the imitation is
decided by a direct comparison with a known and determined
object. It would be the same thing with regard to our passions,
considered as motions of the soul, were these motions of a
nature to be reduced into sensible and determined images. In
this case, therefore, we do not judge of the imitation, as in the
former, by a direct comparison, but by an instantaneous feeling;

---

r. Paradise Lost.

s. Æneid.

t. Samson Agonistes.

u. A modern critic is of opinion, that the Alexandrine is best calculated to exemplify swiftness,
because it most naturally exhibits the act of passing through a long space in a short time. Is it meant,
that we pass through the long space of the Alexandrine in as short a time as we should through the
shorter space of the pentameter? But this cannot be; for, supposing an equal fluency in the syllables
employed in each, their times must be always in the proportion of 12 to 10. That line so often cited
as an example of swiftness, sets this matter in the clearest light:

Αὖτις ἔπειτα πέδονδε κυλίνδετο λᾶας ἀναιδής.   [...and the misbegotten rock came
bounding down again to level ground.]

From whence springs the swiftness in this instance? Is it not from hence, that we pass through a verse
of 17 syllables in the same time that we pass through a verse of 13? But our Alexandrine can never
consist of more or less than 12 syllables. The inference is obvious.

with this additional difference, that we are least sensible of the imitation, when most transported by its effects; for, if the poet is successful in touching the springs of passion, our spirits obey the impression, and run into the same movements with those which accompany the sentiment; thus, while we are under the united influence of the natural motion of the passion, and the artificial movement of the verse, we lose sight of the imitation in the simplicity of the union, and energy of the effect. But in matters of mere description it is not so; in these imitation is professed, and there cannot be a beauty without a manifestation of art. In short, wherever passion is concerned, a coincidence of sound and motion becomes, as it were, the native and proper language of that passion; and our inattention to the art which may be employed on these occasions is so far from contradicting, that it confirms all that has been offered on the origin of verse, and on the natural correspondence between movement and passion.[52]

APPENDIX.

IF the passions, according to the classes assigned them, have their proper and characteristic movements, must not their impressions extend to the imagination? and if so, may we not collect from hence, how far, and under what restrictions, imagery may be the language of passion?

LET us suppose that the imagination may be heated by the movements of quickened and inflamed spirits: hence it may co-

---

52. Using his former arguments, Webb provides an additional insight related to the cognitive reaction to "mere descriptions" compared to passion provoking descriptions. The latter, because of the natural correspondence of movement and passion, make us insensible of the "imitation" — of the trigger which causes the effect. The former, on the other hand, in the absence of the latter, engages us in the artistic object itself. This, Webb suggests, may be the reason why "mere description" is most "celebrated" in literature, despite its being less forceful; nay, its celebrated appearance is a compensation for that lack. On the whole, description and expression are both legitimate as artistic means, as far as Webb is concerned; each, however, dictates its own manner of doing. At the same time Webb insists that a passion provoking effect in poetry has its origin outside the artistic realm. Still related to the Shaftesburian search for an aesthetic faculty, Webb prefers to locate artistic cognition in what amounts to general propensities of mind.

operate with the passions of anger, revenge, and their collaterals. In every such case the image must correspond with the motive; consequently, it should be bold, concise, and decisive, that the fancy may not seem to dwell on her own operations.

THE imagination may be raised by movements of expansion; hence its agreement with pride, wonder, and emulation. But as these passions and their movements tend naturally towards increase, it follows, that the images here employed may be enlarged and dilated. In this case, therefore, contrary to the former, a display of imagination coincides with the nature of the affection.

IF the imagination may be heated or raised into an agreement with the motions of the animal spirits, must it not languish and subside with them; how then can imagery be the language of grief or dejection? the vibrations of relaxed nerves can communicate nothing more than their own languor: accordingly, we shall always find, that, while we are under the influence of a dispiriting passion, our aim will be to express, not to describe, our feelings.

SUCH, I conceive, must be the laws of nature with regard to the influence of passion on the fancy: and yet, I mean not to recommend a strict observance of them. It were a vain and ill-judged attempt to reduce the flights of the imagination under the government of a too rigid philosophy. In this, as in some other subjects, nature seems to sport with our understanding, and lays aside her laws, to wanton in her creations.[53]

THE END

53. In this essay, as we have seen, Webb tried to establish a mutual correspondence of movement and passions. His observations on the correspondence of the arts — poetry and music — rested largely on the natural correspondence which he explicated. In the appendix Webb raises the likelihood of yet another "natural correspondence" — that between the impressions of the characteristic movements (related to the classes of the passions) and the imagination. Though he makes an attempt to show how passions may circumscribe fancy, his attempt remains timid and not fully developed. It does not detract, however, from its suggestive value concerning the operations of the minds and their modes of interrelationships, though he himself did not believe in finding lawfulness in this connection. (For discussion of the relations between affect and imagination see Vol. I: 258-260.)

Thomas Twining

(1735-1804)

The son of a tea merchant from London, Twining was born at Twickenham in 1735 and originally intended for his father's business. Nevertheless, Twining became a revered classical scholar and critic and a knowledgeable and talented musician. He first attended a small school at Twickenham, but upon showing great aptitude for scholarship he was sent to Colchester's Grammar School to prepare for the university. In 1755 he entered Sidney Sussex College, Cambridge, where fellowship followed scholarship and led to an M.A. degree in 1763 and to holy orders in 1764. He spent the remainder of his quiet, studious life at the parsonage of Fordham and Colchester, where he died in 1804.

Though he had already shown remarkable attainment as a classical scholar while at Cambridge, his reputation rests almost entirely on his translation of Aristotle's Poetics, which first appeared in 1789. In retrospect, however, it seems fair to claim that Twining's importance may be attributed not only to his outstanding translation and his critical notes, but also to his dissertations on poetical and musical imitations which accompanied the treatise. The work as a whole was widely acclaimed, for Twining possessed a perfect knowledge of languages, ancient and modern, an exquisite taste, and above all, astute critical insights into poetry and music. Some of the letters he wrote to members of his family were published by his grandnephew in 1882 and a sequel followed in 1887. The 1882 publication entitled "Recreation and Studies of a Country Clergyman of the Eighteenth Century" contains also some letters addressed to Charles Burney in whose History of Music Twining took a keen interest and to which he also contributed of his own knowledge and insights.

Twining represents the cultural heritage of the century as well as the transformation of thought that took place in his lifetime. He considered himself a modernist and has been recognized as such not only by his contemporaries, but by later writers on comparative aesthetics, on the basis of his contribution to ideas regarding the arts.

As far as music is concerned, Twining was interested both in the problem of its signification as well as in the experience which music evokes. In the old Aristoxenian-Pythagorean debate as to what should underlie musical judgment, the perceptual or the mathematical (the issue which was re-invoked in the eighteenth century by people like d'Alembert, Rameau and others), Twining was clearly on the listener's side, arguing that the pleasure and significance of music does not depend on the adequacy and precision of the material of its sound. This was also the reason for his readiness to endorse instrumental music, the significance of which, according to Twining, is by no means pre-established. Like Harris, Avison and others, he challenged the conventional principle of representation in music and focused on what music can do, rather than on what it was supposed to do.

Music, according to Twining, neither simply imitates, nor does it directly express; it is only suggestive. The listener determines the meaning, and he is able to do so because of the enigmatic character of music. Twining argues that the concept of imitation harbors many meanings and varies according to the art to which it is applied. He distinguishes between proper and improper imitation related to the distinction between what he calls "immediacy" and "obviousness," i.e. to a distinction between the perceptual and the cognitive. The first concerns "sameness" between the imitation and the imitated, as far as sensible materials are concerned, while the second applies to the identification of the object to which the imitation refers. As expected, Twining first defines his conceptual scheme in connection with poetic imitation. He suggests that knowledge of the referent necessarily precedes the assessment of the resemblance. In language, we are told, "obviousness" is related to a learned symbolic system, while "immediacy" rests on sensible sense recognition. Music which resembles sound and motion, fits the category of the immediate, but altogether lacks obviousness, i.e. the ability to refer. Consequently, the resemblance created between music and the affections is not between the two, but rather between the effects to which both give rise.

At any rate, resemblance is not enough to establish imitation. Rather, it is achieved once imitation has taken place. Though words may dispel some of music's enigmatic character, they cannot change its very nature which is non-designative and equivocal. Whether Twining did or did not exhaust the entire spectrum of his own argument does not change the fact that he admirably exposed the complexity of artistic norms. Indeed, he is emblematic of all those of his time whose enormous learning and inquisitive minds contributed to our own understanding of the relationship between cognitive processes and modes of symbolization.

DISSERTATION I.

ON POETRY CONSIDERED AS AN IMITATIVE ART.

THE word *Imitation*, like many others, is used, sometimes in a strict and proper sense, and sometimes in a sense more or less extended and improper. Its application to poetry is chiefly of the latter kind. Its precise meaning, therefore, when applied to poetry *in general*, is by no means obvious. No one who has seen a picture is at any loss to understand how painting is imitation. But no man, I believe, ever heard or read, for the first time, that poetry is imitation, without being conscious in some degree, of that "confusion of thought" which an ingenious writer complains of having felt whenever he has attempted to explain the imitative nature of Music.[a] It is easy to see whence this confusion arises, if we consider the process of the mind when words thus extended from their *proper* significations are presented to it. We are told that "Poetry is an imitative art." In order to conceive how it is so, we naturally compare it with painting, sculpture, and such arts as are strictly and clearly imitative. But, in this comparison, the *difference* is so much more obvious and striking than the *resemblance* — we see so much more readily in what respects poetry is *not* properly imitation, than in what respects it is; — that the mind, at last, is left in that sort of perplexity which must always arise from words thus loosely and analogically applied, when the analogy is not sufficiently clear and obvious; that is, when, of that mixture of circum-

---

a. Dr. Beattie, *Essay on Poetry, &c.* ch. vi. §. 1.

stances, *like* and *unlike*, which constitutes analogy, the latter are the most apparent.

In order to understand the following treatise on poetry, in which *imitation* is considered as the very essence of the art,[b] it seems necessary to satisfy ourselves, if possible, with respect to two points; I. In what senses the word *Imitation* is, or *may* be, applied to poetry. II. In what senses it was so applied by Aristotle.[1]

I.

THE only circumstance, I think, common to *everything* we denominate *imitation*, whether properly or improperly, is *resemblance*, of some sort or other.

In every imitation, strictly and properly so called, two conditions seem essential: — the resemblance must be immediate; i.e. between *the imitation, or imitative work, itself,* and the object imitated; — and, it must also be *obvious.* Thus, in sculpture, figure is represented by similar figure; in painting, colour and figure, by similar colour and figure; in personal imitation, or mimicry, voice and gesture, by similar voice and gesture. In all these instances, the resemblance is *obvious;* we recognize

---------- ⌒ ----------

1. Twining saw fit to translate Artistotle's Poetics yet another time because he considered it an unsurpassed statement regarding the construction of art, as well as its relation to perception and its functions. Despite his reverence for Aristotle's great achievement, Twining still wished to address Aristotle's basic concept of imitation as it emerged from the various comparisons among the arts which were undertaken in the eighteenth century. Following Beattie's criticism with regard to the lack of rigor in the use of theoretical concepts in theories of art, he devotes the first part of his dissertation to a clarification of the overall concept of imitation. In retrospect, as it turns out, Twining's attempt is perhaps the profoundest that was undertaken in the eighteenth century.

The two opening paragraphs immediately reveal Twining's independence and lucidity. 'Imitation' for him is a kind of polyseme, for it harbors many extended or transformed meanings when applied to the various arts. Moreover, Twining is aware that the extended meanings of 'imitation,' related to the degree of distance between the object and its imitation, is likely to reveal the different processes of mind which are entailed in its perception as imitation. If painting and sculpture are clearly imitative (according to the conditions he will yet supply), music is the least so; hence the paradigmatic function Twining gives the visual arts in his theory (unlike Aristotle).

---

b. See the *second part* of this Dissertation.

the object imitated: and it is, also, *immediate;* it lies in the imitative *work,* or *energy, itself;* or, in other words, in the very materials, or *sensible media,*c by which the imitation is conveyed. All *these* copies, therefore, are called, strictly and intelligibly, imitations.[2]

1. The materials of poetic imitation are *words.* These may be considered in two views; as sounds *merely,* and as sounds *significant,* or arbitrary and conventional *signs* of ideas. It is evidently, in the *first* view only, that words can bear any real resemblance to the *things expressed;* and, accordingly, that kind of imitation which consists in the resemblance of words considered as mere SOUND, to the *sounds* and *motions* of the objects imitated,d has usually been assigned as the only instance in which the term *imitative* is, in its strict and proper sense, applicable to Poetry.e But setting aside all that is the effect of fancy and of accommodated pronunciation in the reader, to which, I fear, many passages, repeatedly quoted and admired as the happiest coincidences of sound and sense, may be reduced;f setting this aside, even in such words, and

---

c. See Mr. Harris's Treatise on Music, &c. ch. 1.

d. Mr. Harris's Treatise, &c. ch. iii.

e. Mr. Harris. — Lord Kaims, Elements of Criticism, vol. ii. p. I.

f. The reader may see this sufficiently proved by Dr. Johnson in his Lives of the Poets, vol. iv. p. 183. *octavo,* and in the Rambler, N° 92. "In such resemblances," as he well observes, "the mind often governs the ear, and the sounds are estimated "by their meaning." See also Lord Kaims, *El.* of *Crit.* vol. ii. p. 84, 85.

------------- ∽ -------------

2. Twining's philosophical approach is not unlike that which came to be labeled "analytical," for he analyzes the very concepts which he employs, clarifying their status and their relationship to cognitive functions. Thus, he identifies resemblance as the major condition for proper imitation, which itself is conditioned by immediacy and obviousness. While for Harris 'immediacy' stems from sameness between the imitation and the imitated, as far as sensible materials are concerned, for Twining it relates to the recognition of the imitated object in the sensible material, without mediating factors. (The figure is in the sculpture and the still life is in the painting in a sense different from that in which literary characters are in the printed text). 'Obviousness,' on the other hand, concerns the identification of the referred object. In what follows, Twining will examine "improper" imitation with regard to these two conditions, establishing the degree to which they are necessary and sufficient. However, while the scheme itself is fruitful, Twining does not supply adequate justification for it. He does not ask himself, for example, how a picture may come to "obviously" represent that which it pictures, nor does he realize that the immediacy which "proper" imitation entails, involves kinds of mental activities, which go far beyond simple identifications.

William Hogarth: The Enraged Musician

The Enraged Musician was "Design'd, Engrav'd & Publish'd by Wm Hogarth No^er the 30th 1741." Version (1) of the Musician was a trial proof somewhat different than the version (2) which is reproduced here (BM 1868-8-22-1554). The following description of the scene is taken from *Hogarth's Graphic Works*, compiled with commentary by Ronald Paulson (New Haven, Yale University Press, 1965):

The scene, wrote Fielding, is "enough to make a man deaf to look at (*Journal of a Voyage to Lisbon*, ed. H.E. Pagliaro, New York, 1963, p. 46). The itinerant hautboy (oboe) player "was at that time well known about the streets" (*Gen. Works*, 2, 155). The pavior is shown to be Irish by his cap—a beehive shape with the lower edge turned up to make a brim. The man with a basket on his head is a dustman; a sow-gelder on a horse is blowing a cow's horn and a fish-peddler is yelling. The pewterer's was also a noisy business (we see "John Long PEWTERER" on a house in the distance), and cats howl at each other on his rooftop, where a chimneysweep pokes his head out of his chimney. A girl with a milk-pail on her head calls her wares. A ballad-singing woman, pregnant and holding a swathed baby, sings the ballad of "The Ladies Fall," while a parrot alone her head echoes her. The little girl and little boy are making noise in their different ways; the boy has apparently constructed a trap for birds in the roadway. Another boy plays soldier, beating on his drum. A knife-grinder works at his trade, and a dog barks at him.

such arrangements of words, as are actually, in some degree, analogous in sound or motion to the thing signified or described, the resemblance is so faint and distant, and of so general and vague a nature, that it would never, *of itself,* lead us to recognize the object imitated. We discover not the *likeness* till we know the *meaning.* The natural relation of the word to the thing signified, is pointed out only by its arbitrary or conventional relation.g — I do not here mean to deny that such resemblances, however slight and delicate where they really *are,* and however liable to be discovered by fancy where they are *not,* are yet a source of real beauties, of beauties *actually felt* by the reader, when they arise, or appear to arise, spontaneously from the poet's feeling, and their effect is not counteracted by the obviousness of cool intention, and

---

g. See Harris on Music, &c. ch. iii. §.1, 2. This verse of Virgil,

> Stridenti miserum stipula disperdere carmen —
> [...to murder a sorry tune on a scrannel straw... (Virgilius, Ec.3.27)]

is commonly cited as an example of this sort of imitation. I question, however, whether this line would have been remarked by any one as particularly harsh, if a harsh sound had not been described in it. At least, many verses full as harshly constructed might, I believe, be produced, in which no such imitation can be supposed. But, even admitting that such imitation was here intended, it seems to me almost ridiculous to talk of the "*natural relation* between the sound of this verse, and *that of a vile hautboy.*" [Harris, in the chapter above referred to.] All that can be said is, that the sounds are, both of them, harsh sounds; but, certainly no one species of harsh sound can well be more unlike another, than the sound of a rough verse is to the tone of a bad hautboy, or, indeed, of any other musical instrument. — That, in the clearest and most acknowledged instances of such imitative vocal sound, the resemblance is, or can possibly be, so exact as to lead a person unacquainted with the language, *by the sound alone,* to the *signification,* no man in his senses would assert. Yet Dr. Beattie, in a note, p. 304, of his Essay on Poetry, &c. by a mistake for which I am at a loss to account, has ascribed so extravagant a notion to Rousseau. "There is in Tasso's Gierusalemme Liberata, a famous stanza, of which Rousseau says, that a good ear and *sincere heart* are alone able to judge of *it,*" meaning, as appears from what follows, of its *sense;* for he adds, "The imitative harmony and the poetry are indeed admirable; *but I doubt whether a person who understands neither Italian nor Latin, could even guess at the meaning from the sound.*" There can be no room for *doubt* in this matter; — he certainly could not: nor does Rousseau appear to have even hinted the possibility of such a thing. — The passage is in his admirable letter *Sur la Musique Françoise,* where, in order to obviate the prejudices of those who regard the Italian language as wholly soft and effeminate, he produces two stanzas of Tasso, the one as an example of a sweet and tender, the other of a forcible and nervous, combination of sounds: and he adds, that to judge of *this,* i.e. of the *sound* only, not the *sense,* of the stanzas, and also of the impossibility of rendering adequately the sweetness of the one, or the force of the other, in the French language, "it is not necessary to understand Italian — it is sufficient *that we have an ear, and are impartial.*" — "Que ceux qui pensent que l'Italien n'est que le langage de la douceur et de la tendresse, prennent la peine de *comparer entre elles* ces deux strophes du Tasse: — et s'ils desesperent de rendre en François la *douce harmonie* de l'une, qu'ils essayent d'exprimer la *rauque dureté* de l'autre: il n'est pas besoin *pour juger de ceci* d'entendre la langue, il ne faut qu'avoir *des oreilles & de la bonne foi.*" [Let those who think that Italian is a language of but sweetness and tenderness take the trouble and *compare* these two strophes by Tasso: —and if they despair of rendering in French the *sweet harmony* of the one, let them try and express the *rough harshness* of the other: it is not necessary to understand the language in order to *judge this;* one needs to have only an *ear and an unbiased mind.*]

deliberate artifice.[h] Nor do I mean to object to this application of the word *imitative*. My purpose is merely to shew, that when we call this kind of resemblance, imitation, we do not use the word in its *strict* sense — that, in which it is applied to a picture, or a statue. Of the two conditions above mentioned, it wants that which must be regarded as most essential. The resemblance is, indeed, real, *as far as it goes*, and immediate; but, necessarily, from its *generality*, so imperfect, that even when pointed out by the *sense*, it is by no means always *obvious*, and without

---

h. I am persuaded that many very beautiful and striking passages of this kind in the best poets were solely φύσεως αὐτοματιζούσης ἔργα [the works of Nature improvising], not τέχνης μιμήσασθαι τὰ γινόμενα πειρωμένης [art attempting to reproduce a scene] as it is well expressed by *Dion. Hal.* Περὶ συνθέσεως [On Literary Composition], §20. — But the *Critic* is always too ready to transfer his own reflection to the *Poet*, and to consider as the *effects* of art, all those spontaneous strokes of genius which become the *causes* of art by his calm observation and discussion. Scarce any poet has, I think, so many beauties of this kind, fairly produced by strength of imagination, and delicacy of ear, as Virgil. Yet there are some verses frequently cited as fine examples in this way, which appear to me too visibly artificial to be pleasing: such as —

Quadrupedante putrem sonitu quatit ungula campum.
[Hooves with four-footed thunder shook the crumbling plain.]

I am tempted to add to this note a passage from the first dissertation prefixed to the Æneid by that excellent editor, C.G. Heyne; — a man who has honourably distinguished himself from the herd of commentators, by such a degree of taste and philosophy as we do not often find united with laborious and accurate erudition. Speaking of the charms of Virgil's versification, he says, "Illud unum monebimus, in errorem inducere juvenilem animum videri eos qui nimii in eo sunt, ut ad rerum sonos et naturas accommodatos & formatos velint esse versus. Equidem non diffiteor sensum animi me refragantem habere, quotiescunque persuadere mihi volo, magnum aliquem poetam aestu tantarum rerum abreptum et magnorum phantasmatum vi inflammatum, in *sono cursus equestris* vel tubae vel aliarum rerum reddendo laborare; attenuat ea res et deprimit ingenium poetae & artis dignitatem. *Sunt tamen*, ais, *tales versus* in optimo quoque poeta. Recte; sunt utique multi; etsi plures alios ad hoc lusus genus accommodare solet eorum ingenium qui talibus rebus indulgent. Sed mihi ad poetices indolem propius esse videtur statuere, *ipsam orationis naturam* ita esse comparatam, ut multarum rerum sonos exprimat; inflammatum autem phantasmatum specie objecta animum, cum rerum species sibi obversantes ut *oratione vivide exprimat laborat, necessario in ista vocabula incidere, vel orationis proprietate ducente*. Ita graves et celeres, lenes ac duros sonos, *vel non id agens et curans*, ad rerum naturam accommodabit et orator quisque bonus, et multo magis poeta." [We shall mention this one thing, that the young soul seems to be exposed to an error by those who are excessive in wanting the verses to be accommodated and formed by the sounds and nature of things. Indeed, I do not deny that I am opposed to the sensations of the soul, however much I would like to persuade myself that some great poet, carried off by the passion of many matters and inflamed by the power of great phantasies, makes an effort to represent the sound of the cavalry-race, or of the wartrumpet, or of other things; this reduces and degrades the talent of the poet and the merit of the profession. However, you say, there are such verses also in the best poet. Indeed: by all means there are many: moreover it is usual that many others who indulge in such things, accommodate to this playful part of their talent. But in matters of poetics it seems to me more proper that the very nature of the speech should be established so that it would imitate sounds of many things. But when the soul is exposed to the sight of passionate phantasies, while the sights of things hover before it, it should try to express it vividly, using suitable words, or suitable manner of speech. Therefore, any good orator, and much more any poet, will accommodate heavy and swift sounds, soft and harsh sounds, to the nature of things even without thinking or worrying about it.] (Heyne's Virgil, vol. ii. p. 39.)

that, cannot possibly lead to any thing like a clear and certain recognition of the particular object imitated.[i] I must observe farther, that this kind of imitation, even supposing it much more perfect, is, by no means, that which would be likely first to occur to any one, in an enquiry concerning the nature of the imitation attributed to Poetry, were it not, that the circumstance of its real and *immediate* resemblance, has occasioned its being considered, I think not justly, as the strictest sense of the term so applied.

For the most *usual,* and the most *important* senses, and even, as will perhaps appear, for the *strictest* sense, in which Poetry has been, or may be, understood to imitate, we must have recourse to language considered in its most important point of view, as composed, not of sounds merely, but of sounds *significant.*[3]

---

i. The causes of this imperfection are accurately pointed out by Mr. Harris; 1. The "*natural* sounds and motions which Poetry thus imitates, are themselves but *loose* and *indefinite accidents* of those *subjects* to which they belong, and consequently do but *loosely* and *indefinitely* characterise them. 2. *Poetic* sounds and motions do but *faintly* resemble those of *nature,* which are *themselves* confessed to be so *imperfect* and *vague.*" [Treatise on Music, &c. *cb.* iii. §2. See also *cb.* ii. §3.] The following is a famous imitative line of Boileau:

S'en va frapper le mur, & revient en roulant.
[It goes to strike the wall and returns in a roll.]

If this line were read to any one ignorant of the language, he would be so far from guessing *what* was imitated, that it would not, I believe, occur to him that *anything* was imitated at all; unless, indeed, the idea were forced upon his mind by the pronuntiation of the reader. Now, suppose him to understand French: — as the circumstance of *rolling* is mentioned in the line, he might possibly notice the effect of the letter R, and think the poet intended to express the noise of *something* that rolled. And this is all the *real* resemblance than can be discovered in this verse: a resemblance, and that too, but distant and imperfect, in the sound of a letter to the sound of *rolling* in general. For anything beyond this, we must trust to our imagination, assisted by commentator, who assures us, that the poet "a cherché à imiter par le son des mots, *le bruit que fait* UNE ASSIETTE *en roulant."* *Sat.* iii. *v.* 216. [has sought to imitate through the sound of the words the noise made by A PLATE rolling"]

--- ᡈ ---

3. In sub-section 1, Twining applies his conceptual scheme to the role of words in poetic imitation. Transcending Harris's distinction between imitation via sound and imitation via "compact" (Harris' term), he argues that the discovery of likeness in sound imitation lacks obviousness, though it answers to the requirements of immediacy. Not until the meaning is established via words, as signs of ideas, is the likeness perceived. In other words, the referent in language must be known prior to the recognition of the "beauties" of sound resemblances. Note that Twining, unlike Webb and Condillac, does not concern himself with the relation between sound and meaning, as far as the origin of language is concerned, for he refuses to ascribe to it any role in the present understanding of language. Unlike painting, language requires two conditions which

(CONT.)

2. The most general and extensive of these senses, is that in which it is applied to DESCRIPTION, comprehending, not only that poetic land-scape-painting which is *peculiarly* called descriptive Poetry, but all such circumstantial and distinct representation as conveys to the mind a strong and clear idea of its object, whether *sensible* or *mental* .ᵏ Poetry, in this view, is naturally considered as more or less *imitative*, in pro-portion as it is capable of raising an ideal *image* or *picture*, more or less resembling the reality of things. The more distinct and vivid the ideas are of which this picture is composed, and the more closely they corre-spond to the actual *impressions* received from nature, the stronger will be the resemblance, and the more perfect the imitation.

Hence it is evident that, of all description, that of *visible* objects will be the *most* imitative, the ideas of such objects being of all others, the most distinct and vivid. That *such* description, therefore, should have been called imitation, can be no wonder; and, indeed, of all the extend-ed or analogical applications of the word, this is, perhaps, the most

---

k. Nothing is more common than this application of the word to description; though the writers who so apply it have not always explained the ground of the application, or pointed out those precise properties of description which entitle it to be considered as imitation. Mr. Addison makes use of *description* as a general term, comprehending all poetic imitation, or imitation by language, as opposed to that of painting, &c. See *Spectator* N° 416. I.C. Scaliger, though he extended *imitation* to speech in general, did not overlook the circumstances which render description peculiarly imitative. He says, with his usual spirit, speaking of poetic or verbal imitation, — "At *imitatio* non uno modo; quando ne *res* quidem. Alia namque est *simplex designatio,* ut, *Æneas pugnat*: alia *modos* addit et *circumstantias*; verbi gratia — *armatus, in equo, iratus.* Jam hic est pugnantis *etiam facies,* non solum *actio.* Ita *adjunctae circumstantiae, loci ,affectus, occasionis,* &c. *pleniorem* adhuc atque *toro-siorem* efficiunt IMITATIONEM." (*Poet. lib.* vii. *cap.* 2.) [For *simple designation* is one thing, as: *Æneas fights;* another — adds *moods* and *circumstances,* for example: *armed, on a horse, angry.* Now here there is also *character* of the one who fights and not only his *action.* So, *added circumstances, places, affections, occasions,* etc., produce a *far more complete* and also more *muscular* IMITATION.] We must not, however, confound *imitative description* with such description as is merely an *enu-meration of parts.* See *note* m, second part of this dissertation.

(CONT.) ⸺ ∽ ⸺

Twining proposes are related to two different systems; the obvious is related to a learned symbolic system, whereas the immediate is related to a sensible sense recog-nition. (His elaborate footnote clarifies this point.) Altogether, the inner dependence thus revealed between the two conditions is an indication of how Twining's argument will proceed; Twining will try, at all times, to assess the significance of the signs in terms of their symbolic nature.

obvious and natural.¹ There needs no other proof of this than the very language in which we are naturally led to express our admiration of this kind of poetry, and which we perpetually borrow from the arts of strict imitation. We say the poet has *painted* his object; we talk of his *imagery*, of the lively *colours* of his description, and the masterly touches of his *pencil.*ᵐ ⁴

---

1. Τὰ δὲ ῞ΟΨΕΙ γνώριμα, διὰ ποιητικῆ   ς ἑρμηνείας ἐμφαίνεται ΜΙΜΗΤΙΚΩΤΕΡΟΝ· οἷόν, κυμάτων ὄψεις, καὶ τοποθέσιαι, καὶ μάχαι, καὶ περιστάσεις πάθων· ὥστε συνδιατίθεσθαι τὰς ψυχὰς τοῖς εἴδεσι τῶν ἀπαγγελλομένων, ΩΣ ΩΡΩΜΕΝΟΙΣ . *Ptol. Harmon.* 3.3. [The things that are well-known BY THEIR LOOKS, are displayed more IMITATIVELY in the poetic interpretation, such as the looks of waves, and topography, and battles, and circumstances of emotions, so that the souls are exposed to the figures of the reported things, AS IF THEY WERE SEEN.]

m. It cannot be necessary to produce examples of this. They are to be found in almost every page of every writer on the subject of poetry. The reader may see Dr. Hurd's Discourse on Poetical Imitation, p. 10, &c. — Dr. Beattie's Essay on Poetry and Music, p. 97, (*Ed.* 8vo.) and the note. — Dr. Warton on Pope, vol. i. p. 44, 45; vol. ii. 223, 227. — Lord Kaims, Elem. of Criticism, vol. ii. p. 326.

Nor is this manner of speaking peculiar to modern writers. φέρε οὖν, says Ælian, introducing his *description* of the Vale of Tempe: καὶ τὰ καλούμενα Τέμπη, τὰ Θετταλικά, ΔΙΑΓΡΑΨΩΜΕΝ τῷ λόγῳ, καὶ ΔΙΑΠΛΑΣΩΜΕΝ. [Now let us in this work DESCRIBE BY LINES and BY SHAPE the place called Tempe, the Thessalic.] And he adds, as in justification of these expressions, ὡμολόγηται γὰρ καὶ ὁ λόγος, ἐὰν ἔχῃ δύναμιν φραστικήν, μηδὲν ἀσθενέστερον ὅσα βούλεται ΔΕΙΚΝΥΝΑΙ τῶν ἀνδρῶν τῶν κατὰ χειρουργίαν δεινῶν. *Hist. Var. lib.* iii. *cap.* 1. [For the tale, if it has a telling power, gives with the things it wishes *to display* nothing less than the men who are clever at handicraft.] Hence, also, the saying of Simonides, so often repeated, that "a picture is a silent poem, and a poem a speaking picture." Lucian, in that agreeable delineation of a beautiful and accomplished woman, his ΕΙΚΟΝΕΣ, ranks the descriptive poet with the painter and the sculptor: ταῦτα μὲν οὖν ΠΛΑΣΤΩΝ καὶ ΓΡΑΦΕΩΝ, καὶ ΠΟΙΗΤΩΝ παῖδες ἐργάσονται. [this, then, is what SCULPTORS and PAINTERS and POETS can achieve.] Homer, he denominates, τὸν ἄριστον ΤΩΝ ΓΡΑΦΕΩΝ, "the best of PAINTERS;" and calls upon him, even in preference to Polygnotus, Apelles, and the most eminent artists, to paint the charms of his Panthea. See also the treatise Περὶ τῆς ΟΜΗΡΟΥ ποιήσεως, [On Homer's poetry] towards the end. (Εἰ δὲ καὶ Ζωγραφίας διδάσκαλον ῞Ομηρον φαίη τις — κ. τ. ἀλλ) [(If someone says that Homer is a teacher of painting — etc.)]

--- ✍ ---

4. Discussing poetry as imitative, Twining considers language as composed not only of mere sounds but of sounds composed to impart signification. Descriptions carry such signification, Twining tells us, not because they describe literally that which they imitate, but because they are capable of evoking images that are plausible in terms of reality. (Beattie's insistence that plausibility is a condition for credibility has been discussed at great length, Twining was undoubtedly familiar with the latter's arguments.) That language is capable of engendering ideas which have the power to evoke impressions (received, in the first place, unmediated from experience of nature) is the underlying premise of Twining's assertion, which he, of course, takes from the British empiricists. Given his familiarity with the debates regarding the creative imagination, Twining must have taken into account the mental transformations this process entails. Of course, the more distinct and vivid the ideas, the more capable they are of creat-

(CONT.)

The objects of our other senses fall less within the power of description, in proportion as the ideas of those objects are more simple, more fleeting, and less distinct, than those of sight. The description of such objects is, therefore, called with less propriety *imitation*.[n]

Next to visible objects, *sounds* seem the most capable of descriptive imitation. Such description is, indeed, generally aided by real, though imperfect, resemblance of verbal sound; more, or less, according to the nature of the language, and the delicacy of the poet's ear. The following lines of Virgil are, I think, an instance of this.

> Lamentis gemituque et foemineo ululatu
> Tecta fremunt, resonat magnis plangoribus aether.
>
> [Lamentation and sobbing and women's wailing rang
> Through the houses, and high heaven echoed
> with the loud mourning.]

> *Æn. iv. 667–8*

But we are not, now, considering this immediate imitation of sound by sound, but such only as is merely *descriptive*, and operates, like the description of visible objects, only by the *meaning* of the words. Now if we are allowed to call description of visible objects, imitation, when it is such that *we seem to see* the object,[o] I know of no reason why we

---

n. One obvious reason of this is, the want of that natural association just remarked, with *painting*, (the most striking of the *strictly imitative* arts,) which is peculiar to the description of *visible* objects.

o.   ΟΡΩΜΕΝΟΙΣ μᾶλλον ἢ ἀηκουομένοις ἔοικε τὰ ['Ομήρου] ποιήματα
      [The POEMS [of Homer] are more like things seen than things heard.]

> *Treatise de Hom. Poes. loco cit.*

(CONT.)

ing the desired illusion. His differentiation between distinctness and vividness in poetic imitation calls to mind Baumgarten's adoption of the Cartesian distinction. (For Baumgarten, poetical ideas are "clear" though "confused," since they are dictated by the diffuse nature of the workings of the "lower cognitive faculty." Descartes, on the other hand, who was interested in logical ideas, discussed not only their clarity but their distinctness as well; of course, Twining's "distinctness" stands here for Baumgarten's "clarity" and "vividness" for Baumgarten's "confusion," see Part. I). Indeed, both Baumgarten and Twining tried to elucidate the success of the ut pictura poesis paradigm, both assuming the superiority of the sense of vision as far as directness is concerned. In other words, the immediacy that Twining attributes to the visual arts is enlisted as a mediator in poetry which deals with the visual.

may not also consider sounds as imitated,[p] when they are so described that we *seem to hear* them. It would not be difficult to produce from the best poets, and even from prose-writers of a strong and poetical imagination, many instances of sound so imitated. Those readers who are both poetical and musical will, I believe, excuse my dwelling a moment upon a subject which has not, as far as I know, been much considered.[5]

Of our own poets I do not recollect any who have presented *musical* ideas with such feeling, force, and reality of description, as Milton, and Mr. Mason. When Milton speaks of

——Notes with many a winding bout
Of linked sweetness long drawn out.

L'Allegro.

And of "a soft and solemn-breathing sound," that

Rose like a steam of rich distill'd perfumes,
And stole upon the air.

Comus.

Who, that has a truly musical ear, will refuse to consider such description as, in some sort, imitative? [q]

---

p. Lucian, in his *Imagines*, just now cited, has very happily described a fine female voice; and he calls the description, somewhat boldly, καλλιφωνίας καὶ ᾠδῆς ΕΙΚΩΝ. *Tom.* ii. *p.* 13. [IMAGE of beauty of sound and of song] *Ed. Bened.* Πᾶς δὲ ὁ τόνος τοῦ φθέγματος. — κ. τ. αλ. — [All the straining of the voice — etc.——]

q. See also Il Penseroso, 161-166.

5. Here Twining explains the reason for the immediacy he attributes to visual descriptions. 'Immediacy' does not refer to some kind of automatic visual mechanism, but to an essential connection with the ideas which the object imparts. As it turns out, imitation is of ideas, and it is the ideas which may be more clear and distinct regarding what the description is about (i.e. what it means). It is hardly surprising, therefore, that Twining is ready to extend objects of descriptive imitation so as to incorporate the other senses. Even with regard to painting an "as if" situation is created, and this situation is the heart of imitation. In all cases, the description appeals to the imagination, which is expected to suspend disbelief. This explains why Twining finds little interest in imitation of sound by sound, and great interest in verbal descriptions of sound. Here Twining naturally connects with a venerable tradition — the tradition of the harmony of the spheres — in which sound reflected the grand design of the universe. What follows exemplifies various possibilities to vest sound with ideational substance. (Spitzer and Hollander have well explicated the principle ways in which this was brought about. See Part I.)

In the same spirit both of Poetry and of Music are these beautiful lines in CARACTACUS, addressed by the Chorus to the Bards:

————Wond'rous men!
Ye, whose skill'd fingers know how best to lead,
Through all the maze of sound, the wayward step
Of Harmony, recalling oft, and oft
Permitting her unbridled course to rush
Through dissonance to concord, sweetest then
Ev'n when expected harshest.————

It seems scarce possible to convey with greater clearness to the ear of imagination the effect of an artful and well-conducted harmony; of that free and varied range of modulation, in which the ear is ever wandering, yet never lost, and of that masterly and bold intertexture of discord, which leads the sense to pleasure, through paths that lie close upon the very verge of pain.

The general and confused effect of complex and aggregated sound may be said to be *described*, when the most striking and characteristic of the single sounds of which it is compounded are selected and enumerated; just as *single* sounds are described (and they can be described no otherwise) by the selection of their principal *qualities*, or *modifications*. — I cannot produce a finer example of this than the following admirable passage of Dante, in which, with a force of representation peculiar to himself in such subjects, he describes the mingled terrors of those distant sounds that struck his ear as he entered the gates of his imaginary *Inferno;* — : "si mise dentro alle segrete cose." — ["...led him into the secret things."]

Quivi sospiri, pianti, ed alti guai
Risonavan per l'aer senza stelle;

————   ————   ————   ————

Diverse lingue, orribili favelle,
Parole di dolore, accenti d'ira,
Voci alte fioche, e suon di man con elle.

[Here sighs, plaints, and deep wailings
Resounded through the starless air;

————   ————   ————   ————

Strange tongues, horrible outcries,
Words of pain, tones of anger,
Voices deep and hoarse, and sounds of hands amongst them.]
Inferno, Canto III.

The reader may be glad to relieve his imagination from the terrible ENAPΓEIA of this description, by turning his ear to a far different combination of sounds; — to the charming description of "the melodies of morn," in the *Minstrel,* ᴿ or of the *melodies of evening* in the *Deserted Village:* Sweet was the sound, when oft at evening's close,

> Up yonder hill the village murmur rose.
> There as I past with careless steps and slow,
> The mingling notes came soften'd from below;
> The swain responsive as the milk-maid sung,
> The sober herd that low'd to meet their young;
> The noisy geese that gabbled o'er the pool,
> The playful children just let loose from school;
> The watch-dog's voice that bay'd the whisp'ring wind,
> And the loud laugh that spoke the vacant mind.
> These all in soft confusion sought the shade,
> And fill'd each pause the nightingale had made.ˢ

But *single sounds* may also be so described or characterized as to produce a secondary perception, of sufficient clearness to deserve the name of imitation. It is thus that we hear the "far-off Curfeu" of Milton;

> Over some wide-water'd shore

---

r. Book I. *Stanzas* 40, 41.

s. The following Stanza of Spenser has been much admired:

> The joyous birdes, shrouded in cheareful shade,
> Their notes unto the voice attempred sweet,
> Th' angelical soft trembling voices made
> To th' instruments divine, respondence meet;
> The silver-sounding instruments did meet
> With the base murmur of the water's fall;
> The water's fall with difference discreet
> Now soft, now loud, unto the wind did call;
> The gentle warbling wind low answered to all.

> *Fairy Queen, Book* II. *Canto* 12, *Stanza* 71.

Dr. Warton says of these lines, that they "are of themselves a complete concert of the most delicious music." It is unwillingly that I differ from a person of so much taste. I cannot consider as *music*, much less as "delicious music," a mixture of incompatible sounds, if I may so call them — of sounds *musical* with sounds *unmusical.* The singing of birds cannot possibly be "attempred" to the notes of a human voice. The mixture is, and must be, disagreeable. To a person listening to a concert of voices and instruments, the interruption of *singing-birds, wind,* and *waterfalls,* would be little better than the torment of Hogarth's enraged musician.* — Farther — the description itself is, like too many of Spenser's, coldly elaborate, and indiscriminately minute. Of the expressions, some are feeble and without effect — as, "*joyous* birds;" some evidently improper — as, "*trembling* voices," and *cheareful* shade;" for there cannot be a greater fault in a voice than to be tremulous; and *cheareful* is surely an unhappy epithet applied to shade; some cold and laboured, and such as betray too plainly the *necessities of rhyme;* such is,

> "The water's fall with *difference discreet.*"

Swinging slow with sullen roar.[t]

And Mr. Mason's "Bell of Death," that

———pauses now; and now with *rising knell*
Flings to the hollow gale its sullen sound.

Elegy III.

I do not know a happier descriptive line in Homer than the following, in his simile of the nightingale:

'Ήτε θαμὰ τρωπῶσα χέει πολυήχεα φωνήν.[u]
[With how many turns and trills she pours out
her full-throated song]

That which is peculiar in the singing of this bird, the variety, richness,
flexibility, and liquid volubility of its notes, cannot well be more strongly characterized, more *audibly* presented to the mind, than by the
πολυηχεα [many-toned] , the χέει [pouring], and, above all, the θαμὰ
τρωπῶσα [many turns and trills], of this short description.[w] [6] But, to
return — I mentioned also, description of *mental* objects; of the emo-

---

t. The reader who conceives the word "*swinging*," to be merely descriptive of *motion*, will be far, I
think, from feeling the whole force of this passage. They who are accustomed to attend to sounds,
will, I believe, agree with me, that the sound, in this case, is affected by the motion, and that the
swing of a bell is actually *heard in its tone*, which is different from what it would be if the *same* bell
were struck with the *same force*, but *at rest*. The experiment may be easily made with a small hand-
bell.

u. Odyssey, T. 521. I am surprised at Ernestus's interpretation of τρωπῶσα; i.e. "de luscinia inter
canendum SE *versante*," [*Index* to his Homer.] by which the greatest beauty of the description would
be lost; and lost without necessity: for the natural construction is that which *Hesychius* gives: τρωπῶσα — τρέπουσα THN ΦΩNHN [turning THE VOICE].

w. Not a single beauty of this line is preserved in Mr. Pope's translation. The χέει "*pours* her voice,"
is *entirely* dropt; and the strong and rich expression, in θαμὰ τρωπῶσα and πολυηχέα, is diluted into
"*varied* strains." [Book xix. 607.] For the *particular* ideas of a *variety of quick turns* and *inflexions*
[θαμὰ τρωπῶσα] and a *variety of tones*, [πολυηχέα] the translator has substituted the *general*, and therefore weak idea, of *variety* in the abstract — of a song or "strains" simply *varied*. The reader may see
this subject — the importance of *particular* and *determinate* ideas to the force and beauty of description — admirably illustrated in the *Discourse on Poetical Imitation*. [Hurd's Horace, vol. iii. p. 15-19.]

———— ∽ ————

6. Although Twining's examples show how imitation connects with ideas, they differ
as to the kind of description which they involve. The examples from Milton, as expected, derive directly from the tradition of the harmony of the spheres, while Mason's
poem rests on the reader's musical competence, invoking in his/her imagination a kind
of musical "unity amidst variety." The examples from Dante's Inferno and Goldsmith's
Deserted Village describe the effects certain sounds may have ("mingled terrors,"
"sweet sounds"), rather than their musical qualities. Spencer's example (in the footnote) describes an imaginative counterpoint resulting in a "concerted" whole. Here

(CONT.)

tions, passions, and other internal movements and operations of the mind. Such objects may be described, either *immediately*, as they affect the mind, or thorough their *external* and *sensible effects*. Let us take the passion of Dido for an instance:

> At regina gravi jamdudum saucia cura
> Vulnus alit venis, et coeco carpitur igni, &c.
> [But meanwhile Queen Dido, gnawed by love's invisible fire,
> had long suffered from the deep wound draining her life-
> blood.]

> *Æneid* IV.1.

This is *immediate* description. — But when Dido

> Incipit effari, mediaque in voce resistit;
> Nunc eadem, labente die, convivia quaerit,
> Iliacosque iterum, demens, audire labores
> Exposcit, pendetque iterum narrantis ab ore.
> Post, ubi digressi, lumenque obscura vicissim
> Luna premit, suadentque cadentia sidera somnos,
> Sola domo moeret vacua, stratisque relictis
> Incubat.———
> [And she would begin to speak her thoughts,
> but always checked herself with the words half-spoken.
> At day's decline she would want the banqueting
> to begin again as before;
> she would insist beyond all reason on hearing
> yet once more the tale of Troy's anguish,
> and again she would hang breathless on the speaker's words.
> Afterwards, when they had parted,
> as the moon in her turn quenched her lights to darkness
> and the setting stars counselled sleep,

(CONT.) ——— ∽ ———

Twining takes issue with Warton (who considered these lines as a "complete concert"), for he cannot imagine the harmoniousness of the combination described. By addressing the issue literally, Twining contradicts his own position according to which the role of description is to connect with the intended effect and not with real sounds. As for the example of the single sounds, their effect derives from the silence which they alone offset. To repeat and summarize: the imagination does not evoke the sound but rather its perception, i.e. its effect through ideas. Accordingly, imitation comprises three steps: 1) allusion, based on shared knowledge, 2) imagination, which reconstructs the perception of the phenomenon, and 3) the juxtaposition of the reconstruction with the description which gave rise to the whole process to begin with. Imitation is thus achieved through a complicated interaction between the work of art and those to whom it is addressed.

Dido mourned, lonely in the empty banqueting-hall,
and threw herself on the couch which he had left.]

— here, the passion is described, and most exquisitely, by its *sensible effects*. This, indeed, *may* be considered as falling under the former kind of descriptive imitation — that of *sensible* objects. There is this difference, however, between the description of a sensible object, and the description of a mental — of any passion for example — *through* that of a sensible object, that, in the former, the description is considered as terminating in the clear and distinct representation of the sensible object, the landscape, the attitude, the sound, &c.: whereas in the other, the sensible exhibition is only, or chiefly, the *means* of effecting that which is the principal end of such description — the emotion, of whatever kind, that arises from a strong conception of the passion itself. The image carries us on forcibly to the feeling of its internal cause. When this *first* effect is once produced, we may, indeed, return from it to the calmer pleasure, of contemplating the imagery itself with a painter's eye.

It is undoubtedly, *this* description of passions and emotions, by their *sensible* effects, that principally deserves the name of *imitative* ; and it is a great and fertile source of some of the highest and most touching beauties of poetry.[x] With respect to *immediate* descriptions of this kind, they are from their very nature, far more weak and indistinct, and do not, perhaps, often possess that degree of forcible representation that amounts to what we call *imitative* description. — But here some distinctions seem necessary. In a strict and philosophical view, a *single* passion or emotion does not admit of description at all. Considered in itself, it is a simple internal feeling, and, as such, can no more be *described*, than a simple idea can be *defined*. It can be described no otherwise than in its *effects*, of *some* kind or other. But the effects of a passion are of two kinds, *internal* and *external*. Now, popularly speaking, by *the passion* of love, for example, we mean the whole operation of that passion upon the *mind* — we include all its internal workings; and when it is described in the these internal and invisible effects only, we consider it as *immediately* described; these internal effects being included in our general idea of the passion. *Mental objects*, then, admit of immediate

---

x. See the Discourse on Poetical Imitation, of Dr. Hurd, p. 39, &c.

description, only when they are, more or less, complex; and such description may be considered as more or less *imitative*, in proportion as its impression on the mind approaches more or less closely to the real impression of the passion or emotion itself. — Thus, in the passage above referred to as an instance of such immediate description, the mental object described is a complex object — the passion of love, including some of its internal effects; that is, some *other* passions or feelings which it excites, or with which it is accompanied:

> At regina gravi jamdudum saucia cura
> Vulnus alit venis, et coeco carpitur igni.
> Multa viri virtus animo, multusque recursat
> Gentis honos: haerent infixi pectore vultus,
> Verbaque: nec placidam membris dat cura quietem.
> [But meanwhile Queen Dido, gnawed by love's invisible fire,
> had long suffered from the deep wound draining her life-blood.
> Again and again the thought of her hero's valour
> and the high nobility of his descent came forcibly back to her,
> and his countenance and his words stayed imprinted on her mind;
> the distress allowed her no peace and no rest.]
>
> *Æneid IV. initio.*

Reduce this passage to the mere mention of the passion *itself* — the simple feeling or emotion of *love*, in the precise and strict acceptation of the word, abstractedly from its concomitant effects, it will not even be *description*, much less *imitative* description. It will be mere attribution, or predication. It will say only — "Dido was in love."

Thus, again, a complication of *different passions* admits of forcible and *imitative* description:

> ————aestuat ingens
> Imo in corde pudor, mixtoque insania luctu,
> Et furiis agitatus amor, et conscia virtus.
> [In that one heart together there surged a mighty tide of shame,
> madness and misery blending, love tormented by passion for
> revenge, and valour which knew itself true.]
>
> *Æn. XII. 666.*

Here, the mental object described is not any single passion, but the complex passion, if I may call it so, that results from the mixture and fermentation of all the passions *attributed* to Turnus.

To give one example more: —— The mind of a reader can hardly, I think, be flung into an imaginary situation more closely resembling the real situation of a mind distressed by the *complicated* movements of irresolute, fluctuating and anxious deliberation, than it is by these lines of Virgil:

> ———magno curarum fluctuat æstu;
> Atque animum hunc nuc celerem, nunc dividit illuc,
> In partesque rapit varias, perque omnia versat.
> [———was tossed on a heaving tide of anxieties. Rapidly his
> mind leapt this way and that, in the hurried search for different
> viewpoints to help him think out all his problems.]
>
> *Æn. 342 VIII. 19.*

It may be necessary, also, for clearness, to observe, that description, as applied to mental objects, is sometimes used in a more loose and improper sense, and the Poet is said to *describe*, in general, all the passions or manners which he, in any way, exhibits; whether, in the proper sense of the word, *described*, or merely *expressed;* as, for example, in the lines quoted from the opening of the fourth book of the Æneid, the passion of Dido is *described* by the *Poet*. In these ——

> Quis novus hic nostris successit sedibus hospes?
> Quam sese ore ferens! — quam forti pectore et armis! ——
> [What do you think of this new guest who has joined us in our
> home? He has a rare presence, and valiant indeed are his heart
> and his arms.]

— it is *expressed* by herself. But is not this, it may be asked, still *imitation?* It is; but not *descriptive* imitation. As *expressive of passion*, it is no farther imitative, than as the passion expressed is imaginary, and makes a part of the Poet's *fiction*: otherwise, we must apply the word *imitative*, as nobody ever thought of applying it, to *all* cases in which we are made, by sympathy, to feel strongly the passion of another expressed by words. The passage is, indeed, also *imitative* in another view —— as *dramatic*. But for an explanation of both these heads of imitation, I must refer to what follows. —— I shall only add, for fear of mistake, that there is also, in the second of those lines, *descriptive imitation*; but descriptive of *Æneas* only; not of Dido's *passion*, though it strongly *indicates* that passion. —— All I mean to assert is, that those lines are not *descriptive imitation of a mental object*.

So much, then, for the subject of *descriptive imitation*, which has, perhaps, detained us too long upon a single point of our general inquiry.[7]

3. The word *imitation* is also, in a more particular, but well-known, sense, applied to Poetry when considered as FICTION —— to stories, actions, incidents, and characters, as far as they are *feigned* or *invented* by the Poet *in imitation*, as we find it commonly, and obviously enough, expressed, of nature, of real life, of truth, in *general*, as opposed to the individual reality of things which is the province of the historian.[y] Of this imitation the epic and dramatic poems are the principal examples.

That this sense of the term, as applied to fiction, is entirely distinct from that in which it is applied to description, will evidently appear from the following considerations. —— In descriptive imitation, the resemblance is between the ideas raised, and the actual *impressions*, whether external or internal, received from the things themselves. In fictive imitation, the resemblance is, strictly speaking, between the ideas raised, and other ideas; the ideas raised —— the ideas of the *Poem* — — being no other than copies, resemblances, or, more philosophically, new, though similar, combinations of that general stock of ideas, collected from experience, observation, and reading, and reposited in the Poet's mind. —— In description, *imitation* is opposed to actual *impression*, external or internal: in fiction, it is opposed to *fact.* —— In their *effects*, some degree of illusion is implied; but the illusion is not of the

---

y. Μῦθος - λόγος ψευδὴς ΕΙΚΟΝΙΖΩΝ ΤΗΝ ΑΛΗΘΕΙΑΝ. — *Suidas, & Hesychius, voce* Μῦθος. [Mythos — false tale PORTRAYING THE TRUTH.]

——— ∽ ———

7. In the previous paragraphs the mind was the locus of the process of achieving imitation, here Twining dwells on states of mind as objects of imitation. He divides the latter into two kinds — the one entailing descriptions and the other expressions. Descriptions are further divided into "immediate" and "sensible" ones. The "immediate," which relates to designated passions, should resort to psychological complexities in order to yield full descriptions. The "sensible" shares the characteristics of Twining's sensible imitation, except that here it functions as a means "to achieve the end of such a description," i.e. the experience of the passion.

Imitation via expression, on the other hand, diverges almost completely from imitation. It qualifies as imitation only if it is subsumed by an imitative framework. On the whole, like his fellow thinkers, Twining is well aware of the inaccessibility of the emotional as far as simple imitation is concerned, and of the complicated exercises needed to achieve it. It is this inaccessibility, as Webb and Smith showed, that provides room for the unique role of music in treating the passions.

same kind in both. Descriptive imitation may be said to produce *illusive perception,* —— fictive, *illusive belief.*[8]

Farther —— descriptive imitation may subsist without fictive, and fictive, without descriptive. The first of these assertions is too obvious to stand in need of proof. The other may require some explanation. It seems evident that fiction may even subsist in mere *narration,* without any degree of *description,* properly so called; much more, without *such* description as I have called *imitative;* that is, without any greater degree of resemblance to the things expressed, than that which is implied in *all* ideas, and produced by *all* language, considered merely as *intelligible.* Let a story be invented, and related in the plainest manner possible; in short and general expressions, amounting, in the incidents, to mere assertion, and in the account of passions and characters, as far as possible, to mere attribution: this, as fiction, is still *imitation,* —— an invented resemblance of real life, or, if you please, of history,[z] ——

---

8. As already noted (fn. 4), the empiricists' distinction between ideas and impressions is used by Twining, as it was by Harris, Webb and others. Here Twining goes one step further, for he realizes that the mental transformations which art involves are of an illusive kind. To view illusion as a key concept in art is indeed a breakthrough, for it implies that "artificial keys" are required to unlock the mental propensities which create worlds of art, denying that such keys and worlds are naturally given. Hence, a discussion of the arts, necessitates explication of cognitive capabilities along with an understanding of the various artistic media and their constraints. While Smith concentrated on the latter, as we shall see, Twining dwelt on the former: he distinguishes between "fictive imitation," which rests on resemblance between ideas raised and other ideas, and "descriptive imitation," which rests on resemblance between ideas raised and actual impressions. Having subsumed both under illusion, Twining is able to show that ideas, in the first case, are related to belief while ideas in the second are related to perception. Twining is sophisticated enough to analyze 'belief' in terms of a system which connects experience, observation, knowledge etc., a conceptual scheme which, on the whole, constitutes what is generally believed to be factual — the infrastructure of reality. Interestingly, this kind of analysis assumes the artificiality of both artistic procedures as well as of artistic products, and does not lag far behind the recognition that the image that we have of the real world is equally "artificial." Discussing fiction, Twining reminds us of the Aristotelian distinction between the particularity of historical writing compared with the generality of fiction, as far as truth is concerned. The reader may recall that Beattie explained this "general truth" in terms of probabilities. Probabilities, in connection with Twining's conception of illusion, sharpen the kind of mental construction which fiction involves.

though without a single *imitative description*, a single *picture*, a single
instance of strong and visible colouring, throughout the whole.[a]   I
mean, by this, only to shew the distinct and independent senses in
which *imitation* is applied to description and to fiction, by shewing how
each species of imitation *may* subsist without the other; but, that fictive
imitation, though it does not, in any degree, depend on descriptive for
its existence, does, in a very great degree, depend on it for its beauty,
is too obvious to be called in question.[b] [9]

The two senses last mentioned of the word *imitative*, as applied to
description, and to fiction, are manifestly extended, or improper senses,
as well as that first mentioned, in which it is applied to language con-

---

z. "Historiae imitatio ad placitum." [Imitation of history as agreed upon] Bacon, *De augm. Scient.* lib.
ii. c. 13.

a. The Æneid, in this view, is equally *imitation* in every part where it is not, or is not *supposed* to
be, historically true; even in the simplest and barest narration. In point of fiction, "tres littore cervos
prospicit errantes, [He watched three wandering deers on the shore (Æn. I. 184-185)]" is as much
imitation, though not as *poetical*, as the fine description of the storm in the same book, or of Dido's
conflicting passions, in the fourth.

b. Yet even here a distinction obviously suggests itself. A work of fiction may be considered in two
views; in the whole, or in its parts: in the general story, the Μύθος, fable, series of *events*, &c. or, in
the detail and circumstances of the story, the account of such places, persons, and things, as the fable
necessarily involves. Now, in the first view, nothing farther seems requisite to make the fictive imitation *good*, than that the events be, in *themselves*, important, interesting, and affecting, and so *connected* as to appear credible, probable, and natural to the reader, and, by that means, to produce the
illusion, and give the pleasure, that is expected: — and this purpose may be answered by mere *narration*. But in the detail this is not the case. When the Poet proceeds to fill up and distend the outline of his general plan by the exhibition of places, characters, or passions, these also, as well as the
events, must appear probable and natural: but, being more *complex* objects, they can no otherwise
be made to appear so than by some degree of *description*, and that description will not be *good*
description, that is, will not give the pleasure expected from a work of imagination, unless it be *imitative* — such as makes us see the *place*, feel the *passion*, enter thoroughly into the *character*
described. Here, the *fictive* imitation itself cannot produce its proper *effect*, and therefore cannot be
considered as *good*, without the assistance of *descriptive*.

--- ∽ ---

9. This last clarification aims to dispel entrenched conceptions of artistic constraints.
Twining is aware that cognitive dictates were mixed with aesthetic desiderata in the
traditional discussions of art. Relying on his previous analysis of the difference
between descriptive and fictive imitation, Twining argues that fiction contains a coherence of its own and need not resort to description in order to be intelligible. In footnote b. he penetrates into the kind of coherence narrative involves, differentiating
between the general outline of the plot, and the specific events which it discusses.
Maintaining that events must be "well connected" in order to appear credible, he hints
in the direction of an eventual theory of narrative that will differentiate between *fab-
ula* and *sujet*, submitting the former to assumed cognitive abilities and the latter to
effective artistic procedures.

sidered as mere sound. In *all* these imitations, *one* of the essential conditions of whatever is *strictly* so denominated is wanting; — in sonorous
imitation, the resemblance is *immediate*, but not *obvious*; in the others,
it is *obvious*, but not *immediate;* that is, it lies, not in the *words* themselves, but in the *ideas* which they raise as *signs:*c yet as the circumstance of *obvious* resemblance, which may be regarded as the most
striking and distinctive property of Imitation, is here found, this extension of the word seems to have more propriety than that in which it is
applied to those faint and evanescent resemblances which have, not
without reason, been called the echo of sound to sense.d10

4. There seems to be but *one* view in which Poetry can be considered as *Imitation*, in the strict and proper sense of the word. If we look
for both *immediate* and *obvious* resemblance, we shall find it only in
DRAMATIC ———— or to use a more general term —— PERSONATIVE Poetry;
that is, all Poetry in which, whether essentially or occasionally, the Poet
personates; for here, *speech* is imitated by *speech*.e The difference
between this, and mere narration or description, is obvious. When, in
common discourse, we *relate*, or *describe*, in our own persons, we *imitate* in no other sense than as we raise *ideas* which resemble the things
related or described. But when we speak *as another person*, we become
mimics, and not only the ideas we convey, but the words, the discourse
itself, in which we convey them, are imitations; they resemble, or are
supposed to resemble, those of the person we represent. Now this is the
case not only with the Tragic and Comic Poet, but also with the Epic
Poet, and even the Historian, when either of these quits his own character, and *writes* a speech in the character of another person. He is then
an imitator, in as strict a sense as the personal mimic. — In *dramatic*,
and all *personative* Poetry, then, both the conditions of what is *proper-*

---

c. See above, p. 5.

d. Pope's *Essay on Crit.* 365. — Indeed, what Ovid says of the nymph *Echo* [Met. iii. 358.] may be
applied to this echo of imitative words and construction: — Nec *prior ipsa loqui* didicit. [—but yet
has not learned to speak first herself.] The *sense* of the words must *speak first.*

e. The drama, indeed, is said also to imitate *action* by *action;* but this is only in actual representation, where the players are the immediate imitators. In the poem itself nothing but *words* can be
immediately copied. Gravina says well, Non è *imitazione poetica* quella, che non è fatta *dalle parole.*
[That which is not made of words is not poetic imitation.] —(*Della Trag. sect.* 13.)

——— ∽ ———

10. See fn. 3.

ly denominated Imitation, are fulfilled.[11]

And now, the question — "in what senses the word *Imitation* is, or may be applied to Poetry," — seems to have received its answer. It appears, I think, that the term ought not to be extended beyond the *four* different applications which have been mentioned; and that Poetry can be justly considered as *imitative*, only by *sound*, by *description*, by *fiction*, or by *personation*. Whenever the Poet speaks in his own person, and, at the same time, does not either feign, or make "the sound an echo to the sense," or stay to impress his ideas upon the fancy with some degree of that force and distinctness which we call description, he cannot, in any sense that I am aware of, be said to *imitate;* unless we extend imitation to *all* speech — to every mode of expressing our thoughts by words — merely because all words are signs of ideas, and those ideas images of *things.*[f]

It is scarce necessary to observe, that these different species of imitation often run into, and are mixed with, each other. They are, indeed, more properly speaking, only so many distinct, abstracted *views*, in which Poetry may be considered as imitating. It is seldom that any of them are to be found separately; and in some of them, others are necessarily implied. Thus, dramatic imitation implies fiction, and sonorous imitation, description; though conversely, it is plainly otherwise. Descriptive imitation is, manifestly, that which is most independent on all the others. The passages in which they are all united are frequent; and those in which all are excluded, are, in the best Poetry, very rare: for the Poet of genius rarely forgets his proper *language;* and that can scarcely be retained, at least while he *relates*, without more or less of

---

f. See *Hermes, Book* iii. *ch.* 3, p. 329, &c.

———— ∽ ————

11. Having discussed the difference in linguistic imitation between the conditions of immediate resemblances versus obvious resemblances, Twining goes on to show the "obvious," i.e. that direct speech indeed imitates speech, in both its immediate and obvious senses. However, as in the case of painting, Twining again wrongly assumes that the immediate and obvious are sufficient in order to create the "make believe" necessary for theatrical illusion. Had he treated the conditions which this kind of illusion involves, he might have been in a better position to understand the condition of turning "personative music" into a successful illusion. Theatrical conventions, for example, are no more real than are musical ones, and both rest on the suspension of disbelief.

colouring, of imagery, of that *descriptive* force which makes us see and hear. A total suspension of all his functions as an imitator is hardly to be found, but in the simple proposal of his subject,[g] in his invocation,[h] the expression of his own sentiments,[i] or, in those calm beginnings of narration where, now and then, the Poet stoops to *fact*, and becomes, for a moment, little more than a metrical historian.[k]

The full illustration of all this by examples, would draw out to greater length a discussion, which the reader, I fear, has already thought too long. If he will open the Æneid, or any other epic poem, and apply these remarks, he may, perhaps, find it amusing to trace the different kinds of imitation as they successively occur, in their various combinations and degrees; and to observe the Poet varying, from page to page, and sometimes even from line to line, the *quantity*, if I may so speak, of his imitation; sometimes shifting, and sometimes, though rarely and for a moment, throwing off altogether, his imitative form.

It has been often said that ALL *Poetry is Imitation*.[l] But from the preceding inquiry it appears, that, if we take *Poetry* in its common acceptation, for all *metrical composition*, the assertion is not true; not, at least, in any sense of the term *Imitation* but such as will make it equally true

g.   Arma virumque cano, Trojae qui primus ab oris

        Italiam, fato profugus, Lavinaque venit

        Litora.

[This is a tale of arms and of a man. Fated to be an exile, he was the first to sail from the land of Troy and reach Italy, at its Lavinian shore.] *Æneid*, I.

h.   Musa, mihi causas memora, &c.

        [I pray for inspiration, tell how it all began]   *Ibid.*

i.   Tantaene animis caelestibus irae?

        [It is hard to believe Gods in Heaven capable of such rancour] *Ibid.*

        Tantae molis erat Romanam condere gentem.

        [Such was the cost in heavy toil of beginning the life of Rome]   *Ibid.*

k.   Urbs antiqua fuit, (Tyrii tenuere coloni,)

        Carthago, Italiam contra, Tiberinaque longe

        Ostia, &c.

        [Once there was an ancient town called Carthage, inhabited by emigrants from Tyre, and across from Italy, opposite to the mouth of the Tiber but far away, &c.]

                                Ibid.

l. This expression is nowhere, that I know of, used by Aristotle. In the beginning of his treatise he asserts only that the *Epic ,Tagic, Comic,* and *Dithyrambic Poems* are imitations. Le Bossu, not content with saying that "*every sort of Poem in general is an imitation,*" goes so far as even to alter the text of Aristotle in his marginal quotation. He makes him say, ΠΟΙΗΣΕΙΣ πᾶσαι τυγχάνουσιν οὖσαι μιμήσεις τὸ σύνολον. [In general all POEMS are likely to be imitations.]

of *all Speech*.[m] If, on the other hand, we depart from that common acceptation of the word *Poetry*, the assertion that "all Poetry is Imitation," seems only an improper and confused way of saying, that no composition that is not imitative *ought* to be *called* Poetry. To examine the truth of this, would be to engage in a fresh discussion totally distinct from the object of this dissertation. We have not, now, been considering *what* Poetry *is*, or how it should be *defined*; but only, in what sense it is an *Imitative Art*: or, rather, we have been examining the nature and extent of VERBAL IMITATION in general.[n] [12]

---

m. See p. 23, note [f] [p. 340 in this edition].

n. Imitation, in every sense of the word that has been mentioned, is manifestly independent on *metre*, though being more eminently adapted to the nature and end of metrical composition, it has thence been peculiarly denominated *Poetic* imitation, and attributed to the *Poetic Art*.

——————— ∽ ———————

12. Twining's analysis of 'imitation' culminates in his discussion of the philosophical status of the categories he introduced. Warning against extending the meaning of the term 'imitation' so as to encompass the whole field of 'reference,' Twining is guided by his commitment to the historical bond between imitation and illusion. This explains, in part, his descriptive, rather than normative, attitude, i.e. the analysis of the various uses of the term (in the philosophical sense of the word) and the cognitive structures which underlie them. These uses, Twining maintains, are separated only theoretically; in modern terms, they are paradigmatic units. In practice, however, they are interwoven, revealing a flexible "pragmatics." In other words, only the "quality" of the "uses" is cognitively constrained, whereas the "quantities" of their appearance are determined ad hoc. To judge poetry according to the kinds of imitation employed, necessitates argumentation which takes into account stylistic norms and desiderata.

DISSERTATION   II.

ON DIFFERENT SENSES OF THE WORD, IMITATIVE, AS APPLIED TO MUSIC BY THE ANTIENTS, AND BY THE MODERNS.[13]

*T*HE whole power of MUSIC may be reduced, I think, to *three* distinct effects; —— upon the *ear*, the *passions*, and the *imagination*: in other words, it may be considered as simply delighting the *sense*, as raising *emotions*, or, as raising *ideas*. The two last of these effects constitute the whole of what is called the *moral**, or *expressive*, power of Music; and in these only we are to look for anything that can be called *imitation*. Music can be said to imitate, no farther than as it *expresses* something. As far as its effect is merely physical, and confined

---

* *Moral*, merely as opposed to *physical*——as affecting the *mind*; not as *Ethic*, or influencing the *manners*.

——————— ∽ ———————

13. Though primarily concerned with literature, Twining finds the case of imitation in music particularly challenging. Interested in the clarification of "how imitation works," i.e. in the modes of symbolization entailed in achieving artistic illusions, he, of course, rejects accidental associations as irrelevant to musical imitation (cf. Webb on this point). He accepts the observations of former thinkers on the problem of imitation in music, but is able to surpass their theoretical explanations by employing the categories he established in relation to poetry. Thus, music that actually resembles sound and motion (as Harris maintained) fits his category of the immediate, while lacking "obviousness" as a condition. What appeared as convoluted in previous writings, is here stated in unambiguous terms: music lacks referential power. However, given Twining's postulate that "natural deficiencies" may be overcome through artistic manipulation, we may rightly assume that he will attempt to apply the principle to music as well.

to the ear, it gives a simple, original pleasure; it expresses nothing, it *refers* to nothing; it is no more imitative than the smell of a rose, or the flavour of a pine-apple.

Music can raise ideas, *immediately*,[a] only by the actual resemblance of its *sounds* and *motions* to the sounds and motions of the thing suggested.[b] Such Music we call *imitative*, in the same sense in which we apply the word to a similar resemblance of sound and motion in poetry.[c] In both cases, the resemblance, though *immediate*, is so *imperfect*, that it cannot be seen till it is, in some sort, pointed out; and even when it *is* so, is not always very evident. Poetry, indeed, has here a great advantage; it carries with it, of necessity, its own explanation: for the same word that imitates by its *sound*, points out, or hints, at least, the imitation, by its *meaning*. With Music it is not so. It must call in the assistance of language, or something equivalent to language, for its interpreter.[d]

Of all the powers of Music, this of raising ideas by direct resemblance is confessed to be the weakest, and the least important. It is, indeed, so far from being essential to the pleasure of the art, that unless used with great caution, judgment, and delicacy, it will destroy that pleasure, by becoming, to every competent judge, offensive, or ridiculous. It is, however, to Music of *this* kind only that Mr. Harris, and most other modern

---

a. Music *may* raise ideas *immediately*, by mere *association*; but I pass over the effects of this principle, (important and powerful as it is, in Music, as in everything else,) as having nothing to do with *imitation*. If, to raise an idea of any object by casual association, be to *imitate*, any one thing may imitate any other.

I inserted the word, *immediately*, because Music has also a power of raising ideas, to a certain degree, through the *medium* of *emotions*, which naturally suggest correspondent ideas; that is, *such* ideas as usually raise *such* emotions. [See Harris, *on Music, &c.* ch. vi. and below, note [s].]

b. See *Harris, ibid. ch.* ii where this subject is treated with the author's usual accuracy and clearness.

c. See *Dissert.* I.

d. When the idea to be raised is that of a visible object, the imitation of that object by painting, machinery, or other visible representation, may answer the same end.——A visible object strongly characterized by motion, *may* be suggested by such *musical* motion as is analogous to it. Thus, a rapid elevation of sounds, bears, or at least is *conceived* to bear, some analogy to the motion of flame;——but this analogy must be pointed out——"Il faut que l'auditeur soit averti, ou par les *paroles*, ou par le *spectacle*, ou par quelque chose d'equivalent, qu'il doit substituer l'idée du *feu* à celle du *son*." ["It is necessary that the hearer be informed, either by the words, by the spectacle, or by something equivalent to them, if he is to substitute the idea of fire for that of sound."] See M. Dalembert's *Melanges de Literature, vol.* v. *p.* 158,——where the philosophical reader will, perhaps, be pleased with some very ingenious and uncommon observations, on the manner in which the imitative expression even of *Music without words*, may be influenced by the phraseology of the language in which the hearer *thinks*.

writers, allow the word *imitative* to be applied.[e] The highest power of Music, and that from which "it derives its greatest efficacy," is, undoubtedly, its power of raising *emotions*. But this is so far from being regarded by them as *imitation*, that it is expressly *opposed* to it.[f]

The ideas, and the language, of the antients, on this subject, were different. When *they* speak of Music as imitation, they appear to have solely, or chiefly, in view, its power over the *affections*. By *imitation*, they mean, in short, what *we* commonly distinguish from imitation, and oppose to it, under the general term of *expression*.[g] With respect to ARISTOTLE, in particular, this will clearly appear from a few passages which I shall produce from another of his writings; and, at the same time, the expressions made use of in these passages, will help us to *account* for a mode of speaking so different from that of modern writers on the subject.

What Aristotle, in the beginning of his treatise on Poetry,[*] calls ΜΙΜΗΣΙΣ —— IMITATION — he elsewhere, in the same application of it, to *Music*, calls ʹΟΜΟΙΩΜΑ —— RESEMBLANCE. And he, also, clears up his meaning farther, by adding the *thing resembled* or *imitated;*[h] —— ὁμοίωμα ΤΟΙΣ ΗΘΕΣΙ —— ὁμοιώματα ΤΩΝ ΗΘΩΝ[i] —— "resemblance to human *manners*," i.e. *dispositions*, or *tempers*; for what he means by these ἤθη, he has, likewise, clearly explained by *these* expressions —— ὁμοιώματα ΟΡΓΗΣ καὶ ΠΡΑΟΤΗΤΟΣ· ἔτι δ᾽ ΑΝΔΡΙΑΣ καὶ ΣΩΦΡΟ-ΣΥΝΗΣ, &c. "resemblances of the *irascible* and the *gentle* disposition — — of *fortitude* and *temperance*, &c."[k] This resemblance, he expressly tells us, is "in the *rhythm* and the *melody:*" —— ὁμοιώματα —— ἐν τοῖς

e. Dr. Beattie, *On Poetry and Music*, p. 138, & *passim*.——Lord Kaims, *El. of Crit. vol.* ii. *p.* 1. Avison, &c.——There is but *one* branch of this imitation of *sound* by *sound*, that is really important; and *that* has been generally overlooked. I mean, the imitation of the *tones* of *speech*.——Of this, presently.

f. Harris, *On Music, &c.* p. 69, 99, 100.

g. "If we compare *imitation* with *expression*, the superiority of the latter will be evident."——Dr. Beattie, *On Poetry and Music*, p. 139, 140, &c.——Avison, *on Mus. Expression, Part* II. §3.

* καὶ τῆς αὐλητικῆς ἡ πλείστη, καὶ κιθαριστικῆς —— μιμήσεις. [Most forms of flute-playing, and of lyre-playing —— happen to be in general imitations.] ——See *Sect.* I. of the translation.

h. In the same passage he uses the word μίμημα, as synonymous with ὁμοίωμα.

i. Arist. de Repub. lib. viii. cap. 5, p.455, *Ed. Duval.* Plato uses μιμήματα ΤΡΟΠΩΝ in the same sense. *De leg.* lib. ii. p. 655, *Ed. Ser.*

k. The word, ἤθη, taken in its utmost extent, includes *everything* that is *habitual* and *characteristic*; but it is often used in a limited sense, for the *habitual temper*, or *disposition*. That it is here used in that sense appears from Aristotle's own explanation. I therefore thought it necessary to fix the sense of the word *manners*, which has the same *generality* as ἤθη, and is its usual translation, by adding the words "*dispositions* or *tempers*."

PΥΘΜΟΙΣ καὶ τοῖς ΜΕΛΕΣΙΝ, ὀργῆς καὶ πραότητος.[1] In these passages, Aristotle differs only in the *mode* of expression from Mr. Harris, when *he* affirms that "there are sounds to *make us chearful* or *sad, martial* or *tender,* &c.:[m] —— from Dr. Beattie, when he says, "Music may *inspire devotion, fortitude, compassion;* —— may *infuse a sorrow,* &c".[n]

It appears then, in the *first* place, that Music, considered as affecting, or raising *emotions,* was called imitation by the antients, *because* they perceived in it that which is essential to all imitation, and is, indeed, often spoken of as the same thing —— *resemblance.*[o] This resemblance, however, as *here* stated by Aristotle, cannot be *immediate;*[p] for between *sounds themselves,* and *mental affections,* there can be no resemblance. The resemblance can only be a resemblance of *effect:* — — the *general emotions, tempers,* or *feelings* produced in us by certain sounds, are *like* those that accompany actual grief, joy, anger, &c. —— And this, as far, at least, as can be collected from the passage in question, appears to be all that Aristotle meant.[14]

---

l. The same expressions occur in the *Problems, Sect.* xix. *Prob.* 29 and 27.

m. Chap. vi.

n. *On Poet. and Mus.* p. 167.——In another place Dr. Beattie approaches very near indeed to the language of Aristotle; he says, "After all, it must be acknowledged, that there is some *relation,* at least, or *analogy, if not* SIMILITUDE, between certain musical *sounds,* and mental *affections,* &c." [p. 143; p. 220 in this edition.]

o. "Imitations, *or* resemblances, of something else." [Hutcheson's *Inquiry into the Orig.* of *our Ideas of Beauty, &c.* p. 15.] "Taking *imitation* in its *proper sense,* as importing a *resemblance* between two objects." [Lord Kaims, *El.* of *Crit.* ch. xviii. §3.] Imitation, indeed, necessarily implies resemblance; but the converse is not true.

p. See *Dissert.* I. *first pages.*

--- ∽ ---

14. The gap between Twining and his formers looms large in these paragraphs where direct resemblance is excluded from artistic imitation. For Harris or Avison, the lack of direct resemblance sufficed to exclude expressive music from imitation. While agreeing that music "expresses," Twining views expression as a part of imitation. The important question raised by Beattie concerning the lack of immediate resemblance between music and the affections is treated by Twining in the same way in which he treats descriptive poetry, namely, in both cases he assumes that the relationship between sound and mental affections does not constitute a resemblance between two kinds of objects, but rather between the effects which they raise. Altogether, resemblance never suffices for establishing imitation; in fact resemblance is a result of imitation having taken place (see his fn. o.).

But, *secondly;* —— the *expressions* of Music considered in itself, and *without words,* are, (within certain limits), vague, general, and equivocal. What is usually called its power over the *passions,* is, in fact, no more than a power of raising a *general emotion, temper,* or *disposition,* common to several different, though *related,* passions; as pity, love — — anger, courage, &c.q The effect of *words,* is, to strengthen the expression of Music, by confining it —— by giving it a precise direction, supplying it with ideas, circumstances, and an *object,* and, by this means, raising it from a calm and *general* disposition, or emotion, into something approaching, at least, to the stronger feeling of a particular and determinate *passion.* Now, among the antients, Music, it is well known, was scarce ever heard *without* this assistance. Poetry and Music were then far from having reached that state of mutual independence, and separate improvement, in which they have now been long established. When an antient writer speaks of Music, he is, almost always, to be understood to mean *vocal* Music —— Music and Poetry united. This helps greatly to account for the application of the term *imitative,* by Aristotle, Plato, and other Greek writers, to musical *expression,* which modern writers *oppose* to musical *imitations.* That emotions *are* raised by Music, independently of words, is certain;r and it is as certain that these emotions resemble those of actual passion, temper, &c. —— But, in the vague and indeterminate assimilations of Music purely instrumental, though the effect is felt, and the emotion raised, the idea of *resemblance* is far from being necessarily suggested; much less is it likely, that such resemblance, if it did occur, having no *precise* direction, should be considered as *imitation.* s Add *words* to this Music, and the

---

q. The expression of Aristotle seems therefore accurate and philosophical. It is everywhere —— ὁμοίωμα HΘΩN, —— not ΠAΘΩN —— a resemblance "to *manners,* or *tempers,*" not "to *passions.*"

r. This is expressly allowed by Aristotle in the Problem which will presently be produced: —— καὶ γὰρ ἐὰν ᾖ ANEΥ ΛOΓOΥ μέλος, ὅμως ἔχει HΘOΣ.

s. I observed (*Note* a) that Music is capable of raising *ideas,* to a certain degree, through the medium of those *emotions* which it raises *immediately.* But this is an effect so delicate and uncertain — so dependent on the fancy, the sensibility, the musical experience, and even the temporary disposition, of the *hearer,* that to call it *imitation,* is surely going beyond the bounds of all reasonable analogy. Music, here, is not *imitative,* but if I may hazard the expression, merely *suggestive.* But, whatever we may call it, this I will venture to say, —— that in the *best* instrumental Music, expressively *performed,* the very indecision itself of the expression, leaving the hearer to the free operation of his *emotion* upon his *fancy,* and, as it were, to the free *choice* of such ideas as are, to *him,* most adapted to react upon and heighten the emotion which occasioned them, produces a pleasure, which nobody, I believe, who is able to feel it, will deny to be one of the most delicious that Music is capa-

(CONT.)

case will be very different. There is now a precise object of *comparison* presented to the mind; the *resemblance* is pointed out; the thing *imitated* is before us. Farther, one principal use of Music in the time of Aristotle, was to accompany *dramatic* Poetry ——— *that* Poetry which is most peculiarly and strictly *imitative,*[t] and where *manners* and *passions* (ἤθη καὶ πάθη) are peculiarly the *objects* of imitation.

It is, then, no wonder, that the Antients, accustomed to hear the expressions of Music thus constantly *specified*, determined, and referred to a precise object by the ideas of Poetry, should view them in the light of *imitations*; and that even in speaking of *Music, properly* so called, as Aristotle does, they should be led by this association to speak of it in the same terms, and to attribute to it powers, which, in its separate state, do not, in strictness, belong to it. With respect, however, even to the *instrumental* Music of those times, it should be remembered, that we cannot properly judge of it by our *own*, nor suppose it to have been, in that simple state of the art, what it is now, in its state of separate improvement and refinement. It seems highly probable that the Music of the antients, even in performances merely instrumental, retained much of its vocal style and character, and would therefore appear more *imitative* than *our* instrumental Music: and perhaps, after all, a Greek Solo on the flute, or the cithara, was not *much* more than a song without the words, embellished here and there with a little embroidery, or a

---

(CONT.)

ble of affording. But far the greater part even of those who have an ear for Music, have *only* an *ear;* and to *them* this pleasure is unknown. ——— The complaint, so common, of the separation of Poetry and Music, and of the total want of meaning and expression in *instrumental* Music, was never, I believe, the complaint of a man of true musical feeling: and it might, perhaps, be not unfairly concluded, that Aristotle, who expressly allows that "Music, even *without words*, *has expression*," [See the Problem below.] was more of a musician than his master Plato, who is fond of railing at instrumental Music, and asks with Fontenelle, ——— "Sonate, que me *veux* tu? ["Sonata, what would you of me?"] ——— παγχάλεπον, ἄνευ λόγου γιγνόμενον ῥυθμόν τε καὶ ἁρμονίαν γιγνώσκειν, Ὁ, ΤΙ ΒΟΥΛΕ-ΤΑΙ. [It is almost impossible to understand what is intended by this wordless rhythm and harmony.] *De Leg.* ii. p. 669. (The story of Fontenelle is well known. ——— "Je n'oublierai jamais," says Rousseau, "la saillie du célèbre Fontenelle, qui se trouvant excedé de ces eternelles symphonies, s'ecria tout haut dans un transport d'impatience: *Sonate, que me veux tu?*" [I shall never forget...the joke about the celebrated Fontenelle, who wearied by those eternal symphonies, cried out in a transport of impatience: *'Sonate, que me veux tu?'*] *Dict. de Mus.* ——— SONATE.) I would by no means be understood to deny, that there is now, and has been at all times, much unmeaning trash composed for instruments, that would justly provoke such a question. I mean only to say, what has been said for me by a superior judge and master of the art: ——— "There is *some* kind, even of instrumental Music, so divinely composed, and so expressively performed, that it wants no *words* to explain its meaning." ——— Dr. Burney's *Hist.* of *Music*, vol. i. p. 85.

t. Diss. I.

few sprinklings of simple *arpeggio*, such as the fancy, and the fingers, of the player could supply. [15]

But there is another circumstance that deserves to be considered. *Dramatic* Music is, often, *strictly imitative*. It imitates, not only the *effect* of the words, by exciting correspondent *emotions*, but also the *words* themselves *immediately*, by tones, accents, inflexions, intervals, and rhythmical movements, *similar* to those of speech. That this was peculiarly the character of the *dramatic* Music of the antients, seems highly probable, not only from what is said of it by antient authors, but from what we know of their Music *in general*; of their scales, their *genera*, their fondness for *chromatic* and *enharmonic* intervals, which approach so nearly to those sliding and unassignable inflexions, (if I may so speak,) that characterize the melody of *speech*.

——— ◡ ———

15. Compared to people like Estimate John Brown, Twining, like Beattie, does not deplore the separation of music and text, the union of which many considered ideal. (Here, again, Twining discloses his tendency toward the "descriptive" rather than the normative. Like Beattie, he is well aware that aesthetics are conditioned by the artistic practices of the time; one can never fully restore the meaning of an aesthetic theory in the absence of the objects to which it relates.) Writing towards the end of the century, he is not only aware of the development in instrumental music, but is in awe of its momentous achievements. This is part of the new recognition of the second half of the century, which clearly divides our group (Rousseau, in his note on Fontenelle quoted by Twining, attests to this shift). If Twining is still preoccupied by the question of meaning in instrumental music, it is because his basic philosophical questions had not yet been fully resolved. Though he still employs some commonplaces about the relationship between music and text, it is preferable to focus attention on some of his subtler distinctions. These make clear that words may indeed dispel the "vagueness" of music, but that they can never undo its "generality," for music is, by definition, "vague, general and equivocal." Twining implies that the combination of text and music will never yield perfect resemblances like those of descriptive poetry, for otherwise, the uniqueness of music might be obliterated. This, of course, does not diminish the impressive power of music. Twining seems to reformulate the notion, so common in the eighteenth century, of the "non-ideational" nature of music, maintaining that music will never absorb ideas that have been linguistically produced. What is here only suggested, will become central to nineteenth-century aesthetics, particularly to Schopenhauer who will consider the combination of music and a specific text as only one of the possible ways of exemplifying the power of music without exhausting its generality. Like his contemporaries in Germany — the Frühromantiker — Twining submits to the "enigma" of instrumental music, but without resorting to metaphysical overtones.

I am, indeed, persuaded, that the analogy between the melody and rhythm of *Music*, and the melody and rhythm of *speech* ,ᵘ is a principle of greater extent and importance than is commonly imagined. Some writers have extended it so far as to resolve into it the whole power of Music over the affections. Such appears to have been the idea of Rousseau. He divides all Music into *natural* and *imitative;* including, under the latter denomination, all Music that goes beyond the mere pleasure of the sense, and raises any kind or degree of emotion; an effect which he conceives to be wholly owing to an imitation, more or less perceptible, of the accents and inflexions of the voice in animated or passionate speech.ʷ Professor Hutcheson was of the same opinion. In his *Inquiry concerning Beauty, &c.* he says —— "There is also another charm in Music to various persons, which is distinct from the *harmony*, and is occasioned by its *raising agreeable passions. The human voice* is obviously varied by all the stronger passions;ˣ now when our *ear* discerns any *resemblance* between the air of a tune, whether sung, or played upon an instrument, either in its *time* or *modulation*, or any other circumstance, to the *sound of the human voice in any passion*, we shall be touched by it in a very sensible manner, and have *melancholy, joy, gravity, thoughtfulness,* excited in us by a sort of *sympathy* or *contagion.*" [Sect. 6. p. 83.] This ingenious and amiable writer seems to have adopted this opinion from PLATO, to whom, indeed, in a similar passage

---

u. —— λέγεται γὰρ δὴ καὶ ΛΟΓΩΔΕΣ ΤΙ ΜΕΛΟΣ, τὸ συγκείμενον ἐκ τῶν προσῳδιῶν τῶν ἐν τοῖς ὀνόμασι.. [—for there is also a kind of MELODY IN SPEECH which depends upon the accents of words.] [*Aristox. Harm.* i. p. 18. *Ed. Meibom.*] To this he opposes —— ΜΟΥΣΙΚΟΝ ΜΕΛΟΣ. [THE MELODY OF MUSIC.].

w. Dict. de Musique, Art. MUSIQUE — MELODIE, &c.

x. Thus THEOPHRASTUS, in a curious passage cited by Plutarch in his *Symposiacs*, p. 623, *Ed. Xyl.*—— — Μουσικῆς, ἀρχὰς τρεῖς εἶναι, ΛΥΠΗΝ, ΗΔΟΝΗΝ, ΕΝΘΟΥΣΙΑΣΜΟΝ· ὡς ἑκάστου τούτων παρα-τρέποντος ἐκ τοῦ συνήθους καὶ ἐγκλίνοντος τὴν φωνήν. —— "There are *three principles* of Music, *grief, love*, and *enthusiasm;* for each of these passions *turns the voice* from *its usual course*, and gives it inflexions different from those of ordinary speech." —— "Il n'y a que les *passions* qui *chantent*," says Rousseau; "l'entendement ne fait que *parler*." [It is only the passions that sing ... the understanding but speaks.] —— This passage of Theophrastus is introduced to resolve the question —— In what sense *love* is said to *teach Music?* —— "No wonder," says the resolver, "if love, having in itself all these three *principles* of Music, *grief, pleasure*, and *enthusiasm*, should be more prone to vent itself in Music and Poetry than any other passion."—— Aristoxenus, describing the difference between the two motions of the voice, in *speaking* and in *singing*, —— (the motion by *slides*, and that by *intervals*) says —— διόπερ, ἐν τῷ διαλέγεσθαι φεύγομεν τὸ ἱστάναι τὴν φωνήν, ἂν μὴ ΔΙΑ ΠΑΘΟΣ ποτὲ εἰς τοιαύτην κίνησιν ἀναγκασθῶμεν ἐλθεῖν. [— Hence in ordinary conversation we avoid bringing the voice to a standstill, unless occasionally forced by strong feeling to resort to such a motion.] —— p. 9. *Ed. Meibomii.*

in his System of Moral Philosophy,[y] he refers, and who, in the *third* book of his Republic, speaks of a *warlike* melody, inspiring *courage*, as *"imitating* the *sounds* and *accents* of the courageous man;" and, of a *calm* and *sedate* melody, as *imitating* the *sounds* of a man of *such* a character.[z]

With respect to ARISTOTLE —— whether this was *his* opinion, or not, cannot, I think, be determined from anything he has *expressly* said upon the subject. In the passage above produced,* where so much is said of the resemblance of melody and rhythm to manners, or tempers, not a word is said from which it can be inferred, that he meant a resemblance to the tones and accents by which those manners are *expressed* in speech. On the contrary, the expressions there made use of are such as lead us naturally to conclude, that he meant no more than I have above supposed him to mean; *i.e.* that the Music produces in us, immediately, feelings resembling those of real passion, &c. —— For, after having asserted, that there is "a resemblance in rhythms and melodies to the irascible and the gentle disposition," he adds, —— "This is evident from the manner in which we find ourselves affected by the *performance* of such Music; for we perceive *a change produced in the soul* while we listen to it.[a]" And again —— "In melody itself there are *imitations* of human *manners*: this is manifest, from the MELODIES or MODES, which have, evidently, their distinct nature and character; so that, when we hear them, we *feel ourselves affected* by each of them in a different manner. &c.[b]" —— But the passage furnishes, I think, a more decisive proof

---

y. Vol. i. p. 16.

z. *De Rep. lib.* iii. *p.* 399. *Ed. Ser.* The expressions are —— ἡ [sc. ἁρμονία —— i.e. *melody*,] ἐν τῇ πολεμικῇ πράξει ὄντος ἀνδρείου —— πρεπόντως ἂν ΜΙΜΗΣΑΙΤΟ ΦΘΟΓΓΟΥΣ ΤΕ ΚΑΙ ΠΡΟΣΩΙΔΙΑΣ [in the art of war has to do with the essence of the brave]. And again —— σωφρόν- ων, ἀνδρείων, ΦΘΟΓΓΟΥΣ ΜΙΜΗΣΟΝΤΑΙ [WILL IMITATE SOUNDS of wise-men, of brave-men].

* P. 47 [p. 356 in this edition].

a. Δῆλον δὲ ἐκ τῶν ἔργων· ΜΕΤΑΒΑΛΛΟΜΕΝ ΓΑΡ ΤΗΝ ΨΥΧΗΝ ἀκροώμενοι τοιούτων.

b. Ἐν δὲ τοῖς μέλεσιν αὐτοῖς ἔστι μιμήματα τῶν ἠθῶν· καὶ τοῦτ' ἔστι φανερόν· εὐθὺς γὰρ ἡ τῶν Ἁρμονιῶν διέστηκε φύσις· ὥστε ἀκούοντας ΑΛΛΩΣ ΔΙΑΤΙΘΕΣΘΑΙ, καὶ μὴ τὸν αὐτὸν τρόπον ἔχειν πρὸς ἑκάστην αὐτῶν. - κ. τ. αλ. —— [and who..confronts fortune with steadfast endurance and repels her blows] The.Ἁρμονίαι, i.e. *melodies*, (or, more properly perhaps, *enharmonic melodies*) here spoken of, must not be confounded with what are usually called the *modes*, and described by the writers on antient music, under the denomination of τόνοι, i.e. *pitches*, or *keys*:——these were mere transpositions of the *same* scale, or system; the Ἁρμονίαι appear to have been, as the name implies, different *melodies* — scales, in which the arrangement of intervals, and the divisions of the

(CONT.)

that the resemblance here meant, was not a resemblance to *speech*. Aristotle asserts here, as in the *problem* of which I shall presently speak, that, of all that affects the *senses*, Music alone possesses this property of resemblance to human manners. In comparing it with painting, he observes, that this art can imitate, immediately, only *figures* and *colours*; which are not *resemblances* (ὁμοιώματα) of manners and passions, but only *signs* and *indications* of them (σημεῖα) in the human body: whereas, in Music, the resemblance to manners "*is in the melody itself.*ᶜ" Now, whatever may be the meaning of this last assertion —— for it seems not quite philosophical to talk of *such* a resemblance as being *in the sounds themselves* — whatever may be its meaning, it cannot well be, that the melody resembles manners *as expressed by speech*; because this would destroy the distinction between Music and Painting: for *words* are exactly in the same case with *colours* and *figures*; they are not *resemblances* of manners, or passions, but *indications* only. We must then, I fear, be contented to take what Aristotle says as a popular and unphilosophical way of expressing a mere resemblance of *effect*.[16]

(CONT.)

tetrachord (or *genera*) were different. Aristides Quintilianus is the only Greek writer who has given any account of these ἁρμονίαι. (p. 21. Ed. Meib.) He asserts, that it is of *these*, not of the τόνοι, that Plato speaks in the famous passage of his *Republic, lib.* iii. where he rejects some of them, and retains others. *This*, at least, is clear, that whatever the ἁρμονίαι of Plato were, Aristotle here speaks of the same. See his *Rep.* viii. p. 459. —— Their distinctive names, Lydian, Dorian, &c. were the same with those of the τόνοι, that of *syntono-Lydian* excepted, which, I think, is peculiar to the ἁρμονίαι. This coincidence of names seems to have been the chief cause of the confusion we find in the *modern* writers on this subject. The distinction has been pointed out in Dr. Burney's *Hist.* of *Mus.* vol. i. p. 32.——See also Rousseau's Dict art. SYNTONO-LYDIEN, & GENRE.

c. —— οὐκ ἔστι ταῦτα ὁμοιώματα τῶν ἠθῶν, ἀλλὰ ΣΗΜΕΙΑ μᾶλλον, τὰ γινόμενα σχήματα καὶ χρώματα, τῶν ἠθῶν· καὶ ταῦτα ἐστὶν ἐπὶ τοῦ σώματος ἐν τοῖς πάθεσιν. — ἐν δὲ ΤΟΙΣ ΜΕΛΕΣΙΝ ΑΥΤΟΙΣ ἐστι μιμήματα τῶν ἠθῶν. — κ. τ. αλ.. [(Also visual works of art) are not representations of character but rather the FORMS and colors produced are mere indications of character, and these indications are only bodily sensations during the emotions...PIECES OF MUSIC on the contrary do actually contain IN THEMSELVES imitations of character.] —— p. 455. *Ed. Duval.*

------ ✍ ------

16. It is irrelevant whether Twining is accurate in his historical review of voice inflection in music, for all he wishes to do is to relate to a tradition which believed in the vital connection between speech inflection and its musical rendition. This tradition, which heavily rested on assumed Greek theory, was central to the beginnings of opera. It continued into the eighteenth century despite musical practice which proved the contrary. Twining's analysis of the tradition reveals that it simply rested on the imitation of the music of speech by music. In Twining's terms, it is clearly like dramatic poetry — both immediate and obvious. No wonder that this theoretical tradition per-

(CONT.)

In one of his *Musical Problems*, indeed, he advances a step farther, and inquires into the *cause* of this effect of Music upon the mind. The text of these problems is, in general, very incorrect, and often absolutely unintelligible; *this* problem, however, seems not beyond the reach of secure emendation, though it may, possibly, be beyond that of secure *explanation*. As it has not, that I know of, been noticed by any writer on the subject, and may be regarded at least as a curiosity not uninteresting to the musical and philosophical reader, I shall venture to give the entire problem, as I think it *should* be read, and to subjoin a translation.

ΔΙΑ ΤΙ τὸ ἀκουστὸν μόνον ἦθος ἔχει τῶν αἰσθητῶν, (καὶ γὰρ ἐὰν ᾖ ἄνευ λόγου μέλος, ὅμως ἔχει ἦθος) ἀλλ' οὐ τὸ χρῶμα, οὐδὲ ἡ ὀσμή, οὐδὲ ὁ χυμός, ἔχει; ‑ ἤ, ὅτι κίνησιν ἔχει μόνον; οὐχ ἦν ὁ ψόφος ἡμᾶς κινεῖ· τοιαύτη μὲν γὰρ καὶ τοῖς ἄλλοις ὑπάρχει· κινεῖ γὰρ καὶ τὸ χρῶμα τὴν ὄψιν· ἀλλὰ τῆς ἑπομένης τῷ τοιούτῳ ψόφῳ αἰσθανόμεθα κινήσεως αὕτη δὲ ἔχει ὁμοιότητα [τοῖς ἤθεσιν] ἔν τε τοῖς ῥυθμοῖς καὶ ἐν τῇ τῶν φθόγγων τάξει τῶν ὀξέων καὶ βαρέων. (οὐκ ἐν τῇ μίξει· ἀλλ'· ἡ συμφωνία οὐκ ἔχει ἦθος.)᾿Εν δὲ τοῖς ἄλλοις αἰσθητοῖς τοῦτο οὐκ ἔστιν. αἱ δὲ κινήσεις αὗται πρακτικαί εἰσιν· αἱ δὲ πράξεις ἤθους σημασία ἐστί.

[*Problem* xxvii. *of Section 19.*]

(CONT.)

d. The text here, in the Ed. of Duval, stands thus: —— κίνησιν ἔχει μονονουχὶ ἦν ὁ ψόφος —— of which no sense can be made. The emendation appeared to me obvious and certain.

e. I insert —— τοις ἤθεσιν —— as plainly required by the sense of the passage, and fully warranted by Aristotle's repeated expressions of the same kind. See above, p. 47. —— I found no other corrections necessary.

———— ∽ ————

sisted for so long; it simply fits the literal interpretation of mimesis which was so common in those days. However, since it is an inadequate explanation of his own understanding of the effects of music, Twining again enlists Aristotle to provide a competing paradigm. Instead of focusing on "appearances," the latter connects music, though indirectly, with the passions themselves. His sensitivity to the dichotomy between overall effects (revealed in Aristotle's general approach to imitating passions in music) and atomized relationships (manifested in the inflection theory) is evident in his footnote b', in which he distinguishes between the Greek Tonoi (scale transpositions) and the Nomoi (the melody-types).

PROBLEM

"Why, of all that affects the senses, the AUDIBLE only has any *expression* of the manners; (for melody, even *without words*, has this effect —) but colours, smells, and tastes, have no such property? —— Is it because the audible alone affects us by *motion*? —— I do not mean *that* motion by which as mere *sound* it acts upon the *ear;* for *such* motion belongs equally to the objects of our *other* senses; —— thus, colour acts by motion upon the organs of sight, &c. —— But I mean *another motion* which we perceive *subsequent* to that; and *this* motion bears a resemblance to human manners, *both* in the *rhythm*, and in the *arrangement* of *sounds* acute and grave: —— not in their *mixture;* for HARMONY *has no expression.*[f] With the

---

f. This passage is remarkable. It is exactly the *language* of Rousseau—— "il n'y a AUCUN RAPPORT entre des *accords*, & les objets qu'on veut peindre, ou *les passions qu'on veut exprimer.*" [there is no connection between chords and the objects that one wishes to paint, *or the passions that one wishes to express.*] [*Dict de Mus.* art. IMITATION: see also the last paragraph of art. HARMONIE.] Thus, too, Lord Kaims: —— "Harmony, properly so called, though delightful when in perfection, *hath* NO RELATION *to sentiment."* [*El. of Crit.* i. 128.] But how is this? The *same* intervals are the materials both of melody and of harmony. These intervals have, each of them, their peculiar effect and character, and it is by the proper choice of them in *succession*, and by that only, that *melody*, considered abstractedly from rhythm or measure, becomes *expressive*, or has *any* "relation to sentiment." Do these intervals, then, lose at once, as by magic, all their variety and striking difference of character, as soon as they are heard in the simultaneous combinations of harmony? If this be the case, the vocal composer is at once relieved from all care of adapting the harmonies of his accompaniment to the expression of the sentiments conveyed in the words; and it must be matter of perfect indifference whether, for example, he uses the major or minor *third* —— the perfect, or the false, *fifth* —— the common chord, or the chord of the diminished *seventh*, &c: —— With respect to Rousseau, it is not easy to see how this assertion of his can be reconciled with what he has elsewhere said. In his letter *Sur la Musique Françoise*, he expressly allows that every interval, consonant or dissonant, "a son caractere particulier, c'est à dire, une maniere d'*affecter l'ame* qui lui est propre." [has its own peculiar character, that is to say, a manner of affecting the spirit which is proper to it.] —— And upon this depend entirely all the admirable observations he has there made, concerning the ill effects which a crowded harmony, and the "*remplissage*" of chords, have upon musical expression. —— In another article [ACCORD] of his dictionary, this inconsistence is still more striking. One would not think it possible for the same writer, who in *one* place talks of intervals "propres, par leur dureté, à *exprimer l'emportement, la colere*, et LES PASSIONS aigues" ["suitable, by their harshness, for expressing anger, spleen, and the sharper passions"] —— and, of —— "une *harmonie plaintive* qui ATTENDRIT LE COEUR" [a plaintive harmony which softens the heart.] ———— to assert in another part of the same work, that "il n'y a AUCUN RAPPORT entre des *accords*, et LES PASSIONS qu'on veut *exprimer.*"

Had these writers contented themselves with saying, that harmony has much *less relation* to sentiment than melody, they would not have gone beyond the truth. And the reason of this difference in the effect of the *same* intervals, in melody, and in harmony, seems, plainly, this —— that in melody, these intervals being formed by *successive sounds*, have, of course, a much closer, and more obvious *relation* to the tones and inflexions by which sentiments are expressed in *speech*, than they *can* have in harmony, where they are formed by sounds *heard together.*

As to the assertion of Aristotle, it seems only to furnish an additional proof that the antients did not practice anything like our counterpoint, or *continued harmony in different parts.* Where the utmost use of harmony seems to have been confined to unisons, octaves, fourths, and fifths —— where at least no discords, (the most expressive materials of modern harmony) were allowed —— we cannot wonder that the "*mixture*" of sounds in consonance should be thought to have *no relation to sentiment*, and that all the power of Music over the passions, should be confined to melodious and rhythmical *succession.*

objects of our other senses this is not the case. —— Now these motions are analogous to the motion of human *actions*; and those *actions* are the index of the *manners.*"

In this problem, the philosopher plainly attributes the *expressive*
power of musical sounds to their *succession* —— to their *motion* in
measured melody. He also distinguishes the *rhythmical,* from the *melodious,* succession; for he says expressly, that this motion is "*both* in the
rhythm (or *measure,*) *and* in the *order* or *arrangement* of *sounds acute
and grave.*" —— But *whence* the effect of these motions? He answers,
from their analogy to the motions of human *actions,*g by which the manners and tempers of men are expressed in common life. With respect to
the analogy of *rhythmic* movement to the various motions of men in
action, this, indeed, is sufficiently obvious. But Aristotle goes farther,
and supposes, that there is also such analogy in the motion of melody
considered *merely* as a succession of different *tones,* without any
regard to *time;* —— ἐν ΤΕ (sic) τῶν φθόγγων τάξει, τῶν ΟΞΕΩΝ καὶ
ΒΑΡΕΩΝ [by the arrangement of the higher and lower sounds]. He plainly asserts, that this succession of *tones,* also, is analogous to the motion
of human *actions.* Now it seems impossible to assign any human action
to which a succession of *sounds* and *intervals,* merely as such, has, or
can have, any relation or similitude, except the *action* (if the expression
is allowable,) of *speaking,* which *is* such a succession. *If* this be
Aristotle's meaning —— and I confess myself unable to discover any
other —— I do not see how we can avoid concluding, that he agreed
so far with Plato, as to attribute *part* , at least, of the effect of Music upon
the affections to the analogy between melody and speech.

This analogy is, indeed, a curious subject, and deserves, perhaps, a
more thorough examination and development than it has yet received.h

---

g. The original is short, and rather obscure. It says, *literally,* "these motions are *practical motions:*"
πρακτικαὶ εἰσιν. [But that I have given Aristotle's true meaning in my translation, is evident from a
clearer expression in *Prob.* xxix. which is a shorter solution of the same question. His expression
there is —— κινήσεις εἰσιν οἱ ῥυθμοι καὶ τὰ μέλη ΩΣΠΕΡ ΚΑΙ ΑΙ ΠΡΑΞΕΙΣ —— "Rhythm and
melody are *motions, as actions also are.*"

h. Much light has been flung upon this subject, as far as relates to speech, by Mr. Steele, in his curious and ingenious essay *On the Melody and Measure of Speech.* But the object of *his* enquiry was
Speech, not *Music.* His purpose in tracing the resemblance between them, was only to shew that
speech is capable of *notation*; not to examine how far the effect of *Music* on the passions depends
on that resemblance .—— His *notation* is extremely ingenious; but with respect to his project of
accompanying the declamation of Tragedy by a drone bass, I must confess that, for my own part, I
cannot reflect without some comfort upon the improbability that it will ever be attempted.

But I shall not trust myself farther with a speculation so likely to draw me wide from the proper business of this note, than just to observe, that the writers above-mentioned, who resolve *all* the pathetic expression of Music into this principle, though they assert more than it seems possible to prove, are yet much *nearer* to the truth than those, who altogether overlook, or reject, that principle[i]; a principle, of which, instances so frequent and so palpable are to be traced in the works of the best masters of vocal composition —— in those of PURCELL, for example, of HANDEL, and above all, of PERGOLESI —— that I have often wondered it should have been neglected by so exact a writer as Mr. Harris, though it lay directly in his way, and, in one place, he actually touched it as he passed.[k] He seems, here, to have deserted those antients whom, in general, he most delighted to follow. [17]

i. After allowing that "different passions and sentiments do indeed *give different tones* and *accents* to the human voice," Dr. Beattie asks —— "but can the tones of the most pathetic melody be said to bear a resemblance to the voice of a man or woman speaking from the impulse of passion?" I can only answer, that to *my* ear, such a resemblance, in the "*most pathetic melody*," is, *often*, even striking: and I have no doubt that in *many* passages we are affected from a more delicate and latent degree of that resemblance, sufficient to be *felt*, in its effect, though not to be *perceived*. —— Dr. Beattie also asks —— "if there are not melancholy airs in the *sharp key*, and chearful ones in the *flat?*" —— Undoubtedly, the peculiar and opposite characters of these keys, may be variously *modified* and *tempered* by the movement, the accent, and the *manner* of *performance*, in general: but they can never be *destroyed*; much less can they be changed, as Dr. Beattie supposes, to their very *opposites*. A *chearful* air in a *flat* key, I confess, I never heard. If Dr. Beattie thinks the jig in the fifth solo of Corelli *chearful*, because the *movement* is *allegro*, I would beg of him to try an experiment: let him only play the first bar of that jig, (with the bass,) upon a harpsichord, &c. in G *major:* and when he has attended to the effect of that, let him return to the *minor* key, and hear the difference.— —As to "*melancholy* airs in a *sharp* key," the word *melancholy* is, I think, used with considerable latitude, and comprehends different *shades*. In the *lightest* of these shades, it may perhaps be applied to some airs in a major key: that key may, by slowness of movement, softness and smoothness of tone, &c. become solemn, tender, touching, &c. —— but I cannot say I recollect any air in that key which makes an impression that can *properly* be called *melancholy*. But we must be careful in this matter to allow for the magic of *association*, which no one better understands, or has described with more feeling and fancy than Dr. Beattie himself. [See p. 173, &c.] —— With respect to "a transition from the one key to the other" [from major to minor, &c.] "in the *same air, without any sensible change* in the expression," I must also confess that it is, to me, totally unknown. —— One word more:——Dr. Beattie is "at a loss to conceive how it should happen, that a musician overwhelmed with sorrow, for example, should put together a series of notes, whose expression is contrary to that of another series which he had put together when elevated with joy." [p. 180.] —— But is not Dr. Beattie equally at a loss to conceive how it should happen that any man overwhelmed with *sorrow*, should put together, in *speaking*, (as he certainly does) a series of *tones*, whose expression is contrary to that of *another* series which he had put together when elevated with *joy*? —— The two *facts* are equally certain, and, even at the first view, so nearly allied, that whoever can account for the one, need not, I am persuaded, be at the trouble of trying to account separately for the other.

k. Ch. ii. §2. —— particularly note l.

———— ᔕ ————

17. It is to Twining's credit that he should present "The Problem," (even if he wrongly ascribed it to Aristotle rather than to the Peripatetic school), for it contains, in a nut-

(CONT.)

But to return to *Aristotle,* and his treatise on Poetry: —— the reader will observe that he does not there assert in general terms, that *"Music is an Imitative Art,"* but only, that the Music *"of the flute and the lyre* is imitative; and even that, not always, but *"for the most part!"* I just mention this, because I have observed in many of the commentators, as well as in other writers, a disposition to extend and generalize his assertions, by which they have sometimes involved the subject and themselves in unnecessary difficulties.

With respect to *modern* writers, at least, there seems to be a manifest impropriety in denominating Music *an Imitative Art,* while they confine the application of the term *Imitative* to what they confess to be the slightest and least important of all its powers. In this view, consistence and propriety are, certainly, on the side of Dr. Beattie, when he would

---

1. — τῆς αυλητικῆς Η ΠΛΕΙΣΤΗ καὶ κιθαριστικῆς.

(CONT.) ———— ✌ ————

shell, an organic and extremely original conception of music as imitation. It harbors major answers to the problems which Twining himself posed. It is surprising therefore, that Twining should have missed its "novel" approach, for it addresses both the notion of metaphorical movement, which is peculiar to music, as well as the notion of understanding of "actions" as standing for the dynamic and lived part of the passions (see Descartes' discussion to that effect, Part I). He totally misses, therefore, the possibility of relating metaphorical movement to the dynamics of passions, as Webb so brilliantly did.

Instead of seizing upon this gold-mine, so well suited to his basic position, connecting music and affection through shared effects he over-endorsed the inflection of the voice theory which history has already proven barren. (Heightened speech, after all, is where opera began, not where it went in the course of its development; music has its own modes of articulation.) Even if Twining is partially correct about "certain beautiful passages" in Handel or Pergolesi, which somehow lived up to his expectations, he overlooks the fact that, even in these instances the relationship between the natural and the artificial — musical norms and stylistic ones — is what renders it beautiful. His debate with Beattie reveals the same fallacy, not because the major and the minor keys have not become designative for joy and sorrow respectively, but because he overlooks the power of their conventional aspect. Conditioning indeed works! In spite of all his sophistication, Twining missed the central role of artificial norms that Beattie seems to have arrived at "naturally." However, it was Twining who was able to expose the complexity of artistic norms, through his understanding of the cognitive processes of symbolization.

"strike Music off the list of *Imitative Arts.*m" But perhaps even a farther reform may justly be considered as wanting, in our language upon this subject. With whatever propriety, and however naturally and obviously, the arts both of *Music,* and of POETRY, may be, separately, and occasionally, regarded and spoken of as *imitative,* yet, when we arrange and *class* the arts, it seems desirable that a *clearer* language were adopted. The notion, that Painting, Poetry and Musicn are all *Arts of Imitation,* certainly tends to produce, and has produced, much confusion. That they all, in *some* sense of the word, *or other,* imitate, cannot be denied; but the senses of the word when applied to Poetry, or Music, are so different both from each other, and from that in which it is applied to Painting, Sculpture, and the arts of design in general —— the only arts that are *obviously* and *essentially* imitative —— that when we include them all, without distinction, under the same general denomination of *Imitative Arts,* we seem to defeat the only useful purpose of all classing and arrangement; and, instead of producing order and method in our ideas, produce only embarrassment and confusion. [See DISS. I. p. 3,4.][18]

---

m. Page 129 [p. 230 in this edition].

n. What shall we say to those who add ARCHITECTURE to the list of *Imitative Arts?* ——One would not expect to find so absurd a notion adopted by so clear and philosophical a writer as M. d'Alembert. Yet in his *Discours Prel. de l'Encyclop.* he not only makes Architecture an imitative art, but even classes it with *painting* and *sculpture.* He allows, indeed, that the imitation " *de la belle nature,* y est *moins frappante & plus resserrée* que dans les deux autres arts:" ["the imitation of nature is less striking there and more limited than in the two other arts."] —— but how is it any imitation at all? —— only because it imitates "par l'assemblage et l'union des differens corps qu'elle emploie" ["by means of the assembling and union of the different bodies it employs."] —— what?—— "*l'arrangement symmetrique* que *la nature* observe plus ou moins sensiblement dans chaque individu, &c." ["symmetrical arrangement observed by *nature,* more or less sensibly, in each individual, &c."] [*Mel. de lit.* i. 63.] I can only say, that, upon this principle, the joiner, the smith, and the mechanic of almost every kind, have a fair claim to be elevated to the rank of *Imitative Artists:* for if a *regular building* be an imitation of "*la belle nature,*" so is a chair, a table, or a pair of fire tongs.

———— ✧ ————

18. Concluding his essay with an explicit statement concerning the importance of his kind of undertaking is revealing. As much as it illuminates the creative process which has taken place, it reflects its own self-awareness. Indeed, Twining's systematic philosophical search into the concept of 'imitation,' contributed to its collapse as an all-encompassing aesthetic paradigm, making room for competing theories and additional clarifications, which in due course completely replaced its "magic" with scholarly rigor and a sound body of knowledge.

Adam Smith

(1723-1790)

Adam Smith, one of the most influential political economists, was born in 1723 at Kirkcaldy, a fisheries and mining town near Edinburgh.* At the young age of fourteen he was sent to the University of Glasgow where he attended the lectures of Francis Hutcheson. At Glasgow his favorite studies had been mathematics and natural philosophy. In 1740 he entered Balliol College, Oxford, where he remained for seven years. At Oxford he devoted himself almost entirely to moral philosophy and political science. In 1748 he moved to Edinburgh and there, under the patronage of Lord Kames, lectured on rhetoric and belles-lettres. About the same time he made the acquaintance of David Hume which turned into a life-long friendship. In 1751 he was elected professor of logic at the University of Glasgow and in 1752 was transferred to the chair of moral philosophy which had become vacant by the death of Hutcheson's successor. He occupied this position for twelve years. His course of lectures during this period covered the field of natural theology, ethics, morality (as related to justice) and political regulation (founded on the principle of expediency calculated to increase the riches and prosperity of states).

Drawing on his course of lectures, his *Theory of Moral Sentiments*, containing his ethical doctrine, first appeared in 1759. He spent the next ten years at work on the *Wealth of Nations* for which he became famous. This great work appeared in 1776 and was highly acclaimed by his friend David Hume who predicted that the work would only gradually gain in popularity because of the "close attention it requires" and because of its "depth and solidity."

In addition to his books, Smith wrote a number of essays on literary and philosophical subjects most of which appeared posthumously in 1795. Several student reports on Smith's lectures on economics, rhetoric and belles-lettres were also published at various times posthumously.

---

* Since we found that Smith's major concerns throw light on his aesthetic theory, we saw fit to make this introduction somewhat longer than the others.

Smith clearly had a wide range of interests. However, the evidence available suggests, according to scholars, that he reached his methodological and philosophical principles early in his career and that these bestowed a sense of interdependency upon his collected work. Smith was above all guided by his wide and keen observation of social facts, attempting to elicit their significance instead of dwelling on abstract principles of reasoning. Basing himself primarily on premises concerning universal facts of human nature and properties of external objects, Smith wished to study things as they are. Not all of his premises are ascertained by observations, however; some are based on a priori assumptions concerning the provision for social well-being made by nature, which prompts every individual to better his condition. Though interested in his private gain, the individual, according to Smith, is led by an "invisible hand," as it were, to promote the public good. His theory of moral sentiments explains the interrelationship between private and public interest.

'Sympathy' is the mainstay of man's moral sentiments, argued Smith; it is characterized by the analogy between the passion which arises in a person and the emotion which springs up at the thought of his situation. The latter suggests the general idea of some good or evil which has befallen the person whose passion we observe. Sympathy thus provides a basis for our judgements of the merit of other people's feelings and their consequent actions. Thinking of ourselves "as though we were someone else" these mechanisms of sentiment make us judge ourselves from the same point of view from which we judge others. Conscience is "the judge within us" that balances our interests and feelings and those of others. General rules concerning appropriate conduct emerge, according to Smith, from the sentiments. Through sympathy with other individuals responding to a variety of situations, moral rules arise which bring uniformity and stability to one's judgement of others as well as of oneself. Moreover, a person's own conscience is the product of social interaction, since communication with one's own species determines one's sentiments as well as one's conduct.

Like some of his predecessors, Smith clearly rejected self-love as the ultimate basis of behavior, arguing that its proponents have neglected sympathy as a cause of action. Neither is reason a source of the distinction between vice and virtue, for the perception of right and wrong is derived from a sense of the agreeableness or disagreeableness of actions. There is thus no need for a special moral sense, since a basis of sentiment for virtue is already provided by

Nature. In Vol. I we have tried to assess the differences, as far as premises are concerned, between those of Smith and those of Shaftesbury and Hutcheson, and the implications of these differences for our subject (see Vol. I: 240, 242.).

The idea that the general welfare will best be served by permitting each person to pursue his own interests, also looms large in Smith's *Wealth of Nation*. The capitalist, for example, trying to promote his own interests, works willy-nilly to satisfy the needs of others, by producing and selling the goods which satisfy the needs of the greatest number of people. Though Smith recognized the different impacts that different customs and fashions may have on the mode of operation of the moral sentiments, he seems nonetheless to suggest a static kind of social psychology. The latter is assured, according to Smith, by an inherent tendency of the moral sentiments to overcome aberrations. Thus justice, though a moral sentiment, is a sentiment that needs to be strengthened by "rules of justice"; men in fact, have been endowed with the propensity to formulate such rules on the basis of their experiences. Altogether, the moral sentiments operate at different levels of intensity, depending on the "distance" of the external stimuli which impinge upon them. Since the transactions which occur in the market are, as it were, at an extreme distance from each other, there is a limited occasion for any moral sentiments other than the rules of justice to come into operation. By analogy, the rules of conduct apply to the passions, the impact of which may vary according to the closeness of the relationship and the proximity between individuals. In both cases Smith tried to show how the sentiments operate to *socialize* the individual and how the rules operate to assure the maintenance of a social harmonious fabric.

Among other great achievements, Smith has been credited with giving rhetoric a "new look." Deviating from the reverential spirit which the entire rhetorical doctrine enjoyed, he is said to have developed a "theory of communication" (Hogan 1984). From the notes on his lectures on rhetoric (1762, 1763) it emerges that Smith thought that all types of discourse share the goal of the effective transfer of ideas and attitudes to different kinds of audiences in order to achieve different aims. Thus the traditional notion of rhetoric as persuasive speaking became only one of Smith's four classes of communication — historical, poetical, scientific and oratorical. Most important, his prescription for the historian challenged the idea of objectivity by advocating an "indirect description" of the emotions and sentiments of the historical actors. By describing the sentiments of historical actors in various situations, the historian, argued

Smith, could evoke the sympathy of readers with historical actors and allow them to assess their situations by generalizing about right and wrong from historical examples which go beyond their own limited experiences. The analysis of Smith's "indirect description," says Hogan, reveals that Smith aimed at "replicating the manner in which the mind actually comprehends events" (p. 78).

Causes, therefore, must be made clear in order to understand effects. Historical facts, according to Smith, become intelligible only when those who produced them are understood. The description of cause, therefore, should always precede that of the event, though the succession of time should be followed as much as possible given this requirement (p. 83). Smith clearly considered the mere narration of an event inadequate; only indirect description, he maintained, can bring out the effects of history. "Smithian history," says Hogan, "is a human history... a history of perceptions and passions." Smith seemed to have preferred this kind of history, continues Hogan, because he believed 1) that moral judgements stem from "sensations in a multitude of discrete situations" and 2) that the stability of moral rules can be explained through the theory which deems ethical judgement to be "the product of immediate sensations" (pp. 86-91). Altogether the classes of discourse, according to Smith, differ from each other in terms of ends, materials and styles of writing. The ends of the various discourses obviously involve the *intent* of the author, whether he wishes to persuade, entertain or instruct. The formal distinction between prose and verse, accordingly, becomes less important than the distinction between, say, fictional and non-fictional discourse. Thus the goal of instruction, for example, dictates that the materials of history be factual, whereas story tellers may enjoy the freedom of invention provided that the reader is able to recognize the assigned aim of the discourse. The style of writing is likewise affected by the kind of discourse to which it belongs, the aim of which differs from each other. It seems at this point that Smith owes a great deal to Beattie whose writings he knew. His debt to the latter is revealed also in several arguments he developed with regard to music (see our annotations to Smith, particularly 17, 19 and 22). Though Beattie's discussion of historical vs. fictional writing is very similar to that of Smith's, it lacks the latter's sophisticated attitude towards narration at large. Thus history, for example, shares with a well contrived story the narrative style which is distinguished from the "argumentative style" of scientific discourse. In short, the different media differ from each other in the materials they employ as well as in the styles appropriate for each.

For most people familiar with the name of Adam Smith it will come as a surprise to discover that he wrote an essay concerning "The Imitative Arts," trying to delve into the "nature of that imitation." However, given all that was said above and the interdependency which characterizes his work, Smith's aesthetic concerns no longer come as a surprise and one would expect him to start his investigation of the imitative arts from a normative starting point. Moreover, given his novel way of thinking, one would expect Smith to introduce changes in the entrenched legacy of mimesis. Smith does both. As in his other works he attempts to elicit the *nature* and different *modes* of imitation, rather than dwell on abstract principles. Through establishing the "distance" between the original object and the imitating medium, he aims to expose the different modes which enable the "overcoming" of the discrepancies between the two. Thus Smith, in his own unique way, arrives at a Lessing-like conclusion that each artistic medium dictates its subject matter, for he observed that their aims, materials and styles were integrally related to the abilities and possibilities of the medium. The artistic experience depends on the audience's awareness of its participation in a "make believe" situation in which they are allowed to assess the success of the overcoming of the disparity between the real and the fictive by comprehending the manner in which it is produced. Art invariably rests on the unique way in which a work of art solves the problem of disparity. Smith, as expected, turns this deciphering activity concerning art into a normative part of aesthetic contemplation.

Music, as it turns out, is a totally fabricated art. Being however "unnatural" is what makes music potentially the most artistic of all arts, (given Smith's disparity theory). Moreover, music is able to differentiate among different sentiments once designated by a text. This ability of music contributes to clarify any narrative in which the individual psychology of a protagonist is central. At the same time, since music has no model in nature, it is an autonomous, self-contained art, dependent on the structural relations of its parts. While the subject of a poem or a picture is not a part of either, "the subject of a composition of instrumental music *is* a part of that composition." Given the dictates of music, it may assist the imitative arts, but in itself, Smith concludes, it is not an imitative art. Music needs no extra musical content in order to cohere. No wonder Smith in his essay on the arts devotes its largest portion to this independent art.

OF THE

NATURE OF THAT IMITATION

WHICH TAKES PLACE IN WHAT ARE CALLED

THE IMITATIVE ARTS.

NATURE OF THAT IMITATION

WHICH TAKES PLACE IN WHAT ARE CALLED

THE IMITATIVE ARTS

PART I

THE most perfect imitation of an object of any kind must in all cases, it is evident, be another object of the same kind, made as exactly as possible after the same model. What, for example, would be the perfect imitation of the carpet which now lies before me? Another carpet, certainly, wrought as exactly as possible after the same pattern. But, whatever might be the merit or beauty of this second carpet it would not be supposed to derive any from the circumstance of its having been made in imitation of the first. This circumstance of its being not an original, but a copy, would even be considered as some diminution of that merit; a greater or smaller, in proportion as the object was of a nature to lay claim to a greater or smaller degree of admiration. It would not much diminish the merit of a common carpet, because in such trifling objects, which at best can lay claim to so little beauty or merit of any kind, we do not always think it worth while to affect originality: it would diminish a good deal that of a carpet of very exquisite workmanship. In objects of still greater importance, this exact, or, as it would be called, this servile imitation would be considered as the most unpardonable blemish. To build another St. Peter's, or St. Paul's church, of exactly the same dimensions, proportions, and ornaments with the present buildings at Rome, or London, would be supposed to argue such a miserable barrenness of genius and invention as would disgrace the most expensive magnificence.[1]

The exact resemblance of the correspondent parts of the same object is frequently considered as a beauty, and the want of it as a deformity; as in the correspondent members of the human body, in the opposite wings of the same building, in the opposite trees of the same alley, in the correspondent compartments of the same piece of carpet-work, or of the same flower-garden, in the chairs or tables which stand in the correspondent parts of the same room, &c. But in objects of the same kind, which in other respects are regarded as altogether separate and unconnected, this exact resemblance is seldom considered as a beauty, nor the want of it as a deformity. A man, and in the same manner a horse, is handsome or ugly, each of them, on account of his own intrinsic beauty or deformity, without any regard to their resembling or not resembling, the one, another man, or the other, another horse. A set of coach-horses, indeed, is supposed

1. Smith's treatise on the imitative arts, like Twining's, deals with the concept of imitation, its various uses, and other key concepts related to it. Like Twining, Smith begins from a normative starting point, only to deviate from it. However, his normative point is different, for it is divorced from the legacy of mimesis. Looking for the strictest case of imitation, Smith was bound to begin with works of art which imitate other works of art, for only these fully qualify as "perfect imitations" i.e. "copies." [What makes a copy a copy is of course an important question which he, in fact, does not deal with. It is worth noting that imitation in the sense of "art imitating art" was common in Renaissance theories though it was limited to chosen models exemplifying highest aesthetic criteria (Lee 1940/1967: 11). In this latter sense it also appears in Jacob.]

Concerned as he was with economic theory and aware of the potential increase at the time, in the production of works of art, Smith introduced terms which stem from this theory. Thus 'merit,' 'value' and 'originality' became relevant to the assessment of imitation. With the aid of these terms Smith was able to distinguish between works of art which imitate nature and those which copy other works. According to him, the value of the former increases, the more successful the imitation is, whereas the merit of the latter decreases. Originality, in other words, equals value and is by definition related to the traditional concept of imitation, which paradoxically comprises invention.

to be handsomer when they are all exactly matched; but each horse is, in this case, considered not as a separated and unconnected object, or as a whole by himself, but as a part of another whole, to the other parts of which he ought to bear a certain correspondence: Separated from the set, he derives neither beauty from his resemblance, nor deformity from his unlikeness to the other horses which compose it.[2]

Even in the correspondent parts of the same object, we frequently require no more than a resemblance in the general outline. If the inferior members of those correspondent parts are too minute to be seen distinctly, without a separate and distinct examination of each part by itself, as a separate and unconnected object, we should sometimes even be displeased if the resemblance was carried beyond this general outline. In the correspondent parts of a room we frequently hang pictures of the same size; those pictures, however, resemble one another in nothing but the frame, or, perhaps, in the general character of the subject: If the one is a landscape, the other is a landscape too; if the one represents a religious or a Bacchanalian subject, its companion represents another of the same kind. Nobody ever thought of repeating the same picture in each correspondent frame. The frame, and the general character of two or three pictures, is as much as the eye can comprehend at one view, or from one station. Each picture, in order to be seen distinctly, and understood thoroughly, must be viewed from a particular station, and examined by itself as a separate and unconnected object. In a hall or portico, adorned with statues, the nitches, or perhaps the pedestals, may exactly resemble one another, but the statues are always different. Even the masks which are sometimes carried upon the different key-stones of the same arcade, or of the correspondent doors and windows of the same front, though

——— ᴜᴚ ———

2. The first paragraph already implies that resemblance is a potent tool with which to assess imitations. Here Smith distinguishes between internal resemblance, related to the design of the object, and full resemblances across objects. The former is intrinsic to beauty while the latter, as he has already told us, testifies to a lack of invention. The value of resemblance, in other words, is context-dependent while beauty is independent of pre-established models.

they may all resemble one another in the general outline, yet
each of them has always its own peculiar features, and a grimace
of its own. There are some Gothic buildings in which the correspondent windows resemble one another only in the general
outline, and not in the smaller ornaments and subdivisions.
These are different in each, and the architect had considered
them as too minute to be seen distinctly, without a particular and
separate examination of each window by itself, as a separate and
unconnected object. A variety of this sort, however, I think, is not
agreeable. In objects which are susceptible only of a certain inferior order of beauty such as the frames of pictures, the nitches or
the pedestals of statues, &c. there seems frequently to be affectation in the study of variety, of which the merit is scarcely ever
sufficient to compensate the want of that perspicuity and distinctness, of that easiness to be comprehended and remembered,
which is the natural effect of exact uniformity. In a portico of the
Corinthian or Ionic order, each column resembles every other,
not only in the general outline, but in all the minutest ornaments;
though some of them, in order to be seen distinctly, may require
a separate and distinct examination in each column, and in the
entablature of each intercolumnation. In the inlaid tables, which,
according to the present fashion, are sometimes fixed in the correspondent parts of the same room, the pictures only are different
in each. All the other more frivolous and fanciful ornaments are
commonly, so far at least as I have observed the fashion, the same
in them all. Those ornaments, however, in order to be seen distinctly, require a separate and distinct examination of each table.[3]

——————— ✂ ———————

3. Smith's method gains momentum as he proceeds. Each further qualification yields
new aesthetic criteria. Thus the concept of design, which was introduced in the previous paragraph, blossoms into broad aesthetic criteria which include balance, symmetry, "rhythm," completion, etc. Distinguishing between general and particular
designs, Smith succeeds in showing how the former can tolerate copies while the latter requires individuality. This distinction is of major aesthetic value, for when inter-
changed it may produce either boredom or "affectation." In the third part of the present essay which was not included in our selection, Smith makes use of the concept
of affectation to differentiate between "walking and speaking" and "dancing and
singing." Overdoing, he implies there, is likewise a question of context; what is essential to the artistic frame may seem affected in a non-artistic context.

The extraordinary resemblance of two natural objects, of twins, for example, is regarded as a curious circumstance; which, though it does not increase, yet does not diminish the beauty of either, considered as a separate and unconnected object. But the exact resemblance of two productions of art, seems to be always considered as some diminution of the merit of at least one of them; as it seems to prove, that one of them, at least, is a copy either of the other, or of some other original. One may say, even of the copy of the picture, that it derives its merit, not so much from its resemblance to the original, as from its resemblance to the object which the original was meant to resemble. The owner of the copy, so far from setting any high value upon its resemblance to the original, is often anxious to destroy any value or merit which it might derive from this circumstance. He is often anxious to persuade both himself and other people that it is not a copy, but an original, of which what passes for the original is only a copy. But, whatever merit a copy may derive from its resemblance to the original, an original can certainly derive none from the resemblance of its copy.

But though a production of art seldom derives any merit from its resemblance to another object of the same kind, it frequently derives a great deal from its resemblance to an object of a different kind, whether that object be a production of art or of nature. A painted cloth, the work of some laborious Dutch artist, so curiously shaded and coloured as to represent the pile and softness of a woollen one, might derive some merit from its resemblance even to the sorry carpet which now lies before me. The copy might, and probably would, in this case, be of much greater value than the original. But if this carpet was represented as spread, either upon a floor or upon a table, and projecting from the back ground of the picture, with exact observation of perspective, and of light and shade, the merit of the imitation would be still greater.

In Painting, a plain surface of one kind is made to resemble, not only a plain surface of another, but all the three dimensions of a solid substance. In Statuary and Sculpture, a solid substance of one kind, is made to resemble a solid substance of another. The disparity between the object imitating, and the object imitated, is much greater in the one art than in the other; and the pleasure arising from the imitation seems to be greater in proportion as this disparity is greater.

In Painting, the imitation frequently pleases, though the original object be indifferent, or even offensive. In Statuary and Sculpture it is otherwise. The imitation seldom pleases, unless the original object be in a very high degree either great, or beautiful, or interesting. A butcher's stall, or a kitchen-dresser, with the objects which they commonly present, are not certainly the happiest subjects, even for Painting. They have, however, been represented with so much care and success by some Dutch masters, that it is impossible to view the pictures without some degree of pleasure. They would be most absurd subjects for Statuary or Sculpture, which are, however, capable of representing them. The picture of a very ugly or deformed man, such as Aesop, or Scarron, might not make a disagreeable piece of furniture. The statue certainly would. Even a vulgar ordinary man or woman, engaged in a vulgar ordinary action, like what we see with so much pleasure in the pictures of Rembrant, would be too mean a subject for Statuary. Jupiter, Hercules, and Apollo, Venus and Diana, the Nymphs and the Graces, Bacchus, Mercury, Antinous and Meleager, the miserable death of Laocoon, the melancholy fate of the children of Niobe, the Wrestlers, the fighting, the dying gladiator, the figures of gods and goddesses, of heroes and heroines, the most perfect forms of the human body, placed either in the noblest attitudes, or in the most interesting situations which the human imagination is capable of conceiving, are the proper, and therefore have always been the favourite subjects of Statuary: that art cannot, without degrading itself, stoop to represent any thing that is offensive, or mean, or even indifferent. Painting is not so disdainful; and, though capable of representing the noblest objects, it can, without forfeiting its title to please, submit to imitate those of a much more humble nature. The merit of the imitation alone, and without any merit in the imitated object, is capable of supporting the dignity of Painting: it cannot support that of Statuary. There would seem, therefore, to be more merit in the one species of imitation than in the other.[4]

In Statuary, scarcely any drapery is agreeable. The best of the ancient statues were either altogether naked or almost naked; and those of which any considerable part of the body is covered, are represented as clothed in wet linen—a species of clothing which most certainly never was agreeable to the fashion of any country. This drapery too is drawn so tight, as to express beneath its narrow foldings the exact form and outline of any limb, and almost of every muscle of the body. The clothing which thus approached the nearest to no clothing at all, had, it seems, in the judgment of the great artists of antiquity, been that which was most suitable to Statuary. A great painter of the Roman school,

------- ✍ -------

4. Although Smith's preoccupation with imitation reveals an Aristotelian bent, the underlying premise of increasing the "distance" between the original object and its imitations recalls the number of steps Plato places between a work of art and its a priori idea — between mere appearance and the truly real. According to Smith, however, the idea (i.e. the invention) is embedded *in* the work of art; in fact, that is precisely what makes it original. Moreover, the imitation diminishes the value of the imitated object (Plato's second degree of "distance").

Smith turns Plato upside down, for he instills the ideas within the arts themselves, not in their antecedents. This involves a reassessment of the nature of resemblances, since the creative effort required for their *achievement* is of higher value than that of the models upon which they are based; a reassessment of this kind constitutes, in fact, the major part of Smith's aesthetic enquiry, which comprises a thorough investigation of the ways in which resemblances are achieved. The merit of the work of art is gauged by its successful achievement of resemblances. Achieving resemblance, Smith thus implies, is a kind of "problem solving," in which "the disparity between the imitating object and the object imitated" has to be overcome. Moreover, the greater the disparity between the two (i.e. the greater the problem) the greater the challenge and the achievement, when it is obtained. Thus, painting ranks higher than sculpture, since it renders three dimensions in two. Hence also the differences in the choice of subject-matters that is suitable to the constraints of each of the media. What all the arts share is the fact that their merit resides in the *making*, i.e. in the way they proceed to realize the ideas which they intend to impart. Thus, the beauty of the original object, according to Smith, is irrelevant to the merit of the work of art which imitates it. This last assertion runs contrary to the traditional theory of imitation which is still echoed by some of our writers.

who had formed his manner almost entirely upon the study of
the ancient statues, imitated at first their drapery in his pictures;
but he soon found that in Painting it had the air of meanness and
poverty, as if the persons who wore it could scarce afford clothes
enough to cover them; and that larger folds, and a looser and
more flowing drapery, were more suitable to the nature of his
art. In Painting, the imitation of so very inferior an object as a suit
of clothes is capable of pleasing; and, in order to give this object
all the magnificence of which it is capable, it is necessary that the
folds should be large, loose, and flowing. It is not necessary in
Painting that the exact form and outline of every limb, and
almost of every muscle of the body, should be expressed
beneath the folds of the drapery; it is sufficient if these are so disposed as to indicate in general the situation and attitude of the
principal limbs. Painting, by the mere force and merit of its imitation, can venture, without the hazard of displeasing, to substitute, upon many occasions, the inferior in the room of the superior object, by making the one, in this manner cover and entirely conceal a great part of the other. Statuary can seldom venture
to do this, but with the utmost reserve and caution; and the same
drapery, which is noble and magnificent in the one art, appears
clumsy and awkward in the other. Some modern artists, however, have attempted to introduce into Statuary the drapery which
is peculiar to Painting. It may not, perhaps, upon every occasion,
be quite so ridiculous as the marble periwigs in Westminster
Abbey: but, if it does not always appear clumsy and awkward, it
is at best always insipid and uninteresting.[5]

------------ ⟋ ------------

5. By Smith's time the Neoplatonic notion that the arts differ from each other in the
ways they clad the same ideas, had already given way to the Lessingian conception —
though Lessing was not the only one to express it, of course — that each art dictates
its own subject matter (see Vol. I). To this new notion, Smith contributes yet another
angle by separating the issue of medium from the specific aesthetic desiderata which
are still paramount in Lessing who, despite his debate with Winkelmann the classicist,
is committed to the Greek ideal of beauty. Though Smith's analysis of sculpture still
adheres to a very specific conception of that medium (a conception which has long
been superseded by other conceptions), he provides more general and flexible theoretical tools which would deal with a variety of stylistic choices.

It is not the want of colouring which hinders many things from pleasing in Statuary, which please in Painting; it is the want of that degree of disparity between the imitating and the imitated object, which is necessary, in order to render interesting the imitation of an object which is itself not interesting. Colouring, when added to Statuary, so far from increasing, destroys almost entirely the pleasure which we receive from the imitation; because it takes away the great source of that pleasure, the disparity between the imitating and the imitated object. That one solid and coloured object should exactly resemble another solid and coloured object, seems to be a matter of no great wonder or admiration. A painted statue, though it certainly may resemble a human figure much more exactly than any statue which is not painted, is generally acknowledged to be a disagreeable, and even an offensive object; and so far are we from being pleased with this superior likeness, that we are never satisfied with it; and, after viewing it again and again, we always find that it is not equal to what we are disposed to imagine it might have been: though it should seem to want scarce any thing but the life, we could not pardon it for thus wanting what it is altogether impossible it should have. The works of Mrs. Wright, a self-taught artist of great merit, are perhaps more perfect in this way than any thing I have ever seen. They do admirably well to be seen now and then as a show; but the best of them we should find, if brought home to our own house, and placed in a situation where it was to come after into view, would make, instead of an ornamental, a most offensive piece of household furniture. Painted statues, accordingly, are universally reprobated, and we scarce ever meet with them. To colour the eyes of statues is not altogether so uncommon: even this, however, is disapproved by all good judges. "I cannot bear it," (a gentleman used to say, of great knowledge and judgment in this art,) "I cannot bear it; I always want them to speak to me."

Artificial fruits and flowers sometimes imitate so exactly the natural objects which they represent, that they frequently deceive us. We soon grow weary of them, however; and, though they

seem to want nothing but the freshness and the flavour of natural fruits and flowers, we cannot pardon them, in the same
manner, for thus wanting what it is altogether impossible they
should have. But we do not grow weary of a good flower and
fruit painting. We do not grow weary of the foliage of the
Corinthian capital, or of the flowers which sometimes ornament
the frize of that order. Such imitations, however, never deceive
us; their resemblance to the original objects is always much inferior to that of artificial fruits and flowers. Such as it is, however,
we are contented with it; and, where there is such disparity
between the imitating and the imitated objects, we find that it is
as great as it can be, or as we expect that it should be. Paint that
foliage and those flowers with the natural colours, and, instead
of pleasing more, they will please much less. The resemblance,
however, will be much greater; but the disparity between the
imitating and the imitated objects will be so much less, that even
this superior resemblance will not satisfy us. Where the disparity is very great, on the contrary, we are often contented with the
most imperfect resemblance; with the very imperfect resemblance, for example both as to figure and colour, of fruits and
flowers in shell-work.[6]

It may be observed, however, that, though in Sculpture the
imitation of flowers and foliage pleases as an ornament of archi-

6. That Smith was unaware of the fact that Greek sculptures and temples were colored
does not detract from the basic notion of his argument. Here, again, he applies his concept of disparity to the "incompleteness" of the work of art, though in a new sense.
Smith resorts to the imagination, not in order to assist in "rounding up a figure" (as did
Jacob), but as a participant in the *illusion* that causes us to perceive vitality in that
which declares itself as lacking it. This brings to the fore the notion of deception. What
was held in great esteem by ancient and some Renaissance scholars, i.e. the work of
art's ability to deceive (e.g. the grapes of Appeles), is considered by Smith to be inartis-
tic. Works of art should retain an overt disparity with their represented object in order
to allow the beholder to feel that he is participating in a kind of "make believe." The
more the imitating object allows for the illusion to take place (as he will explain later),
despite the avowed disparity between it and the imitated object, the greater the artistic achievement. This kind of Aristotelian argument, contributed no doubt to the rise
of modern art, which altogether discarded resemblance, even the kind which Smith
still insisted on, as an aesthetic criterion.

tecture, as a part of the dress which is to set off the beauty of a different and a more important object, it would not please alone, or as a separate and unconnected object, in the same manner as a fruit and flower painting pleases. Flowers and foliage, how elegant and beautiful soever, are not sufficiently interesting; they have not dignity enough if I may say so, to be proper subjects for a piece of Sculpture, which is to please alone, and not as the ornamental appendage of some other object.

In Tapestry and Needle-work, in the same manner as in Painting, a plain surface is sometimes made to represent all the three dimensions of a solid substance. But both the shuttle of the weaver, and the needle of the embroiderer, are instruments of imitation so much inferior to the pencil of the painter, that we are not surprised to find a proportionable inferiority in their productions. We have all more or less experience that they usually are much inferior; and, in appreciating a piece of Tapestry or Needle-work, we never compare the imitation of either with that of a good picture, for it never could stand that comparison, but with that of other pieces of Tapestry or Needle-work. We take into consideration, not only the disparity between the imitating and the imitated object, but the awkwardness of the instruments of imitation; and if it is as well as any thing that can be expected from these, if it is better than the greater part of what actually comes from them, we are often not only contented but highly pleased.

A good painter will often execute in a few days a subject which would employ the best tapestry-weaver for many years; though, in proportion to his time, therefore, the latter is always much worse paid than the former, yet his work in the end comes commonly much dearer to market. The great expence of good Tapestry, the circumstance which confines it to the palaces of princes and great lords, gives it, in the eyes of the greater part of people, an air of riches and magnificence, which contributes still further to compensate the imperfection of its imitation. In arts which address themselves, not to the prudent and the wise, but to the rich and the great, to the proud and the vain, we ought not to wonder if the appearance of great expence, of being what few people can purchase, of being one of the surest characteristics of great fortune, should often stand in the place of exquisite beauty, and contribute equally to recommend their productions. As the idea of expence seems often to embellish, so that of cheapness seems as frequently to tarnish the lustre even of very agreeable objects. The difference between real and false jewels is what even the experienced eye of a jeweller can sometimes with difficulty distinguish. Let an unknown lady, however, come into a public assembly, with a head-dress which appears to be very richly adorned with diamonds, and let a jeweller only whisper in our ear that they are false stones, not only the lady will immediately sink in our imagination from the rank of a princess to that of a very ordinary woman, but the head-dress, from an object of the most splendid magnificence, will at once become an impertinent piece of tawdry and tinsel finery.[7]

It was some years ago the fashion to ornament a garden with yew and holly trees, clipped into the artificial shapes of pyramids, and columns, and vases, and obelisks. It is now the fash-

——————— *Un* ———————

7. What seems to be a kind of commonsensical description of artistic techniques and their assessment harbors a few critical points. First Smith broadens his concept of the dictates of the medium by including the material and tools employed. Though a needle may increase the disparity between the imitation and the imitated, it cannot compete with the more convincing "painterly" quality of a pencil, for example. The principle of disparity, in other words, can not be considered as a necessary and sufficient condition for artistic achievement, unless the disparity is successfully overcome. Smith thus emphasizes, from yet another angle, how the media affect their subject matter, in line with their possibilities and limitations. To judge one art by the achievements of another, therefore, is out of place (as Voltaire [1772] also insisted in the debate over the comparisons between opera and drama). Smith is also aware of the fact that the judgment of art does not rest only on pure aesthetic considerations. Thus, scarcity or cost, says Smith the economist, may affect aesthetic judgment. (Thorstein Veblen, another great economist, might have applied his "conspicuous consumption" theory to Smith's contention with regard to the tapestries of the rich.) What seems at first to apply only to certain strata of society, turns out to be part and parcel of a general evaluation of objects of art. Although Smith's examples are from the field of economics, the principles he exemplifies are much wider: What we *know* about a work of art is not extraneous to our perception and evaluation of it. This makes Smith an "intentionalist"; little did he know that intentionalism would yet engender hot debates precisely with regard to the evaluation of works of art.

ion to ridicule this taste as unnatural. The figure of a pyramid or obelisk, however, is not more unnatural to a yew-tree than to a block of porphyry or marble. When the yew-tree is presented to the eye in this artificial shape, the gardener does not mean that it should be understood to have grown in that shape: he means, first, to give it the same beauty of regular figure which pleases so much in porphyry and marble; and, secondly, to imitate in a growing tree the ornaments of those precious materials: he means to make an object of one kind resemble another object of a very different kind; and to the original beauty of figure to join the relative beauty of imitation: but the disparity between the imitating and the imitated object is the foundation of the beauty of imitation. It is because the one object does not naturally resemble the other, that we are so much pleased with it, when by art it is made to do so. The shears of the gardener, it may be said, indeed, are very clumsy instruments of Sculpture. They are so, no doubt, when employed to imitate the figures of men, or even of animals. But in the simple and regular forms of pyramids, vases, and obelisks, even the shears of the gardener do well enough. Some allowance too is naturally made for the necessary imperfection of the instrument, in the same manner as in Tapestry and Needle-work. In short, the next time you have an opportunity of surveying those out-of-fashion ornaments, endeavour only to let yourself alone, and to restrain for a few minutes the foolish passion for playing the critic, and you will be sensible that they are not without some degree of beauty; that they give the air of neatness and correct culture at least to the whole garden; and that they are unlike what the "retired leisure, that" (as Milton says) "in trim gardens takes his pleasure," might be amused with. What then, it may be said, has brought them into such universal disrepute among us? In a pyramid or obelisk of marble, we know that the materials are expensive, and that the labour which wrought them into that shape must have been still more so. In a pyramid or obelisk of yew, we know that the materials could cost very little, and the labour still less. The former are ennobled by their expence; the latter degraded by their cheapness. In the cabbage-garden of a tallow-chandler we may sometimes perhaps have seen as many columns and vases, and other ornaments in yew, as there are in marble and porphyry at Versailles: it is this vulgarity which has disgraced them. The rich and the great the proud and the vain, will not admit into their gardens an ornament which the meanest of the people can have as well as they. The taste for these ornaments came originally from France; where, notwithstanding that inconstancy of fashion with which we sometimes reproach the natives of that country, it still continues in good repute. In France, the condition of the inferior ranks of people is seldom so happy as it frequently is in England; and you will there seldom find even pyramids and obelisks of yew in the garden of a tallow-chandler. Such ornaments, not having in that country been degraded by their vulgarity, have not yet been excluded from the gardens of princes and great lords.

The works of the great masters in Statuary and Painting, it is to be observed, never produce their effect by deception. They never are, and it never is intended that they should be mistaken for the real objects which they represent. Painted Statuary may sometimes deceive an inattentive eye: proper Statuary never does. The little pieces of perspective in Painting, which it is intended should please by deception, represent always some very simple, as well as insignificant, object; a roll of paper, for example, or the steps of a staircase, in the dark corner of some passage or gallery. They are generally the works too of some very inferior artists. After being seen once, and producing the little surprise which it is meant they should excite, together with the mirth which commonly accompanies it, they never please more, but appear ever after insipid and tiresome.[8]

——————— ℒ ———————

8. Great artists, Smith tells us, never produce effects by deception; their works never aspire to be "mistaken for the real." This observation serves to reinforce the theory expounded earlier in his essay, concerning the standing of copies in relation to originals. "Sculptured gardens," accordingly, no matter how pleasing, are in fact deceptive, for they literally copy another art, depriving their aesthetic effect of an "invention" of their own, i.e., of a *built-in* permanent-key attribute (which is also related to subtlety of execution and the overcoming of disparity). This also explains why the initial surprise evoked in such cases seems to wane after a while, leaving the beholder uninterested.

The proper pleasure which we derive from those two imitative arts, so far from being the effect of deception, is altogether incompatible with it. That pleasure is founded altogether upon our wonder at seeing an object of one kind represent so well an object of a very different kind, and upon our admiration of the art which surmounts so happily that disparity which Nature had established between them. The nobler works of Statuary and Painting appear to us a sort of wonderful phaenomena, differing in this respect from the Wonderful phaenomena of Nature, that they carry, as it were, their own explication along with them, and demonstrate, even to the eye, the way and manner in which they are produced. The eye, even of an unskilful spectator, immediately discerns, in some measure, how it is that a certain modification of figure in Statuary, and of brighter and darker colours in Painting, can represent, with so much truth and vivacity, the actions, passions, and behaviour of men, as well as a great variety of other objects. The pleasing wonder of ignorance is accompanied with the still more pleasing satisfaction of science. We wonder and are amazed at the effect; and we are pleased ourselves, and happy to find that we can comprehend, in some measure, how that wonderful effect is produced.

A good looking-glass represents the objects which are set before it with much more truth and vivacity than either Statuary or Painting. But, though the science of optics may explain to the understanding, the looking-glass itself does not at all demonstrate to the eye how this effect is brought about. It may excite the wonder of ignorance; and in a clown, who had never beheld a looking-glass before, I have seen that wonder rise almost to rapture and extasy; but it cannot give the satisfaction of science. In all looking-glasses the effects are produced by the same means, applied exactly in the same manner. In every different statue and picture the effects are produced; though by similar, yet not by the same means; and those means too are applied in a different manner in each. Every good statue and picture is a fresh wonder, which at the same time carries, in some measure, its own explication along with it. After a little use and experience, all looking- glasses cease to be wonders altogether; and even the ignorant become so familiar with them, as not to think that their effects require any explication. A looking-glass, besides, can represent only present objects; and, when the wonder is once fairly over, we choose, in all cases, rather to contemplate the substance than to gaze at the shadow. One's own face becomes then the most agreeable object which a looking-glass can represent to us, and the only object which we do not soon grow weary with looking at; it is the only present object of which we can see only the shadow: whether handsome or ugly, whether old or young, it is the face of a friend always, of which the features correspond exactly with whatever sentiment, emotion, or passion we may happen at that moment to feel.[9]

In Statuary, the means by which the wonderful effect is brought about appear more simple and obvious than in Painting; where the disparity between the imitating and the imitated object being much greater, the art which can conquer that greater disparity appears evidently, and almost to the eye, to be founded upon a much deeper science, or upon principles much more abstruse and profound. Even in the meanest subjects we can often trace with pleasure the ingenious means by which Painting surmounts this disparity. But we cannot do this in Statuary, because the disparity not being so great, the means do not

---

9. The pleasure we derive from works of art, explains Smith, stems not only from the *awareness* that they are not the real thing, but from comprehending the *manner* in which they are produced. The latter may be discerned in the work itself, and it is this which creates its permanent wonder. Unlike artistic imitation, the mirror (representing natural phenomena) does not reveal *how* the reflection is brought about, thus shifting interest from the "wonder" of reflection to that which is reflected. Moreover, while mirrors repeat the same wonder again and again, each work of art creates its own wonder. In other words, a work of art invariably rests on the unique way in which it "solves the problem" of disparity, suspending, as it were, the *make*-belief without destroying it. This suspension is entrenched in the work itself, granting art its potency while sustaining, at one and the same time, the interest of its beholders.

Hutcheson was first among the British thinkers to point out this double nature of the artistic experience (see Vol. II: 62), but only with Smith was it fully stated. Embedded in an elaborate theoretical framework, it was able to render the deciphering activity concerning art into a normative part of aesthetic contemplation.

appear so ingenious. And it is upon this account, that in Painting we are often delighted with the representation of many things, which in Statuary would appear insipid, tiresome, and not worth the looking at.

It ought to be observed, however, that though in Statuary the art of imitation appears, in many respects, inferior to what it is in Painting, yet, in a room ornamented with both statues and pictures of nearly equal merit, we shall generally find that the statues draw off our eye from the pictures. There is generally but one, or little more than one, point of view from which a picture can be seen with advantage, and it always presents to the eye precisely the same object. There are many different points of view from which a statue may be seen with equal advantage, and from each it presents a different object. There is more variety in the pleasure which we receive from a good statue, than in that which we receive from a good picture; and one statue may frequently be the subject of many good pictures or drawings, all different from one another. The shadowy relief and projection of a picture, besides, is much flattened, and seems almost to vanish away altogether, when brought into comparison with the real and solid body which stands by it. How nearly soever these two arts may seem to be a-kin, they accord so very ill with one another, that their different productions ought, perhaps, scarce ever to be seen together.[10]

———— ⚬ ————

10. Though sculpture is a "lesser science" in terms of the disparity principle, Smith tells us that it has the advantage of being (literally) seen from different angles, thereby granting sculpture a variety which painting lacks. Letting the beholder choose his "point of view" however, reduces the control of the artist, thus tilting the balance to painting again. Moreover, if we adhere to Smith's own argument, "variety" and "advantage" should not be equalized, for the former applies to all objects regardless of kind, whereas the latter applies only to art. This, in fact, follows from Smith's own argument concerning the three-dimensionality of sculpture which reduces the desired disparity between the imitation and the object imitated, by allowing the imitation to retain one of the key *natural* attributes of the object imitated.

This minor debate with Smith also reveals that the disparity argument needs further elaboration, for the art of sculpture cannot be so easily disparaged. On the whole,

(CONT.)

Part II

AFTER the pleasures which arise from the gratification of the bodily appetites, there seem to be none more natural to man than Music and Dancing. In the progress of art and improvement they are, perhaps, the first and earliest pleasures of his own invention; for those which arise from the gratification of the bodily appetites cannot be said to be of his own invention. No nation has yet been discovered so uncivilized as to be altogether without them. It seems even to be amongst the most barbarous nations that the use and practice of them is both most frequent and most universal, as among the negroes of Africa and the savage tribes of America. In civilized nations, the inferior ranks of people have very little leisure, and the superior ranks have many other amusements; neither the one nor the other, therefore, can spend much of their time in Music and Dancing. Among savage nations, the great body of the people have frequently great intervals of leisure, and they have scarce any other amusement; they naturally, therefore, spend a great part of their time in almost the only one they have.

What the ancients called Rhythmus, what we call Time or Measure, is the connecting principle of those two arts; Music consisting in a succession of a certain sort of sounds, and Dancing in a succession of a certain sort of steps, gestures, and motions, regulated according to time or measure, and thereby formed into a sort of whole or system; which in the one art is called a song or tune, and in the other a dance; the time or measure of the dance corresponding always exactly with that of the song or tune which accompanies and directs it.

(CONT.)　　　　　　———— ♫ ————

Smith's deliberations, insightful and sophisticated as they are, still drag along old notions, which become stumble-blocks. Thus the heated debates of the *paragone* tradition concerning the respective superiority of each of the arts, is still part of Smith's world-view, pushing him to revise their position in his own imaginative "great chain of being" (Schueller rightly connected the traditional comparisons among the arts with the legacy of "the great chain of being" discussed by Lovejoy. See Schueller 1953). Like many of his predecessors, Smith adhered only to one yardstick according to which all the arts ought to be measured. 'Disparity,' sophisticated and novel as it might be, is only one criterion according to which to evaluate an artistic medium.

The human voice, as it is always the best, so it would naturally be the first and earliest of all musical instruments: in singing, or in the first attempts towards singing, it would naturally employ sounds as similar as possible to those which it had been accustomed to; that is, it would employ words of some kind or other, pronouncing them only in time and measure, and generally with a more melodious tone than had been usual in common conversation. Those words, however, might not, and probably would not, for a long time have any meaning, but might resemble the syllables which we make use of in *sol-faing*, or the *derry-down-down* of our common ballads; and serve only to assist the voice in forming sounds proper to be modulated into melody, and to be lengthened or shortened according to the time and measure of the tune. This rude form of vocal Music, as it is by far the most simple and obvious, so it naturally would be the first and earliest.

In the succession of ages it could not fail to occur, that in the room of those unmeaning or musical words, if I may call them so, might be substituted words which expressed some sense or meaning, and of which the pronunciation might coincide as exactly with the time and measure of the tune, as that of the musical words had done before. Hence the origin of Verse or Poetry. The Verse would for a long time be rude and imperfect. When the meaning words fell short of the measure required, they would frequently be eked out with the unmeaning ones, as is sometimes done in our common ballads. When the public ear came to be so refined as to reject, in all serious Poetry, the unmeaning words altogether, there would still be a liberty assumed of altering and corrupting, upon many occasions, the pronunciation of the meaning ones, for the sake of accommodating them to the measure. The syllables which composed them would, for this purpose, sometimes be improperly lengthened, and sometimes improperly shortened; and though no unmeaning words were made use of, yet an unmeaning syllable would sometimes be stuck to the beginning, to the end, or into the middle of a word. All these expedients we find frequently employed in the verses even of Chaucer, the father of the English Poetry. Many ages might pass away before verse was commonly com-

posed with such correctness, that the usual and proper pronunciation of the words alone, and without any other artifice, sub-
jected the voice to the observation of a time and measure, of the
same kind with the time and measure of Music.

The Verse would naturally express some sense which suited
the grave or gay, the joyous or melancholy humour of the tune
which it was sung to; being as it were blended and united with
that tune, it would seem to give sense and meaning to what otherwise might not appear to have any, or at least any which could
be clearly and distinctly understood, without the accompaniment
of such an explication.

A pantomime dance may frequently answer the same purpose,
and, by representing some adventure in love or war, may seem
to give sense and meaning to a Music which might not otherwise
appear to have any. It is more natural to mimic, by gestures and
motions, the adventures of common life, than to express them in
Verse or Poetry. The thought itself is more obvious, and the execution is much more easy. If this mimicry was accompanied by
music, it would of its own accord, and almost without any intention of doing so, accommodate, in some measure, its different
steps and movements to the time and measure of the tune; especially if the same person both sung the tune and performed the
mimicry, as is said to be frequently the case among the savage
nations of Africa and America. Pantomime Dancing might in this
manner serve to give a distinct sense and meaning to Music
many ages before the invention, or at least before the common
use of Poetry. We hear little, accordingly, of the Poetry of the savage nations of Africa and America, but a great deal of their pantomime dances.

Poetry, however, is capable of expressing many things fully
and distinctly, which Dancing either cannot represent at all, or
can represent but obscurely and imperfectly; such as the reasonings and judgments of the understandings; the ideas, fancies, and
suspicions of the imagination; the sentiments, emotions, and passions of the heart. In the power of expressing a meaning with
clearness and distinctness, Dancing is superior to Music, and
Poetry to Dancing.

Of those three Sister Arts, which originally, perhaps, went always together, and which at all times go frequently together, there are two which can subsist alone, and separate from their natural companions, and one which cannot. In the distinct observation of what the ancients called Rhythmus, of what we call Time and Measure, consists the essence both of Dancing and of Poetry or Verse; or the characteristical quality which distinguishes the former from all other motion and action, and the latter from all other discourse. But, concerning the proportion between those intervals and divisions of duration which constitute what is called time and measure, the ear, it would seem, can judge with much more precision than the eye; and Poetry, in the same manner as Music, addresses itself to the ear, whereas Dancing addresses itself to the eye. In Dancing, the rhythmus, the proper proportion, the time and measure of its motions, cannot distinctly be perceived, unless they are marked by the more distinct time and measure of Music. It is otherwise in Poetry; no accompaniment is necessary to mark the measure of good Verse. Music and Poetry, therefore, can each of them subsist alone; Dancing always requires the accompaniment of Music.[11]

———— ⚘ ————

11. The starting point of Smith's short history of the early development of the various arts is the Greek view of the "musical" arts as Plato called them in Book III of *The Republic*. (See also Lippman 1964). Like the Greeks he excludes the art of painting from his short history, viewing *Rhythmus* as the common denominator of the "sister arts" — poetry, music and dancing — or the temporal, *linear* arts, as we would call them nowadays. Smith's classification of the arts is connected with the question of origin. Unlike many of his contemporaries, he does not identify the starting point of music with the inflection of the voice. Furthermore, he does not consider music and language to have come jointly into the world, nor does he believe that music preceded language for purposes of communication.

Smith believes like Harris that, late to develop, the arts were a product of leisure. For Smith, their starting point is the rhythmic organization of sound. Language thus preceded music, lending music its articulated sounds. The exchange between the two eventually yielded prosodic construction to poetry and meaning to musical organization. Music, we learn, has only a most general and vague meaning of its own, which it has probably acquired, in the first place, from dance gestures and motion. However, though music acquires its meaning from without, it is more readily perceived, according to Smith, than is dance which requires music in order to be more "articulate."

(CONT.)

It is Instrumental Music which can best subsist apart, and separate from both Poetry and Dancing. Vocal Music, though it may, and frequently does, consist of notes which have no distinct sense or meaning, yet naturally calls for the support of Poetry. But "Music, married to immortal Verse," as Milton says, or even to words of any kind which have a distinct sense or meaning, is necessarily and essentially imitative. Whatever be the meaning of those words, though, like many of the songs of ancient Greece, as well as some of those of more modern times, they may express merely some maxims of prudence and morality, or may contain merely the simple narrative of some important event, yet even in such didactic and historical songs there will still be imitation; there will still be a thing of one kind, which by art is made to resemble a thing of a very different kind; there will still be Music imitating discourse; there will still be rhythmus and melody, shaped and fashioned into the form either of a good moral counsel, or of an amusing and interesting story.

In this first species of imitation, which being essential to, is therefore inseparable from, all such Vocal Music, there may, and there commonly is, added a second. The words may, and commonly do, express the situation of some particular person, and

———— ♌ ————

(CONT.)

It is interesting to compare Smith with Condillac and Webb. Whereas Smith overlooks the communicative power of musical gestures, Condillac is, of course, one of those who believe that music precedes natural languages as a "language of action" (see Vol. I). It is also of interest to compare Smith's theory of the historical relations between verse and music with Webb's, which is governed by different considerations. Webb's insistence on the function of monosyllables in manipulating flexible and dynamic musical movement yields a more organic picture as far the relations between meaning and rhythm are concerned.

Leaving aside the historical accuracy as well as the eighteenth-century tendency to engage in such speculative matters, Smith's insistence on temporal organization as a parameter more readily perceived is worthy of attention and, indeed, gains support from present-day cognitive studies. It should be borne in mind that Twining recognized the supremacy of vision with regard to its liability for description, relying, as it does, on conceptual schemes. Smith, by contrast, considers audition to be supreme because of its perceptual advantage. The two, of course, do not contradict each other, because they focus on different aspects. Smith himself later shows how the two are intertwined.

all the sentiments and passions which he feels from that situation. It is a joyous companion who gives vent to the gaiety and mirth with which wine, festivity, and good company inspire him. It is a lover who complains, or hopes, or fears, or despairs. It is a generous man who expresses either his gratitude for the favours, or his indignation at the injuries, which may have been done to him. It is a warrior who prepares himself to confront danger, and who provokes or defies his enemy. It is a person in prosperity who humbly returns thanks for the goodness, or one in affliction who with contrition implores the mercy and forgiveness, of that invisible Power to whom he looks up as the Director of all the events of human life. The situation may comprehend, not only one, but two, three, or more persons; it may excite in them all either similar or opposite sentiments; what is a subject of sorrow to one, being an occasion of joy and triumph another; and they may all express, sometimes separately and sometimes together, the particular way in which each of them is affected, as in a duo, trio, or a chorus.

All this it may, and it frequently has been said is unnatural; nothing being more so, than to sing when we are anxious to persuade, or in earnest to express any very serious purpose. But it should be remembered, that to make a thing of one kind resemble another thing of a very different kind, is the very circumstance which, in all the Imitative Arts, constitutes the merits of imitation; and that to shape, and as it were to bend, the measure and the melody of Music, so as to imitate the tone and the language of counsel and conversation, the accent and the style of emotion and passion, is to make a thing of one kind resemble another thing of a very different kind.[12]

——————— ♫ ———————

12. We have learned from Smith that imitation in art requires 1) an awareness of its being an imitation — that is, an awareness of the disparity between art and its objects, and 2) an awareness of the ways in which the disparity is overcome. Smith's disparity theory completely dispels the claim that accompanied the derision of opera — that it is unnatural to use song in a fictive framework as though it were speech. Moreover, it explains why Smith preferred to consider music as the art which was the last to develop. Being unnatural is what makes music potentially the most artistic of all the arts.

(CONT.)

The tone and the movements of Music, tho' naturally very different from those of conversation and passion, may, however, be so managed as to seem to resemble them. On account of the great disparity between the imitating and the imitated object, the mind in this, as in the other cases, cannot only be contented, but delighted, and even charmed and transported, with such an imperfect resemblance as can be had. Such imitative Music, therefore, when sung to words which explain and determine its meaning, may frequently appear to be a very perfect imitation. It is upon this account, that even the incomplete Music of a recitative seems to express sometimes all the sedateness and composure of serious but calm discourse, and sometimes all the exquisite sensibility of the most interesting passion. The more complete Music of an air is still superior, and, in the imitation of the more animated passions, has one great advantage over every sort of discourse, whether Prose or Poetry, which is not sung to Music. In a person who is either much depressed by grief or enlivened by joy, who is strongly affected either with love or hatred, with gratitude or resentment, with admiration or contempt, there is commonly one thought or idea which dwells upon his mind, which continually haunts him, which, when he has chaced it away, immediately returns upon him, and which in company makes him absent and inattentive. He can think but of one object, and he cannot repeat to them that object so frequently as it recurs upon him. He takes refuge in solitude, where he can with freedom either indulge the extasy or give way to the agony of the agreeable or disagreeable passion which agitates him; and where he can repeat to himself, which he does sometimes men-

(CONT.) ———— ⚘ ————

The imitated object with which music is concerned clearly derives from the text which it is called upon to accompany. While the unique role of music in the joint venture will be further clarified, relying on his previous observations, Smith can already claim that music is able to differentiate among different sentiments. This ability to separate the passions from each other is important for the unfolding of a narrative in which the psychological individuality of the protagonists is central. Not unlike historical painting the *opera seria*, with which Smith was undoubtedly familiar, did in fact concentrate on the juxtaposition of different reactions (related to the different protagonists) to a given situation.

tally, and sometimes even aloud, and almost always in the same words, the particular thought which either delights or distresses him. Neither Prose nor Poetry can venture to imitate those almost endless repetitions of passion. They may describe them as I do now, but they dare not imitate them; they would become most insufferably tiresome if they did. The Music of a passionate air not only may, but frequently does, imitate them; and it never makes its way so directly or so irresistibly to the heart as when it does so. It is upon this account that the words of an air, especially of a passionate one, though they are seldom very long, yet are scarce ever sung straight on to the end, like those of a recitative; but are almost always broken into parts, which are transposed and repeated again and again, according to the fancy or judgment of the composer. It is by means of such repetitions only, that Music can exert those peculiar powers of imitation which distinguish it, and in which it excels all the other Imitative Arts. Poetry and Eloquence, it has accordingly been often observed, produce their effect always by a connected variety and succession of different thoughts and ideas: but Music frequently produces its effects by a repetition of the same idea; and the same sense expressed in the same, or nearly the same, combination of sounds, though at first perhaps it may make scarce any impression upon us, yet, by being repeated again and again, it comes at last gradually, and by little and little, to move, to agitate, and to transport us.[13]

------------- ℔ -------------

13. The sound and movement of music may be so managed, says Smith, as to "seem" to resemble conversation and passion, despite their ostensible differences. This statement is still in line with his disparity theory. As far as he is concerned, the more music distances itself from literal resemblance to speech the better; the aria, therefore, is preferable, from an aesthetic point of view, to the recitative. To this Smith adds the profound insight, that music, once "named," i.e. having turned designative by the words to which it is sung, may create a *perfect* imitation. This paradox stems from the fact that music lacks any intrinsic resemblance to that which it aims to imitate, so that it can be "possessed" (allowing music to be especially hospitable to suggestions) by external meanings while lending them its own unique manner of unfolding. (Recall Webb's claim that "Music borrows sentiments from poetry and lends her movement.") Thus music, for example, may be perceived as imitating the *dynamics* of the passion

(CONT.)

To these powers of imitating, Music naturally, or rather necessarily, joins the happiest choice in the objects of its imitation. The sentiments and passions which Music can best imitate are those which unite and bind men together in society; the social, the decent, the virtuous, the interesting and affecting, the amiable and agreeable, the awful and respectable, the noble, elevating, and commanding passions. Grief and distress are interesting and affecting; humanity and compassion, joy and admiration, are amiable and agreeable; devotion is awful and respectable; the generous contempt of danger, the honourable indignation at injustice, are noble, elevating, and commanding. But it is these and such like passions which Music is fittest for imitating, and which it in fact most frequently imitates. They are, if I may say so, all Musical Passions; their natural tones are all clear, distinct, and almost melodious; and they naturally express themselves in a language which is distinguished by pauses at regular, and almost equal, intervals; and which, upon that account, can more easily be adapted to the regular returns of the correspondent periods of a tune. The passions, on the contrary, which drive men from one another, the unsocial, the hateful, the indecent, the vicious passions, cannot easily be imitated by Music. The voice of furious anger, for example, is harsh and discordant; its periods are all irregular, sometimes very long and sometimes very short, and distinguished by no regular pauses. The obscure and almost inarticulate grumblings of black malice and envy, the screaming outcries of dastardly fear, the hideous growlings of brutal and implacable revenge, are all equally discordant. It is with difficulty that Music can imitate any of those

(CONT.)   ———— *m* ————

felt, through the repetitions and transformations which are "natural" to musical succession, but untenable in a succession of ideas.

Though Smith is interested in the nature of the medium, his examples are invariably taken from the musical practice of his day. Thus his main argument relates to the Baroque aria which qualifies because of its motivic elaboration, on the one hand, and the functioning of the text as an overall label (following the reforms of Zeno and Metastasio, whom he himself later mentions), on the other. Smith's contention significantly contributes to the overall attempts of his contemporaries to assess *actual* symbolic ways, which were developed in music since the beginning of the seventeenth century.

passions, and the Music which does imitate them is not the most agreeable. A whole entertainment may consist, without any impropriety, of the imitation of the social and amiable passions. It would be a strange entertainment which consisted altogether in the imitation of the odious and the vicious. A single song expresses almost always some social, agreeable, or interesting passion. In an opera the unsocial and disagreeable are sometimes introduced, but it is rarely, and as discords are introduced into harmony, to set off by their contrast the superior beauty of the opposite passions. What Plato said of Virtue, that it was of all beauties the brightest, may with some sort of truth be said of the proper and natural objects of musical imitation. They are either the sentiments and passions, in the exercise of which consist both the glory and the happiness of human life, or they are those from which it derives its most delicious pleasures, and most enlivening joys; or, at the worst and the lowest, they are those by which it calls upon our indulgence and compassionate assistance to its unavoidable weaknesses, its distresses, and its misfortunes.[14]

To the merit of its imitation and to that of its happy choice in the objects which it imitates, the great merits of Statuary and

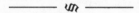

14. With a fair degree of musical sophistication, Smith continues his explanation of why music is especially suited to the imitation of the passions. Like Avison, however, he is trapped in the Platonic tradition, according to which music is supposed to fare better with the "social and amiable" passions than with the disagreeable ones. To the extent that music deviates from its benevolent tendency, Smith observes, it is only in order to create a kind of "unity amidst variety."

It is curious that Smith, who was not afraid of iconoclasm, should so blindly follow a tradition of thought which badly needed re-thinking. We have already explained that music is a synthetic art, i.e. that it invariably has to reconcile its internally established tendencies whether harmonic, contrapuntal and otherwise, in order to create a whole with a distinct import. However, one should not confuse reconciliation, as the British did, with "benevolence" concerning social and psychological matters. In music, even a disagreeable passion has to be communicated via "wholes" which music creates according to its own dictates. However, the musical practice of the eighteenth century reveals a deep conviction that the two are a priori related. Even Mozart's letter to his father, concerning Osmin's rage, reveals the same conviction. Still it may be unfair to expect people to step out of their cultural heritage.

Painting, Music joins another peculiar and exquisite merit of its own. Statuary and Painting cannot be said to add any new beauties of their own to the beauties of Nature which they imitate; they may assemble a greater number of those beauties, and group them in a more agreeable manner than they are commonly, or perhaps ever, to be found in Nature. It may perhaps be true, what the artists are so very fond of telling us, that no woman ever equalled, in all the parts of her body, the beauty of the Venus of Medicis, nor any man that of the Apollo of Belvidere. But they must allow, surely, that there is no particular beauty in any part or feature of those two famous statues, which is not at least equalled, if not much excelled, by what is to be found in many living subjects. But Music, by arranging, and as it were bending to its own time and measure, whatever sentiments and passions it expresses, not only assembles and groups, as well as Statuary and Painting, the different beauties of Nature which it imitates, but it clothes them, besides, with a new and an exquisite beauty of its own; it clothes them with melody and harmony, which, like a transparent mantle, far from concealing any beauty, serve only to give a brighter colour, a more enlivening lustre, and a more engaging grace to every beauty which they infold.[15]

15. As far as its autonomy is concerned, Smith rightly grants music a superiority for it has no model in nature which it imitates. Hardly surprising, in the context of Smith's own theory, it is nevertheless a turning point in the aesthetics of the eighteenth century, which had declared music inferior to the other arts for that very reason. It is interesting, therefore, that Smith should have overlooked the fact that even in sculpture and painting, what is *most* important is not the beauty of the particles assembled, but their organization into an effective whole. (The notion of perfection in art — especially as it was developed by Hutcheson — is indeed marginal in his essay.) As far as music is concerned, however, Smith insists that the traffic music has with sentiments and passions is not necessary for its own constitution, but the other way around — that music subordinates them to its own internal dictates — he implies that content and form are inseparable in music, and that the comprehensibility (not be confused with the meaning) of music does not rest on external factors. In the grand debate whether music serves the text or vice versa, it is clear where Smith stands. It is this kind of thinking which will eventually open the way for theories of the nineteenth century according to which all arts should aspire to the condition of music.

To these two different sorts of imitation—to that general one, by which Music is made to resemble discourse, and to that particular one, by which it is made to express the sentiments and feelings with which a particular situation inspires a particular person, —there is frequently joined a third. The person who sings may join to this double imitation of the singer the additional imitation of the actor; and express, not only by the modulation and cadence of his voice, but by his countenance, by his attitudes, by his gestures, and by his motions, the sentiments and feelings of the person whose situation is painted in the song. Even in private company, though a song may sometimes perhaps be said to be well sung, it can never be said to be well performed, unless the singer does something of this kind; and there is no comparison between the effect of what is sung coldly from a music-book at the end of a harpsichord, and of what is not only sung, but acted with proper freedom, animation, and boldness. An opera actor does no more than this; and an imitation which is so pleasing, and which appears even so natural, in private society, ought not to appear forced, unnatural, or disagreeable upon the stage.

In a good opera actor, not only the modulations and pauses of his voice, but every motion and gesture, every variation, either in the air of his head, or in the attitude of his body, correspond to the time and measure of Music: they correspond to the expression of the sentiment or passion which the Music imitates, and that expression necessarily corresponds to this time and measure. Music is as it were the soul which animates him, which informs every feature of his countenance, and even directs every movement of his eyes. Like the musical expression of a song, his action adds to the natural grace of the sentiment or action which it imitates, a new and peculiar grace of its own; the exquisite and engaging grace of those gestures and motions, of those airs and attitudes which are directed by the movement, by the time and measure of Music; this grace heightens and enlivens that expression. Nothing can be more deeply affecting than the interesting scenes of the serious opera, when to good Poetry and good Music, to the Poetry of Metastasio and the Music of Pergolese, is added the execution of a good actor. In the serious opera, indeed, the action is too often sacrificed to the Music; the castrati, who perform the principal parts, being always the most insipid and miserable actors. The sprightly airs of the comic opera are, in the same manner, in the highest degree enlivening and diverting. Though they do not make us laugh so loud as we sometimes do at the scenes of the common comedy, they make us smile more frequently; and the agreeable gaiety, the temperate joy, if I may call it so, with which they inspire us, is not only an elegant, but a most delicious pleasure. The deep distress and the great passions of tragedy are capable of producing some effect, though it should be but indifferently acted. It is not so with the lighter misfortunes and less affecting situations of comedy: unless it is at least tolerably acted, it is altogether insupportable. But the castrati are scarce ever tolerable actors; they are accordingly seldom admitted to play in the comic opera; which, being upon that account commonly better performed, the serious, appears to many people the better entertainment of the two.[16]

16. In the last two paragraphs Smith connects the imitation in music to the issue of factitiousness. Indeed, we argued in Vol. I that the whole development of music in its relationship to sentiments, passions etc. was caused, in no small measure, by having been "elevated" onto the stage as a major protagonist. The fictive setting lent a habitat to musical imitation in which it could seem natural despite, or perhaps because of, its symbolic functioning. Well versed in opera, Smith is sensitive to fictitious frames and their role in establishing credibility and legitimacy. Moreover, his understanding of the way music adapts itself to function within these frames, leads him to assign to it an informative role, even for the actor who knows the text but does not himself *live* the designated passion. What is implied is that music paradoxically provides more definite connotations (as far as the movements and expression of the actor are concerned) than the text. His observation regarding the difference between the representation of the passions in tragedy and in comedy is also well taken, because of the philosophical nature of the former and the sociological nature of the latter (see Katz 1986). The problem of credibility is indeed for that very reason more acute in comedy; the *opera buffa* took such greater susceptibility into account not only as far as acting is concerned, but in its musical articulation and construction as well.

The imitative powers of Instrumental are much inferior to those of Vocal Music; its melodious but unmeaning and inarticulated sounds cannot, like the articulations of the human voice, relate distinctly the circumstances of any particular story, or describe the different situations which those circumstances produced; or even express clearly, and so as to be understood by every hearer, the various sentiments and passions which the parties concerned felt from these situations: even its imitation of other sounds, the objects which it can certainly best imitate, is commonly so indistinct, that alone, and without any explication, it might not readily suggest to us what was the imitated object. The rocking of a cradle is supposed to be imitated in that concerto of Corelli,* which is said to have been composed for the Nativity: but, unless we were told beforehand, it might not readily occur to us what it meant to imitate, or whether it meant to imitate anything at all; and this imitation (which, though perhaps as successful as any other, is by no means the distinguished beauty of that admired composition) might only appear to us a singular and odd passage in Music. The ringing of bells and the singing of the lark and nightingale are imitated in the symphony of Instrumental Music which Mr. Handel has composed for the Allegro and Penseroso of Milton: these are not only sounds but musical sounds, and may therefore be supposed to be more within the compass of the powers of musical imitation. It is accordingly universally acknowledged, that in these imitations this great master has been remarkably successful; and yet, unless the verses of Milton explained the meaning of the Music, it might not even in this case readily occur to us what it meant to imitate, or whether it meant to imitate any thing at all. With the explication of the words, indeed, the imitation appears, what it certainly is, a very fine one; but without that explication it might perhaps appear only a singular passage, which had less connexion either with what went before or with what came after it, than any other in the Music.

*See example II 1.

Instrumental Music is said sometimes to imitate motion; but in reality it only either imitates the particular sounds which accompany certain motions, or it produces sounds of which the time and measure bear some correspondence to the variations, to the pauses and interruptions, to the successive accelerations and retardations of the motion which it means to imitate: it is in this way that it sometimes attempts to express the march and array of an army, the confusion and hurry of a battle, &c. In all these cases, however, its imitation is so very indistinct, that without the accompaniment of some other art, to explain and interpret its meaning, it would be almost always unintelligible; and we could scarce ever know with certainty, either what it meant to imitate, or whether it meant to imitate any thing at all.

In the imitative arts, though it is by no means necessary that the imitating should so exactly resemble the imitated object, that the one should sometimes be mistaken for the other, it is, however, necessary that they should resemble at least so far, that the one should always readily suggest the other. It would be a strange picture which required an inscription at the foot to tell us, not only what particular person it meant to represent, but whether it meant to represent a man or a horse, or whether it meant to be a picture at all, and to represent any thing. The imitations of instrumental Music may, in some respects, be said to resemble such pictures. There is, however, this very essential difference between them, that the picture would not be much mended by the inscription; whereas, by what may be considered as very little more than such an inscription, instrumental Music, though it cannot always even then, perhaps, be said properly to imitate, may, however, produce all the effects of the finest and most perfect imitation. In order to explain in what manner this is brought about, it will not be necessary to descend into any great depth of philosophical speculation.

That train of thoughts and ideas which is continually passing through the mind does not always move on with the same pace, if I may say so, or with the same order and connection. When we are gay and cheerful, its motion is brisker and more lively, our thoughts succeed one another more rapidly, and those which immediately follow one another seem frequently either to have but little connection, or to be connected rather by their opposition than by their mutual resemblance. As in this wanton and playful disposition of mind we hate to dwell long upon the same thought, so we do not much care to pursue resembling thoughts; and the variety of contrast is more agreeable to us than the sameness of resemblance. It is quite otherwise when we are melancholy and desponding; we then frequently find ourselves haunted, as it were, by some thought which we would gladly chase away, but which constantly pursues us, and which admits no followers, attendants, or companions, but such as are of its own kindred and complexion. A slow succession of resembling or closely connected thoughts is the characteristic of this disposition of mind; a quick succession of thoughts, frequently contrasted and in general very slightly connected, is the characteristic of the other. What may be called the natural state of the mind, the state in which we are neither elated nor dejected, the state of sedateness, tranquillity, and composure, holds a sort of middle place between those two opposite extremes; our thoughts succeed one another more slowly, and with a more distinct connection, than in the one; more quickly, and with a greater variety, than in the other.

Acute sounds are naturally gay, sprightly, and enlivening; grave sounds solemn, awful, and melancholy. There seems too to be some natural connection between acuteness in tune and quickness in time or succession, as well as between gravity and slowness: an acute sound seems to fly off more quickly than a grave one: the treble is more cheerful than the bass; its notes likewise commonly succeed one another more rapidly. But instrumental Music, by a proper arrangement, by a quicker or slower succession of acute and grave, of resembling and contrasted sounds, can not only accommodate itself to the gay, the sedate, or the melancholy mood; but if the mind is so far vacant as not to be disturbed by any disorderly passion, it can, at least for the moment, and to a certain degree, produce every possible modification of each of those moods or dispositions. We all readily distinquish the cheerful, the gay, and the sprightly Music, from the melancholy, the plaintive, and the affecting; and both these from what holds a sort of middle place between them, the sedate, the tranquil, and the composing. And we are all sensible that, in the natural and ordinary state of the mind, Music can, by a sort of incantation, sooth and charm us into some degree of that particular mood or disposition which accords with its own character and temper. In a concert of instrumental Music the attention is engaged, with pleasure and delight, to listen to a combination of the most aqreeable and melodious sounds, which follow one another, sometimes with a quicker, and sometimes with a slower succession; and in which those that immediately follow one another sometimes exactly or nearly resemble, and sometimes contrast with one another in tune, in time, and in order of arrangement. The mind being thus successively occupied by a train of objects, of which the nature, succession, and connection correspond, sometimes to the gay, sometimes to the tranquil, and sometimes to the melancholy mood or disposition, it is itself successively led into each of those moods or dispositions; and is thus brought into a sort of harmony or concord with the Music which so agreeably engages its attention.[17]

It is not, however, by imitation properly, that instrumental Music produces this effect: instrumental Music does not imitate, as vocal Music, as Painting, or as Dancing would imitate, a gay, a sedate, or a melancholy person; it does not tell us, as any of those other arts could tell us, a pleasant, a serious, or a melan-

---

17. From the outset of this part, Smith is suggesting that music has generalized "meanings" of its own, which may gain distinctness by connecting them to external factors. In these last paragraphs he suggests a "coincidence theory" of the more convincing kind we had encountered in Webb, whose works were probably familiar to Smith. (It also seems that he was familiar with Beattie, though he never gives him credit; see, for example, his illustration from Corelli and Handel which are quoted in Beattie's treatise and several other examples which we shall point out.) What he assumes to be universals (certain movements related both to the passions and to music), however, begs the question whether their assigned meanings cannot be attributed just as well to conventions or to the socialization of emotions.

choly story. It is not, as in vocal Music, in Painting, or in Dancing, by sympathy with the gaiety, the sedateness, or the melancholy and distress of some other person, that instrumental Music soothes us into each of these dispositions: it becomes itself a gay, a sedate, or a melancholy object; and the mind naturally assumes the mood or disposition which at the time corresponds to the object which engages its attention. Whatever we feel from instrumental Music is an original, and not a sympathetic feeling: it is our own gaiety, sedateness, or melancholy; not the reflected disposition of another person.[18]

When we follow the winding alleys of some happily situated and well laid out garden, we are presented with a succession of landscapes, which are sometimes gay, sometimes gloomy, and sometimes calm and serene; if the mind is in its natural state, it suits itself to the objects which successively present themselves, and varies in some degree its mood and present humour with every variation of the scene. It would be improper, however, to say that those scenes imitated the gay, the calm, or the melancholy mood of the mind; they may produce in their turn each of those moods, but they cannot imitate any of them. Instrumental Music, in the same manner, though it can excite all those different dispositions, cannot imitate any of them. There are no two things in nature more perfectly disparate than sound and senti-

---

18. Smith here turns to instrumental music in relation to imitation. Though he will concentrate on its connection with fictitious frames, he first ponders whether instrumental music may be an "original," rather than a representation of sympathetic feelings. Smith, however, does not explain what he actually means; had he embedded his statement in a theory of metaphor (à la Goodman), or explained it in terms of the unique cognitive operations that musical movement involves (à la Bergson) he might have given more substance to his claim. At any rate, by this statement he divorces instrumental music from the whole realm of imitation. If he is not disturbed by it, it is because he takes for granted that instrumental music holds something intrinsic of its own, which, in fact, it has absorbed from its long association with the text. Interesting as such is his point that the listener identifies with the music as though it were his own (because it involves, at all times, an imaginary relationship, a kind of illusion which, as he has told us, is what counts, after all, in art).

ment; and it is impossible by any human power to fashion the one into any thing that bears any real resemblance to the other.[19]

This power of exciting and varying the different moods and dispositions of the mind, which instrumental Music really possesses to a very considerable degree, has been the principal source of its reputation for those great imitative powers which have been ascribed to it. "Painting," says an Author, more capable of feeling strongly than of analising accurately, M. Rousseau of Geneva, "Painting, which presents its imitations, not to the imagination, but to the senses, and to only one of the senses, can represent nothing besides the objects of sight. Music, one might imagine, should be equally confined to those of hearing. It imitates, however, every thing, even those objects which are perceivable by sight only. By a delusion that seems almost inconceivable, it can, as it were, put the eye into the ear; and the greatest wonder, of an art which acts only by motion and succession, is, that it can imitate rest and repose. Night, Sleep, Solitude, and Silence are all within the compass of musical imitation. Though all Nature should be asleep, the person who contemplates it is awake; and the art of the musician consists in substituting, in the room of an image of what is not the object of hearing, that of the movements which its presence would excite in the mind of the spectator." — That is, of the effects which it would produce upon his mood and disposition. "The musician" (continues the same Author) "will sometimes, not only agitate the waves of the sea, blow up the flames of a conflagration, make the rain fall, the

———— ⟡ ————

19. Smith's move toward instrumental music involves a turn (as far as ways of symbolization are concerned) from expression to, what Beattie called, "imitation" or to what Twining called, "description." In this connection he emphasizes that music excites, rather than reflects, sentiments (not unlike a succession of changing landscapes). If the supposed natural dispositions of music are denied, one cannot grasp the new factor which Smith introduces into its symbolic functioning unless one assumes a historical process whereby musical idioms became identified with certain emotional categories. Even if this is so, the very turn from effect to effecting is problematic (from a philosophical point of view); *a fortiori* if he strongly believed that music naturally expresses general moods. Already Descartes (and others who followed his thinking) understood that the expression of a certain feeling need not necessarily evoke the same feeling as a response.

rivulets flow and swell the torrents, but he will paint the horrors of a hideous desart, darken the walls of a subterraneous dungeon, calm the tempest, restore serenity and tranquillity to the air and the sky, and shed from the orchestra a new freshness over the groves and the fields. He will not directly represent any of these objects, but he will excite in the mind the same movements which it would feel from seeing them."

Upon this very eloquent description of Mr. Rousseau I must observe, that without the accompaniment of the scenery and action of the opera, without the assistance either of the scene-painter or of the poet, or of both, the instrumental Music of the orchestre could produce none of the effects which are here ascribed to it; and we could never know, we could never even guess, which of the gay, melancholy, or tranquil objects above mentioned it meant to represent to us; or whether it meant to represent any of them, and not merely to entertain us with a concert of gay, melancholy, or tranquil Music; or, as the ancients called them, of the Diastaltic, of the Systaltic, or of the Middle Music. With that accompaniment, indeed, though it cannot always even then, perhaps, be said properly to imitate, yet by supporting the imitation of some other art, it may produce all the same effects upon us as if itself had imitated in the finest and most perfect manner. Whatever be the object or situation which the scene-painter represents upon the theatre, the Music of the orchestra, by disposing the mind to the same sort of mood and temper which it would feel from the presence of that object, or from sympathy with the person who was placed in that situation, can greatly enhance the effect of that imitation: it can accommodate itself to every diversity of scene. The melancholy of the man who, upon some great occasion, only finds himself alone in the darkness, the silence and solitude of the night, is very different from that of one who, upon a like occasion, finds himself in the midst of some dreary and inhospitable desert; and even in this situation his feelings would not be the same as if he was shut up in a subterraneous dungeon. The different degrees of precision with which the Music of the orchestra can accommodate itself to each of those diversities, must depend upon the taste, the sensi-

bility, the fancy and imagination of the composer: it may sometimes, perhaps, contribute to this precision, that it should imitate,
as well as it can, the sounds which either naturally accompany,
or which might be supposed to accompany, the particular objects
represented. The Symphony in the French opera of Alcyone,
which imitated the violence of the winds and the dashing of the
waves, in the tempest which was to drown Ceyx, is much commended by contemporary writers. That in the opera of Isse,
which imitated that murmuring in the leaves of the oaks of
Dodona, which might be supposed to precede the miraculous
pronunciation of the oracle: and that in the opera of Amadis, of
which the dismal accents imitated the sounds which might be
supposed to accompany the opening of the tomb of Ardan,
before the apparition of the ghost of that warrior, are still more
celebrated. Instrumental Music, however, without violating too
much its own melody and harmony, can imitate but imperfectly
the sounds of natural objects, of which the greater part have neither melody nor harmony. Great reserve, great discretion, and a
very nice discernment are requisite, in order to introduce with
propriety such imperfect imitations, either into Poetry or Music;
when repeated too often, when continued too long, they appear
to be what they really are, mere tricks, in which a very inferior
artist, if he will only give himself the trouble to attend to them,
can easily equal the greatest. I have seen a Latin translation of
Mr. Pope's Ode on St. Cecilia's Day, which in this respect very
much excelled the original. Such imitations are still easier in
Music. Both in the one art and in the other, the difficulty is not
in making them as well as they are capable of being made, but
in knowing when and how far to make them at all: but to be able
to accommodate the temper and character of the Music to every
peculiarity of the scene and situation with such exact precision,
that the one shall produce the very same effect upon the mind
as the other, is not one of those tricks in which an inferior artist
can easily equal the greatest; it is an art which requires all the
judgment, knowledge, and invention of the most consummate
master. It is upon this art, and not upon its imperfect imitation,
either of real or imaginary sounds, that the great effects of instru-

mental Music depend; such imitations ought perhaps to be admitted only so far as they may sometimes contribute to ascertain the meaning, and thereby to enhance the effects of this art.[20]

By endeavoring to extend the effects of scenery beyond what the nature of the thing will admit of, it has been much abused; and in the common, as well as in the musical drama, many imitations have been attempted, which, after the first and second time we have seen them, necessarily appear ridiculous: such are, the Thunder rumbling from the Mustard-bowl, and the Snow of Paper and thick Hail of Pease, so finely exposed by Mr. Pope. Such imitations resemble those of painted Statuary; they may surprize at first, but they disgust ever after, and appear evidently such simple and easy tricks as are fit only for the amusement of children and their nurses at a puppet-show.   The thunder of

--------- ⟳ ---------

20. Smith's quotation from Rousseau is indeed in place here, for the latter offers a new conception regarding "musical description." Rousseau understood very well that simple imitations in music — sound by sound and motion by motion — are either partial or unsatisfactory from an aesthetic point of view. He realized that the emotional power of music is linked with its very weakness to "paint," yielding special combinations in which types of musical movement (which are already associated with types of emotional movement), are imbued with "hints" concerning external movements. This variety of connections creates an infinite number of possibilities, all of which are part of the playfulness of the imagination. Rousseau relates his observations to the idea (developed by Baumgarten and others) that art aims at imitating the *effects* the objects have on the beholder, rather than the objects themselves (Twining, as we have seen, made this statement central to his argument). Rousseau, of course, could not anticipate the extensive use that the nineteenth century would make of the possibilities which music is able to engender.

Smith did not think too highly of Rousseau's analytic ability and insisted that a composer who aims to convey the "agitation of the waves of the sea," for example, *must* guide us, in no ambiguous terms, to the idea of the object. Nevertheless, Smith recognizes the ingenuity of Rousseau's argument for it differentiates such sophisticated imitations from literal imitations of "sounds by sound." Though he did not exclude the latter from the province of music, he restricted its use, like so many others, because of its "diminishing returns." On the whole, he indicated a number of possibilities in which instrumental music is able to enrich fictive frames. However, like Twining, he leaves the last word, concerning possible combinations of symbolic procedures, to the judgement, knowledge and inventive power of the artist. Both Twining and Smith understood not only the limits of the arts, but also the limitations of aesthetics as a guide to the individual artist in his/her work.

either theatre ought certainly never to be louder than that which
the orchestre is capable of producing. And their most dreadful
tempests ought never to exceed what the scence painter is capable of representing. In such imitations there may be an art which
merits some degree of esteem and admiration. In the other there
can be none which merits any.

This abuse of scenery has both subsisted much longer, and
been carried to a much greater degree of extravagance, in the
musical than in the common drama. In France it has been long
banished from the latter; but it still continues, not only to be tol-
erated, but to be admired and applauded in the former. In the
French operas, not only thunder and lightning, storms and tempests, are commonly represented in the ridiculous manner above
mentioned, but all the marvellous, all the supernatural of Epic
Poetry, all the metamorphoses of Mythology, all the wonders of
Witchcraft and Magic, every thing that is most unfit to be represented upon the stage, are every day exhibited with the most
complete approbation and applause of that ingenious nation.
The Music of the orchestre producing upon the audience nearly
the same effect which a better and more artful imitation would
produce, hinders them from feeling, at least in its full force, the
ridicule of those childish and aukward imitations which necessarily abound in that extravagant scenery. And in reality such imitations, though no doubt ridiculous every where, yet certainly
appear somewhat less so in the musical than they would in the
common drama. The Italian opera, before it was reformed by
Apostolo Zeno and Metastasio, was in this respect equally extravagant, and was upon that account the subject of the agreeable
raillery of Mr. Addison in several different papers of the
Spectator. Even since that reformation it still continues to be a
rule, that the scene should change at least with every act; and the
unity of place never was a more sacred law in the common
drama, than the violation of it has become in the musical: the latter seems in reality to require both a more picturesque and a
more varied scenery, than is at all necessary for the former. In an
opera, as the Music supports the effect of the scenery, so the
scenery often serves to determine the character, and to explain

the meaning of the Music; it ought to vary therefore as that character varies. The pleasure of an opera, besides, is in its nature more a sensual pleasure, than that of a common comedy or tragedy; the latter produce their effect principally by means of the imagination: in the closet, accordingly, their effect is not much inferior to what it is upon the stage. But the effect of an opera is seldom very great in the closet; it addresses itself more to the external senses, and as it soothes the ear by its melody and harmony, so we feel that it ought to dazzle the eye with the splendour and variety of its scenery.

In an opera the instrumental Music of the orchestre supports the imitation both of the poet and of the actor, as well as of the scene- painter. The overture disposes the mind to that mood which fits it for the opening of the piece. The Music between the acts keeps up the impression which the foregoing had made, and prepares us for that which the following is to make. When the orchestre interrupts, as it frequently does, either the recitative or the air, it is in order either to enforce the effect of what had gone before, or to put the mind in the mood which fits it for hearing what is to come after. Both in the recitatives and in the airs it accompanies and directs the voice, and often brings it back to the proper tone and modulation, when it is upon the point of wandering away from them; and the correctness of the best vocal Music is owing in a great measure to the guidance of instrumental; though in all these cases it supports the imitation of another art, yet in all of them it may be said rather to diminish than to increase the resemblance between the imitating and the imitated object. Nothing can be more unlike to what really passes in the world, than that persons engaged in the most interesting situations, both of public and private life, in sorrow, in disappointment, in distress, in despair, should, in all that they say and do, be constantly accompanied with a fine concert of instrumental Music. Were we to reflect upon it, such accompaniment must in all cases diminish the probability of the action, and render the representation still less like nature than it otherwise would be. It is not by imitation, therefore, that instrumental Music supports and enforces the imitations of the other arts; but it is by produc-

ing upon the mind, in consequence of other powers, the same
sort of effect which the most exact imitation of nature, which the
most perfect observation of probability, could produce. To produce this effect is, in such entertainments, the sole end and purpose of that imitation and observation. If it can be equally well
produced by other means, this end and purpose may be equally
well answered.[21]

But if instrumental Music can seldom be said to be properly
imitative, even when it is employed to support the imitation of
some other art, it is commonly still less so when it is employed
alone. Why should it embarrass its melody and harmony, or constrain its time and measure, by attempting an imitation which,
without the accompaniment of some other art to explain and
interpret its meaning, nobody is likely to understand? In the most
approved instrumental Music, accordingly, in the overtures of
Handel and the concertos of Corelli, there is little or no imitation,
and where there is any, it is the source of but a very small part
of the merit of those compositions. Without any imitation, instrumental Music can produce very considerable effects; though its
powers over the heart and affections are, no doubt, much inferi-
or to those of vocal Music, it has, however, considerable powers:
by the sweetness of its sounds it awakens agreeably, and calls
upon the attention; by their connection and affinity it naturally
detains that attention, which follows easily a series of agreeable
sounds, which have all a certain relation both to a common, fundamental, or leading note, called the key note; and to a certain

——————— ♫ ———————

21. Though it seems that Smith engages at times in commonsensical simple observations, he is, in fact, a keen observer not only of major trends in the arts, but also of
the criticism that accompanied their development. This development lead him to analytic conclusions that illuminate the errors of some historical attempts to realize certain
aesthetic desiderata. His short discussion of the exaggerated "marvels" of the French
or the Italian opera (prior to its reform) may serve as examples. As an observer he recognizes that music is at once more qualified than the other arts to provide sensual sensations, and, at the same time, more fragile with regard to sustaining verisimilitude.
For Smith both these matters are related to his "disparity" theory, for by revealing both
the "power" of music as well as its ambiguity, it exposes the unique seeming paradoxical contribution of music to fictive frames — "immediate" indirectness.

succession or combination of notes, called the song or composition. By means of this relation each foregoing sound seems to
introduce, and as it were prepare the mind for the following: by
its rythmus, by its time and measure, it disposes that succession
of sounds into a certain arrangement, which renders the whole
more easy to be comprehended and remembered. Time and
measure are to instrumental Music what order and method are to
discourse; they break it into proper parts and divisions, by which
we are enabled both to remember better what is gone before,
and frequently to foresee somewhat of what is to come after: we
frequently foresee the return of a period which we know must
correspond to another which we remember to have gone before;
and, according to the saying of an ancient philosopher and musician, the enjoyment of Music arises partly from memory and partly from foresight. When the measure, after having been continued so long as to satisfy us, changes to another, that variety,
which thus disappoints, becomes more agreeable to us than the
uniformity which would have gratified our expectation: but without this order and method we could remember very little of what
had gone before, and we could foresee still less of what was to
come after; and the whole enjoyment of Music would be equal
to little more than the effect of the particular sounds which rung
in our ears at every particular instant. By means of this order and
method it is, during the progress of the entertainment, equal to
the effect of all that we remember, and of all that we foresee; and
at the conclusion, to the combined and accumulated effect of all
the different parts of which the whole was composed.

A well-composed concerto of instrumental Music, by the number and variety of the instruments, by the variety of the parts
which are performed by them, and the perfect concord or correspondence of all these different parts; by the exact harmony or
coincidence of all the different sounds which are heard at the
same time, and by that happy variety of measure which regulates
the succession of those which are heard at different times, presents an object so agreeable, so great, so various, and so interesting, that alone, and without suggesting any other object, either

by imitation or otherwise, it can occupy, and as it were fill up, completely the whole capacity of the mind, so as to leave no part of its attention vacant for thinking of anything else. In the contemplation of that immense variety of agreeable and melodious sounds, arranged and digested, both in their coincidence and in their succession, into so complete and regular a system, the mind in reality enjoys not only a very great sensual, but a very high intellectual, pleasure, not unlike that which it derives from the contemplation of a great system in any other science. A full concerto of such instrumental Music, not only does not require, but it does not admit of any accompaniment. A song or a dance, by demanding an attention which we have not to spare, would disturb, instead of heightening, the effect of the Music; they may often very properly succeed, but they cannot accompany it. That music seldom means to tell any particular story, or to imitate any particular event, or in general to suggest any particular object, distinct from that combination of sounds of which itself is composed. Its meaning, therefore, may be said to be complete in itself, and to require no interpreters to explain it. What is called the subject of such Music is merely, as has already been said, a certain leading combination of notes, to which it frequently returns, and to which all its digressions and variations bear a certain affinity. It is altogether different from what is called the subject of a poem or a picture, which is always something which is not either in the poem or in the picture, or something quite distinct from that combination, either of words on the one hand, or of colours on the other, of which they are respectively com-

———— ⨎ ————

22. Abandoning further discussion of the ways in which music "supports" and "enforces" the imitations of the other arts, Smith now tries to explain the *independence* of instrumental music in producing effects on its own. Given that instrumental music established itself by the second half of the eighteenth century, Smith goes beyond Twining in understanding this independence. Music, he tells us, is a kind of "system" governing the arrangement of sound to take account of "memory" as well as of "foresight" in its unfolding. The "ancient philosopher and musician" to whom he refers without mentioning his name, is Aristoxenus, who described in this manner the

(CONT.)

posed. The subject of a composition of instrumental Music is a part of that composition: the subject of a poem or picture is no part of either.[22]

The effect of instrumental Music upon the mind has been called its expression. In the feeling it is frequently not unlike the effect of what is called the expression of Painting, and is sometimes equally interesting. But the effect of the expression of Painting arises always from the thought of something which, though distinctly and clearly suggested by the drawing and

------- ♫ -------

(CONT.)

uniqueness of *listening* to music; in the eighteenth century this issue was reintroduced through rhetoric and especially through new poetic theories. Baumgarten, in his dealing with literature, was aware of the fact that successions imply both memory and foresight and also permit re-assessment while it is taking place. Smith himself tells us that in this respect music is like "discourse."

The internal "logic" of music is so tight that it may even tolerate, here and there, the "frustration of expectations" (a source for raising emotions, as psychologists tell us; see Meyer 1956) because these are perceived against an ordered background. The whole notion is of course related to the succession whereby smaller units are subsumed by larger sections and sections by even larger segments, eventually leading to the construction of the whole. Though music is an art which does not tell us what it is about, it handles "subjects" — musical subjects — to which its changes and transformations refer. Unlike the subject of a poem or a picture, the subject of a composition is a *built in* part of the composition. Here again Smith is saying that in the case of music, form and content are clearly inseparable and so, for that matter, is the effect of music's formal design, as he will tell us in the following little debate with Avison. Indeed, Smith seems not too far from Hanslick's "tönend bewegte Formen." Moreover, the effect which music produces, because of its own logic, so to speak, is immediate.

The "immediacy" of music is of course one of those attributes, which falls under the whole subject of the powers of music. Though music signifies nothing, it occupies the whole capacity of the mind. Beattie has already hinted in this direction. The nineteenth century, however, beginning with Schopenhauer, gave this particular attribute a new turn. Paradoxically, this immediacy grants music a certain kinship with science, as Smith himself tells us, in that the "secrets" of music are more exposed than are those of the other arts, answering more readily to the aesthetic principles which Smith himself established (see fn. 9 above).

If we bear in mind that Smith set out to discuss the imitative arts, two major points emerge, as far as music is concerned: 1) Given the dictates of the medium, music may assist the imitative arts but is not, in itself, an imitative art. 2) The uniqueness of music resides in its ability to be intelligible without signifying or suggesting extra musical contents.

colouring of the picture, is altogether different from that drawing and colouring. It arises sometimes from sympathy with, sometimes from antipathy and aversion to, the sentiments, emotions, and passions which the countenance, the action, the air and attitude of the persons represented suggest. The melody and harmony of instrumental Music, on the contrary, do not distinctly and clearly suggest any thing that is different from that melody and harmony. Whatever effect it produces is the immediate effect of that melody and harmony, and not of something else which is signified and suggested by them: they in fact signify and suggest nothing. It may be proper to say that the complete art of painting, the complete merit of a picture, is composed of three distinct arts or merits; that of drawing, that of colouring, and that of expression. But to say, as Mr. Avison does, that the complete art of a musician, the complete merit of a piece of Music, is composed or made up of three distinct arts or merits, that of melody, that of harmony, and that of expression, is to say, that it is made up of melody and harmony, and of the immediate and necessary effect of melody and harmony: the division is by no means logical; expression in painting is not the necessary effect either of good drawing or of good colouring, or of both together; a picture may be both finely drawn and finely coloured, and yet have very little expression: but that effect upon the mind which is called expression in Music, is the immediate and necessary effect of good melody. In the power of producing this effect consists the essential characteristic which distinguishes such melody from what is bad or indifferent. Harmony may enforce the effect of good melody, but without good melody the most skilful harmony can produce no effect which deserves the name of expression; it can do little more than fatigue and confound the ear. A painter may possess, in a very eminent degree, the talents of drawing and colouring, and yet possess that of expression in a very inferior degree. Such a painter, too, may have great merit. In the judgment of Du Piles, even the celebrated Titian was a painter of this kind. But to say that a musician possessed the talents of melody and harmony in a very eminent degree, and that of expression in a very inferior one, would be to say, that in his works the cause was not followed by its necessary and proportionable effect. A musician may be a very skilful harmonist, and yet be defective in the talents of melody, air, and expression; his songs may be dull and without effect. Such a musician too may have a certain degree of merit, not unlike that of a man of great learning, who wants fancy, taste, and invention.

Instrumental Music, therefore, though it may, no doubt, be considered in some respects as an imitative art, is certainly less so than any other which merits that appellation; it can imitate but a few objects, and even these so imperfectly, that without the accompaniment of some other art, its imitation is scarce ever intelligible: imitation is by no means essential to it, and the principal effects which it is capable of producing arises from powers altogether different from those of imitation.

Bibliography

The following list includes the historical sources of the present treatises and related contemporary works, modern studies mentioned in our annotations, and a few others which guided our interpretation. For a fuller list see our *Tuning the Mind*.

Addison, Joseph. (1914). *Miscellaneous Works,* edited by A.C. Guthkelch. London: Bell.

Alpers, Svetlana.. (1983). *The Art of Describing: Dutch Art in the Seventeenth Century,* Chicago: The University of Chicago Press.

Aristotle (1968). *Poetics; A Translation and Commentary for Students of Literature,* translated by Leon Golden, commentated by O.B. Hardison (Englewood Cliffs, N.J.: Prentice Hall).

Arnheim, Rudolf. [1957] (1969). *Visual Thinking,* Berkeley: University of California Press.

—— (1974). *Art and Visual Perception,* Berkely: University of California Press.

Auerbach, Erich. [1946] (1953). *Mimesis, The Representation of Reality in Western Literature,* translated W. R. Trask, Princeton: Princeton University Press.

Avison, Charles. [1753] (1967). *An Essay on Musical Expression,* New York: Broude Brothers.

Bacon, Francis. [1627, 1859] (1963). "Sylva Sylvarum or A Natural History," *The Work of Francis Bacon* vol. ii, Stuttgart: Friedrich Fromman Verlag: 339-672.

—— [1605, 1627] (1960). *The Advancement of Learning and New Atlantis,* London: Oxford University Press.

Barasch, Moshe. (1985). *Theories of Art from Plato to Winckelmann,* New York: New York University Press.

Barry, Kevin. (1987). *Language, Music and the Sign: A Study in Aesthetics, Poetics and Poetic Practice from Collins to Colleridge,* Cambridge: Cambridge University Press.

Batteaux, Charles. [1746] (1969). *Les Beaux arts réduits à un même principe,* Geneva: Slatkine Reprints.

Baumgarten, Alexander G. [1735] (1954). *Reflections on Poetry,* (with the original Latin text) translated and edited by K. Aschenbrenner and W.B. Holther, Berkeley: University of California Press.

Bayly, Anslem. (1778). *The Alliance of Music, Poetry and Oratory (Under the Head of Poetry),* London.

Beattie, James. [1760](1778). *Essays on Poetry and Music as the Affect the Mind,* Edinburgh.

Black, Max. (1962). *Models and Metaphors,* Ithaca: Cornell University Press.

Borgerhoff, E.B.O. (1950). *The Freedom of French Classicism,* Princeton: Princeton University Press.

Boyé, Pascal Boyer. [1779] (1973) *L'expression musicale mise au rang des chimères*, Amsterdam., Geneva: Minkoff.

Brown, John. (The Estimate). (1763). *A Dissertation on the Rise, Union and Power, the Progressions, Separations and Corruptions of Poetry and Music*, London.

Brown, John. (The Painter). (1789). *Letters upon the Poetry and Music of Italian Opera*, London.

Bruner, Jerome S. (1965). "Art as a Mode of Knowing," in *On Knowing*, Cambridge, Mass.: Harvard University Press: 59-74.

Bryson, Gladys. [1945] (1968). *Man and Society: The Scottish Inquiry of the Eighteenth Century*, New York: Augustus M. Kelly.

Bukofzer, Manfred F. (1939-40). "Allegory in Baroque Music," *The Journal of the Warburg Institute*, 3: 1-21.

Burke, Edmund. (1958). *A Philosophical Enquiry into the Origin of Our Ideas of the Sublime and Beautiful*, edited by with intro. J.T. Boulton, Notre Dame, Indiana: University of Notre Dame Press.

Burmeister, Joachim. [1601; 1601] (1993). *Musical Poetics*, translated with int. and notes, B. V. Rivera, edited by C. V. Palisca, New Haven: Yale University Press.

Cassirer, Ernst. [1932] (1951). *The Philosophy of the Enlightenment*, translated by F. Köln and J. P. Pettegrove, Princeton: Beacon Press.

—— (1955). *The Philosophy of Symbolic Forms* in 3 vols. translated by R. Manheim, New Haven: Yell University Press.

Caygill, Howard. (1989). *Art of Judgement,* Oxford: Basil Blackwell.

Chabanon, Michel-Paul Guy de. (1785). *De la musique considéré en elle même et dans ses rapports avec la parole, les langues, la poésie et la théâtre*, Paris.

Chastellux, Françios, Jean de. (1765). *Essai surl'union de la poésie et de las musique*, Paris.

Christensen, Thomas (1985). *Science and Music Theory in the Enlightenment: D'Alembert's Critique of Rameau*, an unpublished Ph.D. dissertation, Yale University.

Clynes, Manfred (1980). "The communication of emotion: theory of sentics" *Emotion: Theory, Research, and Experience,* vol. i, edited by R. Plutchik and H. Kellerman, Orlando: Academic Press: 271-301.

Cohen, H.F. (1984). *Quantifying Music: The Science of Music at the First Stage of the Scientific Revolution, 1580-1650,* Dodrecht: Reidel Publishing.

Condillac, Etienne Bonnot de. [1756] (1974). *An Essay on the Origin of Human Knowledge*, translated Th. Nugent, New York: AMS Press.

Cone, Edward T. (1974). *The Composer's Voice*, Berkeley: The University of California Press.

Cooke, Deryck. (1959). *The Language of Music*, London: Oxford University Press.

Cooper, John Gilbert. (1745). *The Power of Harmony*, London.

Dahlhaus, Carl. (1978). *Die Idee der Absoluten Musik*, Kassel: Barenreiter Verlag; translated as (1989) *The idea of Absolute Music* translated R. Lustig, Chicago University press.

—— [1967] (1982). *Esthetics of Music*, translated W. Austin, Cambridge: Cambridge University Press.

Daniel, Samuel. [1930] (1950). *Poems and a Defence of Ryme* , edited by A. Sprague, London: Routledge and Kegan Paul.

Danto, Arthur C. (1981). *The Transfiguration of the Commonplace*, Cambridge, Mass.: Harvard
University Press.

Darenberg, Karl H. (1960). *Studien zur Englischen Musikaesthetik des 18. Jahrhunderts*, Hamburg: Cram, de Gruyter.

Descartes, Rene. [1618] (1961). *Compendium of Music*, translated by W. Robert, New York: The American Institute of Musicology.

—— (1985). *The Philosophical Writings of Descartes*, vol. 1 translated by J. Cottingham, R. Stoothoff, and D. Murdoch, Cambridge: Cambridge University Press.

Dieckman, Liselotte. (1970). *Hieroglyphics*, St. Louis: Washington University Press.

Draper, John W. (1932-33). "Poetry and Music in Eighteenth-Century Aesthetics," *Englische Studien* 67: 70-85.

Dubos, Abbes. [1719] *Réflexions critiques sur la poésie et la peinture* in 3 vols. Paris. translated as [1748] (1978). *Critical Reflections*, translated by Th. Nugent, New York: AMS Press.

Eco, Umberto. (1976). *A Theory of Semiotics,* Bloomington: Indian University Press.

—— (1981). *The Role of the Reader*, Bloomington: Indiana University Press.

Engell, James. (1981). *The Creative Imagination: Enlightenment to Romanticism*, Cambridge, Mass.: Harvard University Press.

Finney, Gretchen L. (1962). *Musical Backgrounds for English Literature*: 1580-1650, New Brunswick: Rutgers University Press.

Flage, Daniel E. (1990). *David Hume's Theory of Mind*, London: Routledge.

Flood, W.H. Grattan. (1916). "An Eighteenth Century Essayist on Poetry and Music," *Musical Quarterly* 2: 191-8.

Foucault, Michel. (1972). *The Order of Things: An Archaeology of the Human Sciences*, New York: Vintage Books.

Gadamer, Hans-Georg. (1976). *Philosophical Hermeneutics,* translated and edited by David E. Linge, Berkeley: University of California Press.

Gardner, Howard. (1985). *The Mind's New Science: A History of the Cognitive Revolution*, New York: Basic Books.

Gay, Peter (1969). *The Enlightenment: An Interpretation* in 2 vols. New York: Alfred Knopf.

Genette, Gerard. [1972] (1980). *Narrative Discourse*, translated by J. Lewin, Ithaca: Cornell University Press.

Georgiades, Thrasysbulos. (1950). "Aus der Musiksprache des Mozarttheaters," *Mozart-Yahrbuch* 1: 76-98.

Godwin, Joscelyn. (1979). *Athanasius Kircher: A Renaissance Man and the Quest for Lost Knowledge*, London: Thames and Hudson.

Gombrich, E.H. [1960] (1977). *Art and Illusion: A Study in the Psychology of Pictorial Representation*, fifth edition, Oxford: Phaidon Press.

Goodman, Nelson. (1968). *Languages of Art*, Indianapolis: The Bobbs-Merrill Company.

—— (1978). *Ways of Worldmaking*, Indianapolis and Cambridge: Hackett Publishing Company.

Grene, Marjorie. (1985). *Descartes*, Brighton: The Harvester Press.

Hagstrum, Jean H. (1958). *The Sister Arts: The Tradition of Literary Pictorialism in English Poetry from Dryden to Gray*, Chicago: The University of Chicago Press.

Hamilton, Kenneth G. (1963). *The Two Harmonies: Poetry and Prose in the Seventeenth Century*, Oxford: Clarendon Press.

Harris, James. [1744] (1792). *Three Treatises. The First Concerning Art. The Second Concerning Music, Painting and Poetry. The Third Concerning Happiness*, in *Miscellanies* vol 1. London: F.Wingrave.

Hatten, Robert. (1994). *Musical Meaning in Beethoven: Markedness, Correlation, Interpretation*, Bloomington: Indiana University Press.

Hausman, Carl R. (1989). *Metaphor and Art: Interactionism and Reference in the Verbal and Nonverbal Arts*, Cambridge: Cambridge University Press.

Hawkins, Sir John. (1776). *A General History of the Science and Practice of Music* in 5 vols. London.

Hecht, Hans. (1920). *Daniel Webb: Ein Beitrag zur englischen Aesthetik des achtzehnten Jahrhunderts*, Hamburg: Verlag von Henri Grand.

Hell, Helmut. (1971). *Die Neapolitanische Opernsinfonie in der ersten Hälfte des 18 Jahrhunderts*, München: Hans Schneider Tutzing.

Herder, Johann Gottfried. (1966). "On the Origin of Language" *On the Origin of Language*, translated and edited by J.H. Moran and A. Gode, New York: Frederick Ungar: 87-176.

Hobbes, Thomas. [1651] (1968). *Leviathan*, edited by C.B. Macpherson, Penguin Books.

Hogan Michael J. (1984). "Historiography and Ethics in Adam Smith's Lectures on Rhetoric, 1762-1763," *Rhetorica* 2: 75-91.

Hollander, John. (1961). *The Untuning of the Sky*, New York: Norton.

Hosler, Bellamy. (1978). *Changing Aesthetic Views of Instrumental Music in 18th-Century Germany*, Ann Arbor, Mich.: UMI Research Press.

Howard, William G. (1909). "Ut pictura poesis," *Publications of the Modern Language Association* 24: 40-123.

Hume, David. (1739). *A Treatise of Human Nature*, London.

Hutcheson, Francis. (1973). *Inquiry Concerning Beauty, Harmony and Design*, edited by P. Kivy, The Hague: Martinus Nijhoff.

Jacob, Hilderbrand. (1734). *Of the Sister Arts, an Essay*, London.

Johnson, Paula. (1972). *Form and Transformation in Music and Poetry of the English Renaissance*, New Haven: Yale University Press.

Jones, Sir William. [1772] [1810] (1971). "On the Arts, Commonly Called Imitative," *The Works of the English Poets* vol. xviii, edited by A. Chalmers, Hildesheim: Georg Olms Verlag: 501-511.

Jones, William of Nayland. (1784). *A Treatise on the Art of Music*, Colchester.

Kallich, Martin. (1970). *The Association of Ideas and Critical Theory in Eighteenth-Century England*, The Hague.

Kant, Emanuel. [1790] (1952) *Critique of Judgement,* translated J. H. Meredith, Oxford: Clarendon Press.

Katz , Ruth. (1986). *Divining the Powers of Music: Aesthetic Theory and the Origins of Opera*, New York: Pendragon Press.

Katz, Ruth and Dahlhaus, Carl. (1987-1991). *Contemplating Music: Source Readings in the Aesthetics of Music* in 4 vols. Vol. i: *Substance*; vol ii: *Import*; vol. iii: *Essence*; vol. iv: *Community of Discourse*. New York: Pendragon Press.

Katz, Ruth and HaCohen, Ruth. (1988). "`Ut Musica Poesis'`: The Crystallization of a Conception Concerning Cognitive Processes and `Well-Made Worlds'`," in *Festschrift Carl Dahlhaus*, edited by H. Danuser et al. Laaber-Verlag: Laaber: 17-37.

Kircher, Athansius [1650] (1970). *Musurgia universalis, zwei Teile in einem Band*, Hildesheim: G. Olms, facsimile of the 1650 edition.

Kilpatrich, Ross Stuart (1990). *Horace, Epistle II and Ars Poetica*, author's translation, Edmonton: University of Alberta Press.

Kivy, Peter. (1976). *The Seventh Sense,* New York: Burt Franklin.

—— (1980). *The Corded Shell: Reflections on Musical Expression*, Princeton: Princeton University Press.

—— (1984). *Sound and Semblance: Reflections on Musical Representation*, Princeton: Princeton University Press.

—— (1988). *Osmin's Rage: Philosophical Reflections on Opera, Drama, and Text*, Princeton: Princeton University Press.

Kristeller, Paul O. (1965). "The Modern System of the Arts," *Renaissance Thought and the Arts*, Princeton: Princeton University Press: 163-227.

Langer, Suzanne K. (1953). *Feeling and Form*, New York: Charles Scribner and Sons.

—— [1942] (1976). *Philosophy in a New Key*, Cambridge, Mass.: Harvard University Press.

Lee, Rensselaer W. [1940] (1967). *Ut pictura poesis: The Humanistic Theory of Painting*, New York: Norton.

Le-Hurray, Peter and Day, James, eds. (1981). *Music and Aesthetics in the Eighteenth and Early NineteenthCenturies*, Cambridge: Cambridge University Press.

Leibniz, Gottfried Wilhelm, Freiherr von. (1969). *Philosophical Papers and Letters*, edited by L. E. Loemker, Dordrecht: Reidel.

Lessing, Gotthold, Ephraim. [1766] (1957). *Laocoon: An Essay Upon the Limits of Painting and Poetry,* translated E. Fothinham, New York: The Noonday Press.

—— [1768-9] (1958). *Hamburgische Dramaturgie*, Stuttgart: Alfred Kröner Verlag.

Levi-Strauss, Claude. [1964] (1969). *The Raw and the Cooked*, translated J. D. Weightman, London: Jonathan Cape.

—— [1963] (1977). *Structural Anthropology*, Translated C. Jacobson, New York: Penguin Books.

Lippman, Edward D. (1964). *Musical Thought in Ancient Greece*, New York: Columbia University Press.

Lipking, Lawrence. (1970). *The Ordering of the Arts in Eighteenth-Century England*, Princeton, N.J.: Princeton University Press.

—— ed. (1986). *Musical Aesthetics: A Historical Reader* in 2 vols. New York: Pendragon Press.

Locke, John. [1690] (1961). *An Essay Concerning Human Understanding*, London: Dent.

Lovejoy, Arthur O., (1960). *Essays in the History of Ideas*, Baltimore: The Johns Hopkins University Press: 69-77.

—— (1933). "Monboddo and Rousseau," *Modern Philology* 3: 275-296.

—— [1936] (1976). *The Great Chain of Being*, Cambridge, Mass.: Harvard University Press.

—— (1904). "Some Eighteenth Century Evolutionists," *Popular Science Monthly* 65: 336-40.

Lowinsky, Edward E. (1965). "Taste, Style and Ideology in Eighteenth-Century Music," *Aspects of the   Eighteenth Century*, edited by E.R. Wasserman, Baltimore: The Johns Hopkins University Press: 163-205.

McCormac, Earl R. (1985). *A Cognitive Theory of Metaphor*, Harvard: MIT Press.

Mace, Dean T.(1952). *English Musical Thought in the Seventeenth Century: A Study of an Art in Decline*, an unpublished Ph.D. dissertation, Columbia University.

Manwaring, Edward. (1744). *Of Harmony and Numbers in Latin and English Prose and in English Poetry*, London.

Mason, John. (1749). *An Essay on the Power of Numbers and the Principles of Harmony in Poetical   Compositions*, London.

Mattheson, Johann. (1739). *Der Volkommene Cappelmeister*, Hamburg: Christian Herald.   translated as (1981). *Der Volkommene Cappelmeister*, by E. Harriss, Ann Arbor: UMI Research Press.

Mendelssohn, Moses. [1929] (1971-2). *Gesammelte Schriften* vol. i-ii, Stuttgart: Friedrich Frommann Verlag.

Mersenne, Marin. [1636]. (1975). *Harmonie Universelle*, Fasc. ed by the Centre National de la Rechereche Scientifique.

Meyer, Leonard B. (1956). *Emotions and Meaning in Music*, Chicago: University of Chicago Press.

Miall, David S. (1987). "Metaphor and Affect: The Problem of Creative Thought," *Metaphor and Symbolic Activity* 2: 81-96.

Michael, Emily. (1984). "Francis Hutcheson on Aesthetic Perception and Aesthetic Pleasure," *British Journal of Aesthetics* 24: 242-255.

Milton, John. (1957). *Complete Poems and Major Prose*, edited by Merritt Y. Hughes, Indianapolis: The Odyssey Press.

Mitford. William. (1774). *Essay upon the Harmony of Language*, London.

Monboddo, James Burnett, Lord. [1773-92] (1809). *On the Origin and Progress of Language* in 5 vols. Edinburgh: A. Smellie.

Murphy, James. (1974). *Rhetoric in the Middle Ages: A History of Rhetorical Theory from Saint Augustine to the Renaissance*, Berkeley: University of California Press.

Nietzche, Friedrich. (1968). *Basic Writings of Nietzche* vol. i, translated and edited by W. Kaufmann, New York: The Modern Library.

Neubauer, John (1986). *The Emancipation of Music from Language*, New Haven: Yale University Press.

Nicolson, Marjorie. (1960). *The Breaking of the Circle: Studies in the Effect of the 'New Science' upon Seventeenth-Century Poetry*, New York: Columbia University Press.

Nisbet, H. B. (1985), edited by *German aesthetic and Literary Criticism: Winckelmann, Lessing, Hamann, Herder, Schiller, Goethe*. Cambridge: Cambridge University Press.

Omond, T.S. (1907). *English Metrists*, London: Oxford University Press.

Osgood, C. E., Suci G. J. & Tannenbaum P. H. (1957). *The measurement of meaning*, Urbana: University of Illinois Press.

Palisca, Claude V. [1968] (1981). *Baroque Music*, New York: Prentice Hall

—— (1985). *Humanism in Italian Renaissance Musical Thought*, New Haven: Yale University Press.

Panofsky, Erwin. [1924] (1968). *Idea, A Concept in Art Theory*, translated by J. S. Peake, New York: Harper Row.

—— [1955] (1983). *Meaning in the Visual Arts*, Penguin Books.

Passmore, John. (1972). *The Perfectibility of Man*, London, Duckworth.

Pater, Walter. [1893] (1980). "The School of Giorgione," *The Renaissance*, the 1893 Text, edited by D.L. Hill, Berkeley: University of California Press: 102-122.

Patey, Douglas L. (1984). *Probability and Literary Form*, Cambridge: Cambridge University Press.

Patrides, edited by (1970). *The Cambridge Platonists*, Cambridge, Massachusetts: Harvard University Press.

Pirro, Andre. (1907). *L'esthétique de Bach*, Paris: Fischbacher.

Pirrota, Nino and Povoledo, Elena. [1969] (1982). *Music and Theater from Poliziano to Monteverdi*, Cambridge: Cambridge University Press.

Plutchik, Robert. (1980) "A General Psychoevolutionary Theory of Emotion" *Emotion: Theory, Research and Experience* vol. i (Theories of Emotions), edited by R. Plutchik and H. Kellerman, Orlando: Academic Press.

The Polite Arts, or, a Dissertation on Poetry, Painting, Musick, Architecture and Eloquence (1749 anon.) London.

Pope, Alexander. [1869] (1911). *The Poetical Works*, London: Macmillan.

Powicke, Fredrick J. [1926] (1971). *The Cambridge Platonists: A Study*, Hamden, Connecticut: Archon Books.

Pribram, Karl H. (1982). "Brain Mechanism in Music: Prolegomena for a Theory of the Meaning of Meaning," *Music, Mind and Brain*, edited by M. Clynes, New York: Plenum: 21-35.

Quintilianus, Aristides. (1983). *On Music* in 3 vols. edited by T. J. Mathiesen, New Haven: Yale University Press.

Rameau, Jean-Philippe. [1722] (1971). *Treatise on Harmony*, translated and edited by Ph. Gossett, New York: Dover Publications.

Ratner, Leonard G. (1956). "Eighteenth-Century Theories of Musical Period Structure," *Musical Quarterly* 42: 439-454.

—— (1970). "Ars Combinatoria: Chance and Choice in Eighteenth-Century Music," in *Studies in Eighteenth-Century Music: A Tribute to Karl Geiringer*, edited by H. C. Robbins Landon, Oxford: Oxford University Press: 343-363.

—— (1980). *Classic Music, Expression, Form and Style*, New York: Scribner Books.

Roberts, Donald Ramsay. (1947). "The Music of Milton," *Philological Quarterly* 26: 328-344.

Robertson, Thomas. (1784). *An Inquiry into the Fine Arts*, London.

Rogerson, Brewster. (1945). *'Ut Musica Poesis': The Parallel of Music and Poetry in Eighteenth Century Criticism*, an unpublished Ph. D. dissertation, Princeton University.

—— (1953). "The Art of Painting the Passions," *Journal of the History of Ideas* 14 :68-94.

Rosen, Charles [1971] (1976). *The Classic Style: Haydn, Mozart, Beethoven*, London: Faber & Faber.

Rousseau, Jean-Jacques. (1827). *Oeuvres complètes* vol. xv, Paris.

—— [1753] (1966). "On the Origin of Languages," *On the Origin of Language*, translated and edited by J.H. Moranand A. Gode, New York: Fredrick Ungar: 3-83.

Saintsbury, George. (1923). *A History of English Prosody from the Twelfth Century to the Present Day*, in 3 vols. London: Macmillan.

Schrade, Leo. (1964). *Tragedy and the Art of Music,* Cambridge Mass.: Harvard University Press.

Schueller, Herbert M. (1948). "'Imitation' and 'Expression' in British Music Criticism in the Eighteenth Century," *Musical Quarterly* 34: 544-566.

—— (1947). "Literature and Music as Sister Arts: An Aspect of Aesthetic Theory in Eighteenth-Century Britain," *Philological Quarterly* 26 :193-205.

—— (1953). "Correspondences between Music and the Sister Arts, According to 18th Century Aesthetic Theory," *Journal of Aesthetics and Art Criticism* 11: 334-359.

Schweitzer, Albert. [1908] (1975). *Johann Sebastian Bach* in 2 vols. translated E. Newman, New York: Dover.

Shaftesbury, Anthony Ashley Cooper, Earl of. (1743). *Characteristics* in 3 vols. London.

Shirlaw, Matthew. [1917] (1969). *The Theory of Harmony*, New York: Da Capo Press.

Smallwood, P. J. edited by (1989). *The Johnson Quotation Book: Based on the Collection of Chartres Bryson*, Bristol: Bristol Classical.

Smith, Adam. (1980). *Essays on Philosophical Subjects*, edited by W.P.D. Wightman, et al., Oxford: Clarendon Press.

—— [1759] (1976). *The Theory of Moral Sentiments,* edited By D. D. Raphael and A.L. Macfie, Oxford: Clarendon Press.

Spitzer, Leo. (1963). *Classical and Christian Ideas of World Harmony*, Baltimore: The Johns Hopkins University Press.

Strunk, Oliver [1950] (1981). *Source Readings in Music History* in 5 vols. New York: Norton.

Townsend, Danbey. (1982). "Shaftesbury's Aesthetic Theory," *Journal of Aesthetic and Art Criticism:* 205-213.

Treitler, Leo. (1988). "Mozart and the Idea of Absolute Music," *Festschrift Carl Dahlhaus*, Laaber: Laaber Verlag: 413-440. Also in Treitler, L. (1989) *Music and the Historical Imagination* Cambridge Mass.: Harvard University Press: 176-214.

Tsur, Reuven. (1998). *Poetic Rhythm: Structure and Performance, an Empirical Study in Cognitive Poetics*, Berne: P. Lang.

Twining, Thomas. (1789). *Two Dissertations: 1) On Poetry Considered as an Imitative Art, 2) On The Different Senses of the World Imitative as Applied to Music by the Antients and by the Moderns*, in Aristotle's *Treatise of Poetry* Translated with Notes, London..

Unger, Hans-Heinrich. (1941). *Die Beziehungen zwischen Musik und Rhetorik im 16.-18. Jahrhundert,* Würzburg.

Verba, Cynthia. (1993). *Music and the French Enlightenment: Reconstruction of a Dialogue 1750- 1764,* Oxford: Clarendon Press.

Verene, D. P. (1981). *Vico's Science of Imagination*, Ithaca: Cornell Universty Press.

Vickers, Brian. (1984). "Figures of Rhetoric/Figures of Music?" *Rhetorica* 2: 1-44.

Vico, Gianbattisata.[1744] (1963). *La scienza nouva* in 2 vols, Milano: Rizzoti.

Voltaire, M. d. (1772). *The Dramatic Works of M. de Voltaire* vol. xxi, translated Rev. Mr. Franklin, Dublin: R. Marchbank.

Walker, D.P. (1941, 1942). "Musical Humanism in the 16th and 17th Centuries," *The Music Review* 2: 1-13; 111-121 221-228; 288-308; 3: 55-71.

—— (1958). *Spiritual and Demonic Magic from Ficino to Campanella*, London: Warburg Institute.

—— (1978). *Studies in Musical Science in the Late Renaissance*, London: Warburg Institute.

Warburton, William. (1738). *The Divine Legation of Moses Demonstrated from the Principles of a Deist*, in 2 vols. London.

Watt, Ian. (1957). *The Rise of the Novel*, Harmondsworth: Chatto & Windus.

Webb, Daniel. (1760). *An Inquiry into the Beauties of Painting*, London.

—— (1762). *Remarks on the Beauties of Poetry*, London.

—— (1769). *Observations on the Correspondence between Poetry and Music*, London.

Weber, Carl. (1921) (1958). *The Rational and Social Foundations of Music*, Southern Illinois University Press.

Weber, William. (1992). *The Rise of Musical Classics in Eighteen-Century England,* Oxford: Oxford University Press.

Weisstein, Ulrich. [1964] (1969). *The Essence of Opera*, New York: Norton.

Wellek, Rene. [1955] (1981). *A History of Modern Criticism 1750-1950* vol. i, Cambridge: Cambridge University Press.

Willy, Basil. [1940] (1961). *The eighteenth Century Background*, Boston: Beacon Press.

Wilson, John. (1959). *Roger North on Music,* London: Novello.

Winn, James Anderson. (1981). *Unsuspected Eloquence: A History of the Relations between Poetry and Music*, New Haven: Yale University Press.

Wolterstorff, Nicholas. (1980). *Works and Worlds of Art*, Oxford: Clarendon Press.

Yolton, John, W. (1985). *Locke - An Introduction*, Oxford: Basil Blackwell.

Zuckerkandl, Victor. [1956] (1973). *Sound and Symbol*, Princeton: Princeton University Press.